Charlotte Mary Yonge

Hopes and fears;

Or, Scenes from the life of a spinster - Vol. 1

Charlotte Mary Yonge

Hopes and fears;
Or, Scenes from the life of a spinster - Vol. 1

ISBN/EAN: 9783337730529

Printed in Europe, USA, Canada, Australia, Japan

Cover: Foto ©ninafisch / pixelio.de

More available books at **www.hansebooks.com**

HOPES AND FEARS;

OR,

SCENES FROM THE LIFE OF A SPINSTER.

BY THE AUTHOR OF 'THE HEIR OF REDCLYFFE,'
'HEARTSEASE,' ETC.

This is the calm of the autumnal eve.
THE BAPTISTERY.

IN TWO VOLUMES.

VOL. I.

LONDON:
JOHN W. PARKER AND SON, WEST STRAND.
1860.

HOPES AND FEARS.

PART I.

CHAPTER I.

Who ought to go then and who ought to stay?
Where do you draw an obvious border line?—
                      Cecil and Mary.

AMONG the numerous steeples counted from the waters of the Thames, in the heart of the City, and grudged by modern economy as cumberers of the soil of Mammon, may be remarked an abortive little dingy cupola, surmounting two large round eyes which have evidently stared over the adjacent roofs ever since the Fire that began at Pie Corner and ended in Pudding Lane.

Strange that the like should have been esteemed the highest walk of architecture, and yet Honora Charlecote well remembered the days when St. Wulstan's was her boast, so large, so clean, so light, so Grecian, so far surpassing damp old Hiltonbury Church. That was at an age when her enthusiasm found indiscriminate food in whatever had a hold upon her affections, the nearer her heart being of course the more admirable in itself, and it would be difficult to say which she loved the most ardently, her city home in Woolstone-lane, or Hiltonbury Holt, the old family seat, where her father was a welcome guest whenever his constitution re-

VOL. I.   B

quired relaxation from the severe toils of a London rector.

Woolstone-lane was a locality that sorely tried the coachmen of Mrs. Charlecote's West-end connexions, situate as it was on the very banks of the Thames, and containing little save offices and warehouses, in the midst of which stood Honora's home. It was not the rectory, but had been inherited from City relations, and it antedated the Fire, so that it was one of the most perfect remnants of the glories of the merchant princes of ancient London. It had a court to itself, shut in by high walls, and paved with round-headed stones, with gangways of flags in mercy to the feet; the front was faced with hewn squares after the pattern of Somerset House, with the like ponderous sashes, and on a smaller scale, the Louis XIV. pediment, apparently designed for the nesting-place of swallows and sparrows. Within was a hall, pannelled with fragrant softly-tinted cedar wood, festooned with exquisite garlands of fruit and flowers, carved by Gibbons himself, with all his peculiarities of rounded form and delicate edge. The staircase and floor were of white stone, tinted on sunny days with reflections from the windows' three medallions of yellow and white glass, where Solomon, in golden mantle and crowned turban, commanded the division of a stout lusty child hanging by one leg; superintended the erection of a temple worthy of Haarlem; or graciously welcomed a recoiling stumpy Vrow of a Queen of Sheba, with golden hair all down her back.

The river aspect of the house had come to perfection at the Elizabethan period, and was sculptured in every available nook with the chevron and three arrows of the Fletchers' Company, and a merchant's mark, like a figure of four with a curly tail. Here were the oriel windows of the best rooms, looking out on a grass plat, small enough in country eyes, but most extensive for the situation, with straight gravelled walks, and low lilac and laburnum trees, that came into profuse blossom long before their country cousins, but which, like the crocuses and snowdrops of the flower borders, had better be looked at than touched by such as dreaded sooty fingers. These shrubs veiled the garden from the great river thoroughfare, to which it sloped down, still showing traces of the handsome stone steps and balustrade that once had formed the access of the gold-chained alderman to his sumptuous barge.

Along those paths paced, book in hand, a tall, well-grown maiden, of good straight features, and clear, pale skin, with eyes and rich luxuriant hair of the same colour, a peculiarly bright shade of auburn, such as painters of old had loved, and Owen Sandbrook called golden, while Humfrey Charlecote would declare he was always glad to see Honor's carrots.

More than thirty years ago, personal teaching at a London parish school or personal visiting of the poor was less common than at present, but Honora had been bred up to be helpful, and she had newly come in from a diligent afternoon of looking at the needlework, and hearing Crossman's Catechism, and Sellon's abridgement from a demurely dressed race of little girls in tall white caps, bibs and tuckers, and very stout indigo blue frocks. She had been working hard at the endeavour to make the little Cockneys, who had never seen a single ear of wheat, enter into Joseph's dreams, and was rather weary of their town sharpness coupled with their indifference and want of imagination, where any nature, save human nature, was concerned. 'I will bring an ear of Hiltonbury wheat home with me —some of the best girls shall see me sow it, and I will take them to watch it growing up—the blade, the ear, the full corn in the ear—poor dears, if they only had a Hiltonbury to give them some tastes that are not all for this hot, busy, eager world! If I could only see one with her lap full of blue bells; but though in this land of Cockaigne of ours, one does not actually pick up gold and silver, I am afraid they are our flowers, and the only ones we esteem worth the picking;

and like old Mr. Sandbrook, we neither understand nor esteem those whose aims are otherwise! Oh! Owen, Owen, may you only not be withheld from your glorious career! May you show this hard, money-getting world that you do really, as well as only in word, esteem one soul to be reclaimed above all the wealth that can be laid at your feet! The nephew and heir of the great Firm voluntarily surrendering consideration, ease, riches, unbounded luxury for the sake of the heathen—choosing a wigwam instead of a West End palace; parched maize rather than the banquet; the backwoods instead of the luxurious park; the Red Indian rather than the club and the theatre; to be a despised minister rather than a magnate of this great city; nay, or to take his place among the influential men of the land. What has this worn, weary old civilization to offer like the joy of sitting beneath one of the glorious aspiring pines of America, gazing out on the blue waters of her limpid inland seas, in her fresh pure air, with the simple children of the forest round him, their princely forms in attitudes of attention, their dark soft liquid eyes fixed upon him, as he tells them 'Your Great Spirit, Him whom ye ignorantly worship, Him declare I unto you,' and then, some glorious old chief bows his stately head, and throws aside his marks of superstition. 'I believe,' he says, and the hearts of all bend with him; and Owen leads them to the lake, and baptizes them, and it is another St. Sacrament! Oh! that is what it is to have nobleness enough truly to overcome the world, truly to turn one's back upon pleasures and honours—what are they to such as this?'

So mused Honora Charlecote, and then ran indoors, with bounding step, to her Schiller, and her hero-worship of Max Piccolomini, to write notes for her mother, and practise for her father the song that was to refresh him for the evening.

Nothing remarkable! No; there was nothing remarkable in Honor, she was neither more nor less than an average woman of the higher type. Refinement and gentleness, a strong appreciation of excellence, and a love of duty, had all been brought out by an admirable education, and by a home devoted to unselfish exertion, varied by intellectual pleasures. Other influences—decidedly traceable in her musings—had shaped her principles and enthusiasms on those of an ardent Oxonian of the early years of William IV.; and so bred up, so led by circumstances, Honora, with her abilities, high cultivation, and tolerable sense, was a fair specimen of what any young lady might be, appearing perhaps somewhat in advance of her contemporaries, but rather from her training than from intrinsic force of character. The qualities of womanhood well developed, were so entirely the staple of her composition, that there is little to describe in her. Was not she one made to learn; to lean; to admire; to support; to enhance every joy; to soften every sorrow of the object of her devotion?

Another picture from Honora Charlecote's life. It is about half after six, on a bright autumnal morning; and, rising nearly due east, out of a dark pine-crowned hill, the sun casts his slanting beams over an undulating country, clothed in grey mist of tints differing with the distance, the farther hills confounded with the sky, the nearer dimly traced in purple, and the valleys between indicated by the whiter, woollier vapours that rise from their streams, a goodly land of fertile field and rich wood, cradled on the bosoms of those soft hills.

Nestled among the woods, clothing its hollows on almost every side, rises a low hill, with a species of table land on the top, scattered over with large thorns and scraggy oaks that cast their shadows over the pale buff bents of the short soft grass of the gravelly soil. Looking southward is a low, irregular, oldfashioned house, with two tall gable ends like eyebrows, and the lesser gable of a porch between them, all covered with large chequers of black timber, filled up with cream-coloured cement. A straight path leads from the porch between beds of scarlet geraniums, their luxuriant horse-shoe leaves weighed down with wet, and china asters, a drop in every quilling, to an oldfashioned sundial, and beside that dial stands Honora Charlecote, gazing joyously out on the bright morning, and trying for the hundredth time to make the shadow of that green old finger point to the same figure as the hand of her watch.

'Oh! down, down, there's a good dog, Fly; you'll knock me down! Vixen, poor little doggie, pray! Look at your paws,' as a blue greyhound and rough black terrier came springing joyously upon her, brushing away the silver dew from the shaven lawn.

'Down, down, lie down, dogs!' and with an obstreperous bound, Fly flew to the new comer, a young man in the robust strength of eight-and-twenty, of stalwart frame, very broad in the chest and shoulders, careless, homely, though perfectly gentlemanlike bearing, and hale, hearty, sunburnt face. It was such a look and such an arm as would win the most timid to his side in certainty of tenderness and protection, and the fond voice gave the same sense of power and of kindness, as he called out 'Holloa, Honor, there you are! Not given up the old fashion?'

'Not till you give me up, Humfrey,' she said, as she eagerly laid her neatly gloved fingers in the grasp of the great, broad, horny palm, 'or at least till you take your gun.'

'So you are not grown wiser?'

'Nor ever will be.'

'Every woman ought to learn to saddle a horse and fire off a gun.'

'Yes, against the civil war squires are always expecting. You shall teach me when the time comes.'

'You'll never see that time, nor any other, if you go out in those thin boots. I'll fetch Sarah's clogs; I suppose you have not a reasonable pair in the world.'

'My boots are quite thick, thank you.'

'Brown paper!' And indeed they were a contrast to his mighty nailed soles, and long, untanned buskins, nor did they greatly resemble the heavy, country-made galoshes which, with an elder brother's authority, he forced her to put on, observing that nothing so completely evinced the Londoner as her obstinacy in never having a pair of shoes that could keep anything out.

'And where are you going?'

'To Hayward's farm. Is that too far for you? He wants an abatement of his rent for some improvements, and I want to judge what they may be worth.'

'Hayward's—oh, not a bit too far!' and holding up her skirts, she picked her way as daintily as her weighty *chaussure* would permit, along the narrow green footway that crossed the expanse of dewy turf in which the dogs careered, getting their noses covered with flakes of thick gossamer, cemented together by dew. Fly scraped it off with a delicate forepaw, Vixen rolled over, and doubly entangled it in her rugged coat. Humfrey Charlecote strode on before his companion with his hands in his pockets, and beginning to whistle, but pausing to observe, over his shoulder, 'A sweet day for getting up the roots! You're not getting wet, I hope?'

'I couldn't through this rhinoceros hide, thank you. How exquisitely the mist is curling up, and showing the church-spire in the valley.'

'And I suppose you have been reading all manner of books?'

'I think the best was a great history of France.'

'France!' he repeated in a contemptuous John Bull tone.

'Ay, don't be disdainful; France was the centre of chivalry in the old time.'

'Better have been the centre of honesty.'

'And so it was in the time of St. Louis and his crusade. Do you know it, Humfrey?'

'Eh?'

That was full permission. Ever since Honora had

been able to combine a narration, Humfrey had been the recipient, though she seldom knew whether he attended, and from her babyhood upwards had been quite contented with trotting in the wake of his long strides, pouring out her ardent fancies, now and then getting an answer, but more often going on like a little singing bird, through the midst of his avocations, and quite complacent under his interruptions of calls to his dogs, directions to his labourers, and warnings to her to mind her feet and not her chatter. In the full stream of crusaders, he led her down one of the multitude of by-paths cleared out in the hazel coppice for sporting; here leading up a rising ground whence the tops of the trees might be overlooked, some flecked with gold, some blushing into crimson, and beyond them the needle point of the village spire, the vane flashing back the sun; there bending into a ravine, marshy at the bottom, and nourishing the lady fern, then again crossing glades, where the rabbits darted across the path, and the battle of Damietta was broken into by stern orders to Fly to come to heel, and the eating of the nuts which Humfrey pulled down from the branches, and held up to his cousin with superior good nature.

'A Mameluke rushed in with a scimitar streaming with blood, and——'

'Take care; do you want help over this fence?'

'Not I, thank you—And said he had just murdered the king——'

'Vic! ah! take your nose out of that. Here was a crop, Nora.'

'What was it?'

'You don't mean that you don't know wheat stubble?'

'I remember it was to be wheat.'

'Red wheat, the finest we ever had in this land; not a bit beaten down, and the colour perfectly beautiful before harvest; it used to put me in mind of your hair. A load to the acre; a fair specimen of the effect of drainage. Do you remember what a swamp it was?'

'I remember the beautiful loose-strifes that used to grow in that corner.'

'Ah! we have made an end of that trumpery.'

'You savage old Humfrey—beauties that they were.'

'What had they to do with my cornfields? A place for everything and everything in its place—French kings and all. What was this one doing wool gathering in Egypt?'

'Don't you understand, it had become the point for the blow at the Saracen power. Where was I? Oh, the Mameluke justified the murder, and wanted St. Louis to be king, but——'

'Ha! a fine covey, I only miss two out of them. These carrots, how their leaves are turned—that ought not to be.'

Honora could not believe that anything ought not to be that was as beautiful as the varied rosy tints of the hectic beauty of the exquisitely shaped and delicately pinked foliage of the field carrots, and with her cousin's assistance she soon had a large bouquet where no two leaves were alike, their hues ranging from the deepest purple or crimson to the palest yellow, or clear scarlet, like seaweed, through every intermediate variety of purple edged with green, green picked out with red or yellow, or *vice versâ*, in never ending brilliancy, such as Humfrey almost seemed to appreciate, as he said, 'Well, you have something as pretty as your weeds, eh, Honor?'

'I can't quite give up mourning for my dear long purples.'

'All very well by the river, but there's no beauty in things out of place, like your Louis in Egypt—well, what was the end of this predicament?'

So Humfrey had really heard, and been interested! With such encouragement, Honora proceeded swimmingly, and had nearly arrived at her hero's ransom, through nearly a mile of field paths, only occasionally interrupted by grunts from her auditor at farming not like his own, when crossing a narrow foot bridge across a clear stream, they stood before a farm-house, timbered and chimneyed much like the Holt, but with new sashes displacing the old lattice.

'Oh! Humfrey, how could you bring me to see such havoc? I never suspected you would allow it.'

'It was without asking leave; an attention to his bride; and now they want an abatement for improvements! Whew!'

'You should fine him for the damage he has done!'

'I can't be hard on him, he is more or less of an ass, and a good sort of fellow, very good to his labourers; he drove Jem Hurd to the infirmary himself, when he broke his arm. No, he is not a man to be hard upon.'

'You can't be hard on any one. Now that window really irritates my mind.'

'Now Sarah walked down to call on the bride, and came home full of admiration at the place being so lightsome and cheerful. Which of you two ladies am I to believe?'

'You ought to make it a duty to improve the general taste! Why don't you build a model farm-house, and let me make the design?'

'Ay, when I want one that nobody can live in. Come, it will be breakfast time.'

'Are not you going to have an interview?'

'No, I only wanted to take a survey of the alterations; two windows, smart door, iron fence, pulled down old barn, talks of another. Hm!'

'So he will get his reduction?'

'If he builds the barn. I shall try to see his wife, she has not been brought up to farming, and whether they get on or not, all depends on the way she may take it up. What are you looking at?'

'That lovely wreath of Traveller's Joy.'

'Do you want it?'

'No, thank you, it is too beautiful where it is.'

'There is a piece, going from tree to tree, by the Hiltonbury Gate, as thick as my arm; I just saved it when West was going to cut it down with the copse wood.'

'Well, you really are improving at last!'

'I thought you would never let me hear the last of it, besides there was a thrush's nest in it.'

By and by the cousins arrived at a field where Humfrey's portly short horns were coming forth after their milking, under the pilotage of an old white-headed man, bent nearly double, uncovering his head as the squire touched his hat in response, and shouted, 'Good morning.'

'If you please, sir,' said the old man, trying to erect himself, 'I wanted to speak to you.'

'Well.'

'If you please, sir, chimney smokes so as a body can scarce bide in the house, and the blacks come down terrible.'

'Wants sweeping,' roared Humfrey, into his deaf ears.

'Have swep it, sir; old woman's been up with her broom.'

'Old woman hasn't been high enough. Send Jack up outside with a rope and a bunch of furze, and let her stand at bottom.'

'That's it, sir!' cried the old man, with a triumphant snap of the fingers over his shoulder. 'Thank ye!'

'Here's Miss Honor, John;' and Honora came forward, her gravity somewhat shaken by the domestic offices of the old woman.

'I'm glad to see you still able to bring out the cows, John. Here's my favourite Daisy as tame as ever.'

'Anan!' and he looked at his master for explanation from the stronger and more familiar voice. 'I be deaf, you see, ma'am.'

'Miss Honor is glad to see Daisy as tame as ever,' shouted Humfrey.

'Ay! ay!' maundered on the old man; 'she ain't done no good of late, and Mr. West and I—us wanted to have fatted her this winter, but the squire, he wouldn't hear on it, because Miss Honor was such a terrible one for her. Says I, when I hears 'em say so, we shall have another dinner on the la-an, and the last was when the old squire was married, thirty-five years ago, come Michaelmas.'

Honora was much disposed to laugh at this freak of the old man's fancy, but to her surprise Humfrey coloured up, and looked so much out of countenance that a question darted through her mind whether he could have any such step in contemplation, and she began to review the young ladies of the neighbourhood, and to decide on each in turn that it would be intolerable to see her as Humfrey's wife; more at home at the Holt than herself. She had ample time for contemplation, for he had become very silent, and once or twice the presumptuous idea crossed her that he might be actually about to make her some confidence, but when he at length spoke, very near the house, it was only to say, 'Honor, I wanted to ask you if you think your father would wish me to ask young Sandbrook here?'

'Oh! thank you, I am sure he would be glad. You know poor Owen has nowhere to go, since his uncle has behaved so shamefully.'

'It must have been a great mortification——'

'To Owen? Of course it was, to be so cast off for his noble purpose.'

'I was thinking of old Mr. Sandbrook——'

'Old wretch! I've no patience with him!'

'Just as he has brought this nephew up and hopes to make him useful, and rest some of his cares upon him in his old age, to find him flying off upon this fresh course, and disappointing all his hopes.'

'But it is such a high and grand course, he ought to have rejoiced in it, and Owen is not his son.'

'A man of his age, brought up as he has been, can hardly be expected to enter into Owen's views.'

'Of course not. It is all sordid and mean, he cannot even understand the missionary spirit of resigning all. As Owen says, half the Scripture must be hyperbole to him, and so he is beginning Owen's persecution already.'

It was one of Humfrey's provoking qualities that no amount of eloquence would ever draw a word of condemnation from him, he would praise readily enough, but censure was very rare with him, and extenuation was always his first impulse, so the more Honora railed at Mr. Sandbrook's interference with his nephew's plans, the less satisfaction she received from him. She seemed to think that in order to admire Owen as he deserved, his uncle must be proportionably reviled, and though Humfrey did not imply a word save in commendation of the young missionary's devotion, she went in-doors feeling almost injured at his not understanding it; but Honora's petulance was a very bright, sunny piquancy, and she only appeared the more glowing and animated for it when she presented herself at the breakfast table, with a preposterous country appetite.

Afterwards she filled a vase very tastefully with her varieties of leaves, and enjoyed taking in her cousin Sarah, who admired the leaves greatly while she thought they came from Mrs. Mervyn's hot-house; but when she found they were the product of her own furrows, voted them coarse, ugly, withered things, such as only the simplicity of a Londoner could bring into civilized society. So Honora stood over her gorgeous feathery bouquet, not knowing whether to laugh or to be scornful, till Humfrey, taking up the vase, inquired, 'May I have it for my study?'

'Oh! yes, and welcome,' said Honora, laughing, and shaking her glowing tresses at him; 'I am thankful to any one who stands up for carrots.'

Good-natured Humfrey, thought she, it is all that I may not be mortified; but after all it is not those very good-natured people who best appreciate lofty actions. He is inviting Owen Sandbrook more because he thinks it would please papa, and because he compassionates him in his solitary lodgings, than because he feels the force of his glorious self-sacrifice.

The northern slope of the Holt was clothed with fir plantations, intersected with narrow paths, which gave admission to the depths of their lonely woodland palace, supported on rudely straight columns, dark save for the snowy exuding gum, roofed in by aspiring beam-like arms, bearing aloft their long tufts of dark blue green foliage, floored by the smooth, slippery, russet needle leaves as they fell, and perfumed by the peculiar fresh smell of turpentine. It was a still and lonely place, the very sounds making the silence more audible (if such an expression may be used), the wind whispering like the rippling waves of the sea in the tops of the pines, here and there the cry of a bird, or far, far away, the tinkle of the sheep bell, or the tone of the church clock, and of movement there was almost as little, only the huge horse ants soberly wending along their highways to their tall hillock thatched with pine leaves, or the squirrel in the ruddy, russet livery of the scene, racing from tree to tree, or sitting up with his feathery tail erect to extract with his delicate paws the seed from the base of the fir cone scale. Squirrels there lived to a good old age, till their plumy tails had turned white, for the squire's one fault in the eyes of keepers and gardeners was that he was soft-hearted towards 'the varmint.'
A Canadian forest on a small scale, an extremely miniature scale indeed, but still Canadian forests are of pine, and the Holt plantation was fir, and firs were pines, and it was a lonely musing place, and so on one of the stillest, clearest days of 'St. Luke's little summer,' the last afternoon of her visit at the Holt, there stood Honora, leaning against a tree stem, deep, deep, very deep in a vision of the primeval woodlands of the West, their red inhabitants, and the white man

who should carry the true, glad tidings westward, westward, ever from east to west. Did she know how completely her whole spirit and soul were surrendered to the worship of that devotion? Worship? Yes, the word is advisedly used; Honora had once given her spirit in homage to Schiller's self-sacrificing Max, the same heart-whole veneration was now rendered to the young missionary, multiplied tenfold by the hero being in a tangible, visible shape, and not by any means inclined to thwart or disdain the allegiance of the golden-haired girl. Nay, as family connexions frequently meeting, they had acted upon each other's minds more than either knew, even when the hour of parting had come, and words had been spoken which gave Honora something more to cherish in the image of Owen Sandbrook than even the hero and saint. There then she stood and dreamt, pensive and saddened indeed, but with a melancholy trenching very nearly on happiness in the intensity of its admiration, and the vague ennobling future of devoted usefulness in which her heart already claimed to share, as her person might in some far away period on which she could not dwell.

A sound approached, a firm footstep, falling with strong elasticity and such regular cadences, that it seemed to chime in with the pine-tree music, and did not startle her till it came so near that there was distinctive character to be discerned in the tread, and then with a strange, new shyness, she would have slipped away, but she had been seen, and Humfrey, with his timber race in his hand, appeared on the path, exclaiming, 'Ah, Honor, is it you come out to meet me, like old times? You have been so much taken up with your friend Master Owen that I have scarcely seen you of late.'

Honor did not move away, but she blushed deeply as she said, 'I am afraid I did not come to meet you, Humfrey.'

'No? What, you came for the sake of a brown

study? I wish I had known you were not busy, for I have been round all the woods marking timber.'

'Ah!' said she, rousing herself with some effort, 'I wonder how many trees I should have saved from the slaughter. Did you go and condemn any of my pets?'

'Not that I know of,' said Humfrey. 'I have touched nothing near the house.'

'Not even the old beech that was scathed with lightning? You know papa says that is the touchstone of influence; Sarah and Mr. West both against me,' laughed Honora, quite restored to her natural manner and confiding ease.

'The beech is likely to stand as long as you wish it,' said Humfrey, with an unaccustomed sort of matter-of-fact gravity, which surprised and startled her, so as to make her bethink herself whether she could have behaved ill about it, been saucy to Sarah, or the like.

'Thank you,' she said; 'have I made a fuss——?'

'No, Honor,' he said, with deliberate kindness, shutting up his knife, and putting it into his pocket; 'only I believe it is time we should come to an understanding.'

More than ever did she expect one of his kind remonstrances, and she looked up at him in expectation, and ready for defence, but his broad, sunburnt countenance looked marvellously heated, and he paused ere he spoke.

'I find I can't spare you, Honora, you had better stay at the Holt for good.' Her cheeks flamed, and her heart galloped, but she could not let herself understand.

'Honor, you are old enough now, and I do not think you need fear. It is almost your home already, and I believe I can make you happy, with the blessing of God——' He paused, but as she could not frame an answer in her consternation, continued, 'Perhaps I should not have spoken so suddenly, but I thought you would not mind me; I should like to have had one word from my little Honor before I go to your father, but don't if you had rather not.'

'O don't go to papa, please don't,' she cried, 'it would only make him sorry.'

Humfrey stood as if under an unexpected shock.

'Oh! how came you to think of it?' she said in her distress; 'I never did, and it can never be—I am so sorry!'

'Very well, my dear, do not grieve about it,' said Humfrey, only bent on soothing her; 'I dare say you are quite right, you are used to people in London much more suitable to you than a stupid, homely fellow like me, and it was a foolish fancy to think it might be otherwise. Don't cry, Honor dear, I can't bear that!'

'O Humfrey, only understand, please! You are the very dearest person in the world to me after papa and mamma; and as to fine London people, oh no, indeed! But——'

'It is Owen Sandbrook; I understand,' said Humfrey, gravely.

She made no denial.

'But Honor,' he anxiously exclaimed, 'you are not going out in this wild way among the backwoods, it would break your mother's heart; and he is not fit to take care of you. I mean he cannot think of it now.'

'O no, no, I could not leave papa and mamma; but some time or other——'

'Is this arranged? Does your father know it?'

'O Humfrey, of course!'

'Then it is an engagement?'

'No,' said Honora, sadly; 'papa said I was too young, and he wished I had heard nothing about it. We are to go on as if nothing had happened, and I know they think we shall forget all about it! As if we could! Not that I wish it to be different. I know it would be wicked to desert papa and mamma while she is so unwell. The truth is, Humfrey,' and her voice sank, 'that it cannot be while they live.'

'My poor little Honor!' he said, in a tone of the most unselfish compassion.

She had entirely forgotten his novel aspect, and only thought of him as the kindest friend to whom she could open her heart.

'Don't pity me,' she said in exultation; 'think what it is to be *his* choice. Would I have him give up his aims, and settle down in the loveliest village in England? No, indeed, for then it would not be Owen! I am happier in the thought of him than I could be with everything present to enjoy.'

'I hope you will continue to find it so,' he said, repressing a sigh.

'I should be ashamed of myself if I did not,' she continued with glistening eyes. 'Should not I have patience to wait while he is at his real glorious labour? And as to home, that's not altered, only better and brighter for the definite hope and aim that will go through everything, and make me feel all I do a preparation.'

'Yes, you know him well,' said Humfrey; 'you saw him constantly when he was at Westminster.'

'O yes, and always! Why, Humfrey, it is my great glory and pleasure to feel that he formed me! When he went to Oxford, he brought me home all the thoughts that have been my better life. All my dearest books we read together, and what used to look dry and cold, gained light and life after he touched it.'

'Yes, I see.'

His tone reminded her of what had passed, and she said, timidly, 'I forgot! I ought not! I have vexed you, Humfrey.'

'No,' he said, in his full tender voice; 'I see that it was vain to think of competing with one of so much higher claims. If he goes on in the course he has chosen, yours will have been a noble choice, Honor; and I believe,' he added, with a sweetness of smile that almost made her forgive the *if*, 'that you are one to be better pleased *so* than with more ordinary happiness. I have no doubt it is all right.'

'Dear Humfrey, you are so good!' she said, struck with his kind resignation, and utter absence of acerbity in his disappointment.

'Forget this, Honora,' he said, as they were coming to the end of the pine wood; 'let us be as we were before.'

Honora gladly promised, and excepting for her wonder at such a step on the part of the cousin whose plaything and pet she had hitherto been, she had no temptation to change her manner. She loved him as much as ever, but only as a kind elder brother, and she was glad hat he was wise enough to see his immeasurable inferiority to the young missionary. It was a wonderful thing, and she was sorry for his disappointment; but after all, he took it so quietly that she did not think it could have hurt him much. It was only that he wanted to keep his pet in the country. He was not capable of love like Owen Sandbrook's.

Years passed on. Rumour had bestowed Mr. Charlecote of Hiltonbury on every lady within twenty miles, but still in vain. His mother was dead, his sister married to an old college fellow, who had waited half a life time for a living, but still he kept house alone.

And open house it was, with a dinner table ever expanding for chance guests, strawberry or syllabub feasts half the summer, and Christmas feasts extending wide on either side of the twelve days. Every one who wanted a holiday was free of the Holt; young sportsmen tried their inexperienced guns under the squire's patient eye; and mammas disposed of their children for weeks together, to enjoy the run of the house and garden, and rides according to age, on pony, donkey, or Mr. Charlecote. No festivity in the neighbourhood was complete without his sunshiny presence; he was wanted wherever there was any family event;

and was godfather, guardian, friend, and adviser of all. Every one looked on him as a sort of exclusive property, yet he had room in his heart for all. As a magistrate, he was equally indispensable in county government, and a charity must be undeserving indeed that had not Humfrey Charlecote, Esq., on the committee. In his own parish he was a beneficent monarch; on his own estate a mighty farmer, owning that his relaxation and delight were his turnips, his bullocks, and machines; and so content with them, and with his guests, that Honora never recollected that walk in the pine woods without deciding that to have monopolized him would have been an injury to the public, and perhaps less for his happiness than this free, open-hearted bachelor life. Seldom did she recal that scene to mind, for she had never been by it rendered less able to trust to him as her friend and protector, and she stood in need of his services and his comfort, when her father's death had left him the nearest relative, who could advise or transact business for her and her mother. Then, indeed, she leant on him as on the kindest and most helpful of brothers.

Mrs. Charlecote was too much acclimatized to the city to be willing to give up her old residence, and Honor not only loved it fondly, but could not bear to withdraw from the local charities where her tasks had hitherto lain; and Woolstone-lane, therefore, continued their home, though the summer and autumn usually took them out of London.

Such was the change in Honora's outward life. How was it with that inmost shrine where dwelt her heart and soul? A copious letter writer, Owen Sandbrook's correspondence never failed to find its way to her, though they did not stand on such terms as to write to one another; and in those letters she lived, doing her day's work with cheerful brightness, and seldom seeming pre-occupied, but imagination, heart, and soul were with his mission.

Very indignant was she when the authorities, instead

of sending him to the interesting children of the forests, thought proper to waste him on mere colonists, some of them Yankee, some Presbyterian Scots. He was asked insolent, nasal questions, his goods were coolly treated as common property, and it was intimated to him on all hands that as Englishman he was little in their eyes, as clergyman less, as gentleman least of all. Was this what he had sacrificed everything for?

By dint of strong complaints and entreaties, after he had quarrelled with most of his flock, he accomplished an exchange into a district where red men formed the chief of his charge; and Honora was happy, and watched for histories of noble braves, gallant hunters, and meek-eyed squaws.

Slowly, slowly she gathered that the picturesque deer skins had become dirty blankets, and that the diseased, filthy, sophisticated savages were among the worst of the pitiable specimens of the effect of contact with the most evil side of civilization. To them, as Owen wrote, a missionary was only a white man who gave no brandy, and the rest of his parishioners were their obdurate, greedy, trading tempters! It had been a shame to send him to such a hopeless set, when there were others on whom his toils would not be thrown away. However, he should do his best.

And Honor went on expecting the wonders his best would work, only the more struck with admiration by hearing that the locality was a swamp of luxuriant vegetation, and equally luxuriant fever and ague; and the letter he wrote thence to her mother on the news of their loss did her more good than all Humfrey's considerate kindness.

Next, he had had the ague, and had gone to Toronto for change of air. Report spoke of Mr. Sandbrook as the most popular preacher who had appeared in Toronto for years, attracting numbers to his pulpit, and sending them away enraptured by his power of language. How beautiful that a man of such talents, always so much stimulated by appreciation, should give up all this most congenial scene, and devote himself to his obscure mission!

Report said more, but Honora gave it no credit till old Mr. Sandbrook called one morning in Woolstone-lane, by his nephew's desire, to announce to his friends that he had formed an engagement with Miss Charteris, the daughter of a general officer there in command.

Honor sat out all the conversation; and Mrs. Charlecote did not betray herself; though, burning with a mother's wrath, she did nothing worse than hope they would be happy.

Yet Honor had not dethroned the monarch of her imagination. She reiterated to herself and to her mother that she had no ground of complaint, that it had been understood that the past was to be forgotten, and that Owen was far more worthily employed than in dwelling on them. No blame could attach to him, and it was wise to choose one accustomed to the country and able to carry out his plans. The personal feeling might go, but veneration survived.

Mrs. Charlecote never rested till she had learnt all the particulars. It was a dashing, fashionable family, and Miss Charteris had been the gayest of the gay, till she had been impressed by Mr. Sandbrook's ministrations. From pope to lover, Honor knew how easy was the transition; but she zealously nursed her admiration for the beauty, who was exchanging her gaieties for the forest missions; she made her mother write cordially, and send out a pretty gift, and treated as a personal affront all reports of the Charteris disapprobation, and of the self-will of the young people. They were married, and the next news that Honora heard was, that the old general had had a fit from passion; thirdly, came tidings that the eldest son, a prosperous M.P., had not only effected a reconciliation, but had obtained a capital living for Mr. Sandbrook, not far from the family-seat.

Mrs. Charlecote declared that her daughter should not stay in town to meet the young couple, and

Honora's resistance was not so much dignity, as a feverish spirit of opposition, which succumbed to her sense of duty, but not without such wear and tear of strained cheerfulness and suppressed misery, that when at length her mother had brought her away, the fatigue of the journey completed the work, and she was prostrated for weeks by low fever. The blow had fallen. He had put his hand to the plough and looked back. Faithlessness towards herself had been passed over unrecognised, faithlessness towards his self-consecration was quite otherwise. That which had absorbed her affections and adoration had proved an unstable, excitable being! Alas! would that long ago she had opened her eyes to the fact that it was her own lofty spirit, not his steadfastness, which had first kept it out of the question that the mission should be set aside for human love. The crash of her idolatry was the greater because it had been so highly pitched, so closely intermingled with the true worship. She was long ill, the past series of disappointments telling when her strength was reduced; and for many a week she would lie still and dreamy, but fretted and wearied, so as to control herself with difficulty when in the slightest degree disturbed, or called upon to move or think. When her strength returned under her mother's tender nursing, the sense of duty revived. She thought her youth utterly gone, with the thinning of her hair and the wasting of her cheeks, but her mother must be the object of her care and solicitude, and she would exert herself for her sake, to save her grief, and hide the wound left by the rending away of the jewel of her heart. So she set herself to seem to like whatever her mother proposed, and she acted her interest so well that insensibly it became real. After all, she was but four-and-twenty, and the fever had served as an expression of the feeling that would have its way: she had had a long rest, which had relieved the sense of pent-up and restrained suffering, and vigour and buoyancy were a part of her character; her tone and manner resumed their cheerfulness, her spirits came back, though still with the dreary feeling that the hope and aim of life were gone, when she was left to her own musings; she was little changed, and went on with daily life, contented and lively over the details, and returning to her interest in reading, in art, poetry, and in all good works, while her looks resumed their brightness, and her mother congratulated herself once more on the rounded cheek and profuse curls.

At the year's end Humfrey Charlecote renewed his proposal. It was no small shock to find herself guilty of his having thus long remained single, and she was touched by his kind forbearance, but there was no bringing herself either to love him, or to believe that he loved her, with such love as had been her vision. The image around which she had bound her heartstrings came between him and her, and again she begged his pardon, and told him she liked him too well as he was to think of him in any other light. Again he, with the most tender patience and humility, asked her to forgive him for having harassed her, and betrayed so little chagrin that she ascribed his offer to generous compassion at her desertion.

CHAPTER II.

'He who lets his feelings run
In soft luxurious flow,
Shrinks when hard service must be done,
And faints at every woe.'

SEVEN years more, and Honora was in mourning for her mother. She was alone in the world, without any near or precious claim, those clinging tendrils of her heart rent from their oldest, surest earthly stay, and her time left vacant from her dearest, most constant occupation. Her impulse was to devote herself and her fortune at once to the good work which most engaged her imagination, but Humfrey Charlecote, her sole relation, since heart complaint had carried off his sister Sarah, interfered with the authority he had always exercised over her, and insisted on her waiting one full year before pledging herself to anything. At one-and-thirty, with her golden hair and light figure, her delicate skin and elastic step, she was still too young to keep house in solitude, and she invited to her home a friendless old governess of her own, sick at heart with standing for the Governess's Institution, promising her a daughter's care and attendance on her old age. Gentle old Miss Wells was but too happy in her new quarters, though she constantly averred that she knew she should not continue there; treated as injuries to herself all Honor's assertions of the dignity of age and old maidishness, and remained convinced that she should soon see her married.

Honora had not seen Mr. Sandbrook since his return from Canada, though his living was not thirty miles from the City. There had been exchanges of calls when he had been in London, but these had only resulted in the leaving of cards ; and from various causes she had been unable to meet him at dinner. She heard of him, however, from their mutual connexion, old Mrs. Sandbrook, who had made a visit at Wrapworth, and came home stored with anecdotes of the style in which he lived, the charms of Mrs. Sandbrook, and the beauty of the children. As far as Honora could gather, and very unwillingly she did so, he was leading the life of an easy-going, well-beneficed clergyman, not neglecting the parish, according to the requirements of the day, indeed slightly exceeding them, very popular, good-natured, and charitable, and in great request in a numerous, demi-suburban neighbourhood, for all sorts of not unclerical gaieties. The Rev. O. Sandbrook was often to be met with in the papers, preaching everywhere and for everything, and whispers went about of his speedy promotion to a situation of greater note. In the seventh year of his marriage, his wife died, and Honora was told of his overwhelming grief, how he utterly refused all comfort or alleviation, and threw himself with all his soul into his parish and his children. People spoke of him as going about among the poor from morning to night, with his little ones by his side, shrinking from all other society, teaching them and nursing them himself, and endeavouring to the utmost to be as both parents in one. The youngest, a delicate infant, soon followed her mother to the grave, and old Mrs. Sandbrook proved herself to have no parent's heart by being provoked with his agonizing grief for the 'poor little sickly thing,' while it was not in Honora's nature not to feel the more tenderly towards the idol of her girlish days, because he was in trouble.

It was autumn, the period when leaves fall off and grow damp, and London birds of passage fly home to their smoky nests. Honora, who had gone to Weymouth chiefly because she saw Miss Wells would be disappointed if she did otherwise ; when there, had grown happily at home with the waves, and in talking to the old fishermen ; but had come back because Miss Wells thought it chilly and dreary, and pined for London warmth and snugness. The noonday sun had found the way in at the oriel window of the drawing-room, and traced the reflection of the merchant's mark upon the upper pane in distorted outline on the wainscoted wall ; it smiled on the glowing tints of Honora's hair, but seemed to die away against the blackness of her dress, as she sat by the table, writing letters, while opposite, in the brightness of the fire, sat the pale, placid Miss Wells with her morning nest of sermon books and needlework around her.

Honor yawned ; Miss Wells looked up with kind anxiety. She knew such a yawn was equivalent to a sigh, and that it was dreary work to settle in at home again this first time without the mother.

Then Honor smiled, and played with her pen wiper.
'Well,' she said, 'it is comfortable to be at home again!'
'I hope you will soon be able to feel so, my dear,' said the kind old governess.
'I mean it,' said Honor cheerfully ; then sighing, 'But do you know? Mr. Askew wishes his curates to visit at the asylum instead of ladies.'

Miss Wells burst out into all the indignation that was in her mild nature. Honor not to visit at the asylum founded chiefly by her own father !

'It is a parish affair now,' said Honor ; 'and I believe those Miss Stones and their set have been very troublesome. Besides, I think he means to change its character.'

'It is very inconsiderate of him,' said Miss Wells ; 'he ought to have consulted you.'

'Everyone loves his own charity the best,' said Honora ; 'Humfrey says endowments are generally a mistake, each generation had better do its own work to the utmost. I wish Mr. Askew had not begun now, it was the work I specially looked to, but I let it alone while——and he cannot be expected——'

'I should have expected it of him though!' exclaimed Miss Wells, 'and he ought to know better! How have you heard it?'

'I have a note from him this morning,' said Honora; 'he asks me Humfrey Charlecote's address; you know he and Mr. Sandbrook are trustees,' and her voice grew the sadder.

'If I am not much mistaken, Mr. Charlecote will represent to him his want of consideration.'

'I think not,' said Honora; 'I should be sorry to make the clergyman's hard task here any harder for the sake of my feelings. Late incumbent's daughters are proverbially inconvenient. No, I would not stand in the way, but it makes me feel as if my work in St. Wulstan's were done,' and the tears dropped fast.

'Dear, dear Honora!' began the old lady, eagerly, but her words and Honora's tears were both checked by the sound of a bell, that bell within the court, to which none but intimates found access.

'Strange! It is the thought of old times, I suppose,' said Honor, smiling, 'but I could have said that was Owen Sandbrook's ring.'

The words were scarcely spoken, ere Mr. Sandbrook and Captain Charteris were announced; and there entered a clergyman leading a little child in each hand. How changed from the handsome, hopeful youth from whom she had parted! Thin, slightly bowed, grief-stricken, and worn, she would scarcely have known him, and as if to hide how much she felt, she bent quickly, after shaking hands with him, to kiss the two children, flaxen-curled creatures in white, with black ribbons. They both shrank closer to their father.

'Cilly, my love, Owen, my man, speak to Miss Charlecote,' he said, 'she is a very old friend of mine. This is my bonny little housekeeper,' he added, 'and here's a sturdy fellow for four years old, is not he?'

The girl, a delicate fairy of six, barely accepted an embrace, and clung the faster to her father, with a gesture as though to repel all advance. The boy took a good stare out of a pair of resolute grey eyes, with one foot in advance, and offered both hands. Honora would have taken him on her knee, but he retreated, and both leant against their father as he sat, an arm round each; after shaking hands with Miss Wells, whom he recollected at once, and presenting his brother-in-law, whose broad, open, sailor countenance, hardy and weather-stained, was a great contrast to his pale, hollow, furrowed cheeks and heavy eyes.

'Will you tell me your name, my dear?' said Honora, feeling the children the easiest to talk to; but the little girl's pretty lips pouted, and she nestled nearer to her father.

'Her name is Lucilla,' he answered with a sigh, recalling that it had been his wife's name. 'We are all somewhat of little savages,' he added, in excuse for the child's silence. 'We have seen few strangers at Wrapworth of late.'

'I did not know you were in London.'

'It was a sudden measure—all my brother's doing,' he said; 'I am quite taken out of my own guidance.'

'I went down to Wrapworth, and found him very unwell, quite out of order, and neglecting himself,' said the captain; 'so I have brought him up for advice, as I could not make him hear reason.'

'I was afraid you were looking very ill,' said Honora, hardly daring to glance at his changed face.

'Can't help being ill,' returned Captain Charteris, 'running about the village in all weathers in a coat like that, and sitting down to play with the children in his wet things. I saw what it would come to, last time.'

Mr. Sandbrook could not repress a cough, which told plainly what it was come to.

Miss Wells asked whom he intended to consult, and there was some talk on physicians, but the subject was turned off by Mr. Sandbrook bending down to point out to little Owen a beautiful carving of a brooding dove on her nest, which formed the central bracket of the fine old mantelpiece.

'There, my man, that pretty bird has been sitting there ever since I can remember. How like it all looks to old times! I could imagine myself running in from Westminster on a saint's day.'

'It is little altered in some things,' said Honor. The last great change was too fresh!

'Yes,' said Mr. Sandbrook, raising his eyes towards her with the look that used to go so deep of old, 'we have both gone through what makes the unchangeableness of these impassive things the more striking.'

'I can't see,' said the little girl, pulling his hand.

'Let me lift you up, my dear,' said Honora; but the child turned her back on her, and said, 'Father.'

He rose, and was bending, at the little imperious voice, though evidently too weak for the exertion, but the sailor made one step forward, and pouncing on Miss Lucilla, held her up in his arms close to the carving. The two little feet made signs of kicking, and she said in anything but a grateful voice, 'Put me down, Uncle Kit.'

Uncle Kit complied, and she retreated under her papa's wing, pouting, but without another word of being lifted, though she had been far too much occupied with struggling to look at the dove. Meantime her brother had followed up her request by saying, 'me,' and he fairly put out his arms to be lifted by Miss Charlecote, and made most friendly acquaintance with all the curiosities of the carving. The rest of the visit was chiefly occupied by the children, to whom their father was eager to show all that he had admired when little older than they were, thus displaying a perfect and minute recollection and affection for the place, which much gratified Honora. The little girl began to thaw somewhat under the influence of amusement, but there was still a curious ungraciousness towards all attentions. She required those of her father as a right, but shook off all others in a manner which might be either shyness or independence; but as she was a pretty and naturally graceful child, it had a somewhat engaging air of caprice. They took leave, Mr. Sandbrook telling the children to thank Miss Charlecote for being so kind to them, which neither would do, and telling her as he pressed her hand, that he hoped to see her again. Honora felt as if an old page in her history had been re-opened, but it was not the page of her idolatry, it was that of the fall of her idol! She did not see in him the champion of the truth, but his presence palpably showed her the excitable weakness which she had taken for inspiration, while the sweetness and sympathy warmed her heart towards him, and made her feel that she had underrated his attractiveness. His implications that he knew she sympathized with him had touched her greatly, and then he looked so ill!

A note from old Mrs. Sandbrook begged her to meet him at dinner the next day, and she was glad of the opportunity of learning the doctor's verdict upon him, though all the time she knew the meeting would be but pain, bringing before her the disappointment not *of* him, but *in* him.

No one was in the drawing-room but Captain Charteris, who came and shook hands with her as if they were old friends; but she was somewhat amazed at missing Mrs. Sandbrook, whose formality would be shocked by leaving her guests in the lurch.

'Some disturbance in the nursery department, I fancy,' said the captain; 'those children have never been from home, and they are rather exacting, poor things.'

'Poor little things!' echoed Honora; then, anxious to profit by the *tête-à-tête*, 'has Mr. Sandbrook seen Dr. L.?'

'Yes, it is just as I apprehended. Lungs very much affected, right one nearly gone. Nothing for it but the Mediterranean.'

'Indeed!'

'It is no wonder. Since my poor sister died he has never taken the most moderate care of his health, perfectly revelled in dreariness and desolateness, I believe! He has had this cough about him ever since the winter, when he walked up and down whole nights with that poor child, and never would hear of any advice till I brought him up here almost by force.'

'I am sure it was time.'

'May it be in time, that's all.'

'Italy does so much! But what will become of the children?'

'They must go to my brother's of course. I have told him I will see him there, but I will not have the children! There's not the least chance of his mending, if they are to be always lugging him about——'

The captain was interrupted by the entrance of Mrs. Sandbrook, who looked a good deal worried, though she tried to put it aside, but on the captain saying, 'I'm afraid that you have troublesome guests, ma'am,' out it all came, how it had been discovered late in the day that Master Owen *must* sleep in his papa's room, in a crib to himself, and how she had been obliged to send out to hire the necessary articles, subject to his nurse's approval; and the captain's sympathy having opened her heart, she further informed them of the inconvenient rout the said nurse had made about getting new milk for them, for which Honor could have found it in her heart to justify her, 'and poor Owen is just as bad,' quoth the old lady; 'I declare those children are wearing his very life out, and yet he will not hear of leaving them behind.'

She was interrupted by his appearance at that moment, as usual, with a child in either hand, and a very sad picture it was, so mournful and spiritless was his countenance, with the hectic tint of decay evident on each thin cheek, and those two fair healthful creatures clinging to him, thoughtless of their past loss, unconscious of that which impended. Little Owen, after one good stare, evidently recognised a friend in Miss Charlecote, and let her seat him upon her knee, listening to her very complacently, but gazing very hard all the time at her, till at last, with an experimental air, he stretched one hand and stroked the broad golden ringlet that hung near him, evidently to satisfy himself whether it really was hair. Then he found his way to her watch, a pretty little one from Geneva, with enamelled flowers at the back, which so struck his fancy that he called out, 'Cilly, look!' The temptation drew the little girl nearer, but with her hands behind her back, as if bent on making no advance to the stranger.

Honora thought her the prettiest child she had ever seen. Small and lightly formed, there was more symmetry in her little fairy figure than usual at her age, and the skin was exquisitely fine and white, tinted with a soft eglantine pink, deepening into roses on the cheeks; the hair was in long flaxen curls, and the eyelashes, so long and fair that at times they caught a glossy light, shaded eyes of that deep blue upon that limpid white, which is like nothing but the clear tints of old porcelain. The features were as yet unformed, but small and delicate, and the upright Napoleon gesture had something peculiarly quaint and pretty in such a soft-looking little creature. The boy was a handsome fellow, with more solidity and sturdiness, and Honora could scarcely continue to amuse him, as she thought of the father's pain in parting with two such beings—his sole objects of affection. A moment's wish flashed across her, but was dismissed the next moment as a mere childish romance.

Old Mr. Sandbrook came in, and various other guests arrived, old acquaintance to whom Owen must be re-introduced, and he looked fagged and worn by the time all the greetings had been exchanged and all the remarks made on his children. When dinner was announced, he remained to the last with them, and did not appear in the dining-room till his uncle had had time to look round for him, and mutter something discontentedly about 'those brats.' The vacant chair was beside Honora, and he was soon seated in it, but at first he did not seem inclined to talk, and leant back, so white and exhausted, that she thought it kinder to leave him to himself.

When, somewhat recruited, he said in a low voice something of his hopes that his little Cilly, as he called her, would be less shy another time, and Honora responding heartily, he quickly fell into the parental strain of anecdotes of the children's sayings and doings, whence Honora collected that in his estimation Lucilla's forte was decision and Owen's was sweetness, and that he was completely devoted to them, nursing and teaching them himself, and finding his whole solace in them. Tender pity moved her strongly towards him, as she listened to the evidences of the desolateness of his home and his heavy sorrow; and yet it was pity alone, admiration would not revive, and indeed, in spite of herself, her judgment *would* now and then respond 'unwise,' or 'weak,' or 'why permit this?' at details of Lucilla's *mutinerie*. Presently she found that his intentions were quite at variance with those of his brother. His purpose was fixed to take the children with him.

'They are very young,' said Honora.

'Yes; but their nurse is a most valuable person, and can arrange perfectly for them, and they will always be under my eye.'

'That was just what Captain Charteris seemed to dread.'

'He little knows,' began Mr. Sandbrook, with a sigh. 'Yes, I know he is most averse to it, and he is one who always carries his point, but he will not do so here; he imagines that they may go to their aunt's nursery, but,' with an added air of confidence, 'that will never do!'

Honora's eyes asked more.

'In fact,' he said, as the flush of pain rose on his cheeks, 'the Charteris children are not brought up as

I should wish to see mine. There are influences at work there not suited for those whose home must be a country parsonage, if—— Little Cilly has come in for more admiration there already than is good for her.'

'It cannot be easy for her not to meet with that.'

'Why, no,' said the gratified father, smiling sadly; 'but Castle Blanch training might make the mischief more serious. It is a gay household, and I cannot believe with Kit Charteris that the children are too young to feel the blight of worldly influence. Do not you think with me, Nora?' he concluded in so exactly the old words and manner as to stir the very depths of her heart, but woe worth the change from the hopes of youth to this premature fading into despondency, and the implied farewell! She did think with him completely, and felt the more for him, as she believed that these Charterises had led him and his wife into the gaieties, which since her death he had forsworn and abhorred as temptations. She thought it hard that he should not have his children with him, and talked of all the various facilities for taking them that she could think of, till his face brightened under the grateful sense of sympathy.

She did not hold the same opinion all the evening. The two children made their appearance at dessert, and there began by insisting on both sitting on his knees; Owen consented to come to her, but Lucilla would not stir, though she put on some pretty little coquettish airs, and made herself extremely amiable to the gentleman who sat on her father's other hand, making smart replies, that were repeated round the table with much amusement.

But the ordinance of departure with the ladies was one of which the sprite had no idea; Honor held out her hand for her; Aunt Sandbrook called her; her father put her down; she shook her curls, and said she should not leave father; it was stupid up in the drawing-room, and she hated ladies, which confession set every one laughing, so as quite to annihilate the effect of Mr. Sandbrook's 'Yes, go, my dear.'

Finally, he took the two up-stairs himself—the stairs which, as he had told Honora that evening, were his greatest enemies, and he remained a long time in their nursery, not coming down till tea was in progress. Mrs. Sandbrook always made it herself at the great silver urn, which had been a testimonial to her husband, and it was not at first that she had a cup ready for him. He looked even worse than at dinner, and Honora was anxious to see him resting comfortably; but he had hardly sat down on the sofa, and taken the cup in his hand, before a dismal childish wail was heard from above, and at once he started up, so hastily as to cough violently. Captain Charteris, breaking off a conversation, came rapidly across the room just as he was moving to the door. 'You're not going to those imps——'

Owen moved his head, and stepped forward.

'I'll settle them.'

Renewed cries met his ears. 'No—— a strange place——' he said. 'I must——'

He put his brother-in-law back with his hand, and was gone. The captain could not contain his vexation, 'That's the way those brats serve him every night!' he exclaimed; 'they will not attempt to go to sleep without him! Why, I've found him writing his sermon with the boy wrapped up in blankets in his lap; there's no sense in it.'

After about ten minutes, during which Mr. Sandbrook did not reappear, Captain Charteris muttered something about going to see about him, and stayed away a good while. When he came down, he came and sat down by Honora, and said, 'He is going to bed, quite done for.'

'That must be better for him than talking here.'

'Why, what do you think I found? Those intolerable brats would not stop crying unless he told them a story, and there was he with his voice quite gone, coughing every two minutes, and romancing on with some allegory about children marching on their little paths, and playing on their little fiddles. So I told Miss Cilly that if she cared a farthing for her father, she would hold her tongue, and I packed her up, and put her into her nursery. She'll mind me when she sees I will be minded; and as for little Owen, nothing would satisfy him but his promising not to go away. I saw that chap asleep before I came down, so there's no fear of the yarn beginning again; but you see what chance there is of his mending while those children are at him day and night.'

'Poor things! they little know.'

'One does not expect them to know, but one does expect them to show a little rationality. It puts one out of all patience to see him so weak. If he is encouraged to take them abroad, he may do so, but I wash my hands of him. I wont be responsible for him—let them go alone!'

Honora saw this was a reproach to her for the favour with which she had regarded the project. She saw that the father's weakness quite altered the case, and her former vision flashed across her again, but she resolutely put it aside for consideration, and only made the unmeaning answer, 'It is very sad and perplexing.'

'A perplexity of his own making. As for their not going to Castle Blanch, they were always there in my poor sister's time a great deal more than was good for any of them, or his parish either, as I told him then; and now, if he finds out that it is a worldly household, as he calls it, why, what harm is that to do to a couple of babies like those? If Mrs. Charteris does not trouble herself much about the children, there are governesses and nurses enough for a score!'

'I must own,' said Honora, 'that I think he is right. Children are never too young for impressions.'

'I'll tell you what, Miss Charlecote, the way he is going on is enough to ruin the best children in the world. That little Cilly is the most arrant little flirt

I ever came across; it is like a comedy to see the absurd little puss going on with the curate, ay, and with every parson that comes to Wrapworth; and she sees nothing else. Impressions! All she wants is to be safe shut up with a good governess, and other children. It would do her a dozen times more good than all his stories of good children and their rocky paths, and boats that never sailed on any reasonable principle.'

'Poor child,' said Honora, smiling, 'she is a little witch.'

'And,' continued the uncle, 'if he thinks it so bad for them, he had better take the only way of saving them from it for the future, or they will be there for life. If he gets through this winter, it will only be by the utmost care.'

Honora kept her project back with the less difficulty, because she doubted how it would be received by the rough captain; but it won more and more upon her, as she rattled home through the gas lights, and though she knew she should learn to love the children only to have the pang of losing them, she gladly cast this foreboding aside as selfish, and applied herself impartially as she hoped to weigh the duty, but trembling were the hands that adjusted the balance. Alone as she stood, without a tie, was not she marked out to take such an office of mere pity and charity? Could she see the friend of her childhood forced either to peril his life by his care of his motherless children, or else to leave them to the influences he so justly dreaded? Did not the case cry out to her to follow the promptings of her heart? Ay, but might not, said caution, her assumption of the charge lead their father to look on her as willing to become their mother? Oh, fie on such selfish prudery imputing such a thought to yonder broken-hearted, sinking widower! He had as little room for such folly as she had inclination to find herself on the old terms. The hero of her imagination he could never be again, but it would be weak consciousness to scruple at offering so obvious an act of compassion. She would not trust herself, she would go by what Miss Wells said. Nevertheless she composed her letter to Owen Sandbrook between waking and sleeping all night, and dreamed of little creatures nestling in her lap, and small hands playing with her hair. How coolly she strove to speak as she described the dilemma to the old lady, and how her heart leapt when Miss Wells, her mind moving in the grooves traced out by sympathy with her pupil, exclaimed, 'Poor little dears, what a pity they should not be with you, my dear, they would be a nice interest for you!'

Perhaps Miss Wells thought chiefly of the brightening in her child's manner, and the alert vivacity of eye and voice such as she had not seen in her since she had lost her mother; but be that as it might, her words were the very sanction so much longed for, and ere long Honora had her writing-case before her, cogitating over the opening address, as if her whole meaning were implied in them.

'My dear Owen,' came so naturally that it was too like an attempt to recur to the old familiarity. 'My dear Mr. Sandbrook?' So formal as to be conscious! 'Dear Owen?' Yes, that was the cousinly medium, and in diffident phrases of restrained eagerness, now seeming too affectionate, now too cold, she offered to devote herself to his little ones, to take a house on the coast, and endeavour to follow out his wishes with regard to them, her good old friend supplying her lack of experience.

With a beating heart she awaited the reply. It was but a few lines, but all Owen was in them.

'MY DEAR NORA—You always were an angel of goodness. I feel your kindness more than I can express. If my darlings were to be left at all, it should be with you, but I cannot contemplate it. Bless you for the thought!

'Yours ever, O. SANDBROOK.'

She heard no more for a week, during which a dread

of pressing herself on him prevented her from calling on old Mrs. Sandbrook. At last, to her surprise, she received a visit from Captain Charteris, the person whom she looked on as least propitious, and most inclined to regard her as an enthusiastic silly young lady. He was very gruff, and gave a bad account of his patient. The little boy had been unwell, and the exertion of nursing him had been very injurious; the captain was very angry with illness, child, and father.

'However,' he said, 'there's one good thing, L. has forbidden the children's perpetually hanging on him, sleeping in his room, and so forth. With the constitutions to which they have every right, poor things, he could not find a better way of giving them the seeds of consumption. That settles it. Poor fellow, he has not the heart to hinder their always pawing him, so there's nothing for it but to separate them from him.'

'And may I have them?' asked Honor, too anxious to pick her words.

'Why, I told him I would come and see whether you were in earnest in your kind offer. You would find them no sinecure.'

'It would be a great happiness,' said she, struggling with tears that might prevent the captain from depending on her good sense, and speaking calmly and sadly; 'I have no other claims, nothing to tie me to any place. I am a good deal older than I look, and my friend, Miss Wells, has been a governess. *She* is really a very wise, judicious person, to whom he may quite trust. Owen and I were children together, and I know nothing that I should like better than to be useful to him.'

'Humph!' said the captain, more touched than he liked to betray; 'well, it seems the only thing to which he can bear to turn!'

'Oh!' she said, breaking off, but emotion and earnestness looked glistening and trembling through every feature.

'Very well,' said Captain Charteris, 'I'm glad, at

least, that there is some one to have pity on the poor things! There's my brother's wife, she doesn't say no, but she talks of convenience and spoilt children—Sandbrook was quite right after all; I would not tell him how she answered me! Spoilt children to be sure they are, poor things, but she might recollect they have no mother—such a fuss as she used to make with poor Lucilla too. Poor Lucilla, she would never have believed that "dear Caroline" would have no better welcome for her little ones! Spoilt indeed! A precious deal pleasanter children they are than any of the lot at Castle Blanch, and better brought up too.'

The good captain's indignation had made away with his consistency, but Honora did not owe him a grudge for revealing that she was his *pis aller*, she was prone to respect a man who showed that he despised her, and she only cared to arrange the details. He was anxious to carry away his charge at once, since every day of this wear and tear of feeling was doing incalculable harm, and she undertook to receive the children and nurse at any time. She would write at once for a house at some warm watering-place, and take them there as soon as possible, and she offered to call that afternoon to settle all with Owen.

'Why,' said Captain Charteris, 'I hardly know. One reason I came alone was, that I believe that little elf of a Cilly has some notion of what is plotting against her. You can't speak a word but that child catches up, and she will not let her father out of her sight for a moment!'

'Then what is to be done? I would propose his coming here, but the poor child would not let him go.'

'That is the only chance. He has been forbidden the walking with them in his arms to put them to sleep, and we've got the boy into the nursery, and he'd better be out of the house than hear them roaring for him. So if you have no objection, and he is tolerable this evening, I would bring him as soon as they are gone to bed.'

Poor Owen was evidently falling under the management of stronger hands than his own, and it could only be hoped that it was not too late. His keeper brought him at a little after eight that evening. There was a look about him as if, after the last stroke that had befallen him, he could feel no more, the bitterness of death was past, his very hands looked woe-begone and astray, without the little fingers pressing them. He could not talk at first; he shook Honor's hand as if he could not bear to be grateful to her, and only the hardest hearts could have endured to enter on the intended discussion. The captain was very gentle towards him, and talk was made on other topics, but gradually something of the influence of the familiar scene, where his brightest days had been passed, began to prevail. All was like old times—the quaint old silver kettle and lamp, the pattern of the china cups, the ruddy play of the fire on the polished panels of the room, and he began to revive and join in the conversation. They spoke of Delaroche's beautiful Madonnas, one of which was at the time to be seen at a print shop—'Yes,' said Mr. Sandbrook, 'and little Owen cried out as soon as he saw it, "That lady, the lady with the flowery watch."'

Honora smiled. It was an allusion to the old jests upon her auburn locks, 'a greater compliment to her than to Delaroche,' she said; 'I saw that he was extremely curious to ascertain what my carrots were made of.'

'Do you know, Nora, I never saw more than one person with such hair as yours,' said Owen, with more animation, 'and oddly enough her name turned out to be Charlecote.'

'Impossible! Humfrey and I are the only Charlecotes left that I know of! Where could it have been?'

'It was at Toronto. I must confess that I was struck by the brilliant hair in chapel. Afterwards I met her once or twice. She was a Canadian born, and had just married a settler, whose name I can't remember, but her maiden name had certainly been Charlecote ; I remembered it because of the coincidence.'

'Very curious ; I did not know there had been any Charlecotes but ourselves.'

'And Humfrey Charlecote has never married ?'

'Never.'

What made Owen raise his eyes at that moment, just so that she met them ; and why did that dreadful uncontrollable crimson heat come mounting up over cheeks and temples, tingling and spreading into her very neck, just because it was the most hateful thing that could happen ? And he saw it. She knew he did so, for he dropped his eyes at once, and there was an absolute silence, which she broke in desperation, by an incoherent attempt to say something, and that ended by blundering into the tender subject—the children ; she found she had been talking about the place to which she thought of taking them, a quiet spot on the northern coast of Somersetshire.

He could bear the pang a little better now, and assented, and the ice once broken, there were so many details and injunctions that lay near his heart that the conversation never flagged. He had great reliance on their nurse, and they were healthy children, so that there was not much instruction as regarded the care of their little persons; but he had a great deal to say about the books they were to be taught from, the hymns they were to learn, and the exact management required by Lucilla's peculiar temper and decided will. The theory was so perfect and so beautifully wise that Honora sat by in reverence, fearing her power of carrying it out ; and Captain Charteris listened with a shade of satire on his face, and at last broke out with a very odd grunt, as if he did not think this quite what he had seen at Wrapworth parsonage.

Mr. Sandbrook coloured, and checked himself. Then, after a pause, he said in a very different tone, 'Perhaps so, Kit. It is only too easy to talk. Nora knows that there is a long way between my intentions and my practice.'

The humble dejection of that tone touched her more than she had been touched since he had wrung her hand, long, long ago.

'Well,' said the captain, perceiving only that he had given pain, 'I will say this for your monkeys, they do *know* what is right at least; they have heard the articles of war, which I don't fancy the other lot ever did. As to the discipline, humph! It is much of a muchness, and I'm not sure but it is not the best at the castle.'

'The children are different at home,' said Owen, quietly; 'but,' he added, with the same sad humility, 'I dare say they will be much the better for the change; I know——'

But he broke off, and put his hand before his eyes.

Honora hoped she should not be left alone with him, but somehow it did happen. The captain went to bring the carriage into the court, and get all imaginable wraps before trusting him out in the air, and Miss Wells disappeared, probably intending kindness. Of course neither spoke, till the captain was almost come back. Then Owen rose from where he had been sitting listlessly, leaning back, and slowly said, 'Nora, we did not think it would end thus when I put my hand to the plough. I am glad to have been here again. I had not remembered what I used to be. I do not ask you to forgive me. You are doing so, returning me good for—shall I say evil?'

Honor could not speak or look, she drooped her head, and her hair veiled her; she held out her hand as the captain came in, and felt it pressed with a feverish, eager grasp, and a murmured blessing.

Honora did not see Mr. Sandbrook again, but Captain Charteris made an incursion on her the next day to ask if she could receive the children on the ensuing morning. He had arranged to set off before daybreak, embarking for Ostend before the children were up, so

as to spare the actual parting, and Honora undertook
to fetch them home in the course of the day. He had
hoped to avoid their knowing of the impending separation, but he could only prevail so far as to extract a
promise that they should not know when it was to
take place. Their father had told them of their destination and his own as they sat on his bed in the morning before he rose, and apparently it had gone off better
than could have been expected; little Owen did not
seem to understand, and his sister was a child who
never shed tears.

The day came, and Honora awoke to some awe at
the responsibility, but with a yearning supplied, a
vacancy filled up. For at least six months she should
be as a mother, and a parent's prayers could hardly
have been more earnest.

She had not long been drest, when a hasty peal was
heard at the bell, and no sooner was the door opened
than in hurried Captain Charteris, breathless, and bearing a large plaid bundle, with tangled flaxen locks
drooping at one end, and at the other rigid white legs,
socks trodden down, one shoe wanting.

He deposited it, and there stood the eldest child, her
chin buried in her neck, her fingers digging fast into
their own palms, her eyes gleaming fiercely at him
under the pent-house she had made of her brows.

'There's an introduction!' he said, panting for
breath. 'Found her in time—the Strand—laid flat on
back seat, under all the plaids and bags—her father
put up his feet and found her—we drove to the lane—
I ran down with her—not a moment—can't stay, good
by, little Cilly goose, to think she could go that figure!'

He advanced to kiss her, but she lifted up her
shoulder between him and her face, much as a pugna-
cious pigeon flaps its wing, and he retreated.

'Wiser not, may be! Look here,' as Honora hurried
after him into the hall to ask after the patient; 'if
you have a bit of sticking plaster, he had better not
see this.'

Lucilla had made her little pearls of teeth meet in the fleshy part of his palm.

Honora recoiled, shocked, producing the plaster from her pocket in an instant.

'Little vixen,' he said, half laughing; 'but I was thankful to her for neither kicking nor struggling!'

'Poor child!' said Honora, 'perhaps it was as much agony as passion!'

He shrugged his shoulders as he held out his hand for her operations, then hastily thanking her and wishing her good by, rushed off again, as the astonished Miss Wells appeared on the stairs. Honor shrank from telling her what wounds had been received, she thought the gentle lady would never get over such a proceeding, and, in fact, she herself felt somewhat as if she had undertaken the charge of a little wild cat, and quite uncertain what the young lady might do next. On entering the breakfast-room, they found her sunk down all in a heap, where her uncle had set her down, her elbows on a low footstool, and her head leaning on them, the eyes still gazing askance from under the brows, but all the energy and life gone from the little dejected figure.

'Poor child! Dear little thing—wont you come to me?' She stirred not.

Miss Wells advanced, but the child's only motion was to shake her frock at her, as if to keep her off; Honora, really afraid of the consequences of touching her, whispered that they would leave her to herself a little. The silver kettle came in and tea was made.

'Lucilla, my dear, the servants are coming in to prayers.'

She did not offer to move, and still Honora let her alone, and she remained in the same attitude while the psalm was read, but afterwards there was a little approximation to kneeling in her position.

'Lucilla, dear child, you had better come to breakfast——' Only another defying glance.

Miss Wells, with what Honor thought defective

judgment, made pointed commendations of the tea, the butter and honey, but they had no effect; Honora, though her heart ached for the wrench the poor child had undergone, thought it best to affect indifference, gave a hint of the kind, and scrupulously avoided looking round at her, till breakfast was finished. When she did so, she no longer met the wary defiant gleam of the blue eyes, they were fast shut, the head had sunk on the arms, and the long breathings of sleep heaved the little frame. 'Poor little dear!' as Miss Wells might well exclaim, she had kept herself wakeful the whole night that her father might not go without her knowledge. And how pretty she looked in that little black frock, so ill and hastily put on, one round white shoulder quite out of it, and the long flaxen locks showing their silky fineness as they hung dispersed and tangled, the pinky flush of sleep upon the little face pillowed on the rosy pair of arms, and with a white unstockinged leg doubled under her. Poor child, there was more of the angel than the tiger-cat in her aspect now, and they had tears in their eyes, and moved softly lest they should startle her from her rest.

But wakened she must be. Honora was afraid of displeasing her domestic vizier, and rendering him for ever unpropitious to her little guests if she deferred his removal of the breakfast things beyond a reasonable hour. How was the awaking to be managed? Fright, tears, passion, what change would come when the poor little maid must awake to her grief? Honora would never have expected so poetical a flight from her good old governess as the suggestion, 'Play to her;' but she took it eagerly, and going to the disused piano, which stood in the room, began a low, soft air. The little sleeper stirred, presently raised her head, shook her hair off her ears, and after a moment, to their surprise, her first word was 'Mamma!' Honora was pausing, but the child said, 'Go on,' and sat for a few moments, as though recovering herself, then rose and came forward slowly, standing at last close to Honora. There was a pause, and she said, 'Mamma did that.'

Never was a sound more welcome! Honora dared to do what she had longed for so much, put an arm round the little creature, and draw her nearer, nor did Lucilla resist, she only said, 'Wont you go on?'

'I can make prettier music in the other room, my dear; we will go there, only you've had no breakfast. You must be very hungry.'

Lucilla turned round, saw a nice little roll cut into slices, and remembered that she *was* hungry; and presently she was consuming it so prosperously under Miss Wells's superintendence, that Honor ventured out to endeavour to retard Jones's desire to 'take away,' by giving him orders about the carriage, and then to attend to her other household affairs. By the time they were ended she found that Miss Wells had brought the child into the drawing-room, where she had at once detected the piano, and looking up at Honora said eagerly, 'Now then!' And Honora fulfilled her promise, while the child stood by softened and gratified, until it was time to propose fetching little Owen, 'your little brother—you will like to have him here.'

'I want my father,' said Lucilla, in a determined voice, as if nothing else were to satisfy her.

'Poor child, I know you do; I am so sorry for you, my dear little woman, but you see the doctors think papa is more likely to get better if he has not you to take care of!'

'I did not want my father to take care of *me*,' said the little lady, proudly; 'I take care of father, I always make his tea, and warm his slippers, and bring him his coffee in the morning. And uncle Kit never *will* put his gloves for him and warm his handkerchief! Oh! what will he do? I can't bear it.'

The violent grief so long kept back was coming now, but not freely; the little girl threw herself on the floor, and in a tumult of despair and passion went on, hurrying out her words, 'It's very hard! It's all Uncle Kit's doing! I hate him! Yes, I do.' And she rolled over and over in her frenzy of feeling.

'My dear! my dear!' cried Honora, kneeling by her, 'this will never do! Papa would be very much grieved to see his little girl so naughty. Don't you know how your uncle only wants to do him good, and to make him get well.'

'Then why didn't he take me?' said Lucilla, gathering herself up, and speaking sullenly.

'Perhaps he thought you gave papa trouble, and tired him.'

'Yes, that's it, and it's not fair,' cried the poor child again; 'why couldn't he tell me? I didn't know papa was ill! he never told me so, nor Mr. Pendy either; or, how I would have nursed him! I wanted to do so much for him; I wouldn't have asked him to tell me stories, nor nothing! No! And now they wont let me take care of him;' and she cried bitterly.

'Yes,' said good, gentle Miss Wells, thinking more of present comfort than of the too possible future; 'but you will go back to take care of him some day, my dear. When the spring comes papa will come back to his little girl.'

Spring! It was a long way off to a mind of six years old, but it made Lucilla look more amiably at Miss Wells.

'And suppose,' proceeded that good lady, 'you were to learn to be as good and helpful a little girl as can be while he is gone, and then nobody will wish to keep you from him. How surprised he would be!'

'And then shall we go home?' said Lucilla.

Miss Wells uttered a somewhat rash assurance to that effect, and the child came near her, pacified and satisfied by the scheme of delightful goodness and progress to be made in order to please her father—as she always called him. Honor looked on, thankful for the management that was subduing and consoling the poor little maid, and yet unable to participate in it, for though the kind old lady spoke in all sincerity, it was impossible to Honora to stifle a lurking fear that the hopes built on the prospect of his return had but a hollow foundation.

However, it attracted Lucilla to Miss Wells, so that Honora did not fear leaving her on going to bring home little Owen. The carriage which had conveyed the travellers, had brought back news of his sister's discovery and capture, and Honora found Mrs. Sandbrook much shocked at the enormity of the proceeding, and inclined to pity Honora for having charge of the most outrageous children she had ever seen. A very long letter had been left for her by their father, rehearsing all he had before given of directions, and dwelling still more on some others, but then apparently repenting of laying down the law, he ended by entreating her to use her own judgment, believe in his perfect confidence, and gratitude beyond expression for most unmerited kindness.

Little Owen, she heard, had made the house resound with cries when his father was nowhere to be found, but his nurse had quieted him, and he came running to Honora with an open, confiding face. 'Are you the lady? And will you take me to Cilly and the sea? And may I have a whale?'

Though Honora did not venture on promising him a tame whale in the Bristol Channel, she had him clinging to her in a moment, eager to set off, to go to Cilly, and the dove he had seen at her house. 'It's a nasty house here—I want to come away,' he said, running backwards and forwards between her and the window to look at the horses, while nurse's interminable boxes were being carried down.

The troubles really seemed quite forgotten; the boy sat on her knee and chattered all the way to Woolstone-lane, and there he and Lucilla flew upon each other with very pretty childish joy; the sister doing the honours of the house in right of having been a little longer an inmate. Nurse caught her, and dressed and combed her, shoed her and sashed her, so that she came down to dinner less picturesque, but more respectable than at her first appearance that morning, and except for the wonderful daintiness of both children, dinner went off very well.

All did go well till night, and then Owen's woes began. Oh! what a piteous sobbing lamentation was it! 'Daddy, daddy!' not to be consoled, not to be soothed, awakening his sister to the same sad cry, stilled only by exhaustion and sleepiness.

Poor little fellow! Night after night it was the same. Morning found him a happy, bright child, full of engaging ways and innocent sayings, and quite satisfied with 'Cousin Honor,' but bedtime always brought back the same wailing. Nurse, a tidy, brisk personage, with a sensible, deferential tone to her superiors, and a caressing one to the children, tried in vain assurances of papa's soon coming back; nay, it might be feared that she held out that going to sleep would bring the morrow when he was to come; but even this delusive promise failed; the present was all; and Cousin Honor herself was only not daddy, though she nursed him, and rocked him in her arms, and fondled him, and told stories or sung his lullaby with nightly tenderness, till the last sobs had quivered into the smooth heavings of sleep.

Might only sea air and exercise act as a soporific! That was a better chance than the new promise which Honora was vexed to find nurse holding out to poor little Owen, that if he would be a good boy, he was going to papa. She was puzzled how to act towards a person not exactly under her authority, but she took courage to speak about these false promises, and found her remonstrance received in good part; indeed, nurse used to talk at much length of the children in a manner that implied great affection for them, coupled with a sense that it would be an excellent thing for them to be in such judicious hands. Honora always came away from nurse in good humour with herself.

The locality she had chosen was a sheltered village on the north coast of Somerset, just where Exmoor began to give grandeur to the outline in the rear, and in front the Welsh hills wore different tints of purple or grey, according to the promise of weather, Lundy Isle and the two lesser ones serving as the most prominent objects, as they rose from——Well, well! Honor counted herself as a Somersetshire woman, and could not brook hearing much about the hue of the Bristol Channel. At any rate, just here it had been so kind as to wash up a small strip of pure white sand, fit for any amount of digging, for her children; and though Sandbeach was watering-place enough to have the lodging-houses, butchers and bakers, so indispensable to the London mind, it was not so much in vogue as to be overrun by fine ladies, spoiling the children by admiring their beauty. So said Miss Charlecote in her prudence—but was not she just as jealous as nurse that people should turn round a second time to look at those lovely little faces?

That was a very happy charge to her and her good old governess, with some drawbacks, indeed, but not such as to distress her over much. The chief was at first Owen's nightly sorrows, his daily idleness over lessons, Lucilla's pride, and the exceeding daintiness of both children, which made their meals a constant vexation and trouble. But what was this compared with the charm of their dependence on her, and of hearing that newly-invented pet name, 'Sweet Honey,' invoked in every little concern that touched them?

It was little Owen's name for her. He was her special favourite—there was no concealing it. Lucilla did not need her as much, and was of a vigorous, independent nature, that would stand alone to the utmost. Owen gave his affection spontaneously; if Lucilla's was won, it must be at unawares. She was living in and for her absent father now, and had nothing to spare for any one else, or if she had, Miss Wells, who had the less claim on her, was preferred to Cousin Honor. 'Father,' was almost her religion; though well taught, and unusually forward in religious knowledge, as far as Honora dared to augur, no motive save her love for him had a substantive existence, as touching her feelings or ruling her actions. For him she said her prayers and learnt her hymns; for him she consented to learn to hem handkerchiefs; for him were those crooked letters for ever being written; nay, at the thought of his displeasure alone could her tears be made to flow when she was naughty; and for him she endeavoured to be less fanciful at dinner, as soon as her mind had grasped the perception that her not eating what was set before her might really hinder him from always having her with him. She was fairly manageable, with very high spirits, and not at all a silly or helpless child; but though she obeyed Miss Charlecote, it was only as obeying her father through her, and his constant letters kept up the strong influence. In her most gracious moods, she was always telling her little brother histories of what they should do when they got home to father and Mr. Prendergast; but to Owen, absence made a much greater difference. Though he still cried at night, his 'Sweet Honey' was what he wanted, and with her caressing him, he only dreaded her leaving him. He lavished his pretty endearments upon her, and missed no one when he held her hand or sat in her lap, stroking her curls, and exchanging a good deal of fondling. He liked his hymns, and enjoyed Scripture stories, making remarks that caused her to reverence him; and though backward, idle, and sometimes very passionate, his was exactly the legitimate character for a child, such as she could deal with and love. She was as complete a slave to the two little ones as their father could have been; all her habits were made to conform to their welfare and pleasure, and very happy she was, but the discipline was more decided than they had been used to; there were habits to be formed, and others to be broken, and she was not weak enough not to act up to her duty in this respect, even though her heart was winding round that sunny-faced boy as fast as it had ever clung to his father. The new Owen Sandbrook, with his innocent earnestness, and the spiritual light in his eyes, should fulfil all her dreams!

Christmas had passed; Mr. Sandbrook had begun to write to his children about seeing them soon; Lucilla's slow hemming was stimulated by the hope of soon making her present; and Honora was marvelling at her own selfishness in dreading the moment when the little ones would be no longer hers; when a hurried note of preparation came from Captain Charteris. A slight imprudence had renewed all the mischief, and his patient was lying speechless under a violent attack of inflammation. Another letter, and all was over.

A shock indeed! but in Honora's eyes, Owen Sandbrook had become chiefly the children's father, and their future was what concerned her most. How should she bear to part with her darlings for ever, and to know them brought up in the way that was not good, and which their father dreaded, and when their orphanhood made her doubly tender over them?

To little Owen it was chiefly that papa was gone 'up there' whither all his hymns and allegories pointed, and at his age, all that he did not actually see was much on a par; the hope of meeting had been too distant for the extinction of it to affect him very nearly, and he only understood enough to prompt the prettiest and most touching sayings, wondering about the doings of papa, mamma, and little baby among the angels, with as much reality as he had formerly talked of papa among the French.

Lucilla heard with more comprehension, but her gay temper seemed to revolt against having sorrow forced on her. She *would* not listen and would not think; her spirits seemed higher than ever, and Honora almost concluded that either she did not feel at all, or that the moment of separation had exhausted all. Her character made Honora especially regret her destiny; it was one only too congenial to the weeds that were more likely to be implanted, than plucked up, at Castle Blanch. Captain Charteris had written to say that he, and probably his brother, should come to Sandbeach to relieve Miss Charlecote from the care of the children, and she prized each day while she still had those dear little voices about the house.

'Sweet Honey,' said Lucilla, who had been standing by the window, apparently watching the rain, 'do Uncle Charteris and Uncle Kit want us to go away from you?'

'I am very much afraid they do, my dear.'

'Nurse said, if you would ask them, we might stay,' said Lucilla, tracing the course of a drop with her finger.

'If asking would do any good, my dear,' sighed Honor; 'but I don't think nurse knows. You see, you belong to your uncles now.'

'I wont belong to Uncle Charteris!' cried Lucilla, passionately. 'I wont go to Castle Blanch! They were all cross to me; Ratia teased me, and father said it was all their fault I was naughty, and he would never take me there again! Don't let Uncle Kit go and take me there!' and she clung to her friend, as if the recollection of Uncle Kit's victory by main force hung about her still.

'I wont, I wont, my child, if I can help it; but it will all be as your dear father may have fixed it, and whatever he wishes I know that his little girl will do.'

Many a dim hope did Honora revolve, and more than ever did she feel as if a piece of her heart would be taken away, for the orphans fastened themselves upon her, and little Owen stroked her face, and said naughty Uncle Kit should not take them away. She found from the children and nurse that about a year ago, just after the loss of the baby, there had been a most unsuccessful visit at Castle Blanch; father and little ones had been equally miserable there in the separation of the large establishment, and Lucilla had been domineeringly petted by her youngest cousin, Horatia, who chose to regard her as a baby, and coerced her by bodily force, such as was intolerable to so highspirited a child, who was a little woman at home. She had resisted and fallen into dire disgrace, and it was almost with horror that she regarded the place and the cousinhood. Nurse appeared to have some private disgust of her own, as well as to have much resented her children's being convicted of naughtiness, and she spoke strongly in confidence to Honora of the ungodly ways of the whole household, declaring that after the advantages she had enjoyed with her dear master, she could not bear to live there, though she might—yes, she *must* be with the dear children just at first, and she ventured to express strong wishes for their remaining in their present home, where they had been so much improved.

The captain came alone. He walked in from the inn just before luncheon, with a wearied, sad look about him, as if he had suffered a good deal; he spoke quietly and slowly, and when the children came in, he took them up in his arms and kissed them very tenderly. Lucilla submitted more placably than Honor expected, but the moment they were set down they sprang to their friend, and held by her dress. Then came the meal, which passed off with small efforts at making talk, but with nothing memorable except the captain's exclamation at the end—'Well, that's the first time I ever dined with you children without a fuss about the meat. Why, Cilly, I hardly know you.'

'I think the appetites are better for the sea air,' said Honor, not that she did not think it a great achievement.

'I'm afraid it has been a troublesome charge,' said the captain, laying his hand on his niece's shoulder, which she at once removed, as disavowing his right in her.

'Oh! it has made me so happy,' said Honor, hardly trusting her voice; 'I don't know how to yield it up.'

Those understanding eyes of Lucilla's were drinking in each word, but Uncle Kit ruthlessly said—'There, it's your walking time, children; you go out now.'

Honora followed up his words with her orders, and Lucilla obeyed, only casting another wistful look, as if she knew her fate hung in the scales. It was showing tact such as could hardly have been expected from the little impetuous termagant, and was the best pleading for her cause, for her uncle's first observation was—'A wonder! Six months back, there would have been an explosion!'

'I am glad you think them improved.'

'Civilized beings, not plagues. You have been very good to them;' and as she intimated her own pleasure in them, he continued—'It will be better for them at Castle Blanch to have been a little broken in; the change from his indulgence would have been terrible.'

'If it were possible to leave them with me, I should be so happy,' at length gasped Honora, meeting an inquiring dart from the captain's eyes, as he only made an interrogative sound, as though to give himself time to think, and she proceeded in broken sentences—'If their uncle and aunt did not so very much wish for them—perhaps—I could—'

'Well,' said Captain Charteris, apparently so little aided by his thoughts as to see no hope of overcoming his perplexity without expressing it, 'the truth is that, though I had not meant to say anything of it, for I think relations should come first, I believe poor Sandbrook would have preferred it.' And while her colour deepened, and she locked her trembling fingers together to keep them still, he went on. 'Yes! you can't think how often I called myself a dozen fools for having parted him from his children! Never held up his head again! I could get him to take interest in nothing—every child he saw he was only comparing to one or other of them. After the year turned, and he talked of coming home, he was more cheerful; but strangely enough, for those last days at Hyères, though he seemed better, his spirits sank unaccountably, and he *would* talk more of the poor little thing that he lost than of these! Then he had a letter from you which set him sighing, and wishing they could always have such care! Altogether, I thought to divert him by taking him on that expedition, but—— Well, I've been provoked with him many a time, but there was more of the *real thing* in him than in the rest of us, and I feel as if the best part of our family were gone.'

'And this was all? He was too ill to say much afterwards?'

'Couldn't speak when he rang in the morning! Was gone by that time next day. Now,' added the captain, after a silence, 'I tell you candidly that my feeling is that the ordinary course is right. I think Charles ought to take the children, and the children ought to be with Charles.'

'If you think so——' began Honor, with failing hopes.

'At the same time,' continued he, 'I don't think they'll be so happy or so well cared for as by you, and knowing poor Owen's wishes, I should not feel justified in taking them away, since you are so good as to offer to keep them.'

Honor eagerly declared herself much obliged, then thought it sounded ironical.

'Unless,' he proceeded, 'Charles should strongly feel it his duty to take them home, in which case——'

'Oh, of course I could say nothing.'

'Very well, then we'll leave it to his decision.'

So it remained, and in trembling Honora awaited the answer. It was in her favour that he was appointed to a ship, since he was thus excluded from exercising any supervision over them at Castle Blanch, and shortly after, letters arrived gratefully acceding to her request. Family arrangements and an intended journey made her proposal doubly welcome, for the present at least, and Mrs. Charteris was full of polite thanks.

Poor little waifs and strays! No one else wanted them, but with her at least they had a haven of refuge, and she loved them the more ardently for their forlorn condition. Her own as they had never before been! and if the tenure were uncertain, she prized it doubly, even though, by a strange fatality, she had never had so much trouble and vexation with them as arose at once on their being made over to her! When all was settled, doubt over, and the routine life begun, Lucilla evidently felt the blank of her vanished hopes, and became fretful and captious, weary of things in general, and without sufficient motive to control her natural taste for the variety of naughtiness! Honor had not undertaken the easiest of tasks, but she neither shrank from her enterprise nor ceased to love the fiery little flighty sprite, the pleasing torment of her life—she loved her only less than that model of childish sweetness, her little Owen.

'Lucy, dear child, don't take your brother there. Owen, dear, come back, don't you see the mud? you'll sink in.'

'I'm only getting a dear little crab, Sweet Honey,' and the four little feet went deeper and deeper into the black mud.

'I can't have it done! come back, children, I desire, directly.'

The boy would have turned, but his sister had hold of his hand. 'Owen, there he is! I'll have him,' and as the crab scuttled sidelong after the retreating tide, on plunged the children.

'Lucy, come here!' cried the unfortunate old hen, as her ducklings took to the black amphibious mass, but not a whit did Lucilla heed. In the ardour of the chase, on she went, unheeding, leaving her brother sticking half way, where having once stopped, he began to find it difficult to withdraw his feet, and fairly screamed to 'Sweet Honey' for help. His progress was not beyond what a few long vigorous steps of hers could come up with, but deeply and blackly did she sink, and when she had lifted her truant out of his two holes, the increased weight made her go ankle deep at the first tread, and just at the same moment a loud shriek proclaimed that Lucilla, in her final assault on the crab, had fallen flat on a yielding surface, where each effort to rise sank her deeper, and Honora almost was expecting in her distress to see her disappear altogether, ere the treacherous mud would allow her to come to the rescue. But in that instant of utmost need, ere she could set down the little boy, a gentleman, with long-legged strides, had crossed the intervening space, and was bearing back the young lady from her mud bath. She raised her eyes to thank him. 'Humfrey!' she exclaimed.

'Honor! so it was you, was it? I'd no notion of it!' as he placed on her feet the little maiden, encrusted with mud from head to foot, while the rest of the party were all apparently cased in dark buskins of the same.

'Come to see me and my children?' she said. 'I am ashamed you should find us under such circumstances! though I don't know what would have become of us otherwise. No, Lucy, you are too disobedient for any one to take notice of you yet—you must go straight home, and be cleaned, and not speak to Mr. Charlecote till you are quite good. Little Owen, here he is—he was quite led into it. But how good of you to come, Humfrey; where are you?'

'At the hotel—I had a mind to come and see how you were getting on, and I'd had rather more than usual to do of late, so I thought I would take a holiday.'

They walked on talking for some seconds, when presently as the squire's hand hung down, a little soft one stole into it, and made him exclaim with a start, 'I thought it was Ponto's nose!'

But though very fond of children, he took up his hand, and did not make the slightest response to the sly overture of the small coquette, the effect as Honor well knew of opposition quite as much as of her strong turn for gentlemen. She pouted a little, and then marched on with 'don't care' determination, while Humfrey and Honora began to talk over Hiltonbury affairs, but were soon interrupted by Owen, who, accustomed to all her attention, did not understand her being occupied by any one else. 'Honey, Honeypots,' and a pull at her hand when she did not immediately attend, 'why don't the little crabs get black legs like mine?'

'Because they only go where they ought,' was the extremely moral reply of the Squire. 'Little boys aren't meant to walk in black mud.'

'The shrimp boys do go in the mud,' shrewdly pleaded Owen, setting Honor off laughing at Humfrey's discomfited look of diversion.

'It wont do to generalize,' she said, merrily. 'Owen must be content to regard crabs and shrimp boys as privileged individuals.'

Owen demanded whether when he was big he might be a shrimp boy, and a good deal of fraternization had taken place between him and Mr. Charlecote before the cottage was reached.

It was a very happy day to Honora; there was a repose and trust to be felt in Humfrey's company, such as she had not experienced since she had lost her parents, and the home sense of kindred was very precious. Only women whose chief prop is gone, can tell the value of one who is still near enough to disapprove without ceremony.

The anxiety that Honor felt to prove to her cousin that it was not a bit of romantic folly to have assumed her present charge, was worth more than all the freedom of action in the world. How much she wanted the children to show off to advantage! how desirous she was that he should not think her injudicious! yes, and how eager to see him pleased with their pretty looks!

Lucilla came down cleaned, curled, and pardoned, and certainly a heart must have been much less tender than Humfrey Charlecote's not to be touched by the aspect of those two little fair waxen-looking beings in the deepest mourning of orphanhood. He was not slow in making advances towards them, but the maiden had been affronted, and chose to be slyly shy and retiring, retreating to the other side of Miss Wells, and there becoming intent upon her story-book, though many a gleam through her eyelashes betrayed furtive glances at the stranger whom Owen was monopolizing. And then she let herself be drawn out, with the drollest mixture of arch demureness and gracious caprice. Honora had never before seen her with a gentleman, and to be courted was evidently as congenial an element to her as to a reigning beauty. She was perfectly irresistible to manhood, and there was no doubt, ere the evening was over, that Humfrey thought her one of the prettiest little girls he had ever seen.

He remained a week at Sandbeach, lodging at the inn, but spending most of his time with Honor. He owned that he had been unwell, and there certainly was a degree of lassitude about him, though Honor suspected that his real motive in coming was brotherly kindness and desire to see whether she were suffering much from the death of Owen Sandbrook. Having come, he seemed not to know how to go away. He was too fond of children to become weary of their petty exactions, and they both had a sort of passion for him; he built castles for them on the beach, presided over their rides, took them out boating, and made them fabulously happy. Lucilla had not been so good for weeks, and the least symptom of an outbreak was at once put down by his good-natured 'No, no!' The evenings at the cottage with Honora and Miss Wells, music and bright talk, were evidently very refreshing to him, and he put off his departure from day to day, till an inexorable matter of county business forced him off.

Not till the day was imminent, did the cousins quit the easy surface of holiday leisure talk. They had been together to the late evening service, and were walking home, when Honora began abruptly, ' Humfrey, I wish you would not object to the children giving me pet names.'

'I did not know that I had shown any objection.'

'As if you did not impressively say Miss Charlecote on every occasion when you mention me to them.'

'Well, and is not it more respectful ?'

'That's not what I want. Where the natural tie is wanting, one should do everything to make up for it.'

'And you hope to do so by letting yourself be called Honeypots !'

'More likely than by sitting up distant and 'awful to be *Miss Charlecoted !*'

'Whatever you might be called must become an endearment,' said Humfrey, uttering unawares one of the highest compliments she had ever received, 'and I own I do not like to hear those little chits make so free with your name.'

'For my sake, or theirs ?'

'For both. There is an old saying about familiarity, and I think you should recollect that, for the children's own good, it is quite as needful to strengthen respect as affection.'

'And you think I can do that by fortifying myself with Miss Charlecote ? Perhaps I had better make it Mrs. Honora Charlecote at once, and get a high cap, a rod, and a pair of spectacles, eh ? No! if they wont respect me out of a buckram suit, depend upon it they would find out it was a hollow one.'

Humfrey smiled. From her youth up, Honor could generally come off in apparent triumph from an argument with him, but the victory was not always where the triumph was.

'Well, Humfrey,' she said, after some pause, 'do you think I am fit to be trusted with my two poor children?'

There was a huskiness in his tone as he said, 'I am sincerely glad you have the pleasure and comfort of them.'

'I suspect there's a reservation there. But really, Humfrey, I don't think I went out searching for the responsibility in the way that makes it dangerous. One uncle did not want them, and the other could not have them, and it would have been mere barbarity in me not to offer. Besides, their father wished——' and her voice faltered with tears.

'No, indeed,' said Humfrey, eagerly, 'I did not in the least mean that it is not the kindest, most generous requital,' and there he broke off, embarrassed by the sincere word that he had uttered, but before she had spoken an eager negative—to what she knew not—he went on. 'And of course I don't mean that you are not one to manage them very well, and all that—only I hope there may not be pain in store—I should not like those people to use you for their nursery governess, and then take the children away just as you had set your heart upon them. Don't do that, Honor,' he added, with an almost sad earnestness.

'Do what? Set my heart on them? Do you think I can help loving the creatures?' she said, with mournful playfulness, 'or that my uncertain tenure does not make them the greater darlings?'

'There are ways of loving without setting one's heart,' was the somewhat grave reply.

He seemed to be taking these words as equivalent to transgressing the command that requires *all* our heart, and she began quickly, 'Oh! but I didn't mean ——' then a sudden thrill crossed her whether there might not be some truth in the accusation. Where had erst the image of Owen Sandbrook stood? First or second? Where was now the image of the boy? She turned her words into 'Do you think I am doing so—in a wrong way?'

'Honor, dear, I could not think of wrong where you are concerned,' he said; 'I was only afraid of your kindness bringing you pain, if you rest your happiness very much upon those children.'

'I see,' said Honor, smiling, relieved. 'Thank you, Humfrey; but you see I can't weigh out my affection in that fashion. They will get it, the rogues!'

'I'm not afraid, as far as the girl is concerned,' said Humfrey. 'You are strict enough with her.'

'But how am I to be strict when poor little Owen never does anything wrong?'

'Yes, he is a particularly sweet child.'

'And not at all wanting in manliness,' cried Honor, eagerly. 'So full of spirit, and yet so gentle. Oh! he is a child whom it is a privilege to train, and I don't think I have spoilt him yet, do you?'

'No, I don't think you have. He is very obedient in general.'

'Oh! if he could be only brought up as I wish. And I do think his innocence is too perfect a thing not to be guarded. What a perfect clergyman he would make! Just fancy him devoting himself to some parish like poor dear old St. Wulstan's—carrying his bright sweetness into the midst of all that black Babel, and spreading light round him! he always says he will be a clergyman like his papa, and I am sure he must be marked out for it. He likes to look at the sheep on the moors, and talk about the shepherd leading them, and I am sure the meaning goes very deep with him.'

She was not going quite the way to show Humfrey that her heart was not set on the boy, and she was checked by hearing him sigh. Perhaps it was for the disappointment he foresaw, so she said, 'Whether I bring him up or not, don't you believe there will be a special care over such a child?'

VOL. I.   F

'There is a special care over every Christian child, I suppose,' he said; 'and I hope it may all turn out so as to make you happy. Here is your door, good night, and good-by.'

'Why, are not you coming in?'

'I think not; I have my things to put up; I must go early to-morrow. Thank you for a very happy week. Good-by, Honor.' There was a shade of disappointment about his tone that she could not quite account for. Dear old Humfrey! Could he be ageing? Could he be unwell? Did he feel himself lonely? Could she have mortified him, or displeased [him? Honor was not a woman of personal vanity, or a solution would sooner have occurred to her. She knew, upon reflection, that it must have been for her sake that Humfrey had continued single, but it was so inconvenient to think of him in the light of an admirer, when she so much needed him as a brother, that it had hardly ever occurred to her to do so; but at last it did strike her whether, having patiently waited so long, this might not have been a visit of experiment, and whether he might not be disappointed to find her wrapped up in new interests —slightly jealous, in fact, of little Owen. How good he had been! Where was the heart that could fail of being touched by so long a course of forbearance and consideration? Besides, Honor had been a solitary woman long enough to know what it was to stand alone. And then how well he would stand in a father's place towards the orphans. He would never decree her parting with them, and Captain Charteris himself must trust him. Yet what a shame it would be to give such a devoted heart nothing better than one worn out, with the power of love, such as he deserved, exhausted for ever. And yet—and yet—something very odd bounded up within her, and told her between shame and exultation, that faithful old Humfrey would not be discontented even with what she had to give. Another time—a little, a very little encouragement, and the pine wood scene would come back again, and then—her heart fainted a little—there should be no concealment—but if she could only have been six months married all at once!

Time went on, and Honora more than once blushed at finding how strong a hold this possibility had taken of her heart, when once she had begun to think of resting upon one so kind, so good, so strong. Every perplexity, every care, every transaction that made her feel her position as a single woman, brought round the yearning to lay them all down upon him, who would only be grateful to her for them. Every time she wanted some one to consult, hope showed her his face beaming sweetly on her, and home seemed to be again opening to her, that home which might have been hers at any time these twelve years. She quite longed to see how glad the dear, kind fellow would be.

Perhaps maidenly shame would have belied her feelings in his actual presence, perhaps she would not have shrunk from him, and been more cold than in her unconsciousness, but he came not; and his absence fanned the spark so tardily kindled. What if she had delayed till too late? He was a man whose duty it was to marry! he had waited till he was some years past forty—perhaps this had been his last attempt, and he was carrying his addresses elsewhere.

Well! Honora believed she had tried to act rightly, and that must be her comfort—and extremely ashamed of herself she was, to find herself applying such a word to her own sensations in such a case—and very much disliking the notion of any possible lady at Hiltonbury Holt.

CHAPTER III.

There is a reaper, his name is Death,
And with his sickle keen
He reaps the bearded grain at a breath,
And the flowers that grow between.
                                   LONGFELLOW.

 LETTER from Humfrey! how Honor's heart fluttered. Would it announce an engagement, or would it promise a visit on which her fate would turn, or would it be only a business letter on her money matters?

Angry at her own trepidation, she opened it. It was none of all these. It told her that Mr. Saville, his brother-in-law, was staying at the Holt with his second wife, and that he begged her to take advantage of this opportunity to come to visit the old place, adding, that he had not been well, and he wished much to see her, if she could spare a few days to him from her children.

Little doubt had she as to the acceptance. The mere words 'going to Hiltonbury,' had power by force of association to make her heart bound. She was a little disappointed that he had not included the children; she feared that it looked as if he were really ill; but it might be on account of the Savilles, or may be he had that to say to her which——oh, nonsense! Were that the case, Humfrey would not reverse the order of things, and make her come to him. At any rate, the children should be her first condition. And then she concentrated her anxieties on his most unusual confession of having been unwell.

Humfrey's substantial person was ready to meet her at the station, and the first glance dispelled her nervous tremors, and calmed the tossings of her mind in the habitual sense of trust and reliance. He thanked her for coming, handed her into the carriage, looked after her goods, and seated himself beside her in so completely his ordinary fashion of taking care of her, that she forgot all her intentions of rendering their meeting momentous. Her first inquiry was for his health, but he put it aside with something about feeling very well now, and he looked so healthy, only perhaps a little more hearty and burly, that she did not think any more of the matter, and only talked in happy desultory scraps, now dwelling on her little Owen's charms, now joyfully recognising familiar objects, or commenting upon the slight changes that had taken place. One thing, however, she observed; Humfrey did not stop the horse at the foot of the steep hill where walking had been a matter of course, when he had been a less solid weight than now. 'Yes, Honor,' he said, smiling, 'one grows less merciful as one grows old and short-breathed.'

'You growing old! you whom I've never left off thinking of as a promising lad, as poor old Mrs. Mervyn used to call you.'

He turned his face towards her as if about to say something very seriously, but apparently changing his intention, he said, 'Poor old Mrs. Mervyn, I wonder how she would like the changes at Beauchamp.'

'Are the Fulmorts doing a great deal?'

'They have quite modernized the house, and laid out the garden—what I should call very prettily, if it were not for my love of the old Dutch one. They see a great deal of company, and go on in grand style.'

'How do you get on with them?'

'Oh! very well; I have dined there two or three times. He is a good-natured fellow enough, and there are some nice children, whom I like to meet with their nurses in the woods. I stood proxy for the last one's sponsor; I could not undertake the office myself.'

'Good-natured!' exclaimed Nora. 'Why, you know how he behaved at St. Wulstan's. No more than 5*l.* a year would he ever give to any charity, though he was making thousands by those gin-shops.'

'Probably he thought he was doing very liberally.'

'Ay, there is no hope for St. Wulstan's till people have left off thinking a guinea their duty, and five very handsome! and that Augusta Mervyn should have gone and married our *bête noire*—our lord of gin-palaces—I do think it must be on purpose for you to melt him. I shall set you at him, Humfrey, next time Mr. Askew writes to me in despair, that something wont go on for lack of means. Only I must be quite sure that you wont give the money yourself, to spare the trouble of dunning.'

'It is not fair to take other people's duties on oneself; besides, as you'll find, Honor, the Holt purse is not bottomless.'

As she would find! This was a very odd way of making sure of her beforehand, but she was not certain that she did not like it. It was comfortable, and would save much preliminary.

The woods were bursting into spring: delicate, deeply creased leaves were joyously emerging to the light on the birches, not yet devoid of the silvery wool where they had been packed, the hazels were fluttering their goslings, the palms were honey sweet with yellow tufts, the primroses peeped out in the banks of moss.

'Oh! Humfrey, this is the great desire of my life fulfilled, to see the Holt in the flush of spring!'

'I have always said you cared for the place more than any one,' said Humfrey, evidently gratified, but with an expression which she did not understand.

'As if I did not! But how strangely differently from my vision my wish has been fulfilled.'

'How strangely!' he repeated, with even greater seriousness than had been in her voice.

The meadow was bright with spring grass, the cattle grazing serenely as in old times, the garden—ah! not quite so gay—either it was better in autumn than in spring, or it wanted poor Sarah's hand; the dogs, not the same individuals, but with much the same manners, dancing round their master—all like, all home. Nothing wanting, but, alas! the good-natured, narrow-minded old mistress of the house to fret her, and notable Sarah to make her comfortable, and wonder at her eccentric tastes. Ah! and how much more was wanting the gentle mother who did all the civility and listening, and the father, so happy to look at green woods, read poetry, and unbend his weary bow! How much more precious was the sight of the one living remnant of those days!

They had a cheerful evening. Mr. Saville had a great deal of old-fashioned Oxford agreeableness; he was very courtly, but a sensible man, with some native fun and many college stories. After many years of donship, his remote parish was somewhat of a solitude to him, and intercourse with a cultivated mind was as pleasant to him now as the sight of a lady had been in his college days. Honor liked conversation too; and Miss Wells, Lucilla, and Owen had been rather barren in that respect, so there was a great deal of liveliness, in which Humfrey took his full share; while good Mrs. Saville looked like what she was, her husband's admiring housekeeper.

'Do you take early walks still, Humfrey?' asked Honor, as she bade him good night. 'If you do, I shall be quite ready to confront the dew;' and therewith came a revulsion of the consciousness within. Was this courting him? and to her great provocation there arose an uncomfortable blush.

'Thank you,' he said, with something of a mournful tone, 'I'm afraid I'm past that, Honor. To-morrow, after breakfast—good night.'

Honor was a little alarmed by all this, and designed a conference with the old housekeeper, Mrs. Stubbs, to inquire into her master's health, but this was not attainable that night, and she could only go to bed in the friendly old wainscoted room, whose white and gold carved monsters on the mantelpiece were well nigh as familiar as the dove in Woolstone-lane; but, oh! how it made her long for the mother whom she used to kiss there.

Humfrey was brisk and cheerful as ever at breakfast, devising what his guests would like to do for the day, and talking of some friends whom he had asked to meet Mr. Saville, so that all the anxieties with which Honora had risen were dissipated, and she took her part gaily in the talk. There was something therefore freshly startling to her, when, on rising, Humfrey gravely said, 'Honor, will you come into my study for a little while?'

The study had always been more of a place for guns and fishing-tackle than for books. It was Humfrey's usual living room when alone, and was of course full besides of justice books, agricultural reports, acts of parliament, piles of papers, little bags of samples of wheat, all in the orderly disorder congenial to the male kind. All this was as usual, but the change that struck her was, that the large red leather lounging chair, hitherto a receptacle for the overflowings of the table, was now wheeled beside the fire, and near it stood a little table with a large print Bible on it, which she well remembered as his mother's. Humfrey set a chair for her by the fire, and seated himself in the easy one, leaning back a little. She had not spoken. Something in his grave preparation somewhat awed her, and she sat upright, watching him.

'It was very kind of you to come, Honor,' he began; 'more kind than you know.'

'I am sure it could be no other than a treat——'

He continued, before she could go farther, 'I wished

particularly to speak to you. I thought it might perhaps spare you a shock.'

She looked at him with a terrified eye.

'Don't be frightened, my dear,' he said, leaning forward, 'there is no occasion. Such things must come sooner or later, and it is only that I wished to tell you that I have been having advice for a good many uncomfortable feelings that have troubled me lately.'

'Well?' she asked, breathlessly.

'And Dixon tells me that it is aneurism.'

Quick and fast came Honora's breath; her hands were clasped together; her eyes cast about with such a piteous, despairing expression, that he started to his feet in a moment, exclaiming—'Honor! Honor dear! don't! there's no need. I did not think you would feel it in this way!'

'Feel! what should I feel if not for you? Oh! Humfrey! don't say it! you are all that is left me— you cannot be spared!' and as he came towards her, she grasped his hand and clung to him, needing the support which he gave in fear of her fainting.

'Dear Honor, do not take it thus. I am very well now—I dare say I shall be so to the last, and there is nothing terrible to the imagination. I am very thankful for both the preparation and the absence of suffering. Will not you be the same?'

'Yes, you,' said Honora, sitting up again, and looking up into his sincere, serene face; 'I cannot doubt that even this is well for you, but it is all selfishness— just as I was beginning to feel what you are to me.'

Humfrey's face lighted up suddenly. 'Then, Honor,' he said, evidently putting strong restraint upon his voice, 'you could have listened to me now.'

She bowed her head—the tears were dropping very fast.

'Thank God!' he said, as again he leant back in his chair; and when she raised her eyes again, he sat with his hands clasped, and a look of heavenly felicity on his face, raised upwards.

'Oh! Humfrey! how thoughtlessly I have trifled away all that might have been the happiness of your life!'

'You never trifled with me,' he said; 'you have always dealt honestly and straightforwardly, and it is best as it is. Had we been together all this time, the parting might have been much harder. I am glad there are so few near ties to break.'

'Don't say so! you, loved by every one, the tower of strength to all that is good!'

'Hush, hush! nonsense, Honor!' said he, kindly. 'I think I have tried,' he went on, gravely, 'not to fall behind the duties of my station; but that would be a bad dependence, were there not something else to look to. As to missing me, the world did very well without me before I was born; it will do as well when I am gone; and as to you, my poor Honor, we have been very little together of late.'

'I had you to lean on.'

'Lean on something stronger,' he said; and as she could not govern her bitter weeping, he went on—'Ah! I am the selfish one now, to be glad of what must make it the worse for you; but if one thing were wanting to make me happy, it was to know that at last you cared for me.'

'I should be a wretch not to do so. So many years of patience and forbearance!——Nobody could be like you.'

'I don't see that,' said Humfrey, simply. 'While you continued the same, I could not well turn my mind to any one else, and I always knew I was much too loutish for you.'

'Now, Humfrey!——'

'Yes, there is no use in dwelling on this,' he said, quietly. 'The reason I asked you to be kind enough to come here, is that I do not think it well to be far from home under the circumstances. There, don't look frightened—they say it may very possibly not come for several months or a year. I hope to have time to put things a little in order for you, and that is one reason I wished to see you; I thought I could make the beginning easier to you.'

But Honora was far too much shaken for such a turn to the conversation; she would not mortify him, but she could neither listen nor understand. He, who was so full of stalwart force, a doomed man, yet calm and happy under his sentence; he, only discovered to be so fondly loved in time to give poignancy to the parting, and yet rejoicing himself in the poor, tardy affection that had answered his manly constancy too late! His very calmness and stillness cut her to the heart, and after some ineffectual attempts to recover herself, she was forced to take refuge in her own room. Weeping, praying, walking restlessly about, she remained there till luncheon time, when Humfrey himself came up to knock at her door.

'Honor dear!' he said, 'come down—try to throw it off—Saville does not wish his wife to be made aware of it while she is here, lest she should be nervous. You must not betray me—and indeed there is no reason for being overcome. Nothing vexes me but seeing you so. Let us enjoy your visit, pray.'

To be commanded to bear up by a strong, manly character so much loved and trusted was perhaps the chief support she could receive; she felt that she must act composure, and coming down in obedience to her cousin, she found the power of doing so. Nay, as she saw him so completely the bright, hospitable host, talking to Mrs. Saville about her poultry, and carrying on quiet jokes with Mr. Saville, she found herself drawn away from the morning's conversation, or remembering it like a dream that had passed away.

They all went out together, and he was apparently as much interested in his young wheat as ever, and even more anxious to make her look at and appreciate crops and cattle, speaking about them in his hearty, simple way, as if his pleasure in them was not flagging, perhaps because it had never been excessive. He had always sat loose to them, and thus they could please and occupy him even when the touch of the iron hand had made itself felt.

And again she saw him engrossed in arranging some petty matter of business for one of the poor people; and when they had wandered down to the gate, pelting the turn-out of the boys' school with a pocket full of apples that he said he had taken up while in conference with the housekeeper, laughing and speaking merrily as the varlets touched their caps to him, and always turning to her for sympathy in his pleasures of success or of good nature, as though her visit were thorough enjoyment to him.

And so it almost was to her. The influence of the dear old scenes was something, and his cheeriness was a great deal more; the peaceful present was not harassed or disturbed, and the foreboding, on which she might not dwell, made it the more precious. That slow wandering about the farm and village, and the desultory remarks, the old pleasant reminiscences, the inquiries and replies about the villagers and neighbours had a quiet charm about them, as free and happy as when, youth and child, they had frisked through the same paths; nay, the old scenes so brought back the old habits that she found herself discoursing to him in her former eager fashion upon the last historical character who had bitten her fancy.

'My old way,' she said, catching herself up; 'dinning all this into your ears as usual, when you don't care.'

'Don't I?' said Humfrey, with his sincere face turned on her in all its sweetness. 'Perhaps I never showed you how much, Honor; and I beg your pardon, but I would not have been without it!'

The Savilles came up, while Honor's heart was brimfull at this compliment, and then it was all commonplace again, except for that sunset light, that rich radiance of the declining day, that seemed unconsciously to pervade all Humfrey's cheerfulness, and to give his mirth and playfulness a solid happiness.

Some mutual friends of long standing came to dinner, and the evening was not unlike the last, quite as free from gloom, and Mr. Charlecote as bright as ever, evidently taking his full share in county business, and giving his mind to it. Only Honor noted that he quietly avoided an invitation to a very gay party which was proposed; and his great ally, Sir John Raymond, seemed rather vexed with him for not taking part in some new and expensive experiment in farming, and asked incredulously whether it were true that he wished to let a farm that he had kept for several years in his own hands. Humfrey agreed that it was so, and said something farther of wishing to come to terms quickly. She guessed that this was for her sake, when she thought all this over in her bedroom.

Such was the effect of his calmness that it had not been a day of agitation. There was more peace than tumult in her mind as she lay down to rest, sad, but not analysing her sadness, and lulled by the present into putting aside the future. So she slept quietly, and awoke with a weight at her heart, but softened and sustained by reverent awe and obedience towards her cousin.

When they met, he scanned her looks with a bright, tender glance, and smiled commendation when he detected no air of sleeplessness. He talked and moved as though his secret were one of untold bliss, and this was not far from the truth; for when, after breakfast, he asked her for another interview in the study, they were no sooner alone than he rubbed his hands together with satisfaction, saying—'So, Honor, you could have had me after all!' looking at her with a broad, undisguised, exulting smile.

'Oh! Humfrey!'

'Don't say it if you don't like it; but you can't guess the pleasure it gives me. I could hardly tell at first what was making me so happy when I awoke this morning.'

'I can't see how it should,' said Honor, her eyes

swimming with tears, 'never to have met with any gratitude for——I have used you too ill—never valued, scarcely even believed in what you lavished on poor silly me—and now, when all is too late, you are glad——'

'Glad! of course I am,' returned Humfrey; 'I never wished to obtrude my feelings on you after I knew how it stood with you. It would have been a shame. Your choice went far above me. For the rest, if to find you disposed towards me at the last makes me so happy,' and he looked at her again with beaming affection, 'how could I have borne to leave you if all had been as I wished? No, no, it is best as it is. You lose nothing in position, and you are free to begin the world again, not knocked down or crushed.'

'Don't talk so, Humfrey! It is breaking my heart to think that I might have been making you happy all this time.'

'Heaven did not will it so,' said Humfrey, reverently, 'and it might not have proved what we fancy. You might not have found such a clodhopper all you wanted, and my stupidity might have vexed you, though now you fancy otherwise. And I have had a very happy life—indeed I have, Honor; I never knew the time when I could not say with all my heart, "The lot is fallen unto me in a fair ground, yea, I have a goodly heritage." Everybody and everything, you and all the rest, have been very kind and friendly, and I have never wanted for happiness. It has been all right. You could fulfil your duty as a daughter undividedly, and now I trust those children will be your object and comfort—only, Honor, not your idols. Perhaps it was jealousy, but I have sometimes fancied that your tendency with their father——'

'Oh! how often I must have given you pain.'

'I did not mean *that*, but, as I say, perhaps I was no fair judge. One thing is well, the relations will be much less likely to take them from you when you are living here.'

She held up her hands in deprecation.

'Honor, dear,' he said pleadingly, yet with authority, 'pray let me talk to you. There are things which I wish very much to say; indeed, without which, I could hardly have asked for this indulgence. It is for your own sake, and that of the place and people.'

'Poor place, poor people.'

He sighed, but then turned his smiling contenance towards her again. 'No one else can care for it or them as you do, Honor. Our "goodly heritage"—it was so when I had it from my father, and I don't think it has got worse under my charge, and I want you to do your duty by it, Honor, and hand it on the same, whoever may come after.'

'For your sake, Humfrey—even if I did not love it. But——'

'Yes, it is a duty,' proceeded Humfrey, gravely. 'It may seem but a bit of earth after all, but the owner of a property has a duty to let it do its share in producing food, or maybe in not lessening the number of pleasant things here below. I mean, it is as much my office to keep my trees and woods fair to look at, as it is not to let my land lie waste.'

She had recovered a good deal while he was moralizing, and became interested. 'I did not suspect you of the poetical view, Humfrey,' she said.

'It is plain sense, I think,' he said, 'that to grub up a fine tree, or a pretty bit of copse without fair reason, only out of eagerness for gain, is a bit of selfishness. But mind, Honor, you must not go and be romantic. You *must* have the timber marked when the trees are injuring each other.'

'Ah! I've often done it with you.'

'I wish you would come out with me to-day. I'm going to the outwood, I could show you.'

She agreed readily, almost forgetting the wherefore.

'And above all, Honor, you must not be romantic about wages! It is not right by other proprietors, nor by the people themselves. No one is ever the better for a fancy price for his labour.'

She could almost have smiled; he was at once so well pleased that she and his 'goodly heritage' should belong to each other, so confident in her love and good intentions towards it, and so doubtful of her discretion and management. She promised with all her heart to do her utmost to fulfil his wishes.

'After all,' he said, thoughtfully, 'the best thing for the place—ay, and for you and every one, would be for you to marry; but there's little chance of that,'I suppose, and it is of no use to distress you by mentioning it. I've been trying to put out of my hands things that I don't think you will be able to manage, but I should like you to keep up the home farm, and you may pretty well trust to Brooks. I dare say he will take his own way, but if you keep a reasonable check on him, he will do very well by you. He is as honest as the day, and very intelligent. I don't know that any one could do better for you.'

'Oh, yes; I will mind all he tells me.'

'Don't show that you mind him. That is the way to spoil him. Poor fellow, he has been a good servant to me, and so have they all. It is a thing to be very thankful for to have had such a set of good servants.'

Honora thought, but did not say that they could not help being good with such a master.

He went on to tell her that he had made Mr. Saville his executor. Mr. Saville had been for many years before leaving Oxford bursar of his college, and was a thorough man of business, whom Humfrey had fixed upon as the person best qualified to be an adviser and assistant to Honora, and he only wished to know whether she wished for any other selection, but this was nearly overpowering her again, for since her father's death, she had leant on no one but Humfrey himself.

One thing more he had to say. 'You know, Honor, this place will be entirely your own. You and I seem to be the last of the Charlecotes, and even if we were not, there is no entail. You may found orphan asylums with it, or leave it to poor Sandbrook's children, just as you please.'

'Oh, I could not do that,' cried Honor, with a sudden revulsion. Love them as she might, Owen Sandbrook's children must not step into Humfrey Charlecote's place. 'And, besides,' she added, 'I want my little Owen to be a clergyman; I think he can be what his father missed.'

'Well, you can do exactly as you think fit. Only what I wanted to tell you is, that there may be another branch, elder than our own. Not that this need make the least difference, for the Holt is legally ours. It seems that our great grandfather had an elder son—a wild sort of fellow—the old people used to tell stories of him. He went on, in short, till he was disinherited, and went off to America. What became of him afterwards I never could make out; but I have sometimes questioned how I should receive any of his heirs if they should turn up some day. Mind you, you need not have the slightest scruple in holding your own. It was made over to my grandfather by will, as I have made it sure for you; but I do think that when you come to think how to dispose of it, the possibility of the existence of these Charlecotes might be taken into consideration.'

'Yankee Charlecotes!' she said.

'Never mind; most likely nothing of the kind will ever come in your way, and they have not the slightest claim on you. I only threw it out, because I thought it right just to speak of it.'

After this commencement, Humfrey, on this and the ensuing days, made it his business to make his cousin acquainted with the details of the management of the estate. He took such pleasure in doing so, and was so anxious she should comprehend, that she was forced to give her whole attention; and, putting all else aside, was tranquilly happy in thus gratifying him.

Those orderly ranges of conscientious accounts were no small testimony to the steady, earnest manner in which Humfrey had set himself to his duty from his early youth, and to a degree they were his honest pride too—he liked to show how good years had made up for bad years, and there was a tenderness in the way he patted their red leather backs to make them even on their shelves, as if they had been good friends to him. No, they must not run into confusion.

The farms and the cottages—the friendly terms of his intercourse, and his large-handed but well-judging almsgiving—all revealed to her more of his solid worth; and the simplicity that regarded all as the merest duty touched her more than all. Many a time did she think of the royal Norwegian brothers, one of whom went to tie a knot in the willows on the banks of the Jordan, while the other remained at home to be the blessing of his people, and from her broken idol wanderer, she turned to worship her steadfast worker at home, as far as his humility and homeliness made it possible, and valued each hour with him as if each moment were of diamond price. And he was so calmly happy, that there was no grieving in his presence. It had been a serene life of simple fulfilment of duty, going ever higher, and branching wider, as a good man's standard gradually rises the longer he lives, the one great disappointment had been borne without sourness or repining, and the affections, deprived of the home channel, had spread in a beneficent flood, and blessed all around. So, though, like every sinful son of man, sensible of many an error, many an infirmity, still the open loving spirit was childlike enough for that blessed sense; for that feeling which St. John expresses as 'if our heart condemn us not, then have we confidence towards God;' confidence in the infinite Merits that atone for the errors of weakness, and occasional wanderings of will; confidence that made the hope a sure and steadfast one, and these sentenced weeks a land of Beulah, where Honora's tardy response to his constant love could be greeted and valued as the precious fulfilment of long-cherished wishes, not dashed aside as giving bitterness to his departure.

The parting was broken by a promise that Honora should again meet the Savilles at the Holt in the autumn. She assured herself that there was no danger before that time, and Humfrey spoke cheerfully of looking forward to it, and seemed to have so much to do, and to be so well equal to doing it, that he would not let them be concerned at leaving him alone.

To worship Humfrey was an easier thing at a distance than when beside him. Honora came back to Sandbeach thoroughly restless and wretched, reproaching herself with having wasted such constant, priceless affection, haunted by the constant dread of each morning's post, and longing fervently to be on the spot. She had self-command enough not to visit her dejection on the children, but they missed both her spirits and her vigilance, and were more left to their nurse; and her chief solace was in long solitary walks, or in evening talks with Miss Wells. Kind Miss Wells perhaps guessed how matters stood between the two last Charlecotes, but she hinted not her suspicions, and was the unwearied recipient of all Honora's histories of his symptoms, of his cheerfulness, and his solicitude for her. Those talks did her good, they set the real Humfrey before her, and braced her to strive against weakness and despondence.

And then the thought grew on her, why, since they were so thoroughly each other's, why should they not marry, and be together to the last? Why should he be left to his solitude for this final year? why should their meetings be so prudentially chaperoned? Suppose the disease should be lingering, how hard it was that she should be absent, and he left to servants! She could well imagine why he had not proposed it, he was too unselfish to think of exposing her to the shock, or making her a widow, but how came she never to have thought of it? She stood beyond all ordinary rules—she had nothing worldly to gain nor to lose by being his wife for these few remaining months—it surely was her part, after the way she had treated him, to meet him more than halfway—she alone could make the proposal—she would—she must. And oh! if the doctors should be mistaken! So spoke the midnight dream—oh! how many times. But what said cool morning? Propriety had risen up, grave decorum objecting to what would shock Humfrey, ay, and was making Honor's cheeks tingle. Yes, and there came the question whether he would not be more distressed than gratified—he who wished to detach himself from all earthly ties—whether he might not be pained and displeased at her thus clinging to him—nay, were he even gratified, might not emotion and agitation be fatal?

Many, many times was all this tossed over in Honor's mind. Often the desperate resolution was definitively taken, and she had seen herself quietly meeting him at dear old Hiltonbury church, with his grave sweet eyes resting satisfied upon her as his darling. As often had the fear of offending him, and the instinct of woman's dignity turned her away when her heart was beating high. That autumn visit—then she would decide. One look as if he wished to retain her, the least air of feebleness or depression, and she would be determined, even if she had to waive all feminine reserves, and set the matter in hand herself. She thought Mr. Saville would highly approve and assist; and having settled into this period for her project, she set herself in some degree at rest, and moved and spoke with so much more of her natural ease, that Miss Wells was consoled about her, and knew not how entirely heart and soul were at Hiltonbury, with such devotion as had never even gone to the back woods.

To meet the Savilles at Hiltonbury in the autumn! Yes—Honor met Mr. Saville, but not as she had intended. By that time the stroke had fallen, just as she had become habituated to the expectation, just as her promised visit had assumed a degree of proximity, and her heart was beating at the prospect of the results.

Humfrey had been scarcely ailing all the summer, he had gone about his occupations with his usual cheerfulness, and had taken part in all the village festivals as genially as ever. Only close observers could have noticed a slackness towards new undertakings, a gradual putting off of old ones, a training of those dependent on his counsel, to go alone, a preference for being alone in the evening, a greater habit of stillness and contemplation.

September had come, and he had merrily sent off two happy boy-sportsmen with the keeper, seeing them over the first field himself, and leaning against the gate, as he sent them away in convulsions of laughing at his droll auguries. The second was a Sunday, a lovely day of clear deep blue sky, and rich sunshine laughing upon the full wealth of harvest fields—part fallen before the hand of the reaper, part waving in their ripe glowing beauty, to which he loved to liken Honora's hair—part in noble redundant shocks of corn in full season. Brooks used afterwards to tell how he overtook the squire slowly strolling to church on that beauteous autumnal morning, and how he paused to remark on the glory of the harvest, and to add, 'Keep the big barn clear, Brooks—let us have all the women and children in for the supper this time —and I say—send the spotted heifer down to-morrow to old Boycotts, instead of his cow that died. With such a crop as this, one can stand something. And,' said Brooks, 'Thank God for it! was as plain written on his face as ever I saw!'

It was the first Sunday in the month, and there was full service. Hiltonbury church had one of those old-fashioned altar-rails which form three sides of a square, and where it was the custom that at the words 'Draw near with faith,' the earliest communicants should advance to the rail and remain till their place was wanted by others, and that the last should not return to their seats till the service was concluded. Mr. Charlecote had for many years been always the first parishioner to walk slowly up the matted aisle, and kneel beside the wall, under the cumbrous old tables of Commandments. There, on this day, he knelt as usual, and harvest labours tending to thin the number of communicants, the same who came up first remained to the end, joined their voices in the Eucharistic Lord's Prayer and Angelic Hymn, and bowed their heads at the blessing of the peace that passeth all understanding.

It was not till the rest were moving away, that the vicar and his clerk remarked that the squire had not risen. Another look, and it was plain that he had sunk somewhat forward on his folded arms, and was only supported by the rail and the wall. The vicar hastily summoned the village doctor, who had not yet left the church. They lifted him, and laid him along on the cushioned step where he had been kneeling, but motion and breath were gone, the strong arms were helpless, and the colour had left the open face. Taken at once from the heavenly Feast on earth to the glory above, could this be called sudden death?

There he lay on the altar step, with hands crossed on his breast, and perfectly blessed repose on his manly countenance, sweetened and ennobled in its stillness, and in every lineament bearing the impress of that Holy Spirit of love who had made it a meet temple.

What an unpremeditated lying in state was that! as by ones and twos, beneath the clergyman's eye, the villagers stole in with slowly, heavily falling tread to gaze in silent awe on their best friend, some sobbing and weeping beyond control, others with grave, almost stolid tranquillity, or the murmured 'He *was* a gentleman,' which, in a poor man's mouth, means 'he was a just man and patient, the friend of the weak and poor.'

His farmers and his own labourers put their shoulders to bear him once more to his own house, through his half-gathered crops—

> The hand of the reaper
> Takes the ears that are hoary,
> But the voice of the weeper
> Wails manhood in glory.

No, bewail him not. It was glory, indeed, but the glory of early autumn, the garnering of the shock of corn in full season. It was well done of the vicar that a few long, full-grained ears of wheat were all that was laid upon his breast in his coffin.

There Honora saw them. The vicar, Mr. Henderson, had written to her at once, as Humfrey had long ago charged him to do, enclosing a letter that he had left with him for the purpose, a tender, soothing farewell, and an avowal such as he could never have spoken of the blessing that his attachment to her had been, in drawing his mind from the narrowness to which he might have been liable, and in elevating the tone of his views and opinions.

She knew what he meant—it was what he had caught from her youthful enthusiasm, second-hand from Owen Sandbrook. Oh! what vivid, vigorous truth not to have been weakened in the transit through two such natures, but to have done its work in the strong, practical mind able and candid enough to adopt it even thus filtered!

There were a few words of affectionate commendation of his people and his land into her keeping, and a parting blessing; and, lastly, written as a postscript— with a blot as if it had been written with hesitation— 'Little children, keep yourselves from idols!'

It was not bitter weeping. It was rather the sense of utter vacancy and hopelessness, with but one fixed purpose—that she would see his face again, and be the nearest to him when he was laid in the grave. She hastily wrote to the housekeeper and to the clergyman that she was coming, and Miss Wells's kind opposition only gave her just wilfulness and determination enough to keep her spirit from sinking.

So she travelled alone, and came to Hiltonbury in the sunset, as the 'last long wains' were slowly bearing their loads of wheat into the farmyard, the waggoners walking dejectedly beside them. Mr. Saville had come before her, and was at the door to receive her. She could not very well bear the presence of any one, nor the talk of cold-blooded arrangements. It seemed to keep away the dreamy living with Humfrey, and was far more dreary than the feeling of desolateness, and when they treated her as mistress of the house that was too intolerable. And yet it was worth something, too, to be the one to authorize that harvest supper in the big barn, in the confidence that it would be anything but revelry. Every one felt that the day was indeed a Harvest Home.

The funeral, according to his expressed wishes, was like those of the farmers of the parish; the coffin borne by his own labourers in their white round frocks; and the labourers were the expected guests for whom provision was made, but far and wide from all the country round, though harvest was at the height, came farmers and squires, poor men and rich, from the peer and county member down to the poor travelling hawker—all had met the sunny sympathy of that smile, all had been aided and befriended, all felt as if a prop, a castle of strength were gone.

Charlecotes innumerable rested in the chancel, and the last heir of the line was laid beneath the same flag where he had been placed on that last Sunday, the spot where Honor might kneel for many more, meeting him in spirit at the feast, and looking to the time when the cry should be, 'Put ye in the sickle, for the harvest is come.'

But ere she could look in thorough hope for that time, another page of Honor's life must be turned, and an alloy, as yet unknown to herself, must be purged from her heart. The last gleam of her youthful sunshine had faded with Humfrey; but youth is but a fraction of human existence, and there were further phases to be gone through and lessons to be learnt; although she was feeling as if all were over with her in this world, and neither hope, love, nor protection were left her, nor any interest save cherishing Humfrey Charlecote's memory, as she sat designing the brass tablet which was to record his name and age in old English illuminated letters, surrounded by a border of ears of corn and grapes.

CHAPTER IV.

> The glittering grass, with dewstars bright,
> Is all astir with twinkling light;
> What pity that such fair array
> In one brief hour should melt away.
> REV. T. WHYTEHEAD.

'THIS is a stroke of good luck!' said Mr. Charteris. 'We must not, on any account, remove the Sandbrook children from Miss Charlecote; she has no relations, and will certainly make the boy her heir.'

'She will marry!' said his wife. 'Some fashionable preacher will swallow her red hair. She is just at the age for it!'

'Less likely when she has the children to occupy her.'

'Well, you'll have them thrown on your hands yet!'

'The chance is worth trying for, though! I would not interfere with her on any account.'

'Oh, no, nor I! but I pity the children.'

'There, Master Owen, be a good boy, and don't worry. Don't you see, I'm putting up your things to go home.'

'Home!' the light glittered in Lucilla's eyes. 'Is it Wrapworth, nursey?'

'Dear me, Miss, not Wrapworth. That's given away, you know; but it's to Hiltonbury you are going—such a grand place, which if Master Owen is only a dear good boy, will all belong to him one of these days.'

'Will there be a pony to ride on ?' asked Owen.

'Oh, yes—if you'll only let those stockings alone—there'll be ponies, and carriages, and horses, and everything a gentleman can have, and all for my own dear little Master Owen !'

'I don't want to go to Hiltonbury,' said Lucilla ; 'I want to go home to the river and the boat, and see Mr. Prendergast and the black cow.'

'I'll give you a black cow, Cilly,' said Owen, strutting about. 'Is Hiltonbury bigger than the Castle ?'

'Oh, ever so big, Master Owen ; such acres of wood, Mr. Jones says, and all your dear cousin's, and sure to be your own in time. What a great gentleman you will be, to be sure, dining thirty gentlefolks twice a week, as they say poor Mr. Charlecote did, and driving four fine horses to your carriage like a gentleman. And then you wont forget poor old nursey-pursey.'

'Oh, no, nurse; I'll give you a ride in my carriage !'

Honora in her listless state had let Mr. Saville think for her, and passively obeyed him when he sent her back to Sandbeach to wind up her affairs there, while he finished off the valuations and other painful business at the Holt, in which she could be of little use, since all she desired was to keep everything as it was. She was anxious to return as soon as possible, so as to take up the reins before there had been time for the relaxation to be felt, the only chance she felt of her being able to fulfil his charge. The removal, the bustle, the talking things over with Miss Wells, and the sight of the children did much to restore her, and her old friend rejoiced to see that necessary occupation was tending to make her time pass more cheerfully than she perhaps knew.

As to the dear old City dwelling : it might have fetched an immense price, but only to become a warehouse, a measure that would have seemed to Honor little short of sacrilege. To let it, in such a locality was impossible, so it must remain unavailable capital, and Honora decided on leaving her old housekeeper therein, with a respectable married niece, who would inhabit the lower regions, and keep the other rooms in order, for an occasional stay in London. She would have been sorry to cut herself off from a month of London in the spring, and the house might farther be useful to friends who did not object to the situation; or could be lent now and then to a curate; and she could well afford to keep it up, so she thought herself justified in following her inclination, and went up for three mournful days of settling matters there, and packing books and ornaments till the rooms looked so dismantled that she could not think how to face them again.

It was the beginning of October when she met Miss Wells, children, and luggage at the station, and fairly was on her way to her home. She tried to call it so, as a duty to Humfrey, but it gave her a pang every time, and in effect she felt far less at home than when he and Sarah had stood in the doorway to greet the arrivals. She had purposely fixed an hour when it would be dark, so that she might receive no painful welcome; she wished no one to greet her, she had rather they were mourning for their master. She had more than once shocked Miss Wells by declaring heiresses to be a mistake; and yet, as she always owned, she could not have borne for any one else to have had the Holt.

Fortunately for her, the children were sleepy, and were rather in a mazy state when lifted out and set on their legs in the wainscoted hall, and she sent them at once with nurse to the cheerful room that Humfrey's little visitors had saved from becoming disused. Miss Wells's fond vigilance was a little oppressive, but she gently freed herself from it, and opened the study door. She had begged that as little change as possible might be made; and there stood, as she had last seen them, the large leathern chair, the little table, the big Bible, and in it the little faded marker she had herself constructed for his twenty-first birthday, when her powers of making presents had not equalled her will. Yet what costly gift could have fulfilled its mission like that one? She opened the heavy book at the place. It was at the first lesson for the last day of his life, the end of the prophet Hosea, and the first words her eyes fell upon were the glorious prophecy—' I will redeem them from death, I will ransom them from the power of the grave.' Her heart beat high, and she stood half musing, half reading: 'They that dwell under His shadow shall return; they shall revive as the corn, and grow as the vine.' How gentle and refreshing the cadence! A longing rose up in her to apply those latter words more closely, by placing them on his tablet; she did not think they would shock his humility, a consideration which had withheld her from choosing other passages of which she always thought in connexion with him. Another verse, and she read: ' Ephraim shall say, What have I to do any more with idols?'

It brought back the postscript. Kind Humfrey must have seen strong cause before he gave any reproof, least of all to her, and she could take his word that the fault had been there. She felt certain of it when she thought of her early devotion to Owen Sandbrook, and the utter blank caused by his defection. Nay, she believed she had begun to idolize Humfrey himself, but now, at her age, chastened, desponding, with nothing before her save the lonely life of an heiress old maid, counting no tie of blood with any being, what had she to engross her affections from the true Object? Alas! Honora's heart was not feeling that Object sufficient! Conscientious, earnest, truly loving goodness, and all connected with it; striving as a faithful, dutiful woman to walk rightly, still the personal love and trust were not yet come. Spent as they had been upon props of earth, when these were taken away the tendrils hung down drearily, unemployed, not fastening on the true support.

Not that she did not kneel beside that little table,

as in a shrine, and entreat earnestly for strength and judgment to do her duty faithfully in her new station, so that Humfrey's charge might be fulfilled, and his people might not suffer; and this done, and her homage paid to his empty throne, she was better able to satisfy her motherly friend by her deportment for the remainder of the evening, and to reply to the welcome of the weeping Mrs. Stubbs. By one of Humfrey's wise acts of foresight, his faithful servant, Reeves, had been provided for as the master of the Union, whither it was certain he would carry the same milk of human kindness as had been so plentiful at Hiltonbury, and the Holt was thus left free for Honora's Mr. Jones, without fear of clashing, though he was divided between pride in his young lady's ownership of a 'landed estate,' and his own dislike to a country residence.

Honora did not sleep soundly. The place was too new, and yet too familiar, and the rattling of the windows, the roaring of the wind in the chimney, and the creaking of the vane, without absolutely wakening her, kept her hearing alive continually, wearing the noises into some harassing dream that Humfrey's voice was calling to her, and hindrances always keeping her from him; and then of Lucilla and Owen in some imminent peril, whence she shrieked to him to save them, and then remembered he would stretch out his hand no more.

Sounder sleep came at last, towards morning, and far later than her usual hour she was wakened by a drumming upon her door, and the boy and girl dashed in, radiant with excitement at the novelty of the place. 'Sweet Honey! Sweet Honey dear, do get up and see. There's a rocking-horse at the end of the passage.' 'And there's a real pony out in the field.' 'There are cows.' 'There's a goat and a little kid, and I want to play with it, and I may, for it is all mine and yours.'

'All yours! Owen, boy,' repeated Honora, sitting up in surprise.

'Nursey said it was all to be Owen's,' said Lucilla.

'And she said I should be as grand a gentleman as poor Mr. Charlecote or uncle Charteris,' proceeded Owen, 'and that I should go out hunting in a red coat, on a beautiful horse; but I want to have the kid now, please Sweet Honey.'

'Nurse does not know anything about it,' said Honora, much annoyed that such an idea should have been suggested in such a manner. 'I thought my little Owen wished for better things—I thought he was to be like his papa, and try to be a good shepherd, praising God and helping people to do right.'

'But can't I wear a red coat too?' said Owen, wistfully.

'No, my dear; clergymen don't go out hunting; or how could they teach the poor little children?'

'Then I wont be a clergyman.'

This was an inconvenient and most undesirable turn; but Honor's first object must be to put the right of heirship out of the little head, and she at once began—'Nurse must have made a mistake, my dear; this place is your home, and will be always so, I hope, while it is mine, but it must not be your own, and you must not think it will. My little boy must work for himself and other people, and that's better than having houses and lands given to him.'

Those words touched the pride in Lucilla's composition, and she exclaimed—'I'll work too;' but the self-consequence of proprietorship had affected her brother more strongly, and he repeated, meditatively, 'Jones said, not mine while she was alive. Jones was cross.'

There might not be much in the words, child as he was, but there was something in his manner of eyeing her which gave her acute, unbearable pain—a look as if she stood in his way and crossed his importance. It was but a baby fit of temper, but she was in no frame to regard it calmly, and with an alteration of countenance that went to his heart, she exclaimed—'Can that be my little Owen, talking as if he wanted his cousin

Honor dead and out of the way? We had better never have come here if you are to leave off loving me.'

Quick to be infected by emotion, the child's arms were at once round her neck, and he was sobbing out that he loved his Sweet Honey better than anything; nurse was naughty; Jones was naughty; he wouldn't hunt, he wouldn't wear a red coat, he would teach little children just like lambs, he would be like dear papa; anything the poor little fellow could think of he poured out with kisses and entreaties to know if he were naughty still; while his sister, after her usual fashion on such occasions, began to race up and down the room with paroxysms, sometimes of stamping, sometimes of something like laughter.

Some minutes passed before Honora could compose herself, or soothe the boy, by her assurances that he was not to blame, only those who put things in his head that he could not understand; and it was not till after much tender fondling that she had calmed him enough for his morning devotions. No sooner were these over than he looked up and said, while the tears still glazed his cheeks, 'Sweet Honey, I'll tell nurse and Mr. Jones that I'm on pilgrimage to the Eastern land, and I'll not turn into by-ways after red coats and little kids to vex you.'

Whether Owen quite separated fact from allegory might have been doubtful to a more prosaic mind than Honora's, but he had brought this dreamy strain with him from his father, and she thought it one of his great charms. She had been obliged to leave him to himself much more than usual of late, and she fervently resolved to devote herself with double energy to watching over him, and eradicating any weeds that might have been sown during her temporary inattention. He clung so fast to her hand, and was so much delighted to have her with him again, so often repeating that she must not go away again, that the genuineness of his affection could not be doubted, and probably he would only retain an impression of having been led to say something very shocking, and the alarm to his sensitive conscience would hinder him from ever even trying to remember what it was.

She spoke, however, to Nurse, telling her that the subject must never be mentioned to the children, since it was by no means desirable for them, and besides she had no intention of the kind. She wished it to be distinctly understood that Master Owen was not to be looked upon as her heir.

'Very true, ma'am, it is too soon to be talking of such things yet, and I must say, I was as sorry as possible to find that the child had had it named to him. People will talk, you see, Miss Charlecote, though I am sure so young a lady as you are . . . . .'

'That has nothing to do with it,' said Honora; 'I consider nothing so bad for a child as to be brought up to expectations to which he has no right, when he is sure to have to provide for himself. I beg that if you hear the subject entered on again in the children's presence, you will put a stop to it.'

'Certainly, ma'am; their poor dear papa never would have wished them to be occupied with earthly things of that sort. As I often said, there never was such an unworldly gentleman; he never would have known if there were a sixpence in the house, nor a joint in the larder, if there had not been cook and me to care for him. I often said to cook—"Well for him that he has honest people about him."'

Honora likewise spoke to Jones, her private retainer. He smiled scorn of the accusation, and answered her as the child he had known in frocks. 'Yes, ma'am, I did tell the young gentleman to hold his tongue, for it never would be his in your lifetime, nor after, in my judgment.'

'Why, certainly. it does seem early days to speak of such a matter,' said Honora, sadly.

'It is unaccountable what people will not put in children's heads,' said Jones, sagely; 'not but what he is a nice quiet young gentleman, and gives very little trouble, but they might let *that* alone. Miss Honora, when will it be convenient to you to take my account of the plate?'

She felt pretty well convinced that Jones had only resented the whole on her account, and that it was not he who had put the notion into the boy's head. As to Nurse, she was far from equally clear. Doubts of Nurse's sincerity had long been growing upon her, and she was in the uncomfortable position of being able to bear neither to think of the children's intercourse with any one tainted with falsehood, nor to dismiss a person implicitly trusted by their father. She could only decide that the first detected act of untruth should be the turning point.

Meantime, painful as was many an association, Honor did not find her position so dreary or so oppressive as she had anticipated. She had a great deal to do, and the tracks had been duly made out for her by her cousin. Mr. Saville, or Humfrey's old friend, Sir John Raymond, were always ready to help her in great matters, and Brooks was an excellent dictatorial deputy in small ones. Her real love for country life, for live animals, and, above all, the power of doing good, all found scope. Humfrey's charge gave her a sense of a fulfilled duty; and mournful and broken-spirited as she believed herself, if Humfrey could have looked at her as she scrupulously made entries in his book, rode out with the children to try to look knowing at the crops, or sat by the fire in the evening with his dogs at her feet, telling stories to the children, he would not have feared too much for his Honor. Living or dead, the love of Humfrey could hardly help being a spring of peace and happiness; and the consciousness of it had been too brief, and the tie never close enough, to lead to a state of crushed spirits. The many little tender observances that she paid to him were a source of mournful sweetness rather than of heartrending.

It was a quietly but fully occupied life, with a

certain severity towards her own comforts, and liberality towards those of other people, which had always been a part of her character, ever since Owen Sandbrook had read sermons with her on self-denial. If Miss Wells had a fire in her bedroom forced upon her, Miss Charlecote had none, and hurried down in the bleak winter morning in shawl and gloves to Humfrey's great Bible, and then to his account books and her business letters. She was fresh with cold when she met the children for their early reading. And then—but it was not soon that she learnt to bear that, though she had gone through the like before, she had to read the household devotions, where every petition seemed to be lacking the manly tone to give it fulness and force.

Breakfast followed, the silver kettle making it homelike, the children chattering, Miss Wells smiling, letters coming in to perplex or to clear up perplexities, amuse or cheer. The children were then turned out for an hour's hoop-driving on the gravel drive, horse-chesnut picking, or whatever might not be mischief, while Honora was conferring with Jones or with Brooks, and receiving her orders for the day. Next followed letter writing, then lessons in general, a real enjoyment, unless Lucilla happened to have picked up a fit of perverseness—some reading to them, or rationalizing of play—the early dinner—the subsequent expedition with them, either walking or riding—for Brooks had soon found ponies for them, and they were gallant little riders. Honor would not give up the old pony, long since trained for her by Humfrey, though, maybe, that was her most undutiful proceeding towards him, as he would certainly have told her that the creature was shaky on the legs. So at last it tumbled down with her, but without any damage, save a hole in her skirt, and a dreadful crying-fit of little Owen, who was frightened out of his wits. She owned that it must be degraded to light cart work, and mounted an animal which Hiltonbury agreed to be more worthy of her. Coming in, the children played; she either did her business or found leisure for reading; then came tea time, then the reading of a story book to the children, and when they were disposed of, of something mildly moral and instructive to suit Miss Wells's taste.

The neighbourhood all mourned Mr. Charlecote as a personal loss, and could hardly help regarding any successor as their enemy. Miss Charlecote had been just enough known in her girlish days not to make her popular in a commonplace neighbourhood; the ladies had criticised her hair and her genius, and the gentlemen had been puzzled by her searching questions into their county antiquities, and obliged to own themselves unaware of a Roman milestone propping their bailiff's pigstye, or of the spur of a champion of one of the Roses being hung over their family pew. But when Mr. Henderson and the Raymonds reported pleasantly of her, and when once or twice she had been seen cantering down the lanes, or shopping in Elverslope, and had exchanged a bow with a familiar face, the gentlemen took to declaring that the heiress was an uncommonly fine woman after all, and the ladies became possessed with the perception that it was high time to call upon Miss Charlecote—what could she be doing with those two children?

So there were calls, which Honor duly returned, and then came invitations, but, to Miss Wells's great annoyance, Honor decided against these. It was not self-denial, but she thought it suitable. She did not love the round of county gaieties, and in her position she did not think them a duty. Retirement seemed to befit the widowhood, which she felt so entirely that when Miss Wells once drove her into disclaiming all possibility of marrying, she called it 'marrying again.' When Miss Wells urged the inexpedience of absolute seclusion, she said she would continue to make morning calls, and she hoped in time to have friends of her own to stay with her; she might ask the Raymonds, or some of the quiet, clerical families (the real *élite*, be it observed) to spend a day or drink tea, but the dinner and ball life was too utterly incongruous for an elderly heiress. When it came to the elderly heiress poor Miss Wells was always shut up in utter despair —she who thought her bright-locked darling only grew handsomer each day of her pride of womanhood.

The brass which Honora had chosen for her cousin's memorial was slow in being executed, and summer days had come in before it was sent to Hiltonbury. She walked down, a good deal agitated, to ascertain whether it were being rightly managed, but, to her great annoyance, found that the church having been left open, so many idle people were standing about that she could not bear to mingle with them. Had it been only the Holt vassalage, either their feeling would have been one with her own, or they would have made way for her, but there were some pert nursery maids gaping about with the children from Beauchamp, whence the heads of the family had been absent all the winter and spring, leaving various nurses and governesses in charge. Honora could not encounter their eyes, and went to the vicarage to send Mr. Henderson, and finding him absent, walked over sundry fields in a vain search for Brooks. Rain came on so violently as to wet her considerably, and, to her exceeding mortification, she was obliged to relinquish her superintendence, either in person or by deputy.

However, when she awoke early and saw the sun laughing through the shining drops, she decided on going down ere the curious world was astir, to see what had been done. It was not far from six, when she let herself out at the porch, and very like a morning with Humfrey, with the tremulous glistening of every spray, and the steamy fragrance rising wherever the sun touched the grass, that seemed almost to grow visibly. The woods were ringing with the songs of birds, circle beyond circle, and there was something in the exuberant merriment of those blackbirds and thrushes that would not let her be sad, though they had been Humfrey's special glory. The thought of such pleasures did not seem out of keeping. The lane was overhung with bushes; the banks, a whole wealth of ferns, climbing plants, tall grasses, and nettles, had not yet felt the sun and were dank and dreary, so she hurried on, and arriving at the clerk's door, knocked and opened. He was gone to his work, and sounds above showed the wife to be engaged on the toilette of the younger branches. She called out that she had come for the keys of the church, and seeing them on the dresser, abstracted them, bidding the good woman give herself no trouble.

She paused under the porch, and ere fitting the heavy key to the lock, felt that strange pressure and emotion of the heart that even if it be sorrow is also an exquisite sensation. If it were mournful that the one last office she could render to Humfrey was over, it was precious to her to be the only one who had a right to pay it, the one whom he had loved best upon earth, round whom she liked to believe that he still might be often hovering—whom he might welcome by and by. Here was the place for communion with him, the spot which had, indeed, been to him none other than the gate of Heaven.

Yet, will it be believed? Not one look did Honora cast at Humfrey Charlecote's monument that morning.

With both hands she turned the reluctant bolts of the lock, and pushed open the nail-studded door. She slowly advanced along the uneven floor of the aisle, and had just reached the chancel arch, when something suddenly stirred, making her start violently. It was still, and after a pause she again advanced, but her heart gave a sudden throb, and a strange chill of awe rushed over her as she beheld a little white face over the altar rail, the chin resting on a pair of folded hands, the dark eyes fixed in a strange, dreamy, spiritual expression of awe.

The shock was but for a moment, the next the blood rallied to her heart, and she told herself that Humfrey would say, that either the state of her spirits had produced an illusion, or else that some child had been left here by accident. She advanced, but as she did so the two hands were stretched out and locked together as in an agony, and the childish, feeble voice cried out, 'Oh! if you're an angel, please don't frighten me; I'll be very good.'

Honora was in a pale, soft, grey dress, that caught the light in a rosy glow from the east window, and her golden hair was hanging in radiant masses beneath her straw bonnet, but she could not appreciate the angelic impression she made on the child, who had been tried so long by such a captivity. 'My poor child,' she said, 'I am no angel; I am only Miss Charlecote. I'm afraid you have been shut up here;' and, coming nearer, she perceived that it was a boy of about seven years old, well dressed, though his garments were disordered. He stood up as she came near, but he was trembling all over, and as she drew him into her bosom, and put her arms round him, she found him quivering with icy cold.

'Poor little fellow,' she said, rocking him, as she sat on the step and folded her shawl round him, 'have you been here all night? How cold you are; I must take you home, my dear. What is your name?'

'I'm Robert Mervyn Fulmort,' said the little boy, clinging to her. 'We came in to see Mr. Charlecote's monument put up, and I suppose they forgot me. I waked up, and everybody was gone, and the door was locked. Oh! please,' he gasped, 'take me out. I don't want to cry.'

She thought it best to take him at once into the cheerful sunlight, but it did not yet yield the warmth that he needed ; and all her soothing words could not check the nervous tremor, though he held her so tight that it seemed as if he would never let her go.

' You shall come home with me, my dear little boy ; you shall have some breakfast, and then I will take you safe home to Beauchamp.'

' Oh, if you please !' said the boy, gratefully.

Exercise was thawing his numbed limbs, and his eyes brightened.

'Whom were you with?' she asked. 'Who could have forgotten you?'

'I came with Lieschen and Nurse and the babies. The others went out with Mademoiselle.'

'And you went to sleep?'

'Yes; I liked to see the mason go chip, chip, and I wanted to see them fit the thing in. I got into that great pew, to see better; and I made myself a nest, but at last they were all gone.'

'And what did you do, then? Were you afraid?'

'I didn't know what to do. I ran all about to see if I could look out at a window, but I couldn't.'

'Did you try to call?'

'Wouldn't it have been naughty?' said the boy; and then, with an impulse of honest truthfulness, 'I did try once; but do you know, there was another voice came back again, and I thought that *die Geistern wachten sich auf.*'

'The what?'

'*Die Geistern das Lieschen sagt in die Gewolben wohnen,*' said little Robert, evidently quite unconscious whether he spoke German or English.

'So you could not call for the echo. Well, did you not think of the bells?'

'Yes; but, oh! the door was shut; and then, I'll tell you—but don't tell Mervyn—I did cry.'

'Indeed, I don't wonder. It must have been very lonely.'

'I didn't like it,' said Robert, shivering; and getting to his German again, he described '*das Gewitter*' beating on the panes, with wind and whirling leaves, and the unearthly noises of the creaking vane. The terror of the lonely, supperless child was dreadful to think of; and she begged to know what he could have done as it grew dark.

'I got to Mr. Charlecote,' said Robert—an answer that thrilled her all over. 'I said I'd be always very good, if he would take care of me, and not let them frighten me. And so I did go to sleep.'

'I'm sure Mr. Charlecote would, my dear little man,' began Honora, then checked by remembering what he would have said. 'But didn't you think of One more sure to take care of you than Mr. Charlecote?'

'Lieschen talks of *der Lieber Gott*,' said the little boy. 'We said our prayers in the nursery, but Mervyn says only babies do.'

'Mervyn is terribly wrong, then,' said Honora, shuddering. 'Oh! Robert, Mr. Charlecote never got up nor went to bed without asking the good God to take care of him, and make him good.'

'Was that why he was so good?' asked Robert.

'Indeed it was,' said she, fervently; 'nobody can be good without it. I hope my little friend will never miss his prayers again, for they are the only way to be manly and afraid of nothing but doing wrong, as he was.'

'I wont miss them,' said Robert, eagerly; then, with a sudden, puzzled look—' Did he send you?'

'Who?'

'Mr. Charlecote.'

'Why—how should....? What made you think so?'

'I—why, once in the night I woke up; and oh! it was so dark, and there were such noises, such rattling and roarings; and then it came all white—white light —all the window-bars and all so plain upon the wall; and then came—bending, bending over—a great grey darkness—oh! so horrible!—and went away, and came back.'

'The shadow of the trees, swaying in the moonlight.'

'Was it? I thought it was the *Nebel Wittwen neckten mir*, and then the *Erlkonung-tochter*. *Wissen sie*— and oh! I did scream once; and then, somehow, it grew quietly darker; and I thought Mr. Charlecote had me folded up so warm on his horse's back, and that we rode ever so far; and they stretched out their long white arms, and could not get me; but somehow he set me down on a cold stone, and said, " Wait here, Robin, and I'll send her to lead you." And then came a creaking, and there were you.'

'Well, little Robin, he did not quite send me; but it was to see his tablet that I came down this morning; so he brought me after all. He was my very dear cousin Humfrey, and I like you for having been his little friend. Will you be mine, too, and let me help you, if I can? and if your papa and mamma give leave, come and see me, and play with the little girl and boy who live with me?'

'Oh, yes!' cried Robert; 'I like you.'

The alliance was sealed with a hearty kiss.

'But,' said Robert, 'you must ask Mademoiselle; papa and mamma are away.'

'And how was it no one ever missed you?'

Robert was far less surprised at this than she was; for, like all children, to be left behind appeared to him a contingency rather probable than otherwise.

He was a fine-looking boy, with dark gray, thoughtful eyes, and a pleasant countenance; but his nerves had been so much shaken that he started, and seemed ready to catch hold of her at every sound.

'What's that?' he cried, as a trampling came along the alley as they entered the garden.

'Only my two little cousins,' said Honora, smiling. 'I hope you will be good friends, though perhaps Owen is too young a playfellow. Here, Lucy, Owen—here is a little friend for you—Robert Fulmort.'

The children came eagerly up, and Lucilla, taking her hand, raised her face to kiss the stranger; but Robert did not approve of the proceeding, and held up his head. Lucilla rose on tip-toe; Robin did the same. As he had the advantage of a whole year's height, he fully succeeded in keeping out of her reach; and very comical was the effect. She gave it up at last, and contented herself with asking, 'And where do you come from?'

'Out of the church,' was Robin's reply.

'Then you are very good and holy, indeed,' said Owen, looking at him earnestly, with clasped hands.

'No!' said Robert, gruffly.

'Poor little man! he was left behind, and shut up in the church all night, without any supper,' said Honora.

'Shut up in the church like Goody Two-Shoes!' cried Lucilla, dancing about. 'Oh, what fun!'

'Did the angels come and sing to you?' asked Owen.

'Don't ask such stupid questions,' cried his sister. 'Oh, I know what I'd have done! Didn't you get up into the pulpit?'

'No!'

'And I do so want to know if the lady and gentleman on the monument have their ruffs the same on the inside, towards the wall, as outside; and, oh! I do so want to get all the dust out of the folds of the lady's ruff. I wish they'd lock me into the church, and I'd soon get out when I was tired.'

Lucilla and Owen decidedly thought Robin had not profited by his opportunities, but he figured better in an examination on his brothers and sisters. There were seven, of whom he was the fourth—Augusta, Juliana, and Mervyn being his elders; Phœbe, Maria, and Bertha, his juniors. The three seniors were under the rule of Mademoiselle, the little ones under that of nurse and Lieschen, and Robert stood on neutral ground, doing lessons with Mademoiselle, whom, he said, in unpicked language which astounded little Owen, 'he morally hated,' and at the same time free of the nursery, where, it appeared, that 'Phœbe was the jolliest little fellow in the world,' and Lieschen was the only 'good-natured body going,' and knew no end of *Mährchen.* The boy spoke a very odd mixture of Lieschen's German and of English, pervaded by stable slang, and was altogether a curious study of the effects of absentee parents; nevertheless Honora and Lucilla both took a considerable fancy to him, the latter patronizing him to such a degree that she hardly allowed him to eat the much-needed breakfast, which recalled colour to his cheek and substance to his voice.

After much thought, Owen delivered himself of the sentiment that 'people's papas and mammas were very funny,' doubtless philosophizing on the inconsistency of the class in being—some so willing, some so reluctant, to leave their children behind them. Honor fully agreed with him, but did not think the discussion profitable for Robin, whom she now proposed to take home in the pony-carriage. Lucilla, always eager for novelty, and ardent for her new friendship, begged to accompany her. Owen was afraid of the strangers, and preferred Miss Wells.

Even as they set out, they found that Robert's disappearance had created some sensation, for the clerk's wife was hurrying up to ask if Miss Charlecote had the keys, that she might satisfy the man from Beauchamp that Master Fulmort was not in the church. At the lodge the woman threw up her hands with joy at the sight of the child; and some way off, on the sward, stood a bigger boy, who, with a loud hurrah, scoured away towards the house as the carriage appeared.

'That's Mervyn,' said Robert; 'he is gone to tell them.'

Beauchamp was many degrees grander since Honor had last visited it. The approach was entirely new. Two fresh wings had been added, and the front was all over scaffolds and cement, in all stages of colour, from rich brown to permanent white. Robert explained that nothing was so nice as to watch the workmen, and showed Lucilla a plasterer on the topmost stage of the scaffolding, who, he said, was the nicest man he knew, and could sing all manner of songs.

Rather nervously Honora drove under the poles to the hall-door, where two girls were seen in the rear of a French woman; and Honor felt as if Robin might have grounds for his 'moral hatred' when her voluble transports of gratitude and affection broke forth, and the desolation in which the loss had left them was described. Robert edged back from her at once, and flew to another party at the bottom of the stairs—a very stout nurse and an uncapped, flaxen-haired mädchen, who clasped him in her arms, and cried, and sobbed over him. As soon as he could release himself, he caught hold of a fat little bundle, which had been coaxing one of his legs all through Lieschen's embrace, and dragging it forwards, cried, ' Here she is—here's Phœbe !' Phœbe, however, was shy, and cried and fought her way back to hide her face in Lieschen's apron ; and meantime a very odd scene took place. School-room and nursery were evidently at most direful war. Each wanted to justify itself lest the lady should write to the parents ; each tried to be too grand to seem to care, and threw all the blame on the other. On the whole, Honor gathered that Mademoiselle believed the boy *enfantin* enough to be in the nursery, the nurses that he was in the schoolroom, and he had not been really missed till bed-time, when each party recriminated instead of seeking him, and neither would allow itself to be responsible for him. Lieschen, who alone had her suspicions where he might be, abstained from naming them in sheer terror of *Kobolden, Geistern*, corpse-candles, and what not, and had lain conjuring up his miseries till morning. Honora did not much care how they settled it amongst them, but tried to make friends with the young people, who seemed to take their brother's restoration rather coolly, and to be chiefly occupied by staring at Lucilla. Augusta and Juliana were self-possessed, and rather *maniérées*, acquitting themselves evidently to the satisfaction of the French governess, and Honor, perceiving her to be a necessary infliction, invited her and her pupils, especially Robin, to spend a day in the next week at the Holt.

The proposal was graciously accepted, and Lucilla spent the intervening time in a tumult of excitement.

Nor was the day entirely unsuccessful; Mademoiselle behaved herself with French tact, and Miss Wells took her off Honora's hands a good deal, leaving them free for the children. Lucilla, always aspiring, began a grand whispering friendship with the two girls, and set her little cap strongly at Mervyn, but that young gentleman was contemptuous and bored when he found no entertainment in Miss Charlecote's stud, and was only to be kept placable by the bagatelle-board and the strawberry-bed. Robert followed his lead more than was satisfactory, but with visible predilections for the Holt ladies, old and young. Honor talked to him about little Phœbe, and he lighted up and began to detail her accomplishments, and to be very communicative about his home vexations and pleasures, and finally, when the children were wishing good night, he bluntly said, 'It would be better fun to bring Lieschen and Phœbe.'

Honor thought so too, and proposed giving the invitation.

'Don't,' said Robert, 'she'd be cross; I'll bring them.'

And so he did. Two days after, the broad German face and the flaxen head appeared, leading that fat ball, Phœbe, and Robin frisking in triumph beside her. Henceforth a great friendship arose between the children. Phœbe soon lost all dread of those who petted her, and favoured them with broad smiles and an incomprehensible patois. Owen made very much of her, and pursued and imitated Robert with the devotion of a small boy to a larger one. Lucilla devoted herself to him for want of better game, and moreover he plainly told her that she was the prettiest little girl he ever saw, and laid all manner of remarkable treasures at her feet. Miss Charlecote believed that he made some curious confidences to her, for once Owen said, 'I want to know why Robin hasn't a Sweet Honey to make him good?'

'Robin has a papa and mamma, and a governess.'

'Robin was telling Lucy he wanted some one to teach him to be good, and she said she would, but I think she is not old enough.'

'Any one who is good is teaching others, my Owen,' said Honor. 'We will ask in our prayers that poor little Robin may be helped.'

When Mr. and Mrs. Fulmort came home, there was an interchange of calls, many thanks for her kindness to the children, and sanction of future intercourse. Mr. Fulmort was a great distiller, who had married a county heiress, and endeavoured to take his place among the country squires, whom he far exceeded in display ; and his wife, a meek, sickly person, lived a life of slavery to the supposed exigencies of fashion. She had always had, in her maiden days, a species of awe of the Charlecotes' London cousin, and was now disposed to be rather gratified by her notice of her children. Mervyn had been disposed of at a tutor's, and Robert was adrift for many hours of the day. As soon as he had discovered the possibility of getting to the Holt alone, he was frequently there, following Honora about in her gardening and farming, as much at home as the little Sandbrooks, sharing in their sports, and often listening to the little books that she read aloud to them. He was very far from being such an angelic little mortal as Owen, with whom indeed his sympathies were few. Once some words were caught from him by both children, which startled Honor exceedingly, and obliged her to tell him that if ever she found him to have repeated the like, she should forbid his coming near them. He looked excessively sullen, and did not come for a week, during which Lucilla was intolerably naughty, and was twice severely punished for using the identical expressions in defiance.

Then he came again, and behaved as if nothing had happened, but the offence never recurred. Some time after, when he boasted of having come away with a lesson unlearnt, in flat disobedience to Mademoiselle, Honor sent him straight home, though Lucilla stamped and danced at her in a frenzy. Another time Owen rushed up to her in great agony at some torture that Robin was inflicting upon a live mouse. Upon this, Honor, full of the spirit of indignation, fairly struck the offender sharply on the fingers with her riding-whip. He scowled at her, but it was only for a moment. She held him tightly by the hand, while she sent the gardener to put his victim out of its misery, and then she talked to him, not sentimentally, her feelings were too strongly stirred, but with all her horror of cruelty. He muttered that Mervyn and the grooms always did it; but he did not hold out long—Lucilla was holding aloof, too much horrified to come near—and finally he burst into tears, and owned that he had never thought!

Every now and then, such outbreaks made Honor wonder why she let him come, perhaps to tempt her children; but she remembered that he and Humfrey had been fond of one another, and she felt drawn towards him, though in all prudence she resolved to lessen the attractions of the Holt by being very strict with all, and rather ungracious to him. Yet, strange to say, the more regulations she made, and the more she flashed out at his faults, the more constant was her visitor, the Robin who seemed to thrive upon the veriest crumbs of good nature.

Positively, Honora was sometimes amazed to find what a dragon she could be upon occasion. Since she had been brought into subordination at six or eight years old, she had never had occasion to find out that she had a spirit of her own, till she found herself astonishing Jones and Brooks for taking the liberty of having a deadly feud; making Brooks understand that cows were not to be sold, nor promises made to tenants, without reference to her; or showing a determined marauder that Humfrey's wood was not to be preyed upon any more than in his own time. They were very feminine explosions to be sure, but they had their effect, and Miss Charlecote's was a real government.

The uproar with nurse came at last, through a

chance discovery that she had taken Owen to a certain forbidden house of gossip, where he had been bribed to secrecy with bread and treacle.

Honora wrote to Mrs. Charteris for permission to dismiss the mischievous woman, and obtained full consent, and the most complete expression of confidence and gratitude. So there ensued a month, when every visit to the nursery seemed to be spent in tears. Nurse was really very fond of the children, and cried over them incessantly, only consoling herself by auguring a brilliant future for them, when Master Owen should reign over Hiltonbury, like the gentleman he was.

'But, nurse, Cousin Honor says I never shall—I'm to be a clergyman like papa. She says......'

Nurse winked knowingly at the housemaid. 'Yes, yes, my darling, no one likes to hear who is to come after them. Don't you say nothing about it; it ain't becoming; but, by and by, see if it don't come so, and if my boy ain't master here.'

'I wish I was, and then nursey would never go.'

However, nurse did go, and after some tears Owen was consoled by promotion to the habits of an older boy.

Lucilla was very angry, and revenged herself by every variety of opposition in her power, all which were put down by the strong hand. It was a matter of necessity to keep a tight grasp on this little wilful sprite, the most fiery morsel of engaging caprice and naughtiness that a quiet spinster could well have lit upon. It really sometimes seemed to Honora as if there were scarcely a fault in the range of possibilities that she had not committed; and indeed a bit of good advice generally seemed to act by contraries, and serve to suggest mischief. Softness and warmth of feeling seemed to have been lost with her father; she did not show any particular affection towards her brother or Honora. Perhaps she liked Miss Wells, but that might be only opposition; nay, Honor would have been almost thankful if she had melted at the departure of the undesirable nurse, but she appeared only hard and cross. If she liked any one it was Robert Fulmort, but that was too much in the way of flirtation.

Vanity was an extremely traceable spring of action. When nurse went, Miss Lucilla gave the household no peace, because no one could rightly curl the long flaxen tresses upon her shoulders, until the worry became so intolerable that Honora, partly as penance, partly because she thought the present mode neither conducive to tidiness nor comfort, took her scissors and trimmed all the ringlets behind, bowl-dish fashion, as her own carrots had figured all the days of her childhood.

Lucilla was held by Mrs. Stubbs during the operation. She did not cry or scream after she felt herself conquered by main strength, but her blue eyes gleamed with a strange, wild light; she would not speak to Miss Charlecote all the rest of the day, and Honora doubted whether she were ever forgiven.

Another offence was the cutting down her name into Lucy. Honor had avoided Cilly from the first; Silly Sandbrook would be too dreadful a sobriquet to be allowed to attach to any one, but Lucilla resented the change more deeply than she showed. Lucy was a housemaid's name, she said, and Honor reproved her for vanity, and called her so all the more. She did not love Miss Charlecote well enough to say that Cilly had been her father's name for her, and that he had loved to wind the flaxen curls round his fingers.

Every new study, every new injunction cost a warfare, disobedience, and passionate defiance and resistance on the one hand, and steady, good-tempered firmness on the other, gradually growing a little stern. The waves became weary of beating on the rock at last. The fiery child was growing into a girl, and the calm will had the mastery of her; she succumbed insensibly; and owing all her pleasures to Cousin Honor, she grew to depend upon her, and mind, manners, and opinions were taking their mould from her.

CHAPTER V.

Too soon the happy child
His nook of heavenward thought must change
For life's seducing wild.
                        Christian Year.

HE summer sun peeped through the Venetian blinds greenly shading the breakfast table.

Only three sides were occupied. For more than two years past good Miss Wells had been lying under the shade of Hiltonbury Church, taking with her Honora Charlecote's last semblance of the dependence and deference of her young ladyhood. The kind governess had been fondly mourned, but she had not left her child to loneliness, for the brother and sister sat on either side, each with a particular pet—Lucilla's, a large pointer, who kept his nose on her knee, Owen's, a white fantailed pigeon, seldom long absent from his shoulder, where it sat quivering and bending backwards its graceful head.

Lucilla, now nearly fourteen, looked younger from the unusual smallness of her stature, and the exceeding delicacy of her features and complexion, and she would never have been imagined to be two years the senior of the handsome-faced, large-limbed young Saxon who had so far outstripped her in height; and yet there was something in those deep blue eyes, that on a second glance proclaimed a keen intelligence as much above her age as her appearance was below it.

'What's the matter?' said she, rather suddenly.

'Yes, sweetest Honey,' added the boy, 'you look bothered. Is that rascal not paying his rent?'

'No!' she said, 'it is a different matter entirely. What do you think of an invitation to Castle Blanch?'

'For us all?' asked Owen.

'Yes, all, to meet your uncle Christopher, the last week in August.'

'Why can't he come here?' asked Lucilla.

'I believe we must go,' said Honora. 'You ought to know both your uncles, and they should be consulted before Owen goes to school.'

'I wonder if they will examine me,' said Owen. 'How they will stare to find Sweet Honey's teaching as good as all their preparatory schools.'

'Conceited boy.'

'I'm not conceited—only in my teacher. Mr. Henderson said I should take as good a place as Robert Fulmort did at Winchester, after four years in that humbugging place at Elverslope.'

'We can't go!' cried Lucilla. 'It's the last week of Robin's holidays!'

'Well done, Lucy!' and both Honor and Owen laughed heartily.

'It is nothing to me,' said she, tossing her head, 'only I thought Cousin Honor thought it good for him.'

'You may stay at home to do him good,' laughed Owen; 'I'm sure I don't want him. You are very welcome, such a bore as he is.'

'Now, Owen.'

'Honey, dear, I do take my solemn affidavit that I have tried my utmost to be friends with him,' said Owen; 'but he is such a fellow—never has the least notion beyond Winchester routine—Latin and Greek, cricket and football.'

'You'll soon be a schoolboy yourself,' said Lucilla.

'Then I shan't make such an ass of myself,' returned Owen.

'Robin is a very good boy, I believe,' said Honor.

'That's the worst of him!' cried Lucilla, running away and clapping the door after her as she went.

'Well, I don't know,' said Owen, very seriously, 'he says he does not care about the Saints' days, because he has no one to get him leave out.'

'I remember,' said Honor, with a sweet smile of tender memory, 'when to me the merit of Saints' days was that they were your father's holidays.'

'Yes, you'll send me to Westminster, and be always coming to Woolstone Lane,' said Owen.

'Your uncles must decide,' she said, half mournfully, half proudly; 'you are getting to be a big boy —past me, Oney.'

It brought her a roughly playful caress, and he added, 'You've got the best right, I'm sure.'

'I had thought of Winchester,' she said. 'Robert would be a friend.'

Owen made a face, and caused her to laugh, while scandalizing her by humming, 'Not there, not there, my child.'

'Well, be it where it may, you had better look over your Virgil, while I go down to my practical Georgics with Brooks.'

Owen obeyed. He was like a spirited horse in a leash of silk. Strong, fearless, and manly, he was still perfectly amenable to her, and had never shown any impatience of her rule. She had taught him entirely herself, and both working together with a thorough good will, she had rendered him a better classical scholar, as all judges allowed, than most boys of the same age, and far superior to them in general cultivation; and she should be proud to convince Captain Charteris that she had not made him the mollycoddle that was obviously anticipated. The other relatives, who had seen the children in their yearly visits to London, had always expressed unqualified satisfaction, though not advancing much in the good graces of Lucy and Owen. But Honor thought the public school ought to be left to the selection of the two uncles, though she wished to be answerable for the expense, both there and at the university. The provision inherited by her charges was very slender, for, contrary to all expectation, old Mr. Sandbrook's property had descended in another quarter, and there was barely 5000*l*. between the two. To preserve this untouched by the expenses of education was Honora's object, and she hoped to be able to smooth their path in life by occasional assistance, but on principle she was determined to make them independent of her, and she had always made it known that she regarded it as her duty to Humfrey, that her Hiltonbury property should be destined—if not to the apocryphal American Charlecote—to a relation of their mutual great grandmother.

Cold invitations had been given and declined, but this one was evidently in earnest, and the consideration of the Captain decided Honora on accepting it, but not without much murmuring from Lucilla. Caroline and Horatia were detestable grown-up young ladies, her aunt was horrid, Castle Blanch was the slowest place in the world; she should be shut up in some abominable school-room, to do fancy-work, and never to get a bit of fun. Even the being reminded of Wrapworth and its associations only made her more cross. She was of a nature to fly from thought or feeling—she was keen to perceive, but hated reflection, and from the very violence of her feelings, she unconsciously abhorred any awakening of them, and steeled herself by levity.

Her distaste only gave way in Robert's presence, when she appeared highly gratified by the change, certain that Castle Blanch would be charming, and her cousin the Lifeguardsman especially so. The more disconsolate she saw Robert, the higher rose her spirits, and his arrival to see the party off sent her away in open triumph, glorifying her whole cousinhood without a civil word to him; but when seated in the carriage, she launched at him a drawing, the favourite work of her leisure hours, broke into unrestrained giggling at his grateful surprise, and, ere the wood was past, was almost strangled with sobs.

Castle Blanch was just beyond the suburbs of London, in complete country, but with an immense neighbourhood, and not half-an-hour by train from town. Honora drove all the way, to enjoy the lovely Thames scenery to the full. They passed through Wrapworth, and as they did so, Lucilla chattered to the utmost, while Honora stole her hand over Owen's and gently pressed it. He returned the squeeze with interest, and looked up in her face with a loving smile —mother and home were not wanting to him!

About two miles further on, and not in the same parish, began the Castle Blanch demesne. The park sloped down to the Thames, and was handsome, and quite full of timber, and the mansion, as the name imported, had been built in the height of pseudo-Gothic, with a formidable keep-looking tower at each corner, but the fortification below consisting of glass; the sham cloister, likewise glass windows, for drawing-room, music-room, and conservatory; and jutting out far in advance, a great embattled gateway, with a sham portcullis, and doors fit to defy an army.

Three men-servants met the guests in the hall, and Mrs. Charteris received them in the drawing-room, with the woman-of-the-world tact that Honora particularly hated—there was always such deference to Miss Charlecote, and such, an assumption of affection for the children, and gratitude for her care of them, and Miss Charlecote had not been an heiress early enough in life for such attentions to seem matters of course.

It was explained that there was no school-room at present, and as a girl of Lucilla's age, who was already a guest, joined the rest of the party at dinner, it was proposed that she and her brother should do the same, provided Miss Charlecote did not object. Honor was really glad of the gratification for Lucilla, and Mrs. Charteris agreed with her before she had time to express her opinion as to girls being kept back or brought forward.

Honor found herself lodged in great state, in a world of looking-glass that had perfectly scared her poor little Hiltonbury maiden, and with a large dressing-room, where she hoped to have seen a bed for Lucilla, but she found that the little girl was quartered in another story, near the cousins; and unwilling to imply distrust, and hating to incite obsequious compliance, she did not ask for any change, but only begged to see the room.

It was in a long passage whence doors opened every way, and one being left ajar, sounds of laughter and talking were heard in tones as if the young ladies were above good breeding in their private moments. Mrs. Charteris said something about her daughter's morning room, and was leading the way thither, when an unguarded voice exclaimed — 'Rouge dragon and all,' and a start and suppressed laughter at the entrance of the new comers gave an air of having been caught.

Four young ladies, in *dégagé* attitudes, were lounging round their afternoon refection of tea. Two, Caroline and Horatia Charteris, shook hands with Miss Charlecote, and kissed Lucilla, who still looked at them ungraciously, followed Honora's example in refusing their offer of tea, and only waiting to learn her own habitation, came down to her room to be dressed for dinner, and to criticise cousins, aunt, house and all. The cousins were not striking—both were on a small scale, Caroline the best looking in features and complexion, but Horatia, the most vivacious and demonstrative, and with an air of dash and fashion that was more effective than beauty. Lucilla, not sensible to these advantages, broadly declared both young ladies to be frights, and commented so freely on them to the willing ears of Owen, who likewise came in to go down under sweet Honey's protection, as to call for a reproof from

Honora, one of whose chief labours ever was to destroy the little lady's faith in beauty, and complacency in her own.

The latter sensation was strong in Honor herself, as she walked into the room between her beautiful pair, and contrasted Lucilla with her contemporary, a formed and finished young lady, all plaits, ribbons, and bracelets—not half so pleasing an object as the little maid in her white frock, blue sash, and short wavy hair, though maybe there was something quaint in such simplicity, to eyes trained by fashion instead of by good taste.

Here was Captain Charteris, just what he had been when he went away. How different from his stately, dull, wife-ridden elder brother. So brisk, and blunt, and eager, quite lifting his niece off her feet, and almost crushing her in his embrace, telling her she was still but a hop-o'-my-thumb, and shaking hands with his nephew with a look of scrutiny that brought the blood to the boy's cheek.

His eyes were never off the children while he was listening to Honora, and she perceived that what she said went for nothing; he would form his judgment solely by what he observed for himself.

At dinner, he was seated between Miss Charlecote and his niece, and Honora was pleased with him for his neglect of her and attention to his smaller neighbour, whose face soon sparkled with merriment, while his increasing animation proved that the saucy little woman was as usual enchanting him. Much that was very entertaining was passing about tiger-hunting, when at dessert, as he stretched out his arm to reach some water for her, she exclaimed, 'Why, Uncle Kit, you *have* brought away the marks! no use to deny it, the tigers did bite you.'

The palm of his hand certainly bore in purple marks resembling those of a set of teeth; and he looked meaningly at Honora, as he quietly replied, 'Something rather like a tigress.'

'Then it was a bite, Uncle Kit?'

'Yes,' in a put-an-end-to-it tone, which silenced Lucilla, her tact being much more ready when concerned with the nobler sex.

In the drawing-room, Mrs. Charteris's civilities kept Honora occupied, while she saw Owen bursting with some request, and, when at length he succeeded in claiming her attention, it was to tell her of his cousin's offer to take him out shooting, and his elder uncle's proviso that it must be with her permission. He had gone out with the careful gamekeeper at Hiltonbury, but this was a different matter, more trying to the nerves of those who stayed at home. However, Honora suspected that the uncle's opinion of her competence to be trusted with Owen would be much diminished by any betrayal of womanly terrors, and she made her only conditions that he should mind Uncle Kit, and not go in front of the guns, otherwise he would never be taken out again, a menace which she judiciously thought more telling than that he would be shot.

By and by Mr. Charteris came to discuss subjects so interesting to her as a farmer, that it was past nine o'clock before she looked round for her children. Healthy as Lucilla was, her frame was so slight and unsubstantial, and her spirits so excitable, that over-fatigue or irregularity always told upon her strength and temper; for which reason Honor had issued a decree that she should go to bed at nine, and spend two hours of every morning in quiet employment, as a counterbalance to the excitement of the visit.

Looking about to give the summons, Honor found that Owen had disappeared. Unnoticed, and wearied by the agricultural dialogue, he had hailed nine o'clock as the moment of release, and crept off with unobtrusive obedience, which Honor doubly prized when she beheld his sister full of eagerness, among cousins and gentlemen, at the racing game. Strongly impelled to end it at once, Honor waited, however, till the little white horseman had reached the goal, and just as challenges to a fresh race were beginning, she came forward with her needful summons.

'O, Miss Charlecote, how cruel!' was the universal cry.

'We can't spare all the life of our game!' said Charles Charteris.

'I solemnly declare we weren't betting,' cried Horatia. 'Come, the first evening—'

'No,' said Honor, smiling. 'I can't have her lying awake to be good for nothing to-morrow, as she will do if you entertain her too much.'

'Another night then, you promise,' said Charles.

'I promise nothing but to do my best to keep her fit to enjoy herself. Come, Lucy.'

The habit of obedience was fixed, but not the habit of conquering annoyance, and Lucilla went off doggedly. Honora would have accompanied her to soothe away her troubles, but her cousin Ratia ran after her, and Captain Charteris stood in the way, disposed to talk.

'Discipline,' he said, approvingly.

'Harsh discipline, I fear, it seemed to her, poor child,' said Honor; 'but she is so excitable that I must try to keep her as quiet as possible.'

'Right,' said the Captain; 'I like to see a child a child still. You must have had some tussles with that little spirit.'

'A few,' she said, smiling. 'She is a very good girl now, but it has been rather a contrast with her brother.'

'Ha!' quoth the Captain; and mindful of the milksop charge, Honora eagerly continued, 'You will soon see what a spirit he has! He rides very well, and is quite fearless. I have always wished him to be with other boys, and there are some very nice ones near us —they think him a capital cricketer, and you should see him run and vault.'

'He is an active-looking chap,' his uncle granted.

'Every one tells me he is quite able to make his

way at school ; I am only anxious to know which public school you and your brother would prefer.'

'How old is he?'

'Only twelve last month, though you would take him for fifteen.'

'Twelve ; then there would be just time to send him to Portsmouth, get him prepared for a naval cadetship, then, when I go out with Sir David Horfield, I could take him under my own eye, and make a man of him at once.'

'Oh! Captain Charteris,' cried Honora, aghast, 'his whole bent is towards his father's profession.'

The Captain had very nearly whistled, unable to conceive any lad of spirit preferring study.

'Whatever Miss Charlecote's wishes may be, Kit,' interposed the diplomatic elder brother, 'we only desire to be guided by them.'

'O no, indeed,' cried Honor; 'I would not think of such a responsibility, it can belong only to his nearer connexions ;' then, feeling as if this were casting him off to be pressed by the sailor the next instant, she added, in haste—'Only I hoped it was understood—if you will let me—the expenses of his education need not be considered. And if he *might* be with me in the holidays,' she proceeded imploringly. 'When Captain Charteris has seen more of him, I am sure he will think it a pity that his talents ......' and there she stopped, shocked at finding herself insulting the navy.

'If a boy have no turn that way, it cannot be forced on him,' said the Captain, moodily.

Honora pitied his disappointment, wondering whether he ascribed it to her influence, and Mr. Charteris blandly expressed great obligation and more complete resignation of the boy than she desired ; disclaimers ran into mere civilities, and she was thankful to the Captain for saying, shortly, 'We'll leave it till we have seen more of the boy.'

Breakfast was very late at Castle Blanch ; and

Honora expected a tranquil hour in her dressing-room with her children, but Owen alone appeared, anxious for the shooting, but already wearying to be at home with his own pleasures, and indignant with everything, especially the absence of family prayers.

The breakfast was long and desultory, and in the midst Lucilla made her appearance with Horatia, who was laughing and saying, 'I found this child wandering about the park, and the little pussy cat wont tell where she has been.'

'Poaching, of course,' responded Charles; 'it is what pussy cats always do till they get shot by the keepers.'

Et cœtera, et cœtera, et cœtera, Lucilla was among all the young people, in the full tide of fun, nonsense, banter, and repartee of a style new to her, but in which she was formed to excel, and there was such a black look when Honor summoned her after the meal, as impressed the awkwardness of enforcing authority among nearer relations; but it was in vain, she was carried off to the dressing-room, and reminded of the bargain for two hours' occupation. She murmured something about Owen going out as he liked.

'He came to me before breakfast; besides, he is a boy. What made you go out in that strange manner?'

There was no answer, but Honor had learnt by experience that to insist was apt to end in obtaining nothing but a collision of wills, and she merely put out the Prayer Books for the morning's reading of the Psalms. By the time it was over Lucilla's fit of temper had past, and she leant back in her chair. 'What are you listening to, Lucy?' said Honor, seeing her fixed eye.

'The river,' said Lucilla, pausing with a satisfied look to attend to the deep, regular rush. 'I couldn't think before what it was that always seemed to be wanting, and now I know. It came to me when I went to bed; it was so nice!'

'The river voice! Yes; it must be one of your oldest friends,' said Honora, gratified at the softening. 'So that carried you out.'

'I couldn't help it! I went home,' said Lucilla.

'Home? To Wrapworth? All alone?' cried Honor, kindly, but aghast.

'I couldn't help it,' again said the girl. 'The river noise was so like everything—and I knew the way—and I felt as if I must go before any one was up.'

'So you really went, and what did you do?'

'I got over the palings our own old way, and there's my throne still in the back of the laurels, and I popped in on old Madge, and oh! she was so surprised! And then I came on Mr. Prendergast, and he walked all the way back with me, till he saw Ratia coming, and then he would not go on any farther.'

'Well, my dear, I can't blame you this time. I am hoping myself to go to Wrapworth with you and Owen.'

'Ratia is going to take me out riding and in the boat,' said Lucy, without a direct answer.

'You like your cousins better than you expected?'

'Rashe is famous,' was the answer, 'and so is Uncle Kit.'

'My dear, you noticed the mark on his hand,' said Honora; 'you do not know the cause?'

'No! Was it a shark or a mad dog?' eagerly asked the child, slightly alarmed by her manner.

'Neither. But do not you remember his carrying you into Woolstone Lane? I always believed you did not know what your little teeth were doing.'

It was not received as Honora expected. Probably the scenes of the girl's infancy had brought back associations more strongly than she was prepared for—she turned white, gasped, and vindictively said, 'I'm glad of it.'

Honora, shocked, had not discovered a reply, when Lucilla, somewhat confused at the sound of her own words, said, 'I know—not quite that—he meant the best—but, Cousin Honor, it was cruel, it was wicked, to part my father and me ! Father—oh, the river is going on still, but not my father !'

The excitable girl burst into a flood of passionate tears, as though the death of her father were more present to her than ever before ; and she had never truly missed him till she was brought in contact with her old home. The fatigue and change, the talking evening and restless night, had produced their effect ; her very thoughtlessness and ordinary *insouciance* rendered the rush more overwhelming when it did come, and the weeping was almost hysterical.

It was not a propitious circumstance that Caroline knocked at the door with some message as to the afternoon's arrangements. Honor answered at haphazard, standing so as to intercept the view, but aware that the long-drawn sobs would be set down to the account of her own tyranny, and nevertheless resolving the more on enforcing the quiescence, the need of which was so evident ; but the creature was volatile as well as sensitive, and by the time the door was shut, stood with heaving breast and undried tears, eagerly demanding whether her cousins wanted her.

' Not at all,' said Honora, somewhat annoyed at the sudden transition ; ' it was only to ask if I would ride.'

' Charles was to bring the pony for me ; I must go,' cried Lucy, with an eye like that of a greyhound in the leash.

' Not yet,' said Honor. ' My dear, you promised.'

' I'll never promise anything again,' was the pettish murmur.

Poor child, these two morning hours were to her a terrible penance, day after day. Practically, she might have found them heavy had they been left to her own disposal, but it was expecting overmuch from human nature to hope that she would believe so without experience, and her lessons were a daily irritation, an apparent act of tyranny, hardening her feelings against the exactor, at the same time that the influence of kindred blood drew her closer to her own family, with a revulsion the stronger from her own former exaggerated dislike.

The nursery at Castle Blanch, and the cousins who domineered over her as a plaything, had been intolerable to the little important companion of a grown man, but it was far otherwise to emerge from the calm seclusion and sober restraints of the Holt into the gaieties of a large party, to be promoted to young ladyhood, and treated on equal terms, save for extra petting and attention. Instead of Robert Fulmort alone, all the gentlemen in the house gave her flattering notice—eye, ear, and helping hand at her disposal, and blunt Uncle Kit himself was ten times more civil to her than to either of her cousins. What was the use of trying to disguise from her the witchery of her piquant prettiness?

Her cousin Horatia had always had a great passion for her as a beautiful little toy, and her affection, once so trying to its object, had taken the far more agreeable form of promoting her pleasures and sympathizing with her vexations. Patronage from two-and-twenty to fourteen, from a daughter of the house to a guest, was too natural to offend, and Lucilla requited it with vehement attachment, running after her at every moment, confiding all her grievances, and being made sensible of many more. Ratia, always devising delights for her, took her on the river, rode with her, set her dancing, opened the world to her, and enjoyed her pleasures, amused by her precocious vivacity, fostering her sauciness, extolling the wit of her audacious speeches, and extremely resenting all poor Honora's attempts to counteract this terrible spoiling, or to put a check upon undesirable diversions and absolute pertness. Every conscientious interference on her part was regarded as duenna-like harshness, and her restrictions as a grievous yoke, and Lucilla made no secret that it was so, treating her to almost unvaried ill-humour and murmurs.

Little did Lucilla know, nor even Horatia, how much of the charms that produced so much effect were due to these very restraints, nor how the droll sauciness and womanly airs were enhanced by the simplicity of appearance, which embellished her far more than the most fashionable air set off her companions. Once Lucilla had overheard her aunt thus excusing her short locks and simple dress—'It is Miss Charlecote's doing. Of course, when so much depends on her, we must give way. Excellent person, rather peculiar, but we are under great obligations to her. Very good property.'

No wonder that sojourn at Castle Blanch was one of the most irksome periods of Honora's life, disappointing, fretting, and tedious. There was a grievous dearth of books and of reasonable conversation, and both she and Owen were exceedingly at a loss for occupation, and used to sit in the boat on the river, and heartily wish themselves at home. He had no companion of his own age, and was just too young and too enterprising to be welcome to gentlemen bent more on amusing themselves than pleasing him. He was roughly admonished when he spoilt sport or ran into danger; his cousin Charles was fitfully goodnatured, but generally showed that he was in the way; his uncle Kit was more brief and stern with him than 'Sweet Honey's' pupil could endure; and Honor was his only refuge. His dreariness was only complete when the sedulous civilities of his aunt carried her beyond his reach.

She could not attain a visit to Wrapworth till the Sunday. The carriage went in state to the parish church in the morning, and the music and preaching furnished subjects for *persiflage* at luncheon, to her great discomfort, and the horror of Owen; and she thought she might venture to Wrapworth in the afternoon. She had a longing for Owen's church, 'for auld lang syne'—no more. Even his bark church in the backwoods could not have rivalled Hiltonbury and the brass.

VOL. I.   K

Owen, true to his allegiance, joined her in good time, but reported that his sister was gone on with Ratia. Whereas Ratia would probably otherwise not have gone to church at all, Honor was deprived of all satisfaction in her annoyance, and the compensation of a *tête-à-tête* with Owen over his father's memory was lost by the unwelcome addition of Captain Charteris. The loss signified the less as Owen's reminiscences were never allowed to languish for want of being dug up and revived, but she could not quite pardon the sailor for the commonplace air his presence cast over the walk.

The days were gone by when Mr. Sandbrook's pulpit eloquence had rendered Wrapworth Church a Sunday show to Castle Blanch. His successor was a cathedral dignitary, so constantly absent that the former curate, who had been continued on at Wrapworth, was, in the eyes of every one, the veritable master. Poor Mr. Prendergast—whatever were his qualifications as a preacher—had always been regarded as a disappointment; people had felt themselves defrauded when the sermon fell to his share instead of that of Mr. Sandbrook, and odious comparison had so much established the opinion of his deficiencies, that Honora was not surprised to see a large-limbed and rather quaint-looking man appear in the desk, but the service was gone through with striking reverence, and the sermon was excellent, though homely and very plain-spoken. The church had been cruelly mauled by churchwardens of the last century, and a few Gothic decorations, intended for the beginning of restoration, only made it the more incongruous. The east window, of stained glass, of a quality left far behind by the advances of the last twenty years, bore an inscription showing that it was a memorial, and there was a really handsome font. Honor could trace the late rector's predilections in a manner that carried her back twenty years, and showed her, almost to her amusement, how her own notions and sympathies had been carried onwards with the current of the world around her.

On coming out, she found that there might have been more kindness in Captain Charteris than she had suspected, for he kept Horatia near him, and waited for the curate, so as to leave her at liberty and unobserved. Her first object was that Owen should see his mother's grave. It was beside the parsonage path, a flat stone, fenced by a low iron border, enclosing likewise a small flower-bed, weedy, ruinous, and forlorn. A floriated cross, filled up with green lichen, was engraven above the name.

Lucilla Horatia
beloved wife of the Reverend Owen Sandbrook
Rector of this parish
and only daughter
of Lieutenant-General Sir Christopher Charteris
She died November the 18th 1837
Aged 29 years.

Mary Caroline
her daughter
Born November 11th 1837
Died April 14th 1838
I shall go to them, but they shall not return to me.

How like it was to poor Owen! that necessity of expression, and the visible presage of weakening health so surely fulfilled! And his Lucilla! It was a melancholy work to have brought home a missionary, and secularized a parish priest! 'Not a generous reflection,' thought Honora, 'at a rival's grave,' and she turned to the boy, who had stooped to pull at some of the bits of groundsel.

'Shall we come here in the early morning, and set it to rights?'

'I forgot it was Sunday,' said Owen, hastily throwing down the weed he had plucked up.

'You were doing no harm, my dear; but we will not leave it in this state. Will you come with us, Lucy?'

Lucilla had escaped, and was standing aloof at the end of the path, and when her brother went towards her, she turned away.

'Come, Lucy,' he entreated, 'come into the garden with us. We want you to tell us the old places.'

'I'm not coming,' was all her answer, and she ran back to the party who stood by the church door, and began to chatter to Mr. Prendergast, over whom she had domineered even before she could speak plain. A silent, shy man, wrapped up in his duties, he was mortally afraid of the Castle Blanch young ladies, and stood ill at ease, talked down by Miss Horatia Charteris, but his eye lighted into a smile as the fairy plaything of past years danced up to him, and began her merry chatter, asking after every one in the parish, and showing a perfect memory of names and faces such as amazed him, in a child so young as she had been at the time when she had left the parish. Honora and Owen meantime were retracing recollections in the rectory garden, eking out the boy's four years old memories with imaginations and moralizings, pondering over the border whence Owen declared he had gathered snowdrops for his mother's coffin; and the noble plane tree by the water-side, sacred to the memory of Bible stories told by his father in the summer evenings—

'That tree!!' laughed Lucilla, when he told her that night as they walked upstairs to bed. 'Nobody could sit there because of the mosquitoes. And I should like to see the snowdrops you found in November?'

'I know there were some white flowers. Were they lilies of the valley for little Mary?'

'It will do just as well,' said Lucilla. She knew that she could bring either scene before her mind with vivid distinctness, but shrinking from the pain almost with horror, she only said, 'It's a pity you aren't a Roman Catholic, Owen; you would soon find a hole in a rock, and say it was where a saint, with his head under his arm, had made a footmark.'

'You are very irreverent, Lucy, and very cross besides. If you would not come and tell us, what could we do?'

'Let it alone.'

'If you don't care for dear papa and mamma, I do,' said Owen, the tears coming into his eyes.

'I'm not going to rake it up to please Honora,' returned his sister. 'If you like to go and poke with her over places where things never happened, you may, but she shan't meddle with my real things.'

'You are very unkind,' was the next accusation from Owen, much grieved and distressed, 'when she is so good and dear, and was so fond of our dear father.'

'I know,' said Lucilla, in a tone he did not understand; then, with an air of eldership, ill-assorting with their respective sizes, 'You are a mere child. It is all very well for you, and you are very welcome to your Sweet Honey.'

Owen insisted on hearing her meaning, and on her refusal to explain, used his superior strength to put her to sufficient torture to elicit an answer. 'Don't, Owen! Let go! There, then! Why, she was in love with our father, and nearly died of it when he married; and Rashe says of course she bullies me for being like my mother.'

'She never bullies you,' cried Owen, indignantly; 'she's much kinder to you than you deserve, and I hate Ratia for putting it into your head, and teaching you such nasty man's words about my own Honor.'

'Ah! you'll never be a man while you are under her. She only wants to keep us a couple of babies for ever—sending us to bed, and making such a figure of me;' and Lucy relieved her feelings by five perpendicular leaps into the air, like an Indianrubber ball, her hair flying out, and her eyes flashing.

Owen was not much astonished, for Lucy's furies often worked off in this fashion; but he was very angry on Honor's account, loving her thoroughly, and perceiving no offence in her affection for his father; and the conversation assumed a highly quarrelsome character. It was much to the credit of masculine discretion that he refrained from reporting it when he joined Honora in the morning's walk to Wrapworth churchyard. Behold! some one was beforehand with them—even Lucilla and the curate!

The wearisome visit was drawing to a close when Captain Charteris began—'Well, Miss Charlecote, have you thought over my proposal?'

'To take Owen to sea? Indeed, I hoped you were convinced that it would never answer.'

'So far from being so, that I see it is his best chance. He will do no good till the priggishness is knocked out of him.'

Honor would not trust herself to answer. Any accusation but this might have been borne.

'Well, well,' said the Captain, in a tone still more provoking, it was so like hushing a petulant child, 'we know how kind you were, and that you meant everything good; but it is not in the nature of things that a lad alone with women should not be cock of the walk, and nothing cures that like a month on board.'

'He will go to school,' said Honor, convinced all this was prejudice.

'Ay, and come home in the holidays, lording it as if he were master and more, like the son and heir.'

'Indeed, Captain Charteris, you are quite mistaken; I have never allowed Owen to think himself in that position. He knows perfectly well that there are nearer claims upon me, and that Hiltonbury can never belong to him. I have always rejoiced that it should be so. I should not like to have the least suspicion that there could be self-interest in his affection for me in the time to come; and I think it presumptuous to interfere with the course of Providence in the matter of inheritances.'

'My good Miss Charlecote,' said the Captain, who had looked at her with somewhat of a pitying smile, instead of attending to her last words, 'do you imagine that you know that boy?'

'I do not know who else should,' she answered, quivering between a disposition to tears at the harshness, and to laughter at the assumption of the stranger uncle to see farther than herself into her darling.

'Ha?' quoth the sailor, 'slippery—slippery fellows.'

'I do not understand you. You do not mean to imply that I have not his perfect confidence, or do you think I have managed him wrongly? If you do, pray tell me at once. I dare say I have.'

'I couldn't say so,' said Captain Charteris. 'You are an excellent good woman, Miss Charlecote, and the best friend the poor things have had in the world; and you have taught them more good than I could, I'm sure; but I never yet saw a woman who could be up to a boy, any more than she could sail a ship.'

'Very likely not,' said Honor, with a lame attempt at a good-humoured laugh; 'but I should be very glad to know whether you are speaking from general experience of woman and boy, or from individual observation of the case in point.'

The Captain made a very odd, incomprehensible little bow; and after a moment's thought, said, 'Plainly speaking, then, I don't think you do get to the bottom of that lad; but there's no telling, and I never had any turn for those smooth chaps. If a fellow begins by being over-precise in what is of no consequence, ten to one but he ends by being reckless in all the rest.'

This last speech entirely reassured Honor, by proving to her that the Captain was entirely actuated by prejudice against his nephew's gentle and courteous manners and her own religious views. He did not believe in the possibility of the success of such an education, and therefore was of course insensible to Owen's manifold excellences.

Thenceforth she indignantly avoided the subject, and made no attempt to discover whether the Captain's eye, practised in midshipmen, had made any positive observations on which to found his dissatisfaction. Wounded by his want of gratitude, and still more hurt by his unkind judgment of her beloved pupil, she transferred her consultations to the more deferential uncle, who was entirely contented with his nephew, transported with admiration of her management, and ready to make her a present of him with all his heart. So readily did he accede to all that she said of schools, that the choice was virtually left to her. Eton was rejected as a fitter preparation for the squirearchy than the ministry; Winchester on account of the distaste between Owen and young Fulmort; and her decision was fixed in favour of Westminster, partly for his father's sake, partly on account of the proximity of St. Wulstan's—such an infinite advantage, as Mr. Charteris observed.

The sailor declared that he knew nothing of schools, and would take no part in the discussion. There had, in truth, been high words between the brothers, each accusing the other of going the way to ruin their nephew, ending by the Captain's exclaiming, ' Well, I wash my hands of it! I can't flatter a foolish woman into spoiling poor Lucilla's son. If I am not to do what I think right by him, I shall get out of sight of it all.'

' His prospects, Kit; how often I have told you it is our duty to consider his prospects.'

' Hang his prospects ! A handsome heiress under forty ! How can you be such an ass, Charles ? He ought to be able to make an independent fortune before he could stand in her shoes, if he were ever to do so, which she declares he never will. Yes, you may look knowing if you will, but she is no such fool in some things; and depend upon it she will make a principle of leaving her property in the right channel; and be that as it may, I warn you that you can't do this lad a worse mischief than by putting any such notion into his head, if it be not there already. There's not a more deplorable condition in the world than to be always dangling after an estate, never knowing if it be to be your own or not, and most likely to be disappointed at last; and, to do Miss Charlecote justice, she is perfectly aware of that; and it will not be her fault if he have any false expectations! So, if you feed him with them, it will all be your fault; and that's the last I mean to say about him.'

Captain Charteris was not aware of a colloquy in which Owen had a share.

'This lucky fellow,' said the young Lifeguardsman, 'he is as good as an eldest son—famous shooting county—capital, well-timbered estate.'

'No, Charles,' said Owen, 'my cousin Honor always says I am nothing like an eldest son, for there are nearer relations.'

'O ha!' said Charles, with a wink of superior wisdom, 'we understand that. She knows how to keep you on your good behaviour. Why, but for cutting you out, I would even make up to her myself—fine-looking, comely woman, and well preserved—and only the women quarrel with that splendid hair. Never mind, my boy, I don't mean it. I wouldn't stand in your light.'

'As if Honor would have *you!*' cried Owen, in fierce scorn.

Charles Charteris and his companions, with loud laughter, insisted on the reasons.

'Because,' cried the boy, with flashing looks, 'she would not be ridiculous; and you are—' He paused, but they held him fast, and insisted on hearing what Charles was.

'Not a good Churchman,' he finally pronounced. 'Yes, you may laugh at me, but Honor shan't be laughed at.'

Possibly Owen's views at present were that 'not to be a good Churchman' was synonymous with all imaginable evil, and that he had put it in a delicate manner. Whether he heard the last of it for the rest of his visit may be imagined. And, poor boy, though he was strong and spirited enough with his own contemporaries, there was no dealing with the full-fledged soldier. Nor, when conversation turned to what 'we' did at Hiltonbury, was it possible always to disclaim standing in the same relation to the Holt as did Charles to Castle Blanch; nay, a certain importance seemed to attach to such an assumption of dignity, of which Owen was not loth to avail himself in his disregarded condition.

PART II.

CHAPTER I.

We hold our greyhound in our hand,
　Our falcon on our glove;
But where shall we find leash or band
　For dame that loves to rove?
　　　　　　　　　Scott.

A JUNE evening shed a slanting light over the greensward of Hiltonbury Holt, and made the western windows glisten like diamonds, as Honora Charlecote slowly walked homewards to her solitary evening meal, alone, except for the nearly blind old pointer who laid his grizzled muzzle upon her knees, gazing wistfully into her face, as seating herself upon the step of the sun-dial, she fondled his smooth, depressed black head.

'Poor Ponto!' she said, 'we are grown old together. Our young ones are all gone!'

Grown old? Less old in proportion than Ponto—still in full vigour of mind and body, but old in disenchantment, and not without the traces of her forty-seven years. The auburn hair was still in rich masses of curl; only on close inspection were silver threads to be detected; the cheek was paler, the brow worn, and the gravely handsome dress was chosen to suit the representative of the Charlecotes, not with regard to lingering youthfulness. The slow movement, subdued tone, and downcast eye, had an air of habitual dejection and patience, as though disappointment had gone deeper, or solitude were telling more on the spirits, than any past blow had done.

She saw the preparations for her tea going on within the window, but ere going indoors, she took out and re-read two letters.

The first was in the irregular decided characters affected by young ladies in the reaction from their grandmothers' pointed illegibilities, and bore a scroll at the top, with the word 'Cilly,' in old English letters of bright blue.

'Lowndes Square, June 14th.

'MY DEAR HONOR,—Many thanks for wishing for your will-o'-th'-wisp again, but it is going to dance off in another direction. Rashe and I are bound to the west of Ireland, as soon as Charles's inauguration is over at Castle Blanch; an odd jumble of festivities it is to be, but Lolly is just cockney enough to be determinedly rural, and there's sure to be some fun to be got out of it; besides, I am pacified by having my special darling, Edna Murrell, the lovely schoolmistress at Wrapworth, to sing to them. How Mr. Calthorpe will admire her, as long as he thinks she is Italian! It will be hard if I can't get a rise out of some of them! This being the case, I have not a moment for coming home; but I send some contributions for the prize-giving, some stunning articles from the Lowther Arcade. The gutta-percha face is for Billy Harrison, *whether in disgrace or not*. He deserves compensation for his many weary hours of Sunday School, and it may suggest a new art for beguiling the time. *Mind* you tell him it is from me, with my love; and bestow the rest on all the chief reprobates. I wish I could see them; but you have no loss, you know how unedifying I am. Kiss Ponto for me, and ask Robin for his commands to Connaught. I know his sulkiness will transpire through Phœbe. Love to that dear little Cinderella, and tell her mamma and Juliana, that if she does not come out this winter, Mrs. Fulmort shall have no peace and Juliana no partners. Please to look in my room for my great nailed boots and hedging-gloves, also for the pig's wool in the left-hand drawer of the cabinet, and send them to me before the end of next week. Owen would give his ears to come with us, but gentlemen would only obstruct Irish chivalry; I am only afraid there is no hope of a faction fight. Mr. Saville called yesterday, so I made him dine here, and sung him into raptures. What a dear old Don he is!

'Your affectionate cousin, CILLY.'

The second letter stood thus :—

'Farrance's Hotel, June 14th.

'MY DEAR MISS CHARLECOTE,—I have seen Lawrence on your business, and he will prepare the leases for your signature. He suggests that it might be more satisfactory to wait, in case you should be coming to town, so that you might have a personal meeting with the parties; but this will be for you to determine. I came up from —— College on Wednesday, having much enjoyed my visit. Oxford is in many respects a changed place, but as long as our old Head remains to us, I am sure of a gratifying welcome, and I saw many old friends. I exchanged cards with Owen Sandbrook, but only saw him as we met in the street, and a very fine-looking youth he is, a perfect Hercules, and the champion of his college in all feats of strength; likely, too, to stand well in the class list. His costume was not what we should once have considered academical; but his is a daring set, intellectual as well as bodily, and the clever young men of the present day are not what they were in my time. It is gratifying to hear how warmly and affectionately he talks of you. I do not know how far you have undertaken the supplies, but I give you a hint that a warning on that subject might not be inappropriate, unless they have come into some great accession of fortune on their uncle's death. I ventured to call upon the young lady in Lowndes Square, and was most graciously received, and asked to dinner by the young Mrs. Charteris. It was a most *récherché* dinner in the new Italian fashion, which does not quite approve itself to me. "Regardless of expense," seems to be the family motto. Your pupil sings better than ever, and knew how to keep her hold of my heart, though I suspected her of patronizing the old parson to pique her more brilliant admirers, whom she possesses in plenty; and no wonder, for she is pretty enough to turn any man's head; and shows to great advantage beside her cousin, Miss Charteris. I hope you will be able to prevent the cousins from really undertaking the wild plan of travelling alone in Ireland, for the sake, they say, of salmon-fishing. I should have thought them not in earnest, but girls are as much altered as boys from the days of my experience, and brothers, too; for Mr. Charteris seemed to view the scheme very coolly; but, as I told my friend Lucilla, I hope you will bring her to reason. I hope your hay-crop promises favourably.

'Yours sincerely, W. SAVILLE.'

No wonder that these letters made loneliness more lonely!

'Oh, that Horatia!' exclaimed she, almost aloud. 'Oh, that Captain Charteris were available! No one else ever had any real power with Lucy! It was an unlucky day when he saw that colonial young lady, and settled down in Vancouver's Island! And yet how I used to wish him away, with the surly independence he was always infusing into Owen. Wanting to take him out there, indeed! And yet, and yet —I sometimes doubt whether I did right to set my personal influence over my dear affectionate boy so much in opposition to his uncle—Mr. Charteris was on my side, though! And I always took care to have it clearly understood that it was his education alone that I undertook. What can Mr. Saville mean?—The supplies? Owen knows what he has to trust to, but I can talk to him. A daring set?—Yes, everything appears daring to an old-world man like Mr. Saville. I am sure of my Owen; with our happy home Sundays. I know I am his Sweet Honey still. And yet' —then hastily turning from that dubious 'and yet'— 'Owen is the only chance for his sister. She does care for him; and he will view this mad scheme in the right light. Shall I meet him at the beginning of the vacation, and see what he can do with Lucy? Mr. Saville thinks I ought to be in London, and I think I might be useful to the Parsonses. I suppose I must; but it *is* a heart-ache to be at St. Wulstan's. One is used to it here; and there are the poor people, and the farm, and the garden—yes, and those dear nightingales—and you, poor Ponto! One is used to it here, but St. Wulstan's is a fresh pain, and so is coming back. But, if it be in the way of right, and to save poor Lucy, it must be, and it is what life is made of. It is a 'following of the funeral' of the hopes that sprang up after my spring-time. Is it my chastisement, or is it my training? Alas! maybe I took those children more for *myself* than for duty's sake! May it all be for their true good in the end, whatever it may be with me. And now I *will* not dream. It is of no use save to unnerve me. Let me go to my book. It must be a story to-night. I cannot fix my attention yet.'

As she rose, however, her face brightened at the sight of two advancing figures, and she went forward to meet them.

One was a long, loosely-limbed youth of two-and-twenty, with broad shoulders, a heavy overhanging brow, dark grey serious eyes, and a mouth scarcely curved, and so fast shut as to disclose hardly any lip.

The hair was dark and lank; the air was of ungainly force, that had not yet found its purpose, and therefore was not at ease; and, but for the educated cast of countenance, he would have had a peasant look, in the brown, homely undress garb, which to most youths of his age would have been becoming.

With him was a girl, tall, slim, and lightly made, though of nicely rounded figure. In height she looked like seventeen, but her dress was more childish than usual at that age; and the contour of her smooth cheeks and short rounded chin, her long neck, her happy blue eyes, fully opened like those of a child; her fair rosy skin and fresh simple air, might almost have belonged to seven years old; and there was all the earnestness, innocence, and careless ease of childhood in her movements and gestures, as she sprang forward to meet Miss Charlecote, exclaiming, 'Robin said I might come.'

'And very right of him. You are both come to tea?' she added, in affirmative interrogation, as she shook hands with the young man.

'No, thank you,' he answered; 'at least I only brought Phœbe, having rescued her from Miss Fennimore's clutches. I must be at dinner. But I will come again for her.' And he yawned wearily.

'I will drive her back; you are tired.'

'No!' he said. 'At least the walk is one of the few tolerable things there is. I'll come as soon as I can escape, Phœbe. Past seven—I must go!'

'Can't you stay? I could find some food for you.'

'No, thank you,' he still said; 'I do not know whether Mervyn will come home, and there must not be too many empty chairs. Good-bye!' and he walked off with long strides, but with stooping shoulders, and an air of dejection almost amounting to discontent.

'Poor Robin!' said Honora, 'I wish he could have stayed.'

'He would have liked it very much,' said Phœbe, casting wistful glances toward him.

'What a pity he did not give notice of his intentions at home!'

'He never will. He particularly dislikes——'

'What?' as Phœbe paused and coloured.

'Saying anything to anybody,' she answered, with a little smile. 'He cannot endure remarks.'

'I am a very sober old body for a visit to me to be the occasion of remarks!' said Honor, laughing more merrily than perhaps Robert himself could have done; but Phœbe answered with grave, straightforward sincerity, 'Yes, but he did not know if Lucy might not be come home.'

Honora sighed, but playfully said, 'In which case he would have stayed?'

'No,' said the still grave girl, 'he would have been still less likely to do so.'

'Ah! the remarks would have been more pointed! But he has brought you at any rate, and that is something! How did he achieve it?'

'Miss Fennimore is really quite ready to be kind,' said Phœbe, earnestly, with an air of defence, 'whenever we have finished all that we have to do.'

'And when is that?' asked Honor, smiling.

'Now, for once,' answered Phœbe, with a bright arch look. 'Yes, I sometimes can; and so does Bertha when she tries; and, indeed, Miss Charlecote, I do like Miss Fennimore; she never is hard upon poor Maria. No governess we ever had made her cry so seldom.'

Miss Charlecote only said it was a comfort. Within herself she hoped that, for Maria's peace and that of all concerned, her deficiency might become an acknowledged fact. She saw that the sparing Maria's tears was such a boon to Phœbe as to make her forgive all overtasking of herself.

'So you get on better,' she said.

'Much better than Robin chooses to believe we do,'

said Phœbe, smiling; 'perhaps it seemed hard at first, but it is comfortable to be made to do everything thoroughly, and to be shown a better best than we had ever thought of. I think it ought to be a help in doing the duty of all one's life in a thorough way.'

'All that thou hast to do,' said Honor, smiling, 'the weekday side of the fourth commandment.'

'Yes, that is just the reason why I like it,' said Phœbe, with bright gladness in her countenance.

'But is that the motive Miss Fennimore puts before you?' said Honor, a little ironically.

'She does not say so,' answered Phœbe. 'She says that she never interferes with her pupils' religious tenets. But, indeed, I do not think she teaches us anything wrong, and there is always Robert to ask.'

This passed as the two ladies were entering the house and preparing for the evening meal. The table was placed in the bay of the open window, and looked very inviting, the little silver tea-pot steaming beside the two quaint china cups, the small crisp twists of bread, the butter cool in ice-plant leaves, and some fresh fruit blushing in a pretty basket. The Holt was a region of Paradise to Phœbe Fulmort; and glee shone upon her sweet face, though it was very quiet enjoyment, as the summer breeze played softly round her cheeks, and danced with a merry little spiral that had detached itself from her glossy folds of light hair.

'How delicious!' she said. 'How sweet the honey-suckle is, dear old thing! You say you have known it all your life, and yet it is fresh as ever.'

'It is a little like you, Phœbe,' said Honor, smiling.

'What! because it is not exactly a pretty flower?'

'Partly; and I could tell you of a few other like-nesses, such as your being Robert's woodbine, yet with a sort of clinging freedom. Yes, and for the qualities you share with the willow, ready to give thanks and live on the least that Heaven may give.'

'But I don't live on the least that Heaven may give,' said Phœbe, in such wonder that Honor smiled at the justice of her simile, without impressing it upon Phœbe, only asking—

'Is the French journey fixed upon, Phœbe?'

'Yes; they start this day fortnight.'

'They—not you?'

'No; there would be no room for me,' with a small sigh.

'How can that be? Who is going? Papa, mamma, two sisters?'

'Mervyn,' added Phœbe, 'the courier, and the two maids.'

'*Two* maids! Impossible!'

'It is always uncomfortable if mamma and my sisters have only one between them,' said Phœbe, in her tone of perfect acquiescence and conviction; and as her friend could not restrain a gesture of indignation, she added eagerly—'But, indeed, it is not only for that reason, but Miss Fennimore says I am not formed enough to profit by foreign travel.'

'She wants you to finish Smith's *Wealth of Nations*, eh?'

'It might be a pity to go away and lose so much of her teaching,' said Phœbe, with persevering contentment. 'I dare say they will go abroad again, and perhaps I shall never have so much time for learning. But, Miss Charlecote, is Lucilla coming home for the Horticultural Show?'

'I am afraid not, my dear. I think I shall go to London to see about her, among other things. The Charterises seem to have quite taken possession of her, ever since she went to be her cousin Caroline's bridesmaid, and I must try to put in my claim.'

'Ah! Robin so much wished to have seen her,' sighed Phœbe. 'He says he cannot settle to anything.'

'Without seeing her?' said Honor, amused, though not without pain.

'Yes,' said Phœbe; 'he has thought so much about Lucilla.'

'And he tells you?'

'Yes,' in a voice expressing of course; while the frank, clear eyes turned full on Miss Charlecote with such honest seriousness, that she thought Phœbe's charm as a confidante might be this absence of romantic consciousness; and she knew of old that when Robert wanted her opinion or counsel, he spared his own embarrassment by seeking it through his favourite sister. Miss Charlecote's influence had done as much for Robert, as he had done for Phœbe, and Phœbe had become his medium of communication with her in all matters of near and delicate interest. She was not surprised when the maiden proceeded—'Papa wants Robin to attend to the office while he is away.'

'Indeed! Does Robin like it?'

'He would not mind it for a time; but papa wants him, besides, to take to the business in earnest. You know, my great-uncle, Robert Mervyn, left Robert all his fortune, quite in his own hands; and papa says that if he were to put that into the distillery it would do the business great good, and that Robert would be one of the richest men in England in ten years' time.'

'But that would be a complete change in his views,' exclaimed Honor, unable to conceal her disapproval and consternation.

'Just so,' answered Phœbe; 'and that is the reason why he wants to see Lucy. She always declared that she could not bear people in business, and we always thought of him as likely to be a clergyman; but, on the other hand, she has become used to London society, and it is only by his joining in the distillery that he could give her what she is accustomed to, and that is the reason he is anxious to see her.'

'So Lucy is to decide his fate,' said Honora. 'I am almost sorry to hear it. Surely, he has never spoken to her.'

'He never does speak,' said Phœbe, with the calm gravity of simplicity which was like a halo of dignity.

'There is no need of speaking. Lucilla knows how he feels as well as she knows that she breathes the air.'

And regards it as little, perhaps, thought Honor, sadly. 'Poor Robin!' she said; 'I suppose he had better get his mind settled; but indeed it is a fearful responsibility for my poor foolish Lucy—' and but for the fear of grieving Phœbe, she would have added, that such a purpose as that of entering Holy Orders ought not to have been made dependent upon the fancy of a girl. Possibly her expression betrayed her sentiments, for Phœbe answered—'There can be no doubt that Lucy will set him at rest. I am certain that she would be shocked at the notion that her tastes were making him doubt whether to be a clergyman.'

'I hope so! I trust so!' said Honora, almost mournfully. 'It may be very good for her, as I believe it is for every woman of any soundness, to be taught that her follies tell upon man's greater aims and purposes. It may be wholesome for her and a check, but——'

Phœbe wondered that her friend paused and looked so sad.

'Oh! Phœbe,' said Honora, after a moment's silence, speaking fervently, 'if you can in any way do so, warn your brother against making an idol! Let nothing come between him and the direct devotion of will and affection to the Higher Service. If he decide on the one or the other, let it be from duty, not with respect to anything else. I do not suppose it is of any use to warn him,' she added, with the tears in her eyes. 'Every one sets the whole soul upon some one object, not the right, and then comes the shipwreck.'

'Dear Robin!' said Phœbe. 'He is so good! I am sure he always thinks first of what is right. But I think I see what you mean. If he undertake the business, it should be as a matter of obedience to papa, not to keep Lucy in the great world. And, indeed, I do not think my father does care much, only he would like the additional capital; and Robert is so much more steady than Mervyn, that he would be more useful. Perhaps it would make him more important at home; no one there has any interest in common with him; and I think that moves him a little; but, after all, those do not seem reasons for not giving himself to God's service," she finished, reverently and considerately.

'No, indeed!' cried Miss Charlecote.

'Then you think he ought not to change his mind?'

'You have thought so all along,' smiled Honor.

'I did not like it,' said Phœbe, 'but I did not know if I were right. I did tell him that I really believed Lucy would think the more highly of him if he settled for himself without reference to her.'

'You did! You were a capital little adviser, Phœbe! A woman worthy to be loved at all had always rather be set second instead of first:—

> I could not love thee, dear, so much,
> Loved I not honour more.

That is the true spirit, and I am glad you judged Lucy to be capable of it. Keep your brother up to that, and all may be well!'

'I believe Robert knows it all the time,' said Phœbe. 'He always is right at the bottom; but his feelings get so much tried that he does not know how to bear it! I hope Lucy will be kind to him if they meet in London, for he has been so much harassed that he wants some comfort from her. If she would only be in earnest!'

'Does he go to London, at all events?'

'He has promised to attend to the office in Great Whittington-street for a month, by way of experiment.'

'I'll tell you what, Phœbe,' cried Honora, radiantly, 'you and I will go too! You shall come with me to Woolstone-lane, and Robin shall be with us every day; and we will try and make this silly Lucy into a rational being.'

'Oh! Miss Charlecote, thank you—thank you.' The quiet girl's face and neck were all one crimson glow of delight.

'If you can sleep in a little brown cupboard of a room in the very core of the City's heart.'

'Delightful! I have so wished to see that house. Owen has told me such things about it. Oh, thank you, Miss Charlecote!'

'Have you ever seen anything in London?'

'Never. We hardly ever go with the rest; and if we do, we only walk in the square. What a holiday it will be!'

'We will see everything, and do it justice. I'll get an order for the print-room at the British Museum. I dare say Robin never saw it either; and what a treat it will be to take you to the Egyptian Gallery!' cried Honora, excited into looking at the expedition in the light of a party of pleasure, as she saw happiness beaming in the young face opposite.

They built up their schemes in the open window, pausing to listen to the nightingales, who, having ceased for two hours, apparently for supper, were now in full song, echoing each other in all the woods of Hiltonbury, casting over it a network of sweet melody. Honora was inclined to regret leaving them in their glory; but Phœbe, with the world before her, was too honest to profess poetry which she did not feel. Nightingales were all very well in their place, but the first real sight of London was more.

The lamp came in, and Phœbe held out her hands for something to do, and was instantly provided with a child's frock, while Miss Charlecote read to her one of Fouqué's shorter tales by way of supplying the element of chivalrous imagination which was wanting in the Beauchamp system of education.

So warm was the evening, that the window remained open, until Ponto erected his crest as a footfall came steadily along, nearer and nearer. Uplifting one of his pendant lips, he gave a low growl through his blunted teeth, and listened again; but apparently satisfied that the step was familiar, he replaced his head on his crossed paws, and presently Robert Fulmort's head and the upper part of his person, in correct evening costume, were thrust in at the window, the moonlight making his face look very white, as he said, 'Come, Phœbe, make haste; it is very late.'

'Is it?' cried Phœbe, springing up; 'I thought I had only been here an hour.'

'Three, at least,' said Robert, yawning; 'six by my feelings. I could not get away, for Mr. Crabbe stayed to dinner; Mervyn absented himself, and my father went to sleep.'

'Robin, only think, Miss Charlecote is so kind as to say she will take me to London!'

'It is very kind,' said Robert, warmly, his weary face and voice suddenly relieved.

'I shall be delighted to have a companion,' said Honora; 'and I reckon upon you, too, Robin, whenever you can spare time from your work. Come in, and let us talk it over.'

'Thank you, I can't. The dragon will fall on Phœbe if I keep her out too late. Be quick, Phœbe.'

While his sister went to fetch her hat, he put his elbows on the sill, and leaning into the room, said, 'Thank you again; it will be a wonderful treat to her, and she has never had one in her life!'

'I was in hopes she would have gone to Germany.'

'It is perfectly abominable! It is all the others' doing! They know no one would look at them a second time if anything so much younger and pleasanter was by! They think her coming out would make them look older. I know it would make them look crosser.'

Laughing was the only way to treat this tirade, knowing, as Honor did, that there was but too much truth in it. She said, however, 'Yet one could hardly wish Phœbe other than she is. The rosebud keeps its charm longer in the shade.'

'I like justice,' quoth Robert.

'And,' she continued, 'I really think that she is much benefited by this formidable governess. Accuracy and solidity and clearness of head are worth cultivating.'

'Nasty latitudinarian piece of machinery,' said Robert, with his fingers over his mouth, like a sulky child.

'May be so; but you guard Phœbe, and she guards Bertha; and whatever your sense of injustice may be, this surely is a better school for her than gaieties as yet.'

'It will be a more intolerable shame than ever if they will not let her go with you.'

'Too intolerable to be expected,' smiled Honora. 'I shall come and beg for her to-morrow, and I do not believe I shall be disappointed.'

She spoke with the security of one not in the habit of having her patronage obstructed by relations; and Phœbe coming down with renewed thanks, the brother and sister started on their way home in the moonlight—the one plodding on moodily, the other unable to repress her glee, bounding on in a succession of little skips, and pirouetting round to clap her hands, and exclaim, 'Oh! Robin, is it not delightful?'

'If they will let you go,' said he, too desponding for hope.

'Do you think they will not?' said Phœbe, with slower and graver steps. 'Do you really think so? But, no! It can't lead to coming out; and I know they like me to be happy when it interferes with nobody.'

'Great generosity,' said Robert, drily.

'Oh, but Robin, you know elder ones come first.'

'A truth we are not likely to forget,' said Robert. 'I wish my uncle had been sensible of it. That legacy of his stands between Mervyn and me, and will never do me any good.'

'I don't understand,' said Phœbe; 'Mervyn has always been completely the eldest son.'

'Ay,' returned Robert, 'and with the tastes of an eldest son. His allowance does not suffice for them, and he does not like to see me independent. If my uncle had only been contented to let us share and share alike, then my father would have had no interest in drawing me into the precious gin and brandy manufacture.'

'You did not think he meant to make it a matter of obedience,' said Phœbe.

'No; he could hardly do that after the way he has brought me up, and what we have been taught all our lives about liberty of the individual, absence of control, and the like jargon.'

'Then you are not obliged ?'

He made no answer, and they walked on in silence across the silvery lawn, the maythorns shining out like flaked towers of snow in the moonlight, and casting abyss-like shadows, the sky of the most deep and intense blue, and the carols of the nightingales ringing around them. Robert paused when he had passed through the gate leading into the dark path down hill through the wood, and setting his elbows on it, leant over it, and looked back at the still and beautiful scene, in all the white mystery of moonlight, enhanced by the white-blossomed trees and the soft outlines of slumbering sheep. One of the birds, in a bush close to them, began prolonging its drawn-in notes in a continuous prelude, then breaking forth into a varied complex warbling, so wondrous that there was no moving till the creature paused.

It seemed to have been a song of peace to Robert, for he gave a long but much softer sigh, and pushed back his hat, saying, 'All good things dwell on the Holt side of the boundary.'

'A sort of Sunday world,' said Phœbe.

'Yes; after this wood one is in another atmosphere.'

'Yet you have carried your cares there, poor Robin.'

'So one does into Sunday, but to get another light thrown on them. The Holt has been the blessing of my life—of both our lives, Phœbe.'

She responded with all her heart. 'Yes, it has made everything happier, at home and everywhere else. I never can think why Lucilla is not more fond of it.'

'You are mistaken,' exclaimed Robert; 'she loves no place so well; but you don't consider what claims her relations have upon her. That cousin Horatia, to whom she is so much attached, losing both her parents, how could she do otherwise than be with her?'

'Miss Charteris does not seem to be in great trouble now,' said Phœbe.

'You do not consider; you have never seen grief, and you do not know how much more a sympathizing friend is needed when the world supposes the sorrow to be over, and ordinary habits to be resumed.'

Phœbe was willing to believe him right, though considering that Horatia Charteris lived with her brother and his wife, she could hardly be as lonely as Miss Charlecote.

'We shall see Lucy in London,' she said.

Robert again sighed heavily. 'Then it will be over,' he said. 'Did you say anything there?' he pursued, as they plunged into the dark shadows of the woodland path, more congenial to the subject than the light.

'Yes, I did,' said Phœbe.

'And she thought me a weak, unworthy wretch for ever dreaming of swerving from my original path.'

'No!' said Phœbe, 'not if it were your duty.'

'I tell you, Phœbe, it is as much my duty to consult Lucilla's happiness as if any words had passed between us. I have never pledged myself to take Orders. It has been only a wish, not a vocation; and if she have become averse to the prospect of a quiet country life, it would not be treating her fairly not to give her the choice of comparative wealth, though procured by means her family might despise.'

'Yes, I knew you would put right and duty first; and I suppose by doing so you make it certain to end rightly, one way or other.'

'A very few years, and I could realize as much as this Calthorpe, the millionaire, whom they talk of as being so often at the Charterises.'

'It will not be so,' said Phœbe. 'I know what she will say;' and as Robert looked anxiously at her, she continued—

'She will say she never dreamt of your being turned from anything so great by any fancies she has seemed to have. She will say so more strongly, for you know her father was a clergyman, and Miss Charlecote brought her up.'

Phœbe's certainty made Robert catch something of her hopes.

'In that case,' he said, 'matters might be soon settled. This fortune of mine would be no misfortune then; and probably, Phœbe, my sisters would have no objection to your being happy with us.'

'As soon as you could get a curacy! Oh, how delightful! and Maria and Bertha would come too.'

Robert held his peace, not certain whether Lucilla would consider Maria an embellishment to his ideal parsonage; but they talked on with cheerful schemes while descending through the wood, unlocking a gate that formed the boundary between the Holt and the Beauchamp properties, crossing a field or two, and then coming out into the park. Presently they were in sight of the house, rising darkly before them, with many lights shining in the windows behind the blinds.

'They are all gone upstairs!' said Phœbe, dismayed. 'How late it must be!'

'There's a light in the smoking-room,' said Robert; 'we can get in that way.'

'No, no! Mervyn may have some one with him. Come in quietly by the servants' entrance.'

No danger that people would not be on foot there! As the brother and sister moved along the long stone passage, fringed with labelled bells, one open door showed two weary maidens still toiling over the plates of the late dinner; and another, standing ajar, revealed various men-servants regaling themselves; and words and tones caught Robert's ear making his brow lower with sudden pain.

Phœbe was proceeding to mount the stone stairs, when a rustling and chattering, as of maids descending, caused her and her brother to stand aside to make way, and down came a pair of heads and candles together over a green bandbox, and then voices in vulgar tones half suppressed. ' I couldn't venture it, not with Miss Juliana—but Miss Fulmort—she never looks over her bills, nor knows what is in her drawers —I told her it was faded, when she had never worn it once!'

And tittering, they passed by the brother and sister, who were still unseen, but Robert heaved a sigh and murmured, 'Miserable work!' somewhat to his sister's surprise, for to her the great ill-regulated household was an unquestioned institution, and she did not expect him to bestow so much compassion on Augusta's discarded bonnet. At the top of the steps they opened a door, and entered a great wide hall. All was exceedingly still. A gas-light was burning over the fire-place, but the corners were in gloom, and the coats and cloaks looked like human figures in the distance. Phœbe waited while Robert lighted her candle for her. Albeit she was not nervous, she started when a door was sharply pushed open, and another figure appeared; but it was nothing worse than her brother Mervyn, in easy costume, and redolent of tobacco.

About three years older than Robert, he was more neatly though not so strongly made, shorter, and with more regular features, but much less countenance. If the younger brother had a worn and dejected aspect, the elder, except in moments of excitement, looked *bored.* It was as if Robert really had the advantage of him in knowing what to be out of spirits about.

'Oh! it's you, is it?' said he, coming forward with a sauntering, scuffling movement in his slippers. 'You larking, Phœbe? What next?'

'I have been drinking tea with Miss Charlecote,' explained Phœbe.

Mervyn slightly shrugged his shoulders, murmuring something about 'Lively pastime.'

'I could not fetch her sooner,' said Robert, 'for my father went to sleep, and no one chose to be at the pains of entertaining Crabbe.'

'Ay—a prevision of his staying to dinner made me stay and dine with the —th mess. Very sagacious—eh, Phœbe?' said he, turning, as if he liked to look into her fresh face.

'Too sagacious,' said she, smiling; 'for you left him all to Robert.'

Manner and look expressed that this was a matter of no concern, and he said ungraciously: 'Nobody detained Robert, it was his own concern.'

'Respect to my father and his guests,' said Robert, with downright gravity that gave it the effect of a reproach.

Mervyn only raised his shoulders up to his ears in contempt, took up his candle, and wished Phœbe good night.

Poor Mervyn Fulmort! Discontent had been his life-long comrade. He detested his father's occupation as galling to family pride, yet was greedy both of the profits and the management. He hated county business and country life, yet chafed at not having the control of his mother's estate, and grumbled at all his father's measures. 'What should an old distiller know of landed property?' In fact he saw the same difference between himself and his father as did the ungracious Plantagenet between the son of a Count and the son of a King: and for want of Provençal troubadours with whom to rebel, he supplied their place by the turf and the billiard-table. At present he was expiating some heavy debts by a forced residence with his parents, and unwilling attention to the office, a most distasteful position, which he never attempted to improve, and which permitted him both the tedium of idleness and complaints against all the employment to which he was necessitated.

The ill-managed brothers were just nearly enough of an age for rivalry, and had never loved one another even as children. Robert's steadiness had been made a reproach to Mervyn, and his grave, rather surly character had never been conciliating. The independence left to the younger brother by their mother's relative was grudged by the elder as an injury to himself, and it was one of the misfortunes of Beauchamp that the two sons had never been upon happy terms together. Indeed, save that Robert's right principles and silent habits hindered him from readily giving or taking offence, there might have been positive outbreaks of a very unbrotherly nature.

CHAPTER II.

Enough of science and of art
Close up those barren leaves!
Come forth, and bring with you a heart
That watches and receives.
WORDSWORTH.

'HALF-PAST five, Miss Phœbe.'
'Thank you ;' and before her eyes were open, Phœbe was on the floor.

Six was the regulation hour. Systematic education had discovered that half an hour was the maximum allowable for morning toilette, and at half-past six the young ladies must present themselves in the schoolroom.

The Bible, Prayer Book, and 'Daily Meditations' could have been seldom touched, had not Phœbe, ever since Robert had impressed on her the duty of such constant study, made an arrangement for gaining an extra half-hour. Cold mornings and youthful sleepiness had received a daily defeat ; and, mayhap, it was such a course of victory that made her frank eyes so blithesome, and her step so free and light.

That bright scheme, too, shone before her, as such a secret of glad hope, that, knowing how uncertain were her chances of pleasure, she prayed that she might not set her heart on it. It was no trifle to her, and her simple spirit ventured to lay her wishes before her loving Father in Heaven, and entreat that she might not be denied, if it were right for her and would be better for Robert; or, if not, that she might be good under the disappointment.

Her orisons sent her forth all brightness, with her small head raised like that of a young fawn, her fresh lips parted by an incipient smile of hope, and her cheeks in a rosy glow of health, a very Hebe, as Mr. Saville had once called her.

Such a morning face as hers was not always met by Miss Fennimore, who, herself able to exist on five hours' sleep, had no mercy on that of her pupils; and she rewarded Phœbe's smiling good-morrow with 'This is better than I expected, you returned home so late.'

'Robert could not come for me early,' said Phœbe.

'How did you spend the evening?'

'Miss Charlecote read aloud to me. It was a delightful German story.'

'Miss Charlecote is a very well-informed person, and I am glad the time was not absolutely lost. I hope you observed the condensation of the vapours on your way home.'

'Robert was talking to me, and the nightingales were singing.'

'It is a pity,' said Miss Fennimore, not unkindly, 'that you should not cultivate the habit of observation. Women can seldom theorize, but they should always observe facts, as these are the very groundwork of discovery, and such a rare opportunity as a walk at night should not be neglected.'

It was no use to plead that this was all very well when there was no brother Robert with his destiny in the scales, so Phœbe made a meek assent, and moved to the piano, suppressing a sigh, as Miss Fennimore set off on a domiciliary visit to the other sisters.

Mr. Fulmort liked his establishment to prove his consequence, and to the old family mansion of the Mervyns he had added a whole wing for the educational department. Above, there was a passage, with pretty little bed-rooms opening from it; below there were two good-sized rooms, with their own door opening into the garden. The elder ones had long ago deserted it, and so completely shut off was it from the rest of the house, that the governess and her pupils were as secluded as though in a separate dwelling. The school-room was no repulsive-looking abode; it was furnished almost well enough for a drawing-room; and only the easels, globes, and desks, the crayon studies on the walls, and a formidable time-table, showed its real destination. The window looked out into a square parterre, shut in with tall laurel hedges, and filled with the gayest and sweetest blossoms. It was Mrs. Fulmort's garden for cut flowers; supplying the bouquets that decked her tables, or were carried to wither at balls; and there were three long, narrow beds, that Phœbe and her younger sisters still called theirs, and loved with the pride of property; but, indeed, the bright carpeting of the whole garden was something especially their own, rejoicing their eyes, and unvalued by the rest of the house. On the like liberal scale were the salaries of the educators. Governesses were judged according to their demands; and the highest bidder was supposed to understand her own claims best. Miss Fennimore was a finishing governess of the highest order, thinking it an insult to be offered a pupil below her teens, or to lose one till nearly beyond them; nor was she far from being the treasure that Mrs. Fulmort pronounced her, in gratitude for the absence of all the explosions produced by the various imperfections of her predecessors.

A highly able woman, and perfectly sincere, she possessed the qualities of a ruler, and had long experience in the art. Her discipline was perfect in machinery, and her instructions admirably complete. No one could look at her keen, sensible, self-possessed countenance, her decided mouth, ever busy hands, and unpretending but well-chosen style of dress, without seeing that her energy and intelligence were of a high order; and there was principle likewise, though no one ever quite penetrated to the foundation of it. Certainly she was not an irreligious person; she conformed, as she said, to the habits of each family she lived with, and she highly estimated moral perfections. Now and then a degree of scorn, for the narrowness of dogma, would appear in reading history, but in general she was understood to have opinions which she did not obtrude.

As a teacher, she was excellent; but her own strong conformation prevented her from understanding that young girls were incapable of such tension of intellect as an enthusiastic scholar of forty-two, and that what was sport to her was toil to a mind unaccustomed to constant attention. Change of labour is not rest, unless it be through gratification of the will. Her very best pupil she had killed. Finding a very sharp sword, in a very frail scabbard, she had whetted the one, and worn down the other, by every stimulus in her power, till a jury of physicians might have found her guilty of manslaughter; but perfectly unconscious of her own agency in causing the atrophy, her dear Anna Webster lived foremost in her affections, the model for every subsequent pupil. She seldom remained more than two years in a family. Sometimes the young brains were over-excited; more often they fell into a dreary state of drilled diligence; but she was too much absorbed in the studies to look close into the human beings, and marvelled when the fathers and mothers were blind enough to part with her on the plea of health and need of change.

On the whole, she had never liked any of her charges since the renowned Anna Webster so well as Phœbe Fulmort; although her abilities did not rise above the 'very fair,' and she was apt to be bewildered in metaphysics and political economy; but then she had none of the eccentricities of will and temper of Miss Fennimore's clever girls, nor was she like most good-humoured ones, recklessly *insouciante*. Her only drawback, in the governess's eyes, was that she never seemed desirous of going beyond what was daily required of her—each study was a duty, and not a subject of zeal.

Presently Miss Fennimore came back, followed by the two sisters, neither of them in the best of tempers. Maria, a stout, clumsily made girl of fifteen, had the same complexion and open eyes as Phœbe, but her colouring was muddled, the gaze full-orbed and vacant, and the lips, always pouting, were just now swelled with the vexation that filled her prominent eyelids with tears. Bertha, two years younger, looked as if nature had designed her for a boy, and the change into a girl was not yet decided. She, too, was very like Maria ; but Maria's open nostrils were in her a droll *retroussé*, puggish little nose ; her chin had a boyish squareness and decision, her round cheeks had two comical dimples, her eyes were either stretched in defiance or narrowed up with fun, and a slight cast in one gave a peculiar archness and character to her face; her skin, face, hands, and all, were uniformly pinky ; her hair in such obstinate yellow curls, that it was to be hoped, for her sake, that the fashion of being *crêpé* might continue. The brow lowered in petulance ; and, as she kissed Phœbe, she muttered in her ear a vituperation of the governess in schoolroom *patois;* then began tossing the lesson-books in the air and catching them again, as a preliminary to finding the places, thus drawing on herself a reproof in German. French and German were alternately spoken in lesson hours by Phœbe and Bertha, who had lived with foreign servants from infancy ; but poor Maria had not the faculty of keeping the tongues distinct, and corrections only terrified her into confusion worse confounded, until Miss Fennimore had in despair decided that English was the best alternative.

Phœbe practised vigorously. Aware that nothing pleasant was passing, and that, be it what it might, she could do no good, she was glad to stop her ears with her music, until eight o'clock brought a pause in the shape of breakfast. Formerly the schoolroom party had joined the family meal, but since the two elder girls had been out, and Mervyn's friends had been often in the house, it had been decided that the home circle was too numerous; and what had once been the play-room was allotted to be the eating-room of the younger ones, without passing the red door, on the other side of which lay the world.

Breakfast was announced by the schoolroom maid, and Miss Fennimore rose. No sooner was her back turned, than Bertha indulged in a tremendous writhing yawn, wriggling in her chair, and clenching both fat fists, as she threatened with each, at her governess's retreating figure, so ludicrously, that Phœbe smiled while she shook her head, and an explosive giggle came from Maria, causing the lady to turn and behold Miss Bertha demure as ever, and a look of disconsolate weariness fast settling down on each of the two young faces. The unbroken routine pressed heavily at those fit moments for family greetings and for relaxation, and even Phœbe would gladly have been spared the German account of the Holt and of Miss Charlecote's book, for which she was called upon. Bertha meanwhile, to whom waggishness was existence, was carrying on a silent drama on her plate, her roll being a quarry, and her knife the workmen attacking it. Now she undermined, now acted an explosion, with uplifted eyebrows and an indicated 'puff!' with her lips, with constant dumb-show directed to Maria, who, without half understanding, was in a constant suppressed titter, sometimes concealed by her pocket-handkerchief.

Quick as Miss Fennimore was, and often as she frowned on Maria's outbreaks, she never could detect their provocative. Over-restraint and want of sympathy were direct instruction in unscrupulous slyness of amusement. A sentence of displeasure on Maria's ill-mannered folly was in the act of again filling her eyes with tears, when there was a knock at the door and all the faces beamed with glad expectation.

It was Robert. This was the time of day when he knew Miss Fennimore could best tolerate him, and he seldom failed to make his appearance on his way down-stairs, the only one of the privileged race who was a wonted object on this side the baize door. Phœbe thought he looked more cheerful, and indeed gravity could hardly have withstood Bertha's face, as she gave a mischievous tweak to his hair behind, under colour of putting her arm round his neck.

'Well, Curlylocks, how much mischief did you do yesterday?'

'I'd no spirits for mischief,' she answered, with mock pitifulness, twinkling up her eyes, and rubbing them with her knuckles as if she were crying. 'You barbarous wretch, taking Phœbe to feast on strawberries and cream with Miss Charlecote, and leaving poor me to poke in that stupid drawing-room, with nothing to do but to count the scollops of mamma's flounce!'

'It is your turn. Will Miss Fennimore kindly let you have a walk with me this evening?'

'And me,' said Maria.

'You, of course. May I come for them at five o'clock?'

'I can hardly tell what to say about Maria. I do not like to disappoint her, but she knows that nothing displeases me so much as that ill-mannered habit of giggling,' said Miss Fennimore, not without concern. Merciful as to Maria's attainments, she was strict as to her manners, and was striving to teach her self-restraint enough to be unobtrusive.

Poor Maria's eyes were glassy with tears, her chest heaved with sobs, and she broke out, 'O pray, Miss Fennimore, O pray!' while all the others interceded for her; and Bertha, well knowing that it was all her fault, avoided the humiliation of a confession, by the apparent generosity of exclaiming, 'Take us both to-morrow instead, Robin.'

Robert's journey was, however, fixed for that day,

and on this plea, licence was given for the walk. Phœbe smiled congratulation, but Maria was slow in cheering up; and when, on returning to the schoolroom, the three sisters were left alone together for a few moments, she pressed up to Phœbe's side, and said, 'Phœbe, I've not said my prayers. Do you think anything will happen to me?'

Her awfully mysterious tone set Bertha laughing. 'Yes, Maria, all the cows in the park will run at you,' she was beginning, when the grave rebuke of Phœbe's eyes cut her short.

'How was it, my dear?' asked Phœbe, tenderly fondling her sister.

'I was so sleepy, and Bertha would blow soap bubbles in her hands while we were washing, and then Miss Fennimore came, and I've been naughty now, and I know I shall go on, and then Robin wont take me.'

'I will ask Miss Fennimore to let you go to your room, dearest,' said Phœbe. 'You must not play again in dressing time, for there's nothing so sad as to miss our prayers. You are a good girl to care so much. Had you time for yours, Bertha?'

'Oh, plenty!' with a toss of her curly head. '*I* don't take ages about things, like Maria.'

'Prayers cannot be hurried,' said Phœbe, looking distressed, and she was about to remind Bertha to whom she spoke in prayer, when the child cut her short by the exclamation, 'Nonsense, Maria, about being naughty. You know I always make you laugh when I please, and that has more to do with it than saying your prayers, I fancy.'

'Perhaps,' said Phœbe, very sadly, 'if you had said yours more in earnest, my poor Bertha, you would either not have made Maria laugh, or would not have left her to bear all the blame.'

'Why do you call me poor?' exclaimed Bertha, with a half-offended, half-diverted look.

'Because I wish so much that you knew better,

or that I could help you better,' said Phœbe, gently.

There Miss Fennimore entered, displeased at the English sounds, and at finding them all, as she thought, loitering. Phœbe explained Maria's omission, and Miss Fennimore allowed her five minutes in her own room, saying that this must not become a precedent, though she did not wish to oppress her conscience.

Bertha's eyes glittered with a certain triumph, as she saw that Miss Fennimore was of her mind, and anticipated no consequences from the neglect, but only made the concession as to a superstition. Without disbelief, the child trained only to reason, and quick to detect fallacy, was blind to all that was not material. And how was the spiritual to be brought before her?

Phœbe might well sigh as she sat down to her abstract of Schlegel's Lectures. 'If any one would but teach them,' she thought; 'but there is no time at all, and I myself do not know half so much of those things as one of Miss Charlecote's lowest classes.'

Phœbe was a little mistaken. An earnest mind taught how to learn, with access to the Bible and Prayer Book, could gain more from these fountainheads than any external teaching could impart; and she could carry her difficulties to Robert. Still it was out of her power to assist her sisters. Surveillance and driving absolutely left no space free from Miss Fennimore's requirements; and all that there was to train those young ones in faith, was the manner in which it *lived* and worked in her. Nor of this effect could she be conscious.

As to dreams or repinings, or even listening to her hopes and fears for her project of pleasure, they were excluded by the concentrated attention that Miss Fennimore's system enforced. Time and capacity were so much on the stretch, that the habit of doing *what* she was doing, and nothing else, had become second nature to the docile and duteous girl; and she had

become little sensible to interruptions; so she went on
with her German, her Greek, and her algebra, scarcely
hearing the repetitions of the lessons, or the counting
as Miss Fennimore presided over Maria's practice, a
bit of drudgery detested by the governess, but necessarily persevered in, for Maria loved music, and had
just voice and ear sufficient to render this single
accomplishment not hopeless, but a certain want of
power of sustained effort made her always break
down at the moment she seemed to be doing best.
Former governesses had lost patience, but Miss Fennimore had early given up the case, and never scolded
her for her failures; she made her attempt less, and
she was improving more, and shedding fewer tears
than under any former dynasty. Even a stern
dominion is better for the subjects than an uncertain
and weak one; regularity gives a sense of reliance,
and constant occupation leaves so little time for being
naughty, that Bertha herself was getting into training,
and on the present day her lessons were exemplary,
always with a view to the promised walk with her
brother, one of the greatest pleasures ever enjoyed by
the denizens of the west wing.

Phœbe's pleasure was less certain, and less dependent
on her merits, yet it invigorated her efforts to do all
she had to do with all her might, even into the statement of the pros and cons of customs and free trade,
which she was required to produce as her morning's
exercise. In the midst, her ear detected the sound of
wheels, and her heart throbbed in the conviction that
it was Miss Charlecote's pony carriage; nay, she found
her pen had indited 'Robin would be so glad,' instead
of 'revenue to the government,' and while scratching
the words out beyond all legibility, she blamed herself
for betraying such want of self-command.

No summons came, no tidings, the wheels went
away; her heart sank, and her spirit revolted against
an unfeeling, unutterably wearisome captivity; but it
was only a moment's fluttering against the bars, the

tears were driven back with the thought, 'After all, the decision is guided from Above. If I stay at home, it *must* be best for me. Let me try to be good!' and she forced her mind back to her exports and her customs. It was such discipline as few girls could have exercised, but the conscientious effort was no small assistance in being resigned; and in the precious minutes granted in which to prepare herself for dinner, she found it the less hard task to part with her anticipations of delight and brace herself to quiet, contented duty.

The meal was beginning when, with a very wide expansion of the door, appeared a short, consequential looking personage, of such plump, rounded proportions, that she seemed ready to burst out of her riding habit, and of a broad, complacent visage, somewhat overblooming. It was Miss Fulmort, the eldest of the family, a young lady just past thirty, a very awful distance from the school-room party, to whom she nodded with good-natured condescension, saying: 'Ah! I thought I should find you at dinner; I'm come for something to sustain nature. The riding party are determined to have me with them, and they wont wait for luncheon. Thank you, yes, a piece of mutton, if there were any under side. How it reminds me of old times. I used so to look forward to never seeing a loin of mutton again.'

'As your chief ambition?' said Miss Fennimore, who, governess as she was, could not help being a little satirical, especially when Bertha's eyes twinkled responsively.

'One does get so tired of mutton and rice pudding,' answered the less observant Miss Fulmort, who was but dimly conscious of any one's existence save her own, and could not have credited a governess laughing at her; 'but really this is not so bad, after all, for a change; and some pale ale. You don't mean that you exist without pale ale?'

'We all drink water by preference,' said Miss Fennimore.

'Indeed! Miss Watson, our finishing governess, never drank anything but claret, and she always had little *pâtés*, or fish, or something, because she said her appetite was to be consulted, she was so delicate. She was very thin, I know; and what a figure you have, Phœbe! I suppose that is water drinking. Bridger did say it would reduce me to leave off pale ale, but I can't get on without it, I get so horridly low, Don't you think that's a sign, Miss Fennimore?'

'I beg your pardon, a sign of what?'

'That one can't go on without it. Miss Charlecote said she thought it was all constitution whether one is stout or not, and that nothing made much difference, when I asked her about German wines.'

'Oh! Augusta, has Miss Charlecote been here this morning?' exclaimed Phœbe.

'Yes; she came at twelve o'clock, and there was I actually pinned down to entertain her, for mamma was not come down. So I asked her about those light foreign wines, and whether they do really make one thinner; you know one always has them at her house.'

'Did mamma see her?' asked poor Phœbe, anxiously.

'Oh yes, she was bent upon it. It was something about you. Oh! she wants to take you to stay with her in that horrible hole of hers in the City—very odd of her. What do you advise me to do, Miss Fennimore? Do you think those foreign wines would bring me down a little, or that they would make me low and sinking?'

'Really, I have no experience on the subject!' said Miss Fennimore, loftily.

'What did mamma say?' was poor Phœbe's almost breathless question.

'Oh! it makes no difference to mamma' (Phœbe's heart bounded); but Augusta went on: 'she always has her soda-water, you know; but of course I should take a hamper from Bass. I hate being unprovided.'

'But about my going to London?' humbly murmured Phœbe.

'What *did* she say?' considered the elder sister, aloud. 'I don't know, I'm sure. I was not attending—the heat does make one so sleepy—but I know we all wondered she should want you at your age. You know some people take a spoonful of vinegar to fine themselves down, and some of those wines *are* very acid,' she continued, pressing on with her great subject of consultation.

'If it be an object with you, Miss Fulmort, I should recommend the vinegar,' said Miss Fennimore. 'There is nothing like doing a thing outright!'

'And, oh! how glorious it would be to see her taking it!' whispered Bertha into Phœbe's ear, unheard by Augusta, who, in her satisfied stolidity, was declaring, 'No, I could not undertake that. I am the worst person in the world for taking anything disagreeable.'

And having completed her meal, which she had contrived to make out of the heart of the joint, leaving the others little but fat, she walked off to her ride, believing that she had done a gracious and condescending action in making conversation with her inferiors of the west wing.

Yet Augusta Fulmort might have been good for something, if her mind and her affections had not lain fallow ever since she escaped from a series of governesses who taught her self-indulgence by example.

'I wonder what mamma said!' exclaimed Phœbe, in her strong craving for sympathy in her suspense.

'I am sorry the subject has been brought forward, if it is to unsettle you, Phœbe,' said Miss Fennimore, not unkindly; 'I regret your being twice disappointed; but, if your mother should refer it to me, as I make no doubt she will, I should say that it would be a great pity to break up our course of studies.'

'It would only be for a little while,' sighed Phœbe; 'and Miss Charlecote is to show me all the museums. I should see more with her than ever I shall when I am come out; and I should be with Robert.'

'I intended asking permission to take you through a systematic course of lectures and specimens when the family are next in town,' said Miss Fennimore. 'Ordinary, desultory sight-seeing leaves few impressions; and though Miss Charlecote is a superior person, her mind is not of a sufficiently scientific turn to make her fully able to direct you. I shall trust to your good sense, Phœbe, for again submitting to defer the pleasure till it can be enhanced.'

Good sense had a task imposed on it for which it was quite inadequate; but there was something else in Phœbe which could do the work better than her unconvinced reason. Even had she been sure of the expediency of being condemned to the schoolroom, no good sense would have brought that resolute smile, or driven back the dew in her eyes, or enabled her voice to say, with such sweet meekness, 'Very well, Miss Fennimore; I dare say it may be right.'

Miss Fennimore was far more concerned than if the submission had been grudging. She debated with herself whether she should consider her resolution irrevocable.

Ten minutes were allowed after dinner in the parterre, and these could only be spent under the laurel-hedge; the sun was far too hot everywhere else. Phœbe had here no lack of sympathy, but had to restrain Bertha, who, with angry gestures, was pronouncing the governess a horrid cross-patch, and declaring that no girls ever were used as they were; while Maria observed, that if Phœbe went to London, she must go too.

'We shall all go some day,' said Phœbe, cheerfully, 'and we shall enjoy it all the more if we are good now. Never mind, Bertha, we shall have some nice walks.'

'Yes, all bothered with botany,' muttered Bertha.

'I thought, at least, you would be glad of me,' said Phœbe, smiling; 'you who stay at home.'

'To be sure, I am,' said Bertha; 'but it is such a shame! I shall tell Robin, and he'll say so too. I shall tell him you nearly cried!'

'Don't vex Robin,' said Phœbe. 'When you go out, you should set yourself to tell him pleasant things.'

'So I'm to tell him you wouldn't go on any account. You like your political economy much too well!'

'Suppose you say nothing about it,' said Phœbe. 'Make yourself merry with him. That's what you've got to do. He takes you out to entertain you, not to worry about grievances.'

'Do you never talk about grievances?' asked Bertha, twinkling up her eyes.

Phœbe hesitated. 'Not my own,' she said, 'because I have not got any.'

'Has Robert, then?' asked Bertha.

'Nobody has grievances who is out of the schoolroom,' opined Maria; and as she uttered this profound sentiment, the tinkle of Miss Fennimore's little bell warned the sisters to return to the studies, which in the heat of summer were pursued in the afternoon, that the walk might be taken in the cool of the evening. Reading aloud, drawing, and sensible plain needlework were the avocations till it was time to learn the morrow's lessons. Phœbe being beyond this latter work, drew on, and in the intervals of helping Maria with her geography, had time to prepare such a bright face as might make Robert think lightly of her disappointment, and not reckon it as another act of tyranny.

When he opened the door, however, there was that in his looks which made her spirits leap up like an elastic spring; and his 'Well, Phœbe!' was almost triumphant.

'Is it—— am I——' was all she could say.

'Has no one thought it worth while to tell you?'

'Don't you know,' interposed Bertha, 'you on the other side the red baize door might be all married, or dead and buried, for aught we should hear. But is Phœbe to go?'

'I believe so.'

'Are you sure?' asked Phœbe, afraid yet to hope.

'Yes. My father heard the invitation, and said that you were a good girl, and deserved a holiday.'

Commendation from that quarter was so rare, that excess of gladness made Phœbe cast down her eyes and colour intensely, a little oppressed by the victory over her governess. But Miss Fennimore spoke warmly. 'He cannot think her more deserving than I do. I am rejoiced not to have been consulted, for I could hardly have borne to inflict such a mortification on her, though these interruptions are contrary to my views. As it is, Phœbe, my dear, I wish you joy.'

'Thank you,' Phœbe managed to say, while the happy tears fairly started. In that chilly land, the least approach to tenderness was like the gleam in which the hardy woodbine leaflets unfold to sun themselves.

Thankful for small mercies, thought Robert, looking at her with fond pity ; but at least the dear child will have one fortnight of a more genial atmosphere, and soon, may be, I shall transplant her to be Lucilla's darling as well as mine, free from task-work, and doing the labours of love for which she is made !

He was quite in spirits, and able to reply in kind to the freaks and jokes of his little sister, as she started, spinning round him like a humming-top, and singing—

Will you go to the wood, Robin a Bobbin?

giving safe vent to an ebullition of spirits that must last her a good while, poor little maiden !

Phœbe took a sober walk with Miss Fennimore, receiving advice on methodically journalizing what she might see, and on the scheme of employments which might prevent her visit from being waste of time. The others would have resented the interference with the holiday ; but Phœbe, though a little sorry to find that tasks were not to be off her mind, was too grateful for Miss Fennimore's cordial consent to entertain any thought except of obedience to the best of her power.

Miss Fennimore was politely summoned to Mrs. Fulmort's dressing-room for the official communication; but this day was no exception to the general custom, that the red baize door was not passed by the young ladies until their evening appearance in the drawing-room. Then the trio descended, all alike in white muslin, made high, and green sashes—a dress carefully distinguishing Phœbe as not introduced, but very becoming to her, with the simple folds and the little net ruche, suiting admirably the tall, rounded slenderness of her shape, her long neck, and short, childish contour of face, where there smiled a joy of anticipation almost inappreciable to those who know not what it is to spend day after day with nothing particular to look forward to.

Very grand was the drawing-room, all amber-coloured with satin-wood, satin and gold, and with everything useless and costly encumbering tables that looked as if nothing could ever be done upon them. Such a room inspired a sense of being in company, and it was no wonder that Mrs. Fulmort and her two elder daughters swept in in as decidedly procession style as if they had formed part of a train of twenty.

The star that bestowed three female sovereigns to Europe seemed to have had the like influence on Hiltonbury parish, since both its squires were heiresses. Miss Mervyn would have been a happier woman had she married a plain country gentleman, like those of her own stock, instead of giving a county position to a man of lower origin and enormous monied wealth. To live up to the claims of that wealth had been her business ever since, and health and enjoyment had been so completely sacrificed to it, that for many years past the greater part of her time had been spent in resting and making herself up for her appearance in the evening, when she conducted her elder daughters to their gaieties. Faded and tallowy in complexion, so as to be almost ghastly in her blue brocade and heavy gold ornaments, she reclined languidly on a large easy-chair, saying, with half-closed eyes—

'Well, Phœbe, Miss Fennimore has told you of Miss Charlecote's invitation.'

'Yes, mamma. I am very, *very* much obliged!'

'You know you are not to fancy yourself come out,' said Juliana, the second sister, who had a good tall figure, and features and complexion not far from beauty, but marred by a certain shrewish tone and air.

'Oh, no,' answered Phœbe; 'but with Miss Charlecote that will make no difference.'

'Probably not,' said Juliana; 'for of course you will see nobody but a set of old maids and clergymen and their wives.'

'She need not go far for old maids,' whispered Bertha to Maria.

'Pray, in which class do you reckon the Sandbrooks?' said Phœbe, smiling; 'for she chiefly goes to meet them.'

'She may go!' said Juliana, scornfully; 'but Lucilla Sandbrook is far past attending to her!'

'I wonder whether the Charterises will take any notice of Phœbe?' exclaimed Augusta.

'My dear,' said Mrs. Fulmort, waking slowly to another idea, 'I will tell Boodle to talk to—what's your maid's name?—about your dresses.'

'Oh, mamma,' interposed Juliana, 'it will be only poking about the exhibitions with Miss Charlecote. You may have that plaid silk of mine that I was going to have worn out abroad, half-price for her.'

Bertha fairly made a little stamp at Juliana, and clenched her fist.

If Phœbe dreaded anything in the way of dress, it was Juliana's half-price.

'My dear, your papa would not like her not to be well fitted out,' said her mother; 'and Honora Charlecote always has such handsome things. I wish Boodle could put mine on like hers.'

'Oh, very well!' said Juliana, rather offended; 'only it should be understood what is to be done if the

Charterises ask her to any of their parties. There will be such mistakes and confusion if she meets any one we know; and you particularly objected to having her brought forward.'

Phœbe's eye was a little startled, and Bertha set her front teeth together on edge, and looked viciously at Juliana.

'My dear, Honora Charlecote never goes out,' said Mrs. Fulmort.

'If she should, you understand, Phœbe,' said Juliana.

Coffee came in at the moment, and Augusta criticised the strength of it, which made a diversion, during which Bertha slipped out of the room, with a face replete with mischievous exultation.

'Are not you going to play to-night, my dears?' asked Mrs. Fulmort. 'What was that duet I heard you practising?'

'Come, Juliana,' said the elder sister, 'I meant to go over it again; I am not satisfied with my part.'

'I have to write a note,' said Juliana, moving off to another table; whereupon Phœbe ventured to propose herself as a substitute, and was accepted.

Maria sat entranced, with her mouth open; and presently Mrs. Fulmort looked up from a kind of doze to ask who was playing. For some moments she had no answer. Maria was too much awed for speech in the drawing-room; and though Bertha had come back, she had her back to her mother, and did not hear. Mrs. Fulmort exerted herself to sit up and turn her head.

'Was that Phœbe?' she said. 'You have a clear, good touch, my dear, as they used to say I had when I was at school at Bath. Play another of your pieces, my dear.'

'I am ready now, Augusta,' said Juliana, advancing.

Little girls were not allowed at the piano when officers might be coming in from the dining-room, so Maria's face became vacant again, for Juliana's music awoke no echoes within her.

Phœbe beckoned her to a remote ottoman, a receptacle for the newspapers of the week, and kept her turning over the *Illustrated News*, an unfailing resource with her, but powerless to occupy Bertha after the first Saturday; and Bertha, turning a deaf ear to the assurance that there was something very entertaining about a tiger-hunt, stood, solely occupied by eyeing Juliana.

Was she studying 'come-out' life as she watched her sisters surrounded by the gentlemen who presently herded round the piano?

It was nearly the moment when the young ones were bound to withdraw, when Mervyn, coming hastily up to their ottoman, had almost stumbled over Maria's foot.

'Beg pardon. Oh, it was only you! What a cow it is!' said he, tossing over the papers.

'What are you looking for, Mervyn?' asked Phœbe.

'An advertisement—*Bell's Life* for the 3rd. That rascal, Mears, must have taken it.'

She found it for him, and likewise the advertisement, which he, missing once, was giving up in despair.

'I say,' he observed, while she was searching, 'so you are to chip the shell.'

'I'm only going to London—I'm not coming out.'

'Gammon!' he said, with an odd wink. 'You need never go in again, like the what's-his-name in the fairy tale, or you are a sillier child than I take you for. They'—nodding at the piano—'are getting a terrible pair of old cats, and we want something young and pretty about.'

With this unusual compliment, Phœbe, seeing the way clear to the door, rose to depart, most reluctantly followed by Bertha, and more willingly by Maria, who began, the moment they were in the hall—

'Phœbe, why do they get a couple of terrible old cats? I don't like them; I shall be afraid.'

'Mervyn didn't mean——' began perplexed Phœbe, cut short by Bertha's boisterous laughter. 'Oh, Maria, what a goose you are! You'll be the death of me, some day! Why, Juliana and Augusta are the cats themselves. Oh, dear! I wanted to kiss Mervyn for saying so. Oh, wasn't it fun! And now, Maria— oh! if I could have stayed a moment longer!'

'Bertha, Bertha, not such a noise in the hall. Come, Maria; mind, you must not tell anybody. Bertha, come,' expostulated Phœbe, trying to drag her sister to the red baize door; but Bertha stood, bending nearly double, exaggerating the helplessness of her paroxysms of laughter.

'Well, at least the cat will have something to scratch her,' she gasped out. 'Oh, I did so want to stay and see!'

'Have you been playing any tricks?' exclaimed Phœbe, with consternation, as Bertha's deportment recurred to her.

'Tricks?—I couldn't help it. Oh, listen, Phœbe!' cried Bertha, with her wicked look of triumph. 'I brought home such a lovely sting-nettle for Miss Fennimore's peacock caterpillar; and when I heard how kind dear Juliana was to you about your visit to London, I thought she really must have it for a reward; so I ran away, and slily tucked it into her bouquet; and I did so hope she would take it up to fiddle with when the gentlemen talk to her,' said the elf, with an irresistibly comic imitation of Juliana's manner towards gentlemen.

'Bertha, this is beyond——' began Phœbe.

'Didn't you sting your fingers?' asked Maria.

Bertha stuck out her fat pink paws, embellished with sundry white lumps. 'All pleasure,' said she, 'thinking of the jump Juliana will give, and how nicely it serves her.'

Phœbe was already on her way back to the drawing-rooms; Bertha sprang after, but in vain. Never would she have risked the success of her trick, could she have guessed that Phœbe would have the temerity to return to the company!

Phœbe glided in without waiting for the sense of awkwardness, though she knew she should have to cross the whole room, and she durst not ask any one to bring the dangerous bouquet to her—not even Robert—he must not be stung in her service.

She met her mother's astonished eye as she threaded her way; she wound round a group of gentlemen, and spied the article of which she was in quest, where Juliana had laid it down with her gloves on going to the piano. Actually she had it! She had seized it unperceived! Good little thief; it was a most innocent robbery; she crept away with a sense of guilt and desire to elude observation, positively starting when she encountered her father's portly figure in the anteroom. He stopped her with 'Going to bed, eh? So Miss Charlecote has taken a fancy to you, has she? It does you credit. What shall you want for the journey?'

'Boodle is going to see,' began Phœbe, but he interrupted.

'Will fifty do? I will have my daughters well turned out. All to be spent upon yourself, mind. Why, you've not a bit of jewellery on! Have you a watch?'

'No, papa.'

'Robert shall choose one for you, then. Come to my room any time for the cash; and if Miss Charlecote takes you anywhere among her set—good connexions she has—and you want to be rigged out extra, send me in the bill—anything rather than be shabby.'

'Thank you, papa! Then, if I am asked out anywhere, may I go?'

'Why, what does the child mean? Anywhere that Miss Charlecote likes to take you, of course.'

'Only because I am not come out.'

'Stuff about coming out! I don't like my girls to be shy and backward. They've a right to show themselves anywhere; and you should be going out with us now, but somehow your poor mother doesn't like the trouble of such a lot of girls. So don't be shy, but make the most of yourself, for you wont meet many better endowed, nor more highly accomplished. Good night, and enjoy yourself.'

Palpitating with wonder and pleasure, Phœbe escaped. Such permission, over-riding all Juliana's injunctions, was worth a few nettle stings and a great fright; for Phœbe was not philosopher enough, in spite of Miss Fenniinore—ay, and of Robert—not to have a keen desire to see a great party.

Her delay had so much convinced the sisters that her expedition had had some fearful consequences, that Maria was already crying lest dear Phœbe should be in disgrace ; and Bertha had seated herself on the balusters, debating with herself whether, if Phœbe were suspected of the trick (a likely story) and condemned to lose her visit to London, she would confess herself the guilty person.

And when Phœbe came back, too much overcome with delight to do anything but communicate papa's goodness, and rejoice in the unlimited power of making presents, Bertha triumphantly insisted on her confessing that it had been a capital thing that the nettles were in Juliana's nosegay !

Phœbe shook her head ; too happy to scold, too humble to draw the moral that the surest way to gratification is to remove the thorns from the path of others.

CHAPTER III.

> She gives thee a garland woven fair,
>   Take care!
> It is a fool's-cap for thee to wear,
>   Beware! Beware!
>   Trust her not,
> She is fooling thee!
>   LONGFELLOW, *from* MÜLLER.

EHOLD Phœbe Fulmort seated in a train on the way to London. She was a very pleasant spectacle to Miss Charlecote opposite to her, so peacefully joyous was her face, as she sat with the wind breathing in on her, in the calm luxury of contemplating the landscape gliding past the windows in all its summer charms, and the repose of having no one to hunt her into unvaried rationality.

Her eye was the first to detect Robert in waiting at the terminus, but he looked more depressed than ever, and scarcely smiled as he handed them to the carriage.

'Get in, Robert, you are coming home with us,' said Honor.

'You have so much to take, I should encumber you.'

'No, the sundries go in cabs, with the maids. Jump in.'

'Do your friends arrive to-night?'

'Yes; but that is no reason you should look so

rueful! Make the most of Phœbe beforehand. Besides, Mr. Parsons is a Wykehamist.'

Robert took his place on the back seat, but still as if he would have preferred walking home. Neither his sister nor his friend dared to ask whether he had seen Lucilla. Could she have refused him? or was her frivolity preying on his spirits?

Phœbe tried to interest him by the account of the family migration, and of Miss Fennimore's promise that Maria and Bertha should have two half hours of real play in the garden on each day when the lessons had been properly done; and how she had been so kind as to let Maria leave off trying to read a French book that had proved too hard for her, not perceiving why this instance of good-nature was not cheering to her brother.

Miss Charlecote's house was a delightful marvel to Phœbe from the moment when she rattled into the paved court, entered upon the fragrant odour of the cedar hall, and saw the Queen of Sheba's golden locks beaming with the evening light. She entered the drawing-room, pleasant-looking already, under the judicious arrangement of the housekeeper, who had set out the Holt flowers and arranged the books, so that it seemed full of welcome.

Phœbe ran from window to mantelpiece, enchanted with the quaint mixture of old and new, admiring carving and stained glass, and declaring that Owen had not prepared her for anything equal to this, until Miss Charlecote, going to arrange matters with her housekeeper, left the brother and sister together.

'Well, Robin!' said Phœbe, coming up to him anxiously.

He only crossed his arms on the mantelpiece, rested his head on them, and sighed.

'Have you seen her?'
'Not to speak to her.'
'Have you called?'
'No.'

'Then where did you see her?'

'She was riding in the Park. I was on foot.'

'She could not have seen you!' exclaimed Phœbe.

'She did,' replied Robert; 'I was going to tell you. She gave me one of her sweetest, brightest smiles, such as only she can give. You know them, Phœbe. No assumed welcome, but a sudden flash and sparkle of real gladness.'

'But why—what do you mean?' asked Phœbe; 'why have you not been to her? I thought from your manner that she had been neglecting you, but it seems to me all the other way.'

'I cannot, Phœbe; I cannot put my poor pretensions forward in the set she is with. I know they would influence her, and that her decision would not be calm and mature.'

'Her decision of what you are to be?'

'That is fixed,' said Robert, sighing.

'Indeed! With papa.'

'No, in my own mind. I have seen enough of the business to find that I could in ten years quadruple my capital, and in the meantime maintain her in the manner she prefers.'

'You are quite sure she prefers it?'

'She has done so ever since she could exercise a choice. I should feel myself doing her an injustice if I were to take advantage of any preference she may entertain for me to condemn her to what would be to her a dreary banishment.'

'Not with you,' cried Phœbe.

'You know nothing about it, Phœbe. You have never led such a life, and you it would not hurt—attract, I mean; but lovely, fascinating, formed for admiration, and craving for excitement as she is, she is a being that can only exist in society. She would be miserable in homely retirement—I mean she would prey on herself. I could not ask it of her. If she consented, it would be without knowing her own tastes. No; all that remains is to find out whether she can submit to owe her wealth to our business.'

'And shall you?'

'I could not but defer it till I should meet her here,' said Robert. 'I shrink from seeing her with those cousins, or hearing her name with theirs. Phœbe, imagine my feelings when, going into Mervyn's club with him, I heard "Rashe Charteris and Cilly Sandbrook" contemptuously discussed by those very names, and jests passing on their independent ways. I know how it is. Those people work on her spirit of enterprise, and she—too guileless and innocent to heed appearances. Phœbe, you do not wonder that I am nearly mad!'

'Poor Robin!' said Phœbe, affectionately. 'But, indeed, I am sure, if Lucy once had a hint—no, one could not tell her, it would shock her too much; but if she had the least idea that people could be so impertinent,' and Phœbe's cheeks glowed with shame and indignation, 'she would only wish to go away as far as she could for fear of seeing any of them again. I am sure they were not gentlemen, Robin.'

'A man must be supereminently a gentleman to respect a woman who does not *make* him do so,' said Robert, mournfully. 'That Miss Charteris! Oh! that she were banished to Siberia!'

Phœbe meditated a few moments; then looking up, said, 'I beg your pardon, Robin, but it does strike me that, if you think that this kind of life is not good for Lucilla, it cannot be right to sacrifice your own higher prospects to enable her to continue it.'

'I tell you, Phœbe,' said he, with some impatience, 'I never was pledged. I may be of much more use and influence, and able to effect more extended good as a partner in a concern like this than as an obscure clergyman. Don't you see?'

Phœbe had only time to utter a somewhat melancholy 'Very likely,' before Miss Charlecote returned to take her to her room, the promised brown cupboard, all wainscoted with delicious cedar, so deeply and uniformly panelled, that when shut, the door was not obvious; and it was like being in a box, for there were no wardrobes, only shelves shut by doors into the wall, which the old usage of the household tradition called awmries (*armoires*). The furniture was reasonably modern, but not obtrusively so. There was a delicious recess in the deep window, with a seat and a table in it, and a box of mignionette along the sill. It looked out into the little high-walled entrance court, and beyond to the wall of the warehouse opposite; and the roar of the great city thoroughfare came like the distant surging of the ocean. Seldom had young maiden's bower given more satisfaction. Phœbe looked about her as if she hardly knew how to believe in anything so unlike her ordinary life, and she thanked her friend again and again with such enthusiasm, that Miss Charlecote laughed as she told her she liked the old house to be appreciated, since it had, like Pompeii, been potted for posterity.

'And thank you, my dear,' she added with a sigh, 'for making my coming home so pleasant. May you never know how I dreaded the finding it full of emptiness.'

'Dear Miss Charlecote!' cried Phœbe, venturing upon a warm kiss, and thrilled with sad pleasure as she was pressed in a warm, clinging embrace, and felt tears on her cheek. 'You have been so happy here!'

'It is not the past, my dear,' said Honora; 'I could live peacefully on the thought of that. The shadows that people this house are very gentle ones. It is the present!'

She broke off, for the gates of the court were opening to admit a detachment of cabs, containing the persons and properties of the new incumbent and his wife. He had been a curate of Mr. Charlecote, since whose death he had led a very hard-working life in various towns; and on his recent presentation to the living of St. Wulstan's, Honora had begged him and his wife to make her house their home while determining on the repairs of the parsonage. She ran down to meet them with gladsome steps. She had never entirely dropped her intercourse with Mr. Parsons, though seldom meeting; and he was a relic of the past, one of the very few who still called her by her Christian name, and regarded her more as the clergyman's daughter of St. Wulstan's than as lady of the Holt. Mrs. Parsons was a thorough clergyman's wife, as active as himself, and much loved and esteemed by Honora, with whom, in their few meetings, she had 'got on' to admiration.

There they were, looking after luggage, and paying cabs so heedfully as not to remark their hostess standing on the stairs; and she had time to survey them with the affectionate curiosity of meeting after long absence, and with pleasure in remarking that there was little change. Perhaps they were rather more gray, and had grown more alike by force of living and thinking together; but they both looked equally alert and cheerful, and as if 50 and 55 were the very prime of years for substantial work.

Their first glances at her were full of the same anxiety for her health and strength, as they heartily shook hands, and accompanied her into the drawing-room, she explaining that Mr. Parsons was to have the study all to himself, and never be disturbed there; then inquiring after the three children, two daughters, who were married, and a son lately ordained.

'I thought you would have brought William to see about the curacy,' she said.

'He is not strong enough,' said his mother. 'He wished it, but he is better where he is; he could not bear the work here.'

'No; I told him the utmost I should allow would be an exchange now and then when my curates were overdone,' said Mr. Parsons.

'And so you are quite deserted,' said Honor, feeling the more drawn towards her friends.

'Starting afresh, with a sort of honeymoon, as I

tell Anne,' replied Mr. Parsons; and such a bright look passed between them, as though they were quite sufficient for each other, that Honor felt there was no parallel between their case and her own.

'Ah! you have not lost your children yet,' said Mrs. Parsons.

'They are not with me,' said Honor, quickly. 'Lucy is with her cousins, and Owen—I don't exactly know how he means to dispose of himself this vacation; but we were all to meet here.' Guessing, perhaps, that Mr. Parsons saw into her dissatisfaction, she then assumed their defence. 'There is to be a grand affair at Castle Blanch, a celebration of young Charles Charteris's marriage, and Owen and Lucy will be wanted for it.'

'Whom has he married?'

'A Miss Mendoza, an immense fortune—something in the stockbroker line. He had spent a good deal, and wanted to repair it; but they tell me she is a very handsome person, very ladylike and agreeable; and Lucy likes her greatly. I am to go to luncheon at their house to-morrow, so I shall treat you as if you were at home.'

'I should hope so,' quoth Mr. Parsons.

'Yes, or I know you would not stay here properly. I'm not alone, either. Why, where's the boy gone? I thought he was here. I have two young Fulmorts, one staying here, the other looking in from the office.'

'Fulmort!' exclaimed Mr. Parsons, with three notes of admiration at least in his voice. 'What! the distiller?'

'The enemy himself, the identical lord of gin-shops— at least his children. Did you not know that he married my next neighbour, Augusta Mervyn, and that our properties touch? He is not so bad by way of squire as he is here; and I have known his wife all my life, so we keep up all habits of good neighbourhood; and though they have brought up the elder ones very ill, they have not succeeded in spoiling this son and daughter. She is one of the very nicest girls I ever knew, and he, poor fellow, has a great deal of good in him.'

'I think I have heard William speak of a Fulmort,' said Mrs. Parsons. 'Was he at Winchester?'

'Yes; and an infinite help the influence there has been to him. I never saw any one more anxious to do right, often under great disadvantages. I shall be very glad for him to be with you. He was always intended for a clergyman, but now I am afraid there is a notion of putting him into the business; and he is here attending to it for the present, while his father and brother are abroad. I am sorry he is gone. I suppose he was seized with a fit of shyness.'

However, when all the party had been to their rooms and prepared for dinner, Robert reappeared, and was asked where he had been.

'I went to dress,' he answered.

'Ah! where do you lodge? I asked Phœbe, but she said your letters went to Whittington-street.'

'There are two very good rooms at the office which my father sometimes uses.'

Phœbe and Miss Charlecote glanced at each other, aware that Mervyn would never have condescended to sleep in Great Whittington-street. Mr. Parsons likewise perceived a straightforwardness in the manner, which made him ready to acknowledge his fellow Wykehamist and his son's acquaintance; and they quickly became good friends over recollections of Oxford and Winchester, tolerably strong in Mr. Parsons himself, and all the fresher on 'William's' account. Phœbe, whose experience of social intercourse was confined to the stately evening hour in the drawing-room, had never listened to anything approaching to this style of conversation, nor seen her brother to so much advantage in society. Hitherto she had only beheld him neglected in his uncongenial home circle, contemning and contemned, or else subjected to the fretting torment of Lucilla's caprice. She had never known what he could be, at his ease, among persons of the same way of thinking. Speaking scarcely ever herself, and her fingers busy with her needle, she was receiving a better lesson than Miss Fennimore had ever yet been able to give. The acquiring of knowledge is one thing, the putting it out to profit another.

Gradually, from general topics, the conversation contracted to the parish and its affairs, known intimately to Mr. Parsons a quarter of a century ago, but in which Honora was now the best informed; while Robert listened as one who felt as if he might have a considerable stake therein, and indeed looked upon usefulness there as compensation for the schemes he was resigning.

The changes since Mr. Parsons's time had not been cheering. The late incumbent had been a man whose trust lay chiefly in preaching, and who, as his health failed, and he became more unable to cope with the crying evils around, had grown despairing, and given way to a sort of dismal, callous indifference; not doing a little, because he could not do much, and quashing the plans of others with a nervous dread of innovation. The class of superior persons in trade, and families of professional men, who in Mr. Charlecote's time had filled many a massively-built pew, had migrated to the suburbs, and preserved only an office or shop in the parish, an empty pew in the church, where the congregation was to be counted by tens instead of hundreds. Not that the population had fallen off. Certain streets which had been a grief and pain to Mr. Charlecote, but over which he had never entirely lost his hold, had become intolerably worse. Improvements in other parts of London, dislodging the inhabitants, had heaped them in festering masses of corruption in these untouched byways and lanes, places where honest men dared not penetrate without a policeman; and report spoke of rooms shared by six families at once.

Mr. Parsons had not taken the cure unknowing of what he should find in it; he said nothing, and looked as simple and cheerful as if his life were not to be a daily course of heroism. His wife gave one long, stifled sigh, and looked furtively upon him with her loving eyes, in something of anxious fear, but with far more of exultation.

Yet it was in no dispirited tone that she asked after the respectable poor—there surely must be some employed in small trades, or about the warehouses. She was answered that these were not many in proportion, and that not only had pew rents kept them out of church, but that they had little disposition to go there. They did send their children to the old endowed charity schools, but as these children grew up, wave after wave lapsed into a smooth, respectable heathen life of Sunday pleasuring. The more religious became dissenters, because the earnest inner life did not approve itself to them in Church teaching as presented to them; the worse sort, by far the most numerous, fell lower and lower, and hovered scarcely above the depths of sin and misery. Drinking was the universal vice, and dragged many a seemingly steady character into every stage of degradation. Men and women alike fell under the temptation, and soon hastened down the descent of corruption and crime.

'Ah!' said Mrs. Parsons, 'I observed gin palaces at the corner of every street.'

There was a pause. Neither her husband nor Honor made any reply. If they had done so, neither of the young Fulmorts would have perceived any connexion between the gin palaces and their father's profession; but the silence caused both to raise their eyes. Phœbe, judging by her sisters' code of the becoming, fancied that their friends supposed their feelings might be hurt by alluding to the distillery, as a trade, and cast about for some cheerful observations, which she could not find.

Robert had received a new idea, one that must be put aside till he had time to look at it.

There was a ring at the door. Honor's face lighted up at the tread on the marble pavement of the hall, and without other announcement, a young man entered the room, and as she sprang up to meet him, bent down his lofty head, and kissed her with half-filial, half-coaxing tenderness.

'Yes, here I am. They told me I should find you here. Ah! Phœbe, I'm glad to see you. Fulmort, how are you?' and a well-bred shake of the hand to Mr. and Mrs. Parsons, with the ease and air of the young master, returning to his mother's house.

'When did you come?'

'Only to-day. I got away sooner than I expected. I went to Lowndes Square, and they told me I should find you here, so I came away as soon as dinner was over. They were dressing for some grand affair, and wanted me to come with them, but of course I must come to see if you had really achieved bringing bright Phœbe from her orbit.'

His simile conveyed the astronomical compliment at once to Honora and Phœbe, who were content to share it. Honora was in a condition of subdued excitement and anxiety, compared to which all other sensations were tame, chequered as was her felicity, a state well known to mothers and sisters. Intensely gratified at her darling's arrival, gladdened by his presence, rejoicing in his endowments, she yet dreaded every phrase lest some dim misgiving should be deepened, and watched for the impression he made on her friends, as though her own depended upon it.

Admiration could not but come foremost. It was pleasant to look upon such a fine specimen of manly beauty and vigour. Of unusual height, his form was so well moulded, that his superior stature was only perceived by comparison with others, and the proportions were those of great strength. The small, well-set head, proudly carried, the short, straight features, and the form of the free massive curls, might have been a model for the bust of a Greek athlete; the colouring was the fresh, healthy bronzed ruddiness of English youth, and the expression had a certain boldness of good-humoured freedom, agreeing with the quiet power of the whole figure. Those bright grey eyes could never have been daunted, those curling, merry lips never at a loss, that smooth brow never been unwelcome, those easy movements never cramped, nor the manners restrained by bashfulness.

The contrast was not favourable to Robert. The fair proportions of the one brought out the irregular build of the other; the classical face made the plain one more homely, the erect bearing made the eye turn to the slouching carriage, and the readiness of address provoked comparison with the awkward diffidence of one disregarded at home. Bashfulness and depression had regained their hold of the elder lad almost as the younger one entered, and in the changes of position consequent upon the new arrival, he fell into the background, and stood leaning, caryatid fashion, against the mantelshelf, without uttering a word, while Owen, in a half recumbent position on an ottoman, a little in the rear of Miss Charlecote and her tea equipage, and close to Phœbe, indulged in the blithe loquacity of a return home, in a tone of caressing banter towards the first lady, of something between good nature and attention to the latter, yet without any such exclusiveness as would have been disregard to the other guests.

'Ponto well! Poor old Pon! how does he get on? Was it a very affecting parting, Phœbe?'

'I didn't see. I met Miss Charlecote at the station.'

'Not even your eyes might intrude on the sacredness of grief! Well, at least you dried them? But who dried Ponto's?' solemnly turning on Honora.

'Jones, I hope,' said she, smiling.

'I knew it! Says I to myself, when Henry opened the door, Jones remains at home for the consolation of Ponto.'

'Not entirely——' began Honora, laughing; but the boy shook his head, cutting her short with a playful frown.

'Cousin Honor, it grieves me to see a woman of your age and responsibility making false excuses. Mr. Parsons, I appeal to you, as a clergyman of the Church of England, is it not painful to hear her putting forward Jones's asthma, when we all know the true fact is that Ponto's tastes are so aristocratic that he can't take exercise with an under servant, and the housekeeper is too fat to waddle. By the by, how is the old thing ?'

'Much more effective than might be supposed by your account, sir, and probably wishing to know whether to get your room ready.'

'My room. Thank you ; no, not to-night. I've got nothing with me. What are you going to do to-morrow. I know you are to be at Charteris's to luncheon ; his Jewess told me so.'

'For shame, Owen.'

'I don't see any shame, if Charles doesn't,' said Owen ; 'only if you don't think yourself at a stall of cheap jewellery at a fair—that's all ! Phœbe, take care. You're a learned young lady.'

'No ; I am very backward.'

'Ah ! it's the fashion to deny it, but mind you don't mention Shakespeare.'

'Why not ?'

'Did you never hear of the *Merchant of Venice ?*'

Phœbe, a little startled, wanted to hear whether Mrs. Charteris were really Jewish, and after a little more in this style, which Honor reasonably feared the Parsonses might not consider in good taste, it was explained that her riches were Jewish, though her grandfather had been nothing, and his family Christian. Owen adding, that but for her origin, she would be very good-looking ; not that he cared for that style, and his manner indicated that such rosy, childish charms as were before him had his preference. But though this was evident enough to all the rest of the world, Phœbe did not appear to have the least perception of his personal meaning, and freely, simply answered, that she admired dark-eyed people, and should be glad to see Mrs. Charteris.

'You will see her in her glory,' said Owen ; 'Tuesday week, the great concern is to come off, at Castle Blanch, and a rare sight she'll be! Cilly tells me she is rehearsing her dresses with different sets of jewels all the morning, and for ever coming in to consult her and Rashe!'

'That must be rather tiresome,' said Honor; 'she cannot be much of a companion.'

'I don't fancy she gets much satisfaction,' said Owen, laughing; 'Rashe never uses much "soft sawder." It's an easy-going place, where you may do just as you choose, and the young ladies appreciate liberty. By the by, what do you think of this Irish scheme?'

Honora was so much ashamed of it, that she had never mentioned it even to Phœbe, and she was the more sorry that it had been thus adverted to, as she saw Robert intent on what Owen let fall. She answered shortly, that she could not suppose it serious.

'Serious as a churchyard,' was Owen's answer. 'I dare say they will ask Phœbe to join the party. For my own part, I never believed in it till I came up to-day, and found the place full of salmon-flies, and the start fixed for Wednesday the 24th.'

'Who?' came a voice from the dark mantelshelf.

'Who? Why, that's the best of it. Who but my wise sister and Rashe? Not a soul besides,' cried Owen, giving way to laughter, which no one was disposed to echo. 'They vow that they will fish all the best streams, and do more than any crack fisherman going, and they would like to see who will venture to warn them off. They've tried that already. Last summer, what did Lucy do, but go and fish Sir Harry Buller's water. You know he's a very tiger about preserving. Well, she fished coolly on in the face of all his keepers; they stood aghast, didn't know what manner of Nixie it was, I suppose; and when Sir Harry came down, foaming at the mouth, she just shook her curls, and made him wade in up to his knees to get her fly out of a bramble!'

'That must be exaggerated,' said Robert.

'Exaggerated! Not a word! It's not possible to

exaggerate Cilly's coolness. I did say something about going with them.'

'You must, if they go at all!' exclaimed Honora.

'Out of the question, Sweet Honey. They reject me with disdain, declare that I should only render them commonplace, and that "rich and rare were the gems she wore," would never have got across Ireland safe if she had a great strapping brother to hamper her. And really, as Charles says, I don't suppose any damage can well happen to them.'

Honora would not talk of it, and turned the conversation to what was to be done on the following day. Owen eagerly proffered himself as escort, and suggested all manner of plans, evidently assuming the entire direction and protection of the two ladies, who were to meet him at luncheon in Lowndes Square, and go with him to the Royal Academy, which, as he and Honora agreed, must necessarily be the earliest object, for the sake of providing innocent conversation.

As soon as the clock struck ten, Robert took leave, and Owen rose, but instead of going, lingered, talking Oxford with Mr. Parsons, and telling good stories, much to the ladies' amusement, though increasing Honora's trepidation by the fear that something in his tone about the authorities, or the slang of his manner, might not give her friends a very good idea of his set. The constant fear of what might come next, absolutely made her impatient for his departure, and at last she drove him away, by begging to know how he was going all that distance, and offering to send Henry to call a cab, a thing he was too good-natured to permit. He bade good night and departed, while Mr. Parsons, in answer to her eager eyes, gratified her by pronouncing him a very fine young man.

'He is very full of spirit,' she said. 'You must let me tell you a story of him. They have a young new schoolmistress at Wrapworth, his father's former living, you know, close to Castle Blanch. This poor thing was obliged to punish a schoolchild, the daughter of one of the bargemen on the Thames, a huge ruffianly man. Well, a day or two after, Owen came upon him in a narrow lane, bullying the poor girl almost out of her life, threatening her, and daring her to lay a finger on his children. What do you think Owen did?'

'Fought him, I suppose,' said Mr. Parsons, 'judging by the peculiar delight ladies take in such exploits. Besides, he has sufficiently the air of a hero to make it incumbent on him to "kill some giant."'

'We may be content with something short of his killing the giant,' said Honor, 'but he really did gain the victory. That lad, under nineteen, positively beat this great monster of a man, and made him ask the girl's pardon, knocked him down, and thoroughly mastered him! I should have known nothing of it, though, if Owen had not got a black eye, which made him unpresentable for the Castle Blanch gaieties, so he came down to the Holt to me, knowing I should not mind wounds gained in a good cause.'

They wished her good night in her triumph.

The receipt of a letter was rare and supreme felicity to Maria; therefore to indite one was Phœbe's first task on the morrow; after which she took up her book, and was deeply engaged, when the door flew back, and the voice of Owen Sandbrook exclaimed, 'Goddess of the silver bow! what, alone?'

'Miss Charlecote is with her lawyer, and Robert at the office.'

'The parson and parsoness parsonically gone to study parsonages, schools, and dilapidations, I suppose. What a bore it is having them here; I'd have taken up my quarters here, otherwise, but I can't stand parish politics.'

'I like them very much,' said Phœbe, 'and Miss Charlecote seems to be happy with them.'

'Just her cut, dear old thing; the same honest, illogical, practical sincerity,' said Owen, in a tone of somewhat superior melancholy; but seeing Phœbe about to resent his words as a disrespectful imputation on their friend, he turned the subject, addressing Phœbe in the manner between teasing and flattering, habitual to a big schoolboy towards a younger child, phases of existence which each had not so long outgrown as to have left off the mutual habits thereto belonging. 'And what is bright Cynthia doing? Writing verses, I declare!—worthy sister of Phœbus Apollo.'

'Only notes,' said Phœbe, relinquishing her paper, in testimony.

'When found make a note of—Summoned by writ —temp. Ed. III.—burgesses—knights of shire. It reads like an act of parliament. Hallam's English Constitution. My eyes! By way of lighter study. It is quite appalling. Pray what may be the occupation of your more serious moments?'

'You see the worst I have with me.'

'Holiday recreation, to which you can just condescend. I say, Phœbe, I have a great curiosity to understand the Zend. I wish you would explain it to me.'

'If I ever read it,' began Phœbe, laughing.

'What, you pretend to deny? You wont put me off that way. A lady who can only unbend so far as to the English Constitution by way of recreation, must——'

'But it is not by way of recreation.'

'Come, I know my respected cousin too well to imagine she would have imposed such a task. That wont do, Phœbe.'

'I never said she had, but Miss Fennimore desired me.'

'I shall appeal. There's no act of tyranny a woman in authority will not commit. But this is a free country, Phœbe, as may be you have gathered from your author, and unless her trammels have reached to your soul——' and he laid his hand on the book to take it away.

'Perhaps they have,' said Phœbe, smiling, but holding it fast, 'for I shall be much more comfortable in doing as I was told.'

'Indeed!' said Owen, pretending to scrutinize her as if she were something extraordinary (really as an excuse for a good gaze upon her pure complexion and limpid eyes, so steady, childlike, and unabashed, free from all such consciousness, as would make them shrink from the playful look). 'Indeed! Now, in my experience the comfort would be in the *not* doing as you were told.'

'Ah! but you know I have no spirit.'

'I wish to heaven other people had none!' cried Owen, suddenly changing his tone, and sitting down opposite to Phœbe, his elbow on the table, and speaking earnestly. 'I would give the world that my sister were like you. Did you ever hear of anything so preposterous as this Irish business?'

'She cannot think of it, when Miss Charlecote has told her of all the objections,' said Phœbe.

'She will go the more,' returned Owen; 'I say to you, Phœbe, what I would say to no one else. Lucilla's treatment of Honora Charlecote is abominable—vexes me more than I can say. They say some nations have no words for gratitude. One would think she had come of them.'

Phœbe looked much shocked, but said, 'Perhaps Miss Charlecote's kindness has seemed to her like a matter of course, not as it does to us, who have no claim at all.'

'We had no claim,' said Owen; 'the connexion is nothing, absolutely nothing. I believe, poor dear, the attraction was that she had once been attached to my father, and he was too popular a preacher to *keep* well as a lover. Well, there were we, a couple of orphans, a nuisance to all our kith and kin—nobody with a bit of mercy for us but that queer coon, Kit Charteris, when she takes us home, treats us like her own children, feels for us as much as the best mother living could; undertakes to provide for us. Now, I put it to you, Phœbe, has she any right to be cast off in this fashion?'

'I don't know in what fashion you mean.'

'Don't you. Haven't you seen how Cilly has run restive from babyhood? A pretty termagant she was, as even I can remember. And how my poor father spoilt her! Any one but Honor would have given her up, rather than have gone through what she did, so firmly and patiently, till she had broken her in fairly well. But then come in these Charterises, and Cilly runs frantic after them, her own *dear* relations. Much they had cared for us when we were troublesome little pests. But it's all the force of blood. Stuff! The whole truth is that they are gay, and Honora quiet; they encourage her to run riot. Honora keeps her in order.'

'Have you spoken to her?'

'As well speak to the wind. She thinks it a great favour to run down to Hiltonbury for the Horticultural Show, turn everything topsy-turvy, keep poor dear Sweet Honey in a perpetual ferment, then come away to Castle Blanch, as if she were rid of a troublesome duty.'

'I thought Miss Charlecote sent Lucy to enjoy herself? We always said how kind and self-denying she was.'

'Denied, rather,' said Owen; 'only that's her way of carrying it off. A month or two in the season might be very well; see the world, and get the tone of it; but to racket about with Ratia, and leave Honor alone for months together, is too strong for me.'

Honora came in, delighted at her boy's visit, and well pleased at the manner in which he was engrossed. Two such children needed no chaperon, and if that sweet crescent moon were to be his guiding light, so much the better.

'Capital girl, that,' he said, as she left the room. 'This is a noble achievement of yours.'

'In getting my youngest princess out of the castle. Ay! I do feel in a beneficent enchanter's position.'

'She has grown up much prettier than she promised to be.'

'And far too good for a Fulmort. But that is Robert's doing.'

'Poor Robert! how he shows the old distiller in grain. So he is taking to the old shop?—best thing for him.'

'Only by way of experiment.'

'Pleasant experiment to make as much as old Fulmort! I wish he'd take me into partnership.'

'You, Owen?'

'I am not proud. These aren't the days when it matters how a man gets his tin, so he knows what to do with it. Ay! the world gets beyond the dear old Hiltonbury views, after all, Sweet Honey, and you see what City atmosphere does to me.'

'You know I never wished to press any choice on you,' she faltered.

'What!' with a good-humoured air of affront, 'you thought me serious? Don't you know I'm the ninth, instead of the nineteenth-century man, under your wing? I'd promise you to be a bishop, only, you see, I'm afraid I couldn't be mediocre enough.'

'For shame, Owen!' and yet she smiled. That boy's presence and caressing sweetness towards herself were the greatest bliss to her, almost beyond that of a mother with a son, because more uncertain, less her right by nature.

Phœbe came down as the carriage was at the door, and they called in Whittington Street for her brother, but he only came out to say he was very busy, and would not intrude on Mrs. Charteris—bashfulness for which he was well abused on the way to Lowndes Square.

Owen, with his air of being at home, put aside the servants as they entered the magnificent house, replete with a display of state and luxury analogous to that of

Beauchamp, but with better taste and greater ease. The Fulmorts were in bondage to ostentation; the Charterises were lavish for their own enjoyment, and heedless alike of cost and of appearance.

The great drawing-room was crowded with furniture, and the splendid marqueterie tables and crimson ottomans were piled with a wild confusion of books, prints, periodicals, papers, and caricatures, heaped over ornaments and bijouterie, and beyond, at the doorway of a second room, even more miscellaneously filled, a small creature sprang to meet them, kissing Honora, and exclaiming, 'Here you are! Have you brought the pig's wool? Ah! but you've brought something else! No—what's become of that Redbreast?' as she embraced Phœbe.

'He was so busy that he could not come.'

'Ill-behaved bird; a whole month without coming near me.'

'Only a week,' said Phœbe, speaking less freely, as she perceived two strangers in the room, a gentleman in moustaches, who shook hands with Owen, and a lady, whom from her greeting to Miss Charlecote (for introductions were not the way of the house), she concluded to be the formidable Rashe, and therefore regarded with some curiosity.

Phœbe had expected her to be a large masculine woman, and was surprised at her dapper proportions and not ungraceful manner. Her face, neither handsome nor the reverse, was one that neither in features nor complexion revealed her age, and her voice was pitched to the tones of good society, so that but for a certain 'don't care' sound in her words, and a defiant freedom of address, Phœbe would have set down all she had heard as a mistake, in spite of the table covered with the brilliant appliances of fly-making, over which both she and Lucilla were engaged. It was at the period when ladies affected coats and waistcoats, and both cousins followed the fashion to the utmost; wearing tightly-fitting black coats, plain linen collars, and shirt-like under-sleeves, with black ties round the neck. Horatia was still in mourning for her mother, and wore a black skirt, but Lucilla's was of rich deep gentianella-coloured silk, and the buttons of her white vest were of beautiful coral. The want of drapery gave a harshness to Miss Charteris's appearance, but the little masculine affectations only rendered Lucy's miniature style of feminine beauty still more piquant. Less tall than many girls of fourteen, she was exquisitely formed; the close-fitting dress became her taper waist, the ivory fairness of the throat and hands shone out in their boyish setting, and the soft delicacy of feature and complexion were enhanced by the vivid sparkling of those porcelain blue eyes, under the long lashes, still so fair and glossy as to glisten in the light, like her profuse flaxen tresses, arranged in a cunning wilderness of plaits and natural ringlets. The great charm was the minuteness and refinement of the mould containing the energetic spirit that glanced in her eyes, quivered on her lips, and pervaded every movement of the elastic feet and hands, childlike in size, statuelike in symmetry, elfin in quickness and dexterity. 'Lucile la Fée,' she might well have been called, as she sat manipulating the gorgeous silk and feathers with an essential strength and firmness of hands such as could hardly have been expected from such small members, and producing such lovely specimens that nothing seemed wanting but a touch of her wand to endow them with life. It was fit fairy work, and be it farther known, that few women are capable of it; they seldom have sufficient accuracy of sustained attention and firmness of finger combined, to produce anything artistic or durable, and the accomplishment was therefore Lucilla's pride. Her cousin could prepare materials, but could not finish.

'Have you brought the pig's wool?' repeated Lucy, as they sat down. 'No? That *is* a cruel way of testifying. I can't find a scrap of that shade, though I've nearly broke my heart in the tackle-shops. Here's my last fragment, and this butcher will be a wreck for want of it.'

'Let me see,' quoth the gentleman, bending over with an air of intimacy.

'You may see,' returned Lucilla, 'but that will do no good. Owen got this at a little shop at Elverslope, and we can only conclude that the father of orange pigs is dead, for we've tried every maker, and can't hit off the tint.'

'I've seen it in a shop in the Strand,' he said, with an air of depreciation, such as set both ladies off with an ardour inexplicable to mere spectators, both vehemently defending the peculiarity of their favourite hue, and little personalities passing, exceedingly diverting apparently to both parties, but which vexed Honora and dismayed Phœbe by the coolness of the gentleman, and the ease with which he was treated by the ladies.

Luncheon was announced in the midst, and in the dining-room they found Mrs. Charteris, a dark, aquiline beauty, of highly-coloured complexion, such as permitted the glowing hues of dress and ornament in which she delighted, and large languid dark eyes of Oriental appearance.

In the scarlet and gold net confining her sable locks, her ponderous earrings, her massive chains and bracelets, and gorgeous silk, she was a splendid ornament at the head of the table; but she looked sleepily out from under her black-fringed eyelids, turned over the carving as a matter of course to Owen, and evidently regarded the two young ladies as bound to take all trouble off her hands in talking, arranging, or settling what she should do with herself or her carriage.

'Lolly shall take you there,' or 'Lolly shall call for that,' passed between the cousins without the smallest reference to Lolly herself (otherwise Eloïsa), who looked serenely indifferent through all the plans proposed for her, only once exerting her will sufficiently to say, 'Very well, Rashe, dear, you'll tell the coachman—

only don't forget that I must go to Storr and Mortimer's.'

Honora expressed a hope that Lucilla would come with her party to the Exhibition, and was not pleased that Mr. Calthorp exclaimed that there was another plan.

'No, no, Mr. Calthorp, I never said any such thing!'

'Miss Charteris, is not that a little too strong?'

'You told me of the Dorking,' cried Lucilla, 'and you said you would not miss the sight for anything; but I never said you should have it.'

Rashe meanwhile clapped her hands with exultation, and there was a regular clatter of eager voices—'I should like to know how you would get the hackles out of a suburban poultry fancier.'

'Out of him?—no, out of his best Dorking. Priced at 120*l.* last exhibition—two years old—wouldn't take 200*l.* for him now.'

'You don't mean that you've seen him?'

'Hurrah!' Lucilla opened a paper, and waved triumphantly five of the long tippet-plumes of chanticleer.

'You don't mean——'

'Mean! I more than mean! Didn't you tell us that you had been to see the old party on business, and had spied the hackles walking about in his yard?'

'And I had hoped to introduce you.'

'As if we needed that! No, no. Rashe and I started off at six o'clock this morning, to shake off the remains of the ball, rode down to Brompton, and did our work. No, it was not like the macaw business, I declare. The old gentleman held the bird for us himself, and I promised him a dried salmon.'

'Well, I had flattered myself—it was an unfair advantage, Miss Sandbrook.'

'Not in the least. Had you gone, it would have cast a general clumsiness over the whole transaction, and not left the worthy old owner half so well satisfied.

I believe you had so little originality as to expect to engage him in conversation while I captured the bird ; but once was enough of that.'

Phœbe could not help asking what was meant ; and it was explained that, while a call was being made on a certain old lady with a blue and yellow macaw, Lucilla had contrived to abstract the prime glory of the creature's tail—a blue feather lined with yellow— an irresistible charm to a fisherwoman. But here even the tranquil Eloïsa murmured that Cilly must never do so again when she went out with HER.

'No, Lolly, indeed I wont. I prefer honesty, I assure you, except when it is too commonplace. I'll meddle with nothing at Madame Sonnini's this afternoon.'

'Then you cannot come with us ?'

'Why, you see, Honor, here have Rashe and I been appointed band-masters, Lord Chamberlains, masters of the ceremonies, major-domos, and I don't know what, to all the Castle Blanch concern ; and as Rashe neither knows nor cares about music, I've got all that on my hands ; and I must take Lolly to look on while I manage the programme.'

'Are you too busy to find a day to spend with us at St. Wulstan's ?'

A discussion of engagements took place, apparently at the rate of five per day ; but Mrs. Charteris interposed an invitation to dinner for the next evening, including Robert; and farther, it appeared that all the three were expected to take part in the Castle Blanch festivities. Lolly had evidently been told of them as settled certainties among the guests, and Lucilla, Owen, and Rashe vied with each other in declaring that they had imagined Honor to have brought Phœbe to London with no other intent, and that all was fixed for the ladies to sleep at Castle Blanch the night before, and Robert Fulmort to come down in the morning by train.

Nothing could have been farther from Honora's

predilections than such gaieties, but Phœbe's eyes were growing round with eagerness, and there would be unkindness in denying her the pleasure, as well as churlishness in disappointing Lucy and Owen, who had reckoned on her in so gratifying a manner. Without decidedly accepting or refusing, she let the talk go on.

'Miss Fulmort,' said Ratia, 'I hope you are not too religious to dance.'

Much surprised, Phœbe made some reply in the negative.

'Oh, I forgot, that's not your sisters' line; but I thought....' and she gave an expressive glance to indicate Miss Charlecote.

'Oh, no,' again said Phœbe, decidedly.

'Yes, I understand. Never mind, I ought to have remembered; but when people are *gone in*, one is apt to forget whether they think "promiscuous dancing" immoral or praiseworthy. Well, you must know some of my brother's constituents are alarmingly excellent—fat, suburban, and retired; and we have hatched a juvenile hay-making, where they may eat and flirt without detriment to decided piety; and when they go off, we dress for a second instalment for an evening party.'

To Phœbe it sounded like opening Paradise, and she listened anxiously for the decision; but nothing appeared certain except the morrow's dinner, and that Lucilla was to come to spend the Sunday at Miss Charlecote's; and this being fixed, the luncheon party broke up, with such pretty bright affection on Lucilla's part, such merry coaxing of Honor, and such orders to Phœbe to 'catch that Robin to-morrow,' that there was no room left for the sense of disappointment that no rational word had passed.

'Where?' asked Owen, getting into the carriage.

'Henry knows—the Royal Academy.'

'Ha! no alteration in consequence of the invitation? no finery required? you must not carry Hiltonbury philosophy *too* far.'

'I have not accepted it.'

'That is not required; it is your fate, Phœbe; why don't you speak, or are you under an embargo from any of the wicked enchanters? Even if so, you might be got off among the pious juveniles.'

'Papa was so kind as to say I might go wherever Miss Charlecote liked,' said Phœbe; 'but, indeed, I had rather do exactly what suits her; I dare say the morning party will suit her best——'

'The oily popular preachers!'

'Thank you, Owen,' laughed Honor.

'No, now you must accept the whole. There's room to give the preachers a wide berth, even should they insist on "concluding with prayer," and it will be a pretty sight. They have the Guards' band coming.'

'I never heard a military band,' ejaculated Phœbe.

'And there are to be sports for the village children, I believe,' added Owen; 'besides, you will like to meet some of the lions—the Archdeacon and his wife will be there.'

'But how can I think of filling up Mrs. Charteris's house, without the least acquaintance?'

'Honey-sweet philosopher, Eloïsa heeds as little how her house is filled, so it *be* filled, as Jessica did her father's ring. Five dresses a-day, with accoutrements to match, and for the rest she is sublimely indifferent. Fortune played her a cruel trick in preventing her from being born a fair sultana.'

'Not to be a Mahometan?' said Phœbe.

'I don't imagine she is far removed from one;' then, as Phœbe's horror made her look like Maria, he added —'I don't mean that she was not bred a Christian, but the Oriental mind never distinctly embraces tenets contrary to its constitution.'

'Miss Charlecote, is he talking in earnest?'

'I hope not,' Honora said, a little severely, 'for he would be giving a grievous account of the poor lady's faith——'

'Faith! no, my dear, she has not reflection enough for faith. All that enters into the Eastern female mind is a little observance.'

'And you are not going to lead Phœbe to believe that you think it indifferent whether those observances be Christian or Pagan?' said Honora, earnestly.

There was a little pause, and then Owen rather hesitatingly said—'It is a hard thing to pronounce that three-fifths of one's fellow-creatures are on the high road to Erebus, especially when ethnologically we find that certain aspects of doctrine never have approved themselves to certain races, and that climate is stronger than creed. Am I not talking Fennimorically, Phœbe?'

'Much more Fennimorically than I wish her to hear, or you to speak,' said Honora; 'you talk as if there were no such thing as truth.'

'Ah! now comes the question of subjective and objective, and I was as innocent as possible of any intention of plunging into such a sea, or bringing those furrows into your forehead, dear Honor! See what it is to talk to you and Miss Fennimore's pupil. All things, human and divine, have arisen out of my simple endeavour to show you that you must come to Castle Blanch, the planners of the feast having so ordained, and it being good for all parties, due from the fairy godmother to the third princess, and seriously giving Cilly another chance of returning within the bounds of discretion.'

Honora thought as much. She hoped that Robert would by that time have assumed his right to plead with Lucilla, and that in such a case she should be a welcome refuge, and Phœbe still more indispensable; so her lips opened in a yielding smile, and Phœbe thanked her rapturously, vague hopes of Robert's bliss adding zest to the anticipation of the lifting of the curtain which hid the world of brightness.

'There's still time,' said Owen, with his hand on

the check-string; 'which do you patronize? Redmayne or——'

'Nonsense,' smiled Honor, 'we can't waste our escort upon women's work.'

'Ladies never want a gentleman more than when their taste is to be directed.'

'He is afraid to trust us, Phœbe.'

'Conscience has spoken,' said Owen; 'she knows how she would go and disguise herself in an old dowager's gown to try to look like sixty!'

'As for silk gowns——'

'I positively forbid it,' he cried, cutting her short, 'it is five years old!'

'A reason why I should not have another too grand to wear out.'

'And you never ought to have had it. Phœbe, it was bought when Lucy was seventeen, on purpose to look as if she was of a fit age for a wall-flower, and so well has the poor thing done its duty, that Lucy hears herself designated as the pretty girl who belongs to the violet and white! If she had known *that* was coming after her, I wont answer for the consequence.'

'If it *does* annoy Lucy—we do not so often go out together——don't Owen, I never said it was to be now, I am bent on Landseer.'

'But I said so,' returned Owen, 'for Miss Charlecote regards the distressed dress-makers—four dresses—think of the fingers that must ache over them.'

'Well, he does what he pleases,' sighed Honor; 'there's no help for it, you see, Phœbe. Shall you dislike looking on?' For she doubted whether Phœbe had been provided with means for her equipment, and might not require delay and correspondence, but the frank answer was, 'Thank you, I shall be glad of the opportunity. Papa told me I might fit myself out in case of need.'

'And suppose we are too late for the Exhibition.'

'I never bought a dress before,' quoth Phœbe.

Owen laughed. 'That's right, Phœbe! Be strong-minded and original enough to own that some decorations surpass " Raffaelles, Correggios, and stuff "——'

'No,' said Phœbe, simply, and with no affectation of scorn, 'they only interest me more at this moment.'

Honor smiled to Owen her love for the honesty that never spoke for effect, nor took what it believed it ought to feel, for what it really felt. Withal, Owen gained his purpose, and conducted the two ladies into one of the great shops of ladies' apparel.

Phœbe followed Miss Charlecote with eyes of lively anticipation. Miss Fennimore had taught her to be *real* when she could not be philosophical, and scruples as to the 'vain pomp and glory of the world,' had not presented themselves; she only found herself admitted to privileges hitherto so jealously withheld as to endow them with a factitious value, and in a scene of real beauty. The textures, patterns, and tints were, as Owen observed, such as approved themselves to the æsthetic sense, the miniature embroidery of the brocades was absolute art, and no contemptible taste was displayed in the apparently fortuitous yet really elaborate groupings of rich and delicate hues, fine folds, or ponderous draperies.

'Far from it,' said Honor; 'the only doubt is whether such be a worthy application of æsthetics. Were they not given us for better uses?'

'To diffuse the widest amount of happiness?'

'That is one purpose.'

'And a fair woman well dressed is the sight most delightful to the greatest number of beholders.'

Honor made a playful face of utter repudiation of the maxim, but meeting him on his own ground emphasized 'FAIR and WELL dressed — that is, appropriately.'

'That is what brings me here,' said Owen, turning round, as the changeful silks, already asked for, were laid on the counter before them.

It was an amusing shopping. The gentleman's

object was to direct the taste of both ladies, but his success was not the same. Honora's first affections fell upon a handsome black, enlivened by beautiful blue flowers in the flounces; but her tyrant scouted it as 'a dingy dowager,' and overruled her into choosing a delicate lavender, insisting that if it were less durable, so much the better for her friends, and domineering over the black lace accompaniments with a solemn tenderness that made her warn him in a whisper that people were taking her for his ancient bride, thus making him some degrees more drolly attentive; settling her headgear with the lady of the shop, without reference to her! After all, it was very charming to be so affectionately made a fool of, and it was better for her children as well as due to the house of Charlecote that she should not be a dowdy country cousin.

Meantime, Phœbe stood by amused, admiring, assisting, but not at all bewildered. Miss Fennimore had impressed the maxim : 'Always know what you mean to do, and do it.' She had never chosen a dress before, but that did not hinder her from having a mind and knowing it; she had a reply for each silk that Owen suggested, and the moment her turn came, she desired to see a green glacé. In vain he exclaimed, and drew his favourites in front of her, in vain appealed to Miss Charlecote and the shopman; she laughed him off, took but a moment to reject each proffered green which did not please her, and in as brief a space had recognised the true delicate pale tint of ocean. It was one that few complexions could have borne, but their connoisseur, with one glance from it to her fresh cheek, owned her right, though much depended on the garniture, and he again brought forward his beloved lilac, insinuating that he should regard her selection of it as a personal attention. No; she laughed, and said she had made up her mind and would not change; and while he was presiding over Honora's black lace, she was beforehand with him, and her bill was being made out for her white muslin worked mantle, white

bonnet with a tuft of lady grass, white evening dress
and wreath of lilies of the valley.

'Green and white, forsaken quite,' was the best
revenge that occurred to him, and Miss Charlecote
declared herself ashamed that the old lady's dress had
caused so much more fuss than the young lady's.

It was of course too late for the Exhibition, so they
applied themselves to further shopping, until Owen
had come to the farthest point whence he could con-
veniently walk back to dine with his cousins, and go
with them to the opera, and he expended some
vituperation upon Ratia for an invitation which had
prevented Phœbe from being asked to join the party.

Phœbe was happy enough without it, and though
not morbidly bashful, felt that at present it was more
comfortable to be under Miss Charlecote's wing than
that of Lucilla, and that the quiet evening was more
composing than fresh scenes of novelty.

The Woolstone Lane world was truly very different
from that of which she had had a glimpse, and quite as
new to her. Mr. Parsons, after his partial survey,
was considering of possibilities, or more truly of en-
deavours at impossibilities, a mission to that dreadful
population, means of discovering their sick, of reclaim-
ing their children, of causing the true Light to shine
in that frightful gross darkness that covered the people.
She had never heard anything yet discussed save on
the principle of self-pleasing or self-aggrandizement;
here, self-spending was the axiom on which all the pro-
blems were worked.

After dinner, Mr. Parsons retired into the study,
and while his wife and Miss Charlecote sat down for a
friendly gossip over the marriages of the two daughters,
Phœbe welcomed an unrestrained *tête-à-tête* with her
brother. They were one on either seat of the old
oriel window, she, with her work on her lap, full of
pleasant things to tell him, but pausing as she looked
up, and saw his eyes far far away, as he knelt on the

cushion, his elbows on the sill of the open lattice, one hand supporting his chin, the other slowly erecting his hair into the likeness of the fretful porcupine. He had heard of, but barely assented to, the morrow's dinner, or the *fête* at Castle Blanch; he had not even asked her how Lucilla looked; and after waiting for some time, she said, as a feeler—' You go with us to-morrow ?'

'I suppose I must.'

' Lucy said so much in her pretty way about catching the robin, that I am sure she was vexed at your not having called.'

No answer : his eyes had not come home.

Presently he mumbled something so much distorted by the compression of his chin, and by his face being out of window, that his sister could not make it out. In answer to her sound of inquiry, he took down one hand, removed the other from his temple, and emitting a modicum more voice from between his teeth, said, ' It is plain—it can't be——'

' What can't be ? Not—Lucy ?' gasped Phœbe.

' I can't take shares in the business.'

Her look of relief moved him to explain, and drawing himself in, he sat down on his own window-seat, stretching a leg across, and resting one foot upon that where she was placed, so as to form a sort of barrier, shutting themselves into a sense of privacy.

' I can't do it,' he repeated, ' not if my bread depended on it.'

' What is the matter ?'

' I have looked into the books, I have gone over it with Rawlins.'

' You don't mean that we are going to be ruined ?'

' Better that we were than to go on as we do! Phœbe, it is wickedness.' There was a long pause. Robert rested his brow on his hand, Phœbe gazed intently at him, trying to unravel the idea so suddenly presented. She had reasoned it out before he looked up, and she roused him by softly saying, 'You mean that you do not like the manufacture of spirits because they produce so much evil.'

Though he did not raise his head, she understood his affirmation, and went on with her quiet logic, for, poor girl, hers was not the happy maiden's defence—'What my father does cannot be wrong.' Without condemning her father, she instinctively knew that weapon was not in her armoury, and could only betake herself to the merits of the case. 'You know how much rather I would see you a clergyman, dear Robin,' she said; 'but I do not understand why you change your mind. We always knew that spirits were improperly used, but that is no reason why none should be made, and they are often necessary.'

'Yes,' he answered; 'but, Phœbe, I have learnt to-day that our trade is not supported by the lawful use of spirits. It is the ministry of hell.'

Phœbe raised her startled eyes in astonished inquiry.

'I would have credited nothing short of the books, but there I find that not above a fifth part of our manufacture goes to respectable houses, where it is applied properly. The profitable traffic, which it is the object to extend, is the supply of the gin palaces of the city. The leases of most of those you see about here belong to the firm, it supplies them, and gains enormously on their receipts. It is to extend the dealings in this way that my legacy is demanded.'

The enormity only gradually beginning to dawn upon Phœbe, all she said was a meditative—'You would not like that.'

'You did not realize it,' he said, nettled at her quiet tone. 'Do not you understand? You and I, and all of us, have eaten and drunk, been taught more than we could learn, lived in a fine house, and been made into ladies and gentlemen, all by battening on the vice and misery of this wretched population. Those unhappy men and women are lured into the gaudy palaces at the corners of the streets to purchase a moment's oblivion of conscience, by stinting their children of bread, that we may wear fine clothes, and call ourselves county people.'

'Do not talk so, Robert,' she exclaimed, trembling; 'it cannot be right to say such things——'

'It is only the bare fact! it is no pleasure to me to accuse my own father, I assure you, Phœbe, but I cannot blind myself to the simple truth.'

'He cannot see it in that light.'

'He *will* not.'

'Surely,' faltered Phœbe, 'it cannot be so bad when one does not know it is——'

'So far true. The conscience does not waken quickly to evils with which our lives have been long familiar.'

'And Mervyn was brought up to it——'

'That is not my concern,' said Robert, too much in the tone of 'Am I my brother's keeper?'

'You will at least tell your reasons for refusing.'

'Yes, and much I shall be heeded! However, my own hands shall be pure from the wages of iniquity. I am thankful that all I have comes from the Mervyns.'

'It is a comfort, at least, that you see your way.'

'I suppose it is;' but he sighed heavily, with a sense that it was almost profanation to have set such a profession in the balance against the sacred ministry.

'I know *she* will like it best.'

Dear Phœbe! in spite of Miss Fennimore, faith must still have been much stronger than reason if she could detect the model parsoness in yonder firefly.

Poor child, she went to bed, pondering over her brother's terrible discoveries, and feeling as though she had suddenly awakened to find herself implicated in a web of iniquity; her delightful parcel of purchases lost their charms, and oppressed her as she thought of them in connexion with the rags of the squalid children the Rector had described, and she felt as if there were no escape, and she could never be happy again under the knowledge of the price of her luxuries, and the dread of judgment. 'Much good had their wealth done them,' as Robert truly said. The house of Beauchamp had never been nearly so happy as if their means had been moderate. Always paying court to their own station, or they were disunited among themselves, and not yet amalgamated with the society to which they had attained, the younger ones passing their elders in cultivation, and every discomfort of change of position felt, though not acknowledged. Even the mother, lady as she was by birth, had only belonged to the second-rate class of gentry, and while elevated by wealth, was lowered by connexion, and not having either mind or strength enough to stand on her own ground, trod with an ill-assured foot on that to which she aspired.

Not that all this crossed Phœbe's mind. There was merely a dreary sense of depression, and of living in the midst of a grievous mistake, from which Robert alone had the power of disentangling himself, and she fell asleep sadly enough; but, fortunately, sins, committed neither by ourselves, nor by those for whom we are responsible, have not a lasting power of paining; and she rose up in due time to her own calm sunshiny spirit of anticipation of the evening's meeting between Robin and Lucy—to say nothing of her own first dinner party.

CHAPTER IV.

And instead of 'dearest Miss,'
Jewel, honey, sweetheart, bliss,
And those forms of old admiring,
Call her cockatrice and siren.
     C. LAMB.

HE ladies of the house were going to a ball, and were in full costume : Eloïsa a study for the Arabian Nights, and Lucilla in an azure gossamer-like texture surrounding her like a cloud, turquoises on her arms, and blue and silver ribbons mingled with her blonde tresses.

Very like the clergyman's wife !

O sage Honor, were you not provoked with yourself for being so old as to regard that bewitching sprite, and marvel whence comes the cost of those robes of the woof of Faerie ?

Let Oberon pay Titania's bills.

That must depend on who Oberon is to be.

Phœbe, to whom a doubt on that score would have appeared high treason, nevertheless hated the presence of Mr. Calthorp as much as she could hate anything, and was in restless anxiety as to Titania's behaviour. She herself had no cause to complain, for she was at once singled out and led away from Miss Charlecote, to be shown some photographic performances, in which Lucy and her cousin had been dabbling.

'There, that horrid monster is Owen—he never will come out respectable. Mr. Prendergast, he is better, because you don't see his face. There's our school, Edna Murrell and all ; I flatter myself that *is* a work of art ; only this little wretch fidgeted, and muddled himself.'

'Is that the mistress ? She does not look like one.'

'Not like Sally Page ? No; she would bewilder the Hiltonbury mind. I mean you to see her ; I would not miss the shock to Honor. No, don't show it to her! I wont have any preparation.'

'Do you call that preparation ?' said Owen, coming up, and taking up the photograph indignantly. 'You should not do such things, Cilly!'

'Tisn't I that do them—it's Phœbe's brother—the one in the sky I mean, Dan Phœbus, and if he wont flatter, I can't help it. No, no, I'll not have it broken; it is an exact likeness of all the children's spotted frocks, and if it be not of Edna, it ought to be.'

'Look, Robert,' said Phœbe, as she saw him standing shy, grave, and monumental, with nervous hands clasped over the back of a chair, neither advancing nor retreating, 'what a beautiful place this is!'

'Oh! that's from a print—Glendalough! I mean to bring you plenty of the real place.'

'Kathleen's Cave,' said the unwelcome millionaire.

'Yes, with a comment on Kathleen's awkwardness! I should like to see the hermit who could push me down.'

'You! You'll never tread in Kathleen's steps!'

'Because I shan't find a hermit in the cave.'

'Talk of skylarking on "the lake whose gloomy shore!"' They all laughed except the two Fulmorts.

'There's a simpler reason,' said one of the Guardsmen, 'namely, that neither party will be there at all.'

'No, not the saint——'

'Nor the lady. Miss Charteris tells me all the maiden aunts are come up from the country.' (How angry Phœbe was!)

'Happily, it is an article I don't possess.'

'Well, we will not differ about technicalities, as long as the fact is the same. You'll remember my words when

you are kept on a diet of Hannah More and Miss
Edgeworth till you shall have abjured hounds, balls,
and salmon-flies.'

'The woman lives not who has the power!'

'What bet will you take, Miss Sandbrook?'

'What bet will you take, Lord William, that, maiden
aunts and all, I appear on the 3rd, in a dress of salmon-
flies?'

'A hat trimmed with goose feathers to a pocket-
handkerchief, that by that time you are in the family
mansion, repenting of your sins.'

Phœbe looked on like one in a dream, while the terms
of the wager were arranged with playful precision.
She did not know that dinner had been announced, till
she found people moving, and in spite of her antipathy
to Mr. Calthorp, she rejoiced to find him assigned to
herself—dear, good Lucy must have done it to keep
Robin to herself, and dear, good Lucy she shall be, in
spite of the salmon, since in the progress downstairs
she has cleared the cloud from his brow.

It was done by a confiding, caressing clasp on his arm,
and the few words, 'Now for old friends! How
charming little Phœbe looks!'

How different were his massive brow and deep-set
eyes without their usual load, and how sweet his gratified smile!

'Where have you been, you Robin? If I had not
passed you in the Park, I should never have guessed
there was such a bird in London. I began to change
my mind, like Christiana—"I thought Robins were
harmless and gentle birds, wont to hop about men's
doors, and feed on crumbs, and such like harmless food."'

'And have you seen me eating worms?'

'I've not seen you at all.'

'I did not think you had leisure—I did not believe
I should be welcome.'

'The cruellest cut of all; positive irony——'

'No, indeed! I am not so conceited as——'

'As what?'

'As to suppose you could want me.'

'And there was I longing to hear about Phœbe! If you had only come, I could have contrived her going to the *Zauberflote* with us last night, but I didn't know the length of her tether.'

'I did not know you were so kind.'

'Be kinder yourself another time. Don't I know how I have been torn to pieces at Hiltonbury, without a friend to say one word for the poor little morsel!' she said piteously.

He was impelled to an eager 'No, no!' but recalling facts, he modified his reply into, 'Friends enough, but very anxious!'

'There, I knew none of you trusted me,' she said, pretending to pout.

'When play is so like earnest——'

'Slow people are taken in! That's the fun! I like to show that I can walk alone sometimes, and not be snatched up the moment I pop my head from under my leading-strings.'

Her pretty gay toss of the head prevented Robert from thinking whether woman is meant to be without leading-strings.

'And it was to avoid countenancing my vagaries that you stayed away?' she said, with a look of injured innocence.

'I was very much occupied,' answered Robert, feeling himself in the wrong.

'That horrid office! You aren't thinking of becoming a Clarence, to drown yourself in brandy—that would never do.'

'No, I have given up all thoughts of that!'

'You *thought*, you wretched Redbreast! I *thought* you knew better.'

'So I ought,' said Robert, gravely, 'but my father wished me to make the experiment, and I must own, that before I looked into the details, there were considerations which—which——'

'Such considerations as £ s. d.? For shame!'

'For shame, indeed,' said the happy Robert. 'Phœbe judged you truly. I did not know what might be the effect of habit——' and he became embarrassed, doubtful whether she would accept the assumption on which he spoke; but she went beyond his hopes.

'The only place I ever cared for is a very small old parsonage,' she said, with feeling in her tone.

'Wrapworth? that is near Castle Blanch.'

'Yes! I must show it you. You shall come with Honor and Phœbe on Monday, and I will show you everything.'

'I should be delighted—but is it not arranged?'

'I'll take care of that. Mr. Prendergast shall take you in, as he would a newly arrived rhinoceros, if I told him. He was our curate, and used to live in the house even in our time. Don't say a word, Robin, it is to be. I must have you see my river, and the stile where my father used to sit when he was tired. I've never told any one which that is.'

Ordinarily Lucilla never seemed to think of her father, never named him, and her outpouring was doubly prized by Robert, whose listening face drew her on.

'I was too much of a child to understand how fearfully weak he must have been, for he could not come home from the castle without a rest on that stile, and we used to play round him, and bring him flowers. My best recollections are all of that last summer—it seems like my whole life at home, and much longer than it could really have been. We were all in all to one another. How different it would have been if he had lived! I think no one has believed in me since.'

There was something ineffably soft and sad in the last words, as the beautiful, petted, but still lonely orphan, cast down her eyelids with a low long sigh, as though owning her errors, but pleading this extenuation. Robert, much moved, was murmuring something incoherent, but she went on. 'Rashe does, perhaps. Can't you see how it is a part of the general disbelief in me to suppose that I come here only for London seasons, and such like? I must live where I have what the dear old soul there has not got to give.'

'You cannot doubt of her affection. I am sure there is nothing she would not do for you.'

"'Do!' that is not what I want. It can't be done, it must be *felt*, and that it never will be. When there's a mutual antagonism, gratitude becomes a fetter, intolerable when it is strained.'

'I cannot bear to hear you talk so; revering Miss Charlecote as I do, and feeling that I owe everything to her notice.'

'Oh, I find no fault, I reverence her too! It was only the nature of things, not her intentions, nor her kindness, that was to blame. She meant to be justice and mercy combined towards us, but I had all the one, and Owen all the other. Not that I am jealous! Oh, no! Not that she could help it; but no woman can help being hard on her rival's daughter.'

Nothing but the sweet tone and sad arch smile could have made this speech endurable to Robert, even though he remembered many times when the trembling of the scale in Miss Charlecote's hands had filled him with indignation. 'You allow that it was justice,' he said, smiling.

'No doubt of that,' she laughed. 'Poor Honor! I must have been a grievous visitation, but I am very good now; I shall come and spend Sunday as gravely as a judge, and when you come to Wrapworth, you shall see how I can go to the school when it is not forced down my throat—no merit either, for our mistress is perfectly charming, with *such* a voice! If I were Phœbe I would look out, for Owen is desperately smitten.'

'Phœbe!' repeated Robert, with a startled look.

'Owen and Phœbe! I considered it *une affaire arrangée* as much as——' She had almost said you and me: Robert could supply the omission, but he was only blind of *one* eye, and gravely said, 'It is well there is plenty of time before Owen to tame him down.'

'Oney,' laughed Lucilla; 'yes, he has a good deal to do in that line, with his opinions in such a mess that I really don't know what he does believe.'

Though the information was not new to Robert, her levity dismayed him, and he gravely began, 'If you have such fears—' but she cut him off short.

'Did you ever play at bagatelle?'

He stared in displeased surprise.

'Did you never see the ball go joggling about before it could settle into its hole, and yet abiding there very steadily at last? Look on quietly, and you will see the poor fellow as sober a parish priest as yourself.'

'You are a very philosophical spectator of the process,' Robert said, still displeased.

'Just consider what a capacious swallow the poor boy had in his tender infancy, and how hard it was crammed with legends, hymns, and allegories, with so many scruples bound down on his poor little conscience that no wonder, when the time of expansion came, the whole concern should give way with a jerk.'

'I thought Miss Charlecote's education had been most anxiously admirable.'

'Precisely so! Don't you see? Why, how dull you are for a man who has been to Oxford!'

'I should seriously be glad to hear your view, for Owen's course has always been inexplicable to me.'

'To you, poor Robin, who lived gratefully on the crumbs of our advantages! The point was that to you they were crumbs, while we had a surfeit.'

'Owen never seemed overdone. I used rather to hate him for his faultlessness, and his familiarity with what awed my ignorance.'

'The worse for him! He was too apt a scholar, and received all unresisting, unsifting—Anglo-Catholicism, slightly touched with sentiment, enthusiasm for the Crusades, passive obedience—acted faithfully up to it; imagined that to be 'not a good Churchman,' as he told Charles, expressed the seven deadly sins, and that reasoning was the deadliest of all!'

'As far as I understand you, you mean that there was not sufficient distinction between proven and non-proven—important and unimportant.'

'You begin to perceive. If Faith be overworked, Reason kicks; and, of course, when Owen found the Holt was not the world; that thinking was not the exclusive privilege of demons; that habits he considered as imperative duties were inconvenient, not to say impracticable; that his articles of faith included much of the apocryphal,—why, there was a general downfall!'

'Poor Miss Charlecote,' sighed Robert, 'it is a disheartening effect of so much care.'

'She should have let him alone, then, for Uncle Kit to make a sailor of. Then he would have had something better to do than to *think!*'

'Then you are distressed about him?' said Robin, wistfully.

'Thank you,' said she, laughing; 'but you see I am too wise ever to think or distress myself. He'll think himself straight in time, and begin a reconstruction from his scattered materials, I suppose, and meantime he is a very comfortable brother, as such things go; but it is one of the grudges I can't help owing to Honora, that such a fine fellow as that is not an independent sailor or soldier, able to have some fun, and not looked on as a mere dangler after the Holt.'

'I thought the reverse was clearly understood?'

'She ought to have 'acted as sich.' How my relatives, and yours too, would laugh if you told them so! Not that I think, like them, that it is Elizabethan dislike to naming a successor, nor to keep him on his good behaviour; she is far above that, but it is plain how it will be. The only other relation she knows in the world is farther off than we are—not a bit more of a Charlecote, and twice her age; and when she has waited twenty or thirty years longer for the auburn-haired lady my father saw in a chapel at Toronto, she will bethink herself that Owen, or Owen's eldest son, had better have it than the Queen. That's the sense of it; but I hate the hanger-on position it keeps him in.'

'It is a misfortune,' said Robert. 'People treat him as a man of expectations, and at his age it would not be easy to disown them, even to himself. He has an eldest son air about him, which makes people impose on him the belief that he is one; and yet, who could have guarded against the notion more carefully than Miss Charlecote?'

'I'm of Uncle Kit's mind,' said Lucilla, 'that children should be left to their natural guardians. What! is Lolly really moving before I have softened down the edge of my ingratitude?'

'So!' said Miss Charteris, as she brought up the rear of the procession of ladies on the stairs.

Lucilla faced about on the step above, with a face where interrogation was mingled with merry defiance.

'So that is why the Calthorp could not get a word all the livelong dinner-time!'

'Ah! I used you ill; I promised you an opportunity of studying 'Cock Robin,' but you see I could not help keeping him myself—I had not seen him for so long.'

'You were very welcome! It is the very creature that baffles me. I can talk to any animal in the world except an incipient parson.'

'Owen, for instance?'

'Oh! if people choose to put a force on nature, there can be no general rules. But, Cilly, you know I've always said you should marry whoever you liked; but I require another assurance—on your word and honour —that you are not irrevocably Jenny Wren as yet!'

'Did you not see the currant wine?' said Cilly, pulling leaves off a myrtle in a tub on the stairs, and scattering them over her cousin.

'Seriously, Cilly! Ah, I see now—your exclusive attention to him entirely reassures me. You would never have served him so, if you had meant it.'

'It was commonplace in me,' said Lucilla, gravely, 'but I could not help it; he made me feel so good— or so bad—that I believe I shall——'

'Not give up the salmon,' cried Horatia. 'Cilly, you will drive me to commit matrimony on the spot.'

'Do,' said Lucilla, running lightly up, and dancing into the drawing-room, where the ladies were so much at their ease, on low couches and ottomans, that Phœbe stood transfixed by the novelty of a drawing-room treated with such freedom as was seldom permitted in even the schoolroom at Beauchamp, when Miss Fennimore was in presence.

'Phœbe, bright Phœbe!' cried Lucilla, pouncing on both her hands, and drawing her towards the other room, 'it is ten ages since I saw you, and you must bring your taste to aid my choice of the fly costume. Did you hear, Rashe? I've a bet with Lord William that I appear at the ball all in flies. Isn't it fun?'

'Oh, jolly!' cried Horatia. 'Make yourself a pike-fly.'

'No, no; not a guy for any one. Only wear a trimming of salmon-flies, which will be lovely.'

'You do not really mean it?' said Phœbe.

'Mean it? With all my heart, in spite of the tremendous sacrifice of good flies. Where honour is concerned——'

'There, I knew you would not shirk.'

'Did I ever say so?'—in a whisper, not unheard by Phœbe, and affording her so much satisfaction that she only said, in a grave, puzzled voice, 'The hooks?'

'Hooks and all,' was the answer. 'I do nothing by halves.'

'What a state of mind the fishermen will be in!' proceeded Horatia. 'You'll have every one of them at your feet.'

'I shall tell them that two of a trade never agree.

Come, and let us choose.' And opening a drawer, Lucilla took out her long parchment book, and was soon eloquent on the merits of the doctor, the butcher, the duchess, and all her other radiant fabrications of gold pheasants' feathers, parrot plumes, jays' wings, and the like. Phœbe could not help admiring their beauty, though she was perplexed all the while, uncomfortable on Robert's account, and yet not enough assured of the usages of the London world to be certain whether this were unsuitable. The Charteris family, though not of the most *élite* circles of all, were in one to which the Fulmorts had barely the *entrée*, and the ease and dash of the young ladies, Lucilla's superior age, and caressing patronage, all made Phœbe in her own eyes too young and ignorant to pass an opinion. She would have known more about the properties of a rectangle or the dangers of a paper currency.

Longing to know what Miss Charlecote thought, she stood, answering as little as possible, until Rashe had been summoned to the party in the outer room, and Cilly said, laughing, 'Well, does she astonish your infant mind?'

'I do not quite enter into her,' said Phœbe, doubtfully.

'The best-natured, and most unappreciated girl in the world. Up to anything, and only a victim to prejudice. You, who have a strong-minded governess, ought to be superior to the delusion that it is interesting to be stupid and helpless.'

'I never thought so,' said Phœbe, feeling for a moment in the wrong, as Lucilla always managed to make her antagonists do.

'Yes, you do, or why look at me in that pleading, perplexed fashion, save that you have become possessed with the general prejudice. Weigh it, by the light of Whately's logic, and own candidly wherefore Rashe and I should be more liable to come to grief, travelling alone, than two men of the same ages.'

'I have not grounds enough to judge,' said Phœbe,

beginning as though Miss Fennimore were giving an exercise to her reasoning powers; then, continuing with her girlish eagerness of entreaty; 'I only know that it cannot be right, since it grieves Robin and Miss Charlecote so much.'

'And all that grieves Robin and Miss Charlecote must be shocking, eh? Oh, Phœbe, what very women all the Miss Fennimores in the world leave us, and how lucky it is!'

'But I don't think you are going to grieve them,' said Phœbe, earnestly.

'I hate the word!' said Lucilla. 'Plaguing is only fun, but grieving, that is serious.'

'I do believe this is only plaguing!' cried Phœbe, 'and that this is your way of disposing of all the flies. I shall tell Robin so!'

'To spoil all my fun,' exclaimed Lucilla. 'No, indeed!'

Phœbe only gave a nod and smile of supreme satisfaction.

'Ah! but Phœbe, if I'm to grieve nobody, what's to become of poor Rashe, you little selfish woman?'

'Selfish, no?' sturdily said Phœbe. 'If it be wrong for you, it must be equally wrong for her; and perhaps,' she added, slowly, 'you would both be glad of some good reason for giving it up. Lucy, dear, do tell me whether you really like it, for I cannot fancy you do.'

'Like it? Well, yes! I like the salmons, and I dote on the fun and the fuss. I say, Phœbe, can you bear the burden of a secret? Well—only mind, if you tell Robin or Honor, I shall certainly go; we never would have taken it up in earnest if such a rout had not been made about it, that we were driven to show we did not care, and could be trusted with ourselves.'

'Then you don't mean it?'

'That's as people behave themselves. Hush! Here comes Honor. Look here, Sweet Honey, I am in a process of selection. I am pledged to come out at the ball in a unique trimming of salmon-flies.'

'My dear!' cried poor Honor, in consternation, 'you can't be so absurd.'

'It is so slow not to be absurd.'

'At fit times, yes; but to make yourself so conspicuous!'

'They say I can't help that,' returned Lucy, in a tone of comical melancholy.

'Well, my dear, we will talk it over on Sunday, when I hope you may be in a rational mood.'

'Don't say so,' implored Lucilla, 'or I shan't have the courage to come. A rational mood! It is enough to frighten one away; and really I do want very much to come. I've not heard a word yet about the Holt. How is the old dame, this summer?'

And Lucy went on with unceasing interest about all Hiltonbury matters, great and small, bewitching Honora more than would have seemed possible under the circumstances. She was such a winning fairy that it was hardly possible to treat her seriously, or to recollect causes of displeasure, when under the spell of her caressing vivacity, and unruffled, audacious fun.

So impregnable was her gracious good-humour, so untameable her high spirits, that it was only by remembering the little spitfire of twelve or fourteen years ago that it was credible that she had a temper at all; the temper erst wont to exhale in chamois bounds and dervish pirouettes, had apparently left not a trace behind, and the sullen ungraciousness to those who offended her had become the sunniest sweetness, impossible to disturb. Was it real improvement? Concealment it was not, for Lucilla had always been transparently true. Was it not more probably connected with that strange levity, almost insensibility, that had apparently indurated feelings which in early childhood had seemed sensitive even to the extent of violence. Was she only good-humoured because nothing touched her? Had that agony of parting with her gentle father seared her affections, till she had become like a polished gem, all bright glancing beauty, but utterly unfeeling?

CHAPTER V.

Reproof falleth on the saucy as water.
                              FEEJEE PROVERB.

ONSIDERATE of the slender purses of her children, Honora had devoted her carriage to fetch them to St. Wulstan's on the Sunday morning, but her offer had been declined, on the ground that the Charteris conveyances were free to them, and that it was better to make use of an establishment to which Sunday was no object, than to cloud the honest face of the Hiltonbury coachman by depriving his horses of their day of rest. Owen would far rather take a cab than so affront Grey! Pleased with his bright manner, Honora had yet reason to fear that expense was too indifferent to both brother and sister, and that the Charteris household only encouraged recklessness. Wherever she went, she heard of the extravagance of the family, and in the shops the most costly wares were recommended as the choice of Mrs. Charteris. Formerly, though Honor had equipped Lucilla handsomely for visits to Castle Blanch, she had always found her wardrobe increased by the gifts of her uncle and aunt. The girl had been of age more than a year, and in the present state of the family, it was impossible that her dress could be still provided at their expense, yet it was manifestly far beyond her means, and what could be the result? She would certainly brook no in-

terference, and would cast advice to the winds. Poor Honor could only hope for a crash that would bring her to reason, and devise schemes for forcing her from the effects of her own imprudence without breaking into her small portion. The great fear was lest false pride, and Charteris influence, should lead her to pay her debts at the cost of a marriage with the millionaire; and Honor could take little comfort in Owen's assurance that the Calthorp had too much sense to think of Cilly Sandbrook, and only promoted and watched her vagaries for the sake of amusement and curiosity. There was small satisfaction to her wellwishers in hearing that no sensible man could think seriously of her.

Anxiously was that Sunday awaited in Woolstone Lane, the whole party feeling that this was the best chance of seeing Lucilla in a reasonable light, and coming to an understanding with her. Owen was often enough visible in the interim, and always extremely agreeable; but Lucilla never, and he only brought an account of her gaieties, shrugging his shoulders over them.

The day came; the bells began, they chimed, they changed, but still no Sandbrooks appeared. Mr. Parsons set off, and Robert made an excursion to the corner of the street. In vain Miss Charlecote still lingered; Mrs. Parsons, in despair, called Phœbe on with her as the single bell rang, and Honor and Robert presently started with heads turned over their shoulders, and lips laying all blame on Charteris' delays of breakfast. A last wistful look, and the church porch engulfed them; but even when enclosed in the polished square pew, they could not resign hope at every tread on the matted floor, and finally subsided into a trust that the truants might after service emerge from a seat near the door. There were only too many to choose from.

That hope baffled, Honora still manufactured excuses which Phœbe greedily seized and offered to her brother, but she read his rejection of them in his face, and to her conviction that it was all accident, he answered, as she took his arm, 'A small accident would suffice for Sandbrook.'

'You don't think he is hindering his sister!'

'I can't tell. I only know that he is one of the many stumbling-blocks in her way. He can do no good to any one with whom he associates intimately. I hate to see him reading poetry with you.'

'Why did you never tell me so!' asked the startled Phœbe.

'You are so much taken up with him that I can never get at you, when I am not devoured by that office.'

'I am sure I did not know it,' humbly answered Phœbe. 'He is very kind and amusing, and Miss Charlecote is so fond of him that, of course, we must be together; but I never meant to neglect you, Robin, dear.'

'No, no, nonsense, it is no paltry jealousy; only now I can speak to you, I must,' said Robert, who had been in vain craving for this opportunity of getting his sister alone, ever since the alarm excited by Lucilla's words.

'What is this harm, Robin?'

'Say not a word of it. Miss Charlecote's heart must not be broken before its time, and at any rate it shall not come through me."

'What, Robert?'

'The knowledge of what he is. Don't say it is prejudice. I know I never liked him, but you shall hear why. You ought now——'

Robert's mind had often of late glanced back to the childish days when, with their present opinions reversed, he thought Owen a muff, and Owen thought him a reprobate. To his own blunt and reserved nature, the expressions, so charming to poor Miss Charlecote, had been painfully distasteful. Sentiment, profession, obtrusive reverence, and fault-finding scruples had revolted him, even when he thought it a proof of his own irreligion to be provoked. Afterwards, when both were schoolboys, Robert had yearly increased in conscientiousness under good discipline and training, but, in their holiday meetings, had found Owen's standard receding as his own advanced, and heard the once-deficient manly spirit asserted by boasts of exploits and deceptions repugnant to a well-conditioned lad. He saw Miss Charlecote's perfect confidence abused and trifled with, and the more he grew in a sense of honour, the more he disliked Owen Sandbrook.

At the University, where Robert's career had been respectable and commonplace, Owen was at once a man of mark. Mental and physical powers alike rendered him foremost among his compeers; he could compete with the fast, and surpass the slow on their own ground; and his talents, ready celerity, good-humoured audacity, and quick resource, had always borne him through with the authorities, though there was scarcely an excess or irregularity in which he was not a partaker; and stories of Sandbrook's daring were always circulating among the under-graduates. But though Robert could have scared Phœbe with many a history of lawless pranks, yet these were not his chief cause for dreading Owen's intimacy with her. It was that he was one of the youths on whom the spirit of the day had most influence, one of the most adventurous thinkers and boldest talkers: wild in habits, not merely from ebullition of spirits, but from want of faith in the restraining power.

All this Robert briefly expressed in the words, 'Phœbe, it is not that his habits are irregular and unsteady; many are so whose hearts are sound. But he is not sound—his opinions are loose, and he only respects and patronizes Divine Truth as what has approved itself to so many good, great, and beloved human creatures. It is not denial—it is patronage. It is the common-sense heresy——'

'I thought we all ought to learn common sense.'

'Yes, in things human, but in things Divine it is the subtle English form of rationalism. This is no time to explain, Phœbe; but human sense and intellect are made the test, and what surpasses them is only admired as long as its stringent rules do not fetter the practice.'

'I am sorry you told me,' said Phœbe, thoughtfully, 'for I always liked him; he is so kind to me.'

Had not Robert been full of his own troubles he would have been reassured, but he only gave a contemptuous groan.

'Does Lucy know this?' she asked.

'She told me herself what I well knew before. She does not reflect enough to take it seriously, and contrives to lay the blame upon the narrowness of Miss Charlecote's training.'

'Oh, Robin! When all our best knowledge came from the Holt!'

'She says, perhaps not unjustly, that Miss Charlecote overdid things with him, and that this is reaction. She observes keenly. If she would only *think!* She would have been perfect had her father lived, to work on her by affection.'

'The time for that is coming——'

Robert checked her, saying, 'Stay, Phœbe. The other night I was fooled by her engaging ways, but each day since I have become more convinced that I must learn whether she be only using me like the rest. I want you to be a witness of my resolution, lest I should be tempted to fail. I came to town, hesitating whether to enter the business for her sake. I found that this could not be done without a great sin. I look on myself as dedicated to the ministry, and thus bound to have a household suited to my vocation. All must turn on her willingness to conform to this standard. I shall lay it before her. I can bear the suspense no longer. My temper and resolution are going, and I am good for nothing. Let the touchstone be, whether she will resign her expedition to Ireland,

and go quietly home with Miss Charlecote. If she will so do, there is surely that within her that will shine out brighter when removed from irritation on the one side, or folly on the other. If she will not, I have no weight with her; and it is due to the service I am to undertake, to force myself away from a pursuit that could only distract me. I have no right to be a clergyman and choose a hindrance not a help—one whose tastes would lead back to the world, instead of to my work!'

As he spoke, in stern, rigid resolution—only allowing himself one long, deep, heavy sigh at the end—he stood still at the gates of the court, which were opened as the rest of the party came up; and, as they crossed and entered the hall, they beheld, through the open door of the drawing-room, two figures in the window—one, a dark torso, perched outside on the sill; the other, in blue skirt and boy-like bodice, negligently reposing on one side of the window-seat, her dainty little boots on the other; her coarse straw bonnet, crossed with white, upon the floor; the wind playing tricks with the silky glory of her flaxen ringlets; her cheek flushed with lovely carnation, declining on her shoulder; her eyes veiled by their fair fringes.

'Hallo!' she cried, springing up, 'almost caught asleep!' And Owen, pocketing his pipe, spun his legs over the window-sill, while both began, in rattling, playful vindication and recrimination—

'It wasn't my fault { he wouldn't.'
{ she wouldn't.'

'Indeed, I wasn't a wilful heathen; Mr. Parsons, it was he——'

'It was she who chose to take the by-ways, and make us late. Rush into church before a whole congregation, reeking from a six miles' walk! I've more respect for the Establishment.'

'You walked!' cried five voices.

'See her Sabbatarianism!'

'Nonsense! I should have driven Charlie's cab.'

'Charlie has some common sense where his horse is concerned.'

'He wanted it himself, you *know*.'

'She grew sulky, and victimized me to a walk.'

'I'm sure it was excellent fun.'

'Ay, and because poor Calthorp had proffered his cab for her to drive to Jericho, and welcome, she drags me into all sorts of streets of villanous savours, that he might not catch us up.'

'Horrid hard mouth that horse of his,' said Lucilla, by way of dashing the satisfaction on Miss Charlecote's face.

'I do not wonder you were late.'

'Oh! that was all Owen's doing. He vowed that he had not nerve to face the pew-opener!'

'The grim female in weeds—no, indeed!' said Owen. 'Indeed, I objected to entering in the guise of flaming meteors, both on reverential and sanatory grounds.'

'Insanatory, methinks,' said Miss Charlecote; 'how could you let her sleep, so much heated, in this thorough draught?'

'Don't flatter yourself,' said Cilly, quaintly shaking her head; 'I'm not such a goose as to go and catch cold! Oh! Phœbe, my salmon-flies are loveliness itself; and I hereby give notice, that a fine of three pairs of thick boots has been proclaimed for every pun upon sisters of the angle and sisters of the angels! So beware, Robin!'—and the comical audacity with which she turned on him, won a smile from the grave lips that had lately seemed so remote from all peril of complimenting her whimsies.

Even Mr. Parsons said 'the fun was tempting.'

'Come and get ready for luncheon,' said the less fascinated Honora, moving away.

'Come and catch it!' cried the elf, skipping upstairs before her, and facing round her 'Dear old Honeyseed.' 'I honour your motives; but wouldn't it be for the convenience of all parties, if you took *Punch's* celebrated advice—" don't"?'

'How am I to speak, Lucy,' said Honora, 'if you come with the avowed intention of disregarding what I say ?'

'Then hadn't you better not,' murmured the girl, in the lowest tone, drooping her head, and peeping under her eyelashes, as she sat with a hand on each elbow of her arm-chair, as though in the stocks.

'I would not, my child,' was the mournful answer, 'if I could help caring for you.'

Lucilla sprang up and kissed her. 'Don't, then ; I don't like anybody to be sorry,' she said. 'I'm sure I'm not worth it.'

'How can I help it, when I see you throwing away happiness—welfare—the good opinion of all your friends?'

'My dear Honora, you taught me yourself not to mind Mrs. Grundy ! Come, never mind, the reasonable world has found out that women are less dependent than they used to be.'

'It is not what the world thinks, but what is really decorous.'

Lucilla laughed—though with some temper—'I wonder what we are going to do otherwise !'

'You are going beyond the ordinary restraints of women in your station ; and a person who does so, can never tell to what she may expose herself. Liberties are taken when people come out to meet them.'

'That's as they choose !' cried Lucilla, with such a gesture of her hand, such a flash of her blue eyes, that she seemed trebly the woman, and it would have been boldness indeed to presume with her.

'Yes ; but a person who has even had to protect herself from incivility, to which she has wilfully exposed herself, does not remain what she might be behind her screen.'

'*Omne ignotum pro terribili*,' laughed Lucilla, still not to be made serious. 'Now, I don't believe that the world is so flagrantly bent on annoying every pretty girl. People call me vain, but I never was so vain as that. I've always found them very civil; and Ireland is the land of civility. Now, seriously, my good cousin Honor, do you candidly expect any harm to befal us?'

'I do not think you likely to meet with absolute injury.' Lucilla clapped her hands, and cried, 'An admission, an admission! I told Rashe you were a sincere woman.' But Miss Charlecote went on, 'But there is harm to yourself in the affectation of masculine habits; it is a blunting of the delicacy suited to a Christian maiden, and not like the women whom St. Paul and St. Peter describe. You would find that you had forfeited the esteem—not only of ordinary society—but of persons whose opinion you do value; and in both these respects you would suffer harm. You, my poor child, who have no one to control you, or claim your obedience as a right, are doubly bound to be circumspect. I have no power over you; but if you have any regard for her to whom your father confided you—nay, if you consult what you know would have been his wishes—you will give up this project.'

The luncheon-bell had already rung, and consideration for the busy clergyman compelled her to go down with these last words, feeling as if there were a leaden weight at her heart.

Lucilla remained standing before the glass, arranging her wind-tossed hair; and, in her vehemence, tearing out combfuls, as she pulled petulantly against the tangled curls. 'Her old way—to come over me with my father! Ha!—I love him too well, to let him be Miss Charlecote's engine for managing me!—her *dernier ressort* to play on my feelings. Nor will I have Robin set at me! Whether I go or not, shall be as I please, not as any one else does; and if I stay at home, Rashe shall own it is not for the sake of the conclave here. I told her she might trust me.'

Down she went, and at luncheon devoted herself to the captivation of Mr. Parsons; afterwards insisting on going to the schools—she, whose aversion to them was Honora's vexation at home. Strangers to make a sensation were contrary to the views of the Parsonses; but the wife found her husband inconsistent—'one lady, more or less, could make no difference on this first Sunday;' and, by and by, Mrs. Parsons found a set of little formal white-capped faces, so beaming with entertainment at the young lady's stories, and the young lady herself looking so charming, that she, too, fell under the enchantment.

After church, Miss Charlecote proposed a few turns in the garden; dingy enough, but a marvel for the situation: and here the tacit object of herself and Phœbe was to afford Robert an opportunity for the interview on which so much depended. But it was like trying to catch a butterfly; Lucilla was here, there, everywhere; and an excuse was hardly made for leaving her beside the grave, silent young man, ere her merry tones were heard chattering to some one else. Perhaps Robert, heart-sick and oppressed with the importance of what trembled on his tongue, was not ready in seizing the moment; perhaps she would not let him speak; at any rate, she was aware of some design; since, baffling Phœbe's last attempt, she danced up to her bedroom after her, and throwing herself into a chair, in a paroxysm of laughter, cried, 'You abominable little pussycat of a manœuvrer; I thought you were in a better school for the proprieties! No, don't make your round eyes, and look so dismayed, or you'll kill me with laughing! Cooking *tête-à-têtes*, Phœbe—I thought better of you. Oh, fie!' and holding up her finger, as if in displeasure, she hid her face in ecstasies of mirth at Phœbe's bewildered simplicity.

'Robert wanted to speak to you,' she said, with puzzled gravity.

'And you would have set us together by the ears! No, no, thank you, I've had enough of that sort of thing for one day. And what shallow excuses. Oh! what fun to hear your pretexts. Wanting to see what

Mrs. Parsons was doing, when you knew perfectly well she was deep in a sermon, and wished you at the antipodes. And blushing all the time, like a full-blown poppy,' and off she went on a fresh score—but Phœbe, though disconcerted for a moment, was not to be put out of countenance when she understood her ground, and she continued with earnestness, undesired by her companion—' Very likely I managed badly, but I know you do not really think it improper to see Robert alone, and it is very important that you should do so. Indeed it is, Lucy,' she added—the youthful candour and seriousness of her pleading, in strong contrast to the flighty, mocking carelessness of Lucilla's manners; 'do pray see him; I know he would make you listen. Will you be so very kind! If you would go into the little cedar room, I could call him at once.'

'Point blank! Sitting in my cedar parlour! Phœbe, you'll be the death of me,' cried Cilly, between peals of merriment. 'Do you think I have nerves of brass?'

'You would not laugh, if you knew how much he feels.'

'A very good thing for people to feel! It saves them from torpor.'

'Lucy, it is not kind to laugh when I tell you he is miserable.'

'That's only proper, my dear,' said Lucilla, entertained by teasing.

'Not miserable from doubt,' answered Phœbe, disconcerting in her turn. 'We know you too well for that;' and as an expression, amused, indignant, but far from favourable, came over the fair face she was watching, she added in haste, 'It is this project, he thought you had said it was given up.'

'I am much indebted,' said Lucilla, haughtily, but again relapsing into laughter; 'but to find myself so easily disposed of.....Oh! Phœbe, there's no scolding such a baby as you; but if it were not so absurd——'

'Lucy, Lucy, I beg your pardon; is it all a mistake,

or have I said what was wrong? Poor Robin will be so unhappy.'

Phœbe's distress touched Lucilla.

'Nonsense, you little goose; aren't you woman enough yet to know that one flashes out at finding oneself labelled, and made over before one's time.'

'I'm glad if it was all my blundering,' said Phœbe. 'Dear Lucy, I was very wrong, but you see I always was so happy in believing it was understood!'

'How stupid,' cried Lucilla; 'one would never have any fun; no, you haven't tasted the sweets yet, or you would know one has no notion of being made sure of till one chooses! Yes, yes, I saw he was primed and cocked, but I'm not going to let him go off.'

'Lucy, have you no pity?'

'Not a bit! Don't talk commonplaces, my dear."

'If you knew how much depends upon it.'

'My dear, I know that,' with an arch smile.

'No, you do not,' said Phœbe, so stoutly that Lucilla looked at her in some suspense.

'You think,' said honest Phœbe, in her extremity, 'that he only wants to make——to propose to you! Now, it is not only that, Lucilla,' and her voice sank, as she could hardly keep from crying; 'he will never do that if you go on as you are doing now; he does not think it would be right for a clergyman.'

'Oh, I dare say!' quoth Lucilla, and then a silence. 'Did Honor tell him so, Phœbe?'

'Never, never!' cried Phœbe; 'no one has said a word against you! only don't you know how quiet and good any one belonging to a clergyman should be?"

'Well, I've heard a great deal of news to-day, and it is all my own fault, for indulging in sentiment on Wednesday. I shall know better another time.'

'Then you don't care!' cried Phœbe, turning round, with eyes flashing as Lucilla did not know they could lighten. 'Very well! If you don't think Robert worth it, I suppose I ought not to grieve, for you can't be what I used to think you; and it will be better for him when he once has settled his mind—than if—if afterwards you disappointed him and were a fine lady—but oh! he will be so unhappy,' her tears were coming fast; 'and, Lucy, I did like you so much!'

'Well, this is the funniest thing of all,' cried Lucilla, by way of braving her own emotion; 'little Miss Phœbe gone into the heroics!' and she caught her two hands, and holding her fast, kissed her on both cheeks; 'a gone coon, am I, Phœbe, no better than one of the wicked; and Robin, he grew angry, hopped upon a twig, did he! I beg your pardon, my dear, but it makes me laugh to think of his dignified settling of his mind. Oh! how soon it could be unsettled again! Come, I wont have any more of this; let it alone, Phœbe, and trust me that things will adjust themselves all the better for letting them have their swing. Don't you look prematurely uneasy, and don't go and make Robin think that I have immolated him at the altar of the salmon. Say nothing of all this; you will only make a mess in narrating it."

'Very likely I may,' said Phœbe; 'but if you will not speak to him yourself, I shall tell him how you feel.'

'If you can,' laughed Lucilla.

'I mean, how you receive what I have told you of his views; I do not think it would be fair or kind to keep him in ignorance.'

'Much good may it do him,' said Lucy; 'but I fancy you will tell him, whether I give you leave or not, and it can't make much difference. I'll tackle him, as the old women say, when I please, and the madder he may choose to go, the better fun it will be.'

'I believe you are saying so to tease me,' said Phœbe; 'but as I know you don't mean it, I shall wait till after the party; and then, unless you have had it out with him, I shall tell him what you have said.'

'Thank you,' said Lucilla, ironically, conveying to Phœbe's mind the conviction that she did not believe that Robert's attachment could suffer from what had here passed. Either she meant to grant the decisive interview, or else she was too confident in her own power to believe that he could relinquish her; at all events, Phœbe had sagacity enough to infer that she was not indifferent to him, though, as the provoking damsel ran down-stairs, Phœbe's loyal spirit first admitted a doubt whether the tricksy sprite might not prove as great a torment as a delight to Robin. 'However,' reflected she, 'I shall make the less mischief, if I set it down while I remember it.'

Not much like romance, but practical sense was both native and cultivated in Miss Fennimore's pupil. Yet as she recorded the sentences, and read them over bereft of the speaker's caressing grace, she blamed herself as unkind, and making the worst of gay retorts which had been provoked by her own home thrusts. 'At least,' she thought, 'he will be glad to see that it was partly my fault, and he need never see it at all if Lucy will let him speak to her himself.'

Meantime, Honora had found from Owen that the young ladies had accepted an invitation to a very gay house in Cheshire, so that their movements would for a fortnight remain doubtful. She recurred to her view that the only measure to be taken was for him to follow them, so as to be able to interpose in any emergency, and she anxiously pressed on him the funds required.

'Shouldn't I catch it if they found me out?' said Owen, shrugging his shoulders. 'No, but indeed, sweet Honey, I meant to have made up for this naughty girl's desertion. You and I would have had such rides and readings together : I want you to put me on good terms with myself.'

'My dear boy! But wont that best be done by minding your sister? She does want it, Owen; the less she will be prudent for herself, the more we must think for her!'

'She can do better for herself than you imagine,' said Owen. 'Men say, with all her free ways, they could not go the least bit farther with her than she pleases. You wouldn't suppose it, but she can keep out of scrapes better than Rashe can—never has been in one yet, and Rashe in twenty. Never mind, your Honor, there's sound stuff in the bonny scapegrace; all the better for being free and unconventional. The world owes a great deal to those who dare to act for themselves; though, I own, it is a trial when one's own domestic womankind take thereto.'

'Or one's mankind to encouraging it,' said Honor, smiling, but showing that she was hurt.

'I don't encourage it; I am only too wise to give it the zest of opposition. Was Lucy ever bent upon a naughty trick without being doubly incited by the pleasure of showing that she cared not for her younger brother?'

'I believe you are only too lazy! But, will you go? I don't think it can be a penance. You would see new country, and get plenty of sport.'

'Come with me, Honey,' said he, with the most insinuating manner, which almost moved her. 'How jolly it would be!'

'Nonsense! an elderly spinster,' she said, really pleased, though knowing it impossible.

'Stuff!' he returned, in the same tone. 'Make it as good as a honeymoon. Think of Killarney, Honor!'

'You silly boy, I can't. There's harvest at home; besides, it would only aggravate that mad girl doubly to have me coming after her.'

'Well, if you will not take care of me on a literal wild goose chase,' said Owen, with playful disconsolateness, 'I'll not answer for the consequences.'

'But, you go?'

'Vacation rambles are too tempting to be resisted; but, mind, I don't promise to act good genius save at the last extremity, or else I shall never get forgiven, and I shall keep some way in the rear.'

So closed the consultation; and after an evening which Lucilla perforce rendered lively, she and her brother took their leave. The next day they were to accompany the Charterises to Castle Blanch to prepare for the festivities : Honor and her two young friends following on the Wednesday afternoon.

CHAPTER VI.

> He who sits by haunted well
> Is subject to the Nixie's spell;
> He who walks on lonely beach
> To the mermaid's charmed speech;
> He who walks round ring of green
> Offends the peevish Fairy Queen.—SCOTT.

AT the station nearest to Castle Blanch stood the tall form of Owen Sandbrook, telling Honor that he and his sister had brought the boat; the river was the longer way, but they would prefer it to the road; and so indeed they did, for Phœbe herself had had enough of the City to appreciate the cool verdure and calm stillness of the meadow pathway, by which they descended to the majestic river, smoothly sleeping in glassy quiet, or stealing along in complacently dimpling ripples.

On the opposite bank, shading off the sun, an oak copse sloped steeply towards the river, painting upon the surface a still shimmering likeness of the summit of the wood, every mass of foliage, every blushing spray receiving a perfect counterpart, and full in the midst of the magic mirror floated what might have been compared to the roseate queen lily of the waters on her leaf.

There, in the flat, shallow boat reclined the maiden, leaning over the gunwale, gazing into the summer wavelets with which one bare pinkly-tinted hand was toying, and her silken ringlets all but dipping in, from beneath the round black hat, archly looped up on one side by a carnation bow, and encircled by a series of the twin jetty curls of the mallard; while the fresh rose colour of the spreading muslin dress was enhanced by the black scarf that hung carelessly over it. There was a moment's pause, as if no one could break the spell; but Owen, striding on from behind, quickly dissolved the enchantment.

'You monkey, you've cast off. You may float on to Greenwich next!' he indignantly shouted.

She started, shaking her head saucily. ''Twas so slow there, and so broiling,' she called back, 'and I knew I should only drift down to meet you, and could put in when I pleased.'

Therewith she took the sculls and began rowing towards the bank, but without force sufficient to prevent herself from being borne farther down than she intended.

'I can't help it,' she exclaimed, fearlessly laughing as she passed them.

'Robert was ready to plunge in to stem her progress, lest she should meet with some perilous eddy, but Owen laid hold on him, saying, 'Don't be nervous, she's all right; only giving trouble, after the nature of women. There; are you satisfied?' he called to her, as she came to a stop against a reed bed, with a tall fence interposed between boat and passengers. 'A nice ferrywoman you.'

'Come and get me up again,' was all her answer.

'Serve you right if I never picked you up till London-bridge,' he answered. 'Stand clear, Fulmort,' and with a run and a bound, he vaulted over the high hedge, and went crackling through the nodding bulrushes and reed-maces; while Lucy, having accomplished pulling up one of the latter, was pointing it lancewise at him, singing,

With a bulrush for his spear, and a thimble for a hat,
Wilt thou fight a traverse with the castle cat.

'Come, come; 'tis too squashy here for larking,' he said, authoritatively, stepping into the boat, and bringing it up with such absence of effort that when a few minutes after he had brought it to the landing-place, and the freight was seated, Robert had no sooner taken the other oar than he exclaimed at the force of the stream with which Owen had dealt so easily, and Lucilla so coolly.

'It really was a fearful risk,' he said reproachfully to her.

'Oh!' she said; 'I know my Thames, and my Thames knows me!'

'Now's the time to improve it,' said Owen; 'one or other should preach about young ladies getting loose, and not knowing where they may be brought up.'

'But you see I did know; besides, Phœbe's news from Paris will be better worth hearing,' said Lucilla, tickling her friend's face with the soft long point of her dark velvety mace.

'My news from Paris?'

'For shame, Phœbe! Your face betrays you.'

'Lucy; how could you know? I had not even told Miss Charlecote!'

'It's true! it's true!' cried Lucilla. 'That's just what I wanted to know!'

'Lucy, then it was not fair,' said Phœbe, much discomposed. 'I was desired to tell no one, and you should not have betrayed me into doing so.'

'Phœbe, you always were a green oasis in a wicked world!'

'And now, let me hear,' said Miss Charlecote. 'I can't flatter you, Phœbe; I thought you were labouring under a suppressed secret.'

'Only since this morning,' pleaded Phœbe, earnestly; 'and we were expressly forbidden to mention it; I cannot imagine how Lucy knows.'

'By telegraph!'

Phœbe's face assumed an expression of immeasurable wonder.

'I almost hope to find you at cross purposes, after all,' said Honora.

'No such good luck,' laughed Lucilla. 'Cinderella's seniors never could go off two at a time. Ah! there's the name, I beg your pardon, Phœbe.'

'But, Lucy, what can you mean? Who can have telegraphed about Augusta?'

'Ah! you knew not the important interests involved, nor Augusta how much depended on her keeping the worthy admiral in play. It was the nearest thing— had she only consented at the end of the evening instead of the beginning, poor Lord William would have had the five guineas that he wants so much more than Mr. Calthorp.'

'Lucy!'

'It was a bet that Sir Nicholas would take six calendar months to supply the place of Lady Bannerman. It was the very last day. If Augusta had only waited till twelve!'

'You don't mean that he has been married before. I thought he was such an excellent man!' said Phœbe, in a voice that set others besides Lucilla off into irresistible mirth.

'Once, twice, thrice!' cried Lucilla. 'Catch her, Honor, before she sinks into the river in disgust with this treacherous world.'

'Do you know him, Lucy?' earnestly said Phœbe.

'Yes, and two of the wives; we used to visit them because he was an old captain of Uncle Kit's.'

'I would not believe in number three, Phœbe, if I were you,' said Owen, consolingly; 'she wants confirmation.'

'Two are as bad as three,' sighed Phœbe; 'and Augusta did not even call him a widower.'

'Cupid bandaged! It was a case of love at first sight. Met at the *Trois Frères Provençaux*, heard each other's critical remarks, sought an introduction, compared notes; he discovered her foresight with regard to pale ale; each felt that here was a kindred soul!'

'That could not have been telegraphed!' said Phœbe, recovering spirit and incredulity.

'No; the telegraph was simply 'Bannerman, Fulmort. 8.30 p.m., July 10th.' The other particulars followed by letter this morning.'

'How old is he?' asked Phœbe, with resignation.

'Any age above sixty. What, Phœbe, taking it to heart? I was prepared with congratulations. It is only second best, to be sure; but don't you see your own emancipation?'

'I believe that had never occurred to Phœbe,' said Owen.

'I beg your pardon, Lucy,' said Phœbe, thinking that she had appeared out of temper; 'only it had sounded so nice in Augusta's letter, and she was so kind, and somehow it jars that there should have been that sort of talk.'

Cilly was checked. In her utter want of thought it had not occurred to her that Augusta Fulmort could be other than a laughing-stock, or that any bright anticipations could have been spent by any reasonable person on her marriage. Perhaps the companionship of Rashe, and the satirical outspoken tone of her associates, had somewhat blunted her perception of what might be offensive to the sensitive delicacy of a young sister; but she instantly perceived her mistake, and the carnation deepened in her cheek, at having distressed Phœbe, and.... Not that she had deigned any notice of Robert after the first cold shake of the hand, and he sat rowing with vigorous strokes, and a countenance of set gravity, more as if he were a boatman than one of the party; Lucilla could not even meet his eye when she peeped under her eyelashes to recover defiance by the sight of his displeasure.

It was a relief to all when Honora exclaimed, 'Wrapworth! how pretty it looks.'

It was, indeed, pretty, seen through the archway of the handsome stone bridge. The church tower and picturesque village were set off by the frame that closed them in ; and though they lost somewhat of the enchantment when the boat shot from under the arch, they were still a fair and goodly English scene.

Lucilla steered towards the steps leading to a smooth shaven lawn, shaded by a weeping willow, well known to Honor.

'Here we land you and your bag, Robert,' said Owen, as he put in. 'Cilly, have a little sense, do.'

But Lucilla, to the alarm of all, was already on her feet, skipped like a chamois to the steps, and flew dancing up the sward. Ere Owen and Robert had helped the other two ladies to land in a more rational manner, she was shaking her mischievous head at a window, and thrusting in her sceptral reed-mace.

'Neighbour, oh, neighbour, I'm come to torment you! Yes, here we are in full force, ladies and all, and you must come out and behave pretty. Never mind your slippers; you ought to be proud of the only thing I ever worked. Come out, I say; here's your guest, and you must be civil to him.'

'I am very glad to see Mr. Fulmort,' said Mr. Prendergast, his only answer in words to all this, though while it was going on, as if she were pulling him by wires, as she imperiously waved her bulrush, he had stuck his pen into the inkstand, run his fingers in desperation through his hair, risen from his seat, gazed about in vain for his boots, and felt as fruitlessly on the back of the door for a coat to replace the loose alpaca article that hung on his shoulders.

'There. You've gone through all the motions,' said Cilly, 'that'll do ; now, come out and receive them.'

Accordingly, he issued from the door, shy and slouching ; rusty where he wore cloth, shiny where he wore alpaca, wild as to his hair, gay as to his feet, but, withal, the scholarly gentleman complete, and not a day older or younger, apparently, then when Honor had last seen him, nine years since, in bondage then to the child playing at coquetry, as now to the coquette playing at childhood. It was curious, Honor thought, to see how, though so much more uncouth and negligent than Robert, the indefinable signs of good blood made themselves visible, while they were wanting in one as truly the Christian gentleman in spirit and in education.

Mr. Prendergast bowed to Miss Charlecote, and shook hands with his guest, welcoming him kindly; but the two shy men grew more bashful by contact, and Honor found herself, Owen, and Lucilla sustaining the chief of the conversation, the curate apparently looking to the young lady to protect him and do the honours, as she did by making him pull down a cluster of his roses for her companions, and conducting them to eat his strawberries, which she treated as her own, flitting, butterfly like, over the beds, selecting the largest and ruddiest specimens, while her slave plodded diligently to fill cabbage-leaves, and present them to the party in due gradation.

Owen stood by amused, and silencing the scruples of his companions.

'He is in Elysium,' he said; 'he had rather be plagued by Cilly than receive a mitre! Don't hinder him, Honey; it is his pride to treat us as if we were at home and he our guest.'

'Wrapworth has not been seen without Edna Murrell,' said Lucilla, flinging the stem of her last strawberry at her brother, 'and Miss Charlecote is a woman of schools. What, aren't we to go, Mr. Prendergast?'

'I beg your pardon. I did not know.'

'Well; what is it?'

'I do sometimes wish Miss Murrell were not such an attraction.'

'You did not think that of yourself.'

'Well, I don't know; Miss Murrell is a very nice young woman,' he hesitated, as Cilly seemed about to thrust him through with her reed; 'but couldn't you, Cilla, now, give her a hint that it would be better if she would associate more with Mrs. Jenkyns, and——'

'Couldn't, Mr. Prendergast; I've more regard for

doing as I would be done by. When you see Edna, Honor——'

'They are very respectable women,' said the curate, standing his ground; 'and it would be much better for her than letting it be said she gives herself airs.'

'That's all because we have had her up to the castle to sing.'

'Well, so it is, I believe. They do say, too—I don't know whether it is so—that the work has not been so well attended to, nor the children so orderly.'

'Spite, spite, Mr. Prendergast; I had a better opinion of you than to think you could be taken in by the tongues of Wrapworth.'

'Well, certainly I did hear a great noise the other day.'

'I see how it is! This is a systematic attempt to destroy the impression I wished to produce.'

He tried to argue that he thought very well of Miss Murrell, but she would not hear; and she went on with her pretty, saucy abuse, in her gayest tones, as she tripped along the churchyard path, now, doubtless, too familiar to renew the associations that might have tamed her spirits. Perhaps the shock her vivacity gave to the feelings of her friends was hardly reasonable, but it was not the less real; though, even in passing, Honora could not but note the improved condition of the two graves, now carefully tended, and with a lovely white rose budding between them.

A few more steps, and from the open window of the school-house there was heard a buzz and hum, not outrageous, but which might have caused the item of discipline not to figure well in an inspector's report; but Mr. Prendergast and Lucilla appeared habituated to the like, for they proceeded without apology.

It was a handsome gable-ended building, Elizabethan enough to testify to the taste that had designed it, and with a deep porch, where Honor had advanced, under Lucilla's guidance, so as to have a moment's view of the whole scene before their arrival had disturbed it.

The children's backs were towards the door, as they sat on their forms at work. Close to the oriel window, the only person facing the door, with a table in front of her, there sat, in a slightly reclining attitude, a figure such as all reports of the new race of schoolmistresses had hardly led Honor to imagine to be the *bonâ fide* mistress. Yet the dress was perfectly quiet, merely lilac cotton, with no ornament save the small bow of the same colour at the throat, and the hair was simply folded round the head, but it was magnificent raven hair; the head and neck were grandly made; the form finely proportioned, on a large scale; the face really beautiful, in a pale, dark, Italian style; the complexion of the clearest olive, but as she became aware of the presence of the visitors it became overspread with a lovely hue of red; while the eyelids revealed a superb pair of eyes, liquid depths of rich brown, soft and languid, and befitting the calm dignity with which she rose, curtseyed, and signed to her scholars to do the same; the deepening colour alone betraying any sense of being taken by surprise.

Lucilla danced up to her, chattering with her usual familiar, airy grace. 'Well, Edna, how are you getting on? Have I brought a tremendous host to invade you? I wanted Miss Charlecote to see you, for she is a perfect connoisseur in schools.'

Edna's blush grew more carnation, and the fingers shook so visibly with which she held the work, that Honora was provoked with Lucy for embarrassing the poor young thing by treating her as an exhibition, especially as the two young gentlemen were present, Robert with his back against the door-post in a state of resignation, Owen drawing Phœbe's attention to the little ones whom he was puzzling with incomprehensible remarks and questions. Hoping to end the scene, Honor made a few commonplace inquiries as to the numbers and the habits of the school; but the mistress, though preserving her dignity of attitude, seemed hardly able to speak, and the curate replied for her.

'I see,' said Lucilla, 'your eye keeps roaming to the mischief my naughty brother is doing among the fry down there.'

'Oh, no! ma'am. I beg your pardon——'

'Never mind, I'll remove the whole concern in a moment, only we must have some singing first.'

'Don't, Lucy!' whispered Honor, looking up from an inspection of some not first-rate needlework; 'it is distressing her, and displays are contrary to all rules of discipline.'

'Oh! but you must,' cried Cilly. 'You have not seen Wrapworth without. Come, Edna, my bonniebell,' and she held out her hand in that semi-imperious, semi-caressing manner which very few had ever withstood.

'One song,' echoed Owen, turning towards the elder girls. 'I know you'll oblige me; eh, Fanny Blake?'

To the scholars the request was evidently not distasteful; the more tuneful were gathering together, and the mistress took her station among them, all as if the exhibition were no novelty. Lucilla, laying her hand on the victim's arm, said, 'Come, don't be nervous, or what will you do to-morrow? Come.'

'"Goddess of the Silver Bow,"' suggested Owen. 'Wasn't it that which your mother disapproved, Fanny, because it was worshipping idols to sing about great Diana of the Ephesians?'

'Yes, sir,' said rather a conceited voice from the prettiest of the elder girls; 'and you told us it was about Phœbe Bright, and gave her the blue and silver ribbon.'

'And please, sir,' said another less prepossessing damsel, 'Mrs. Jenkyns took it away, and I said I'd tell you.'

Owen shrugged up his shoulders with a comical look, saying, as he threw her a shilling, 'Never mind; there's a silver circle instead of a bow—that will do as well. Here's a rival goddess for you, Phœbe; two moons in a system.'

VOL. I.   S

The girls were in a universal titter, the mistress with her eyes cast down, blushing more than ever. Lucilla muttered an amused but indignant, 'For shame, Owen!' and herself gave the key-note. The performance was not above the average of National School melody, but no sooner was it over, than Owen named, in an under tone, another song, which was instantly commenced, and in which there joined a voice that had been still during the first, but which soon completely took the lead. And such a voice, coming as easily as the notes of the nightingale from the nobly formed throat, and seeming to fill the room with its sweet power! Lucilla's triumph was complete; Honor's scruples were silenced by the admiring enjoyment, and Phœbe was in a state of rapture. The nervous reluctance had given way to the artistic delight in her own power, and she readily sang all that was asked for, latterly such pieces as needed little or no support from the children—the 'Three Fishers' Wives' coming last, and thrilling every one with the wondrous pathos and sadness of the tones that seemed to come from her very heart.

It seemed as if they would never have come away, had not Mr. Prendergast had pity on the restless movements of some of the younglings who, taking no part in the display, had leisure to perceive that the clock had struck their hour of release, and at the close of 'The Fishers' Wives,' he signed to Lucilla to look at the hour.

'Poor little things!' said she, turning round to the gaping and discontented collection, 'have we used you so ill? Never mind.' Again using her bulrush to tickle the faces that looked most injured, and waken them into smiles—'Here's the prison house open,' and she sprang out. 'Now—come with a whoop and come with a call—I'll give my club to anybody that can catch me before I get down to the vicarage garden.'

Light as the wind, she went bounding, flying across the churchyard like a butterfly, ever and anon pausing to look round, nod, and shake her sceptre, as the urchins tumbled confusedly after, far behind, till closing the gate, she turned, poised the reed javelin-wise in the air, and launched it among them.

'It is vain to try to collect them again,' sighed Mr. Prendergast, 'we must shut up. Good night, Miss Murrell;' and therewith he turned back to his garden, where the freakish sprite, feigning flight, took refuge in the boat, cowering down, and playfully hiding her face in deprecation of rebuke, but all she received was a meekly melancholy, 'O Cilla! prayers.'

'One day's less loathing of compulsory devotion,' was her answer in saucy defiance. 'I owed it to them for the weariness of listening for ten minutes to the "Three Fishers' Wives," which they appreciated as little as their pastor did!'

'I know nothing about songs, but when one wants them—poor things—to look to something better than sleep.'

'Oh, hush! Here are Miss Charlecote and Mr. Fulmort on your side, and I can't be crushed with united morality in revenge for the tears Edna caused you all to shed. There, help Miss Charlecote in; where can Owen be dawdling? You can't pull, Phœbe, or we would put off without him. Ah, there!' as he came bounding down, 'you intolerable loiterer, I was just going to leave you behind.'

'The train starting without the engine,' he said, getting into his place; 'yes, take an oar if you like, little gnat, and fancy yourself helping.'

The gay warfare, accompanied by a few perilous tricks on Lucilla's part, lasted through the further voyage. Honora guessed at a purpose of staving off graver remonstrance, but Phœbe looked on in astonishment. Seventeen is often a more serious time of life than two-and-twenty, and the damsel could not comprehend the possibility of thoughtlessness when there was anything to think about. The ass's bridge was nothing compared with Lucy! Moreover the habits of persiflage of a lively family often are confusing to one not used to the tone of jest and repartee, and Phœbe had as little power as will to take part in what was passing between the brother and sister; she sat like the spectator of a farce in a foreign tongue, till the boat had arrived at the broad open extent of park gently sweeping down towards the river, the masses of trees kept on either side so as to leave the space open where the castle towered in pretentious grandeur, with a flag slowly swaying in the summer wind on the top of the tallest turret.

The trees made cool reaches of shade, varied by intervals of hot sunshine, and much longer did the way appear, creeping onward in the heat, than it had looked when the eye only took in the simple expanse of turf, from river to castle. Phœbe looked to her arrival there, and to bedroom conferences, as the moment of recovering a reasonable Lucy, but as they neared the house, there was a shout from the wire fence enclosing the shrubbery on the eastern side, and Horatia was seen standing at the gate calling them to come into the cloisters and have some sustenance.

Passing the screen of shrubs, a scene lay before them, almost fit for the gardens of Seville. Three sides of an extensive square were enclosed by the semi-gothic buildings, floridly decorated with stone carving; one consisted of the main edifice, the lower windows tented with striped projecting blinds; a second of the wing containing the reception rooms, fronted by the imitative cloister, which was continued and faced with glass on the third side—each supporting column covered with climbing plants, the passion flower, the tropæolum, the trumpet honeysuckle, or even the pomegranate, opening their gay blooms on every side. The close-shaven turf was broken by small patches of gorgeously-tinted flower beds, diversified by vases filled with trailing plants, and lines of orange trees and fuchsias, with here and there a deep-belled datura, all converging towards the central marble fountain, where the water played high, and tinkled coolly in sparkling jets. Between it and the house, there were placed in the shade some brightly-tinted cushions and draperies, lounging chairs, and a low table, bearing an oriental-looking service of tiny cups of all kinds of bright and fantastic hues, no two alike. Near it reclined on her cushions a figure in perfect keeping with the scene, her jetty hair contrasting with her gold and coral net, her scarlet gold-embroidered slipper peeping out from her pale buff-coloured dress, deeply edged with rich purple, and partly concealed by a mantle of the unapproachable pink which suggests Persia, all as gorgeous in apparel as the blue and yellow macaw on his pole, and the green and scarlet lories in their cage. Owen made a motion of smoking with Honor's parasol, whispering, 'Fair Fatima! what more is wanting?'

'There! I've got Lolly out!' cried Horatia, advancing with her vehement cordiality, and grasping their hands with all her might; 'I would have come and pulled you up the river, Miss Charlecote, but for imperative claims. Here's some tea for you; I know you must be parched.'

And while Mrs. Charteris, scarcely rising, held out her ring-encrusted fingers, and murmured a greeting, Ratia settled them all, pushed a chair behind Miss Charlecote, almost threw Phœbe on a cushion, handed tea, scolded Owen, and rattled away to Lucilla with an impetus that kept Phœbe in increased wonder. It was all about the arrangements for the morrow, full of the utmost good-nature and desire to secure every one's pleasure, but all discussed in a broad, out-spoken way, with a liberal use of slang phrases, and of unprefaced surnames, a freedom of manner and jovial carelessness of voice that specially marked Rashe Charteris at home.

Phœbe had a good deal of opportunity for these observations, for as soon as her stream of information was exhausted, Rashe jumped up and insisted on conducting the guests round the hot-houses and pleasure-grounds. She knew Miss Charlecote was a famous hand at such things. Lucilla remained on the grass, softly teasing Lolly about the exertions of the morrow, and Owen applying himself to the care of Honor, Rashe took possession of Phœbe with all the tyrannous good-nature that had in baby days rendered her hateful to Lucilla. She showed off the parrots and gold fish as to a child, she teased the sensitive plant, and explained curiosities down to the level of the youthful intellect; and Phœbe, scientific enough to know if she went wrong in botany or locality, began a word or two of modest suggestion, only to be patronizingly enlightened, and stopt short, in the fear of pedantry. Phœbe had yet to learn the ignorance of the world.

At last, with a huge torrent of explanations and excuses, Ratia consigned the two guests to share the same bedroom and dressing-room. The number of gentlemen visitors had necessitated close packing, and Cilly, she said, had come to sleep in her room. Another hope had failed ! But at the moment when the door was shut, Phœbe could only sink into a chair, untie her bonnet, and fan herself. Such oppressive good-nature was more fatiguing than a ten miles' walk, or than the toughest lesson in political economy.

'If nature have her own ladies,' was Honora's comment on her young friend's exhaustion, 'she likewise has her own dairy-maids!'

'Miss Charteris *is* a lady,' said Phœbe, her sense of the intended kindness of her hostess calling her to speak in vindication.

'Yes,' said Honor, hesitating; 'it is station that emboldens her. If she had been a dairy-maid, she would have been a bouncing rude girl; if a farmer's daughter, she would be hearty and useful; if one of the boasters of gentility, she would think it worth while to restrain herself; as she is, her acknowledged birth and breeding enable her to follow her inclinations without fear of opinion.'

'I thought refinement was one great characteristic of a lady,' said Phœbe.

'So it is, but affectation and false shame are the contrary. Refinement was rather overworked, and there has been a reaction of late ; simplicity and unconstraint have been the fashion, but unfortunately some dispositions are not made to be unconstrained.'

'Lucy is just as unrestrained as her cousin,' said Phœbe, ' but she never seems like her. She offends one's judgment sometimes, but never one's taste—at least hardly ever ;' and Phœbe blushed as she thought of what had passed about her sister that day.

' Poor Lucy ! it is one misfortune of pretty people, that they can seldom do what is taken amiss. She is small and feminine, too, and essentially refined, whatever she can do. But I was very sorry for you to-day, Phœbe. Tell me all about your sister, my dear.'

'They knew more than I did, if all that is true,' said Phœbe. 'Augusta wrote—oh ! so kindly—and seemed so glad, that it made me very happy. And papa gave his consent readily to Robert's doing as he pleased, and almost said something about his taking me to the wedding at Paris. If Lucy should—should accept Robin, I wonder if she would go, too, and be bridesmaid ! '

So they comforted themselves with a few pretty auguries, dressed, and went down to dinner, where Phœbe had made sure that, as before, Lucy would sit next Robin, and be subdued. Alas, no ! Ladies were far too scarce articles for even the last but one to be the prize of a mere B.A. To know who were Phœbe's own neighbours would have been distraction to Juliana, but they were lost on one in whom the art of conversation was yet undeveloped, and who was chiefly intent on reading her brother's face, and catching what Lucy was saying. She had nearly given up listening in despair, when she heard, ' Pistols ? oh, of course. Rashe has gone to the expense of a revolver, but I extracted grandpapa's from the family armoury—such little darlings. I'm strongly tempted to send a challenge, just to keep them in use—that's because you despise me—I'm a crack shot—we practised every day last winter—women shoot much better than men, because they don't make their hands unsteady—what can be better than the guidance of Ratia, the feminine of Ratio, reason, isn't it?'

It is not quite certain that this horrible Latinity did not shock Miss Fennimore's discreet pupil more than all the rest, as a wilful insult to Miss Charlecote's education!

She herself was not to escape 'the guidance of Ratia,' after dinner. Her silence had been an additional proof to the good-natured Rashe that she was a child to be protected and entertained, so she paraded her through the rooms, coaxed her to play when no one was listening, showed her illustrated books and new-fashioned puzzles, and domineered over her so closely, that she had not a moment in which to speak a word to her brother, whom she saw disconsolately watching the hedge of gentlemen round Lucy. Was it wrong to feel so ungrateful to a person exclusively devoted to her entertainment for that entire evening?

Phœbe had never known a room-mate nor the solace of a bed-time gossip, and by the time Miss Charlecote began to think of opening the door between their rooms, and discussing the disgusts of the day, the sounds of moving about had ceased. Honor looked in, and could not help advancing to the bedside to enjoy the sight of the rosy face in the sound healthful sleep, the lips unclosed, and the silken brown hair wound plainly across the round brow, the childish outline and expression of the features even sweeter in sleep than awake. It rested Honora's wearied anxious spirit to watch the perfect repose of that innocent young face, and she stood still for some minutes, breathing an ejaculation that the child might ever be as guileless and peaceful as now, and then sighing at the thought of other young sleepers, beside whose couches even fonder prayers had been uttered, only, as it seemed, to be blown aside.

She was turning away, when Phœbe suddenly awoke, and was for a moment startled, half rising, asking if anything were the matter.

'No, my dear; only I did not think you would have been in bed so quickly. I came to wish you good night, and found you asleep.' And with the strong tender impulse of a gentle wounded spirit, Honor hung over the maiden, recomposing the clothes, and fondling her, with a murmured blessing.

'Dear Miss Charlecote,' whispered Phœbe, 'how nice it is! I have so often wondered what it would be like, if any one came in to pet us at night, as they do in books; and oh! it is so nice! Say *that* again, please.'

That was the blessing which would have made Lucilla in angry reserve hide her head in the clothes!

CHAPTER VII.

> But, ah me! she's a heart of stone,
> Which Cupid uses for a hone,
>   I verily believe;
> And on it sharpens those eye-darts,
> With which he wounds the simple hearts
>   He bribes her to deceive.
>   *A Coquette, by X.*

BREAKFAST was late, and lengthened out by the greater lateness of many of the guests, and the superlative tardiness of the lady of the house, who had repudiated the cares of the hostess, and left the tea equipage to her sister-in-law. Lucilla had been downstairs among the first, and hurried away again after a rapid meal, forbidding any one to follow her, because she had so much to do, and on entering the drawing-room, she was found with a wilderness of flowers around her, filling vases and making last arrangements.

Honora and Phœbe were glad to be occupied, and Phœbe almost hoped to escape from Rashe. Speaking to Lucilla was not possible, for Eloïsa had been placed by Rashe in a low chair, with a saucer before her, which she was directed to fill with verbenas, while the other four ladies, with Owen, whom his cousin had called to their aid, were putting last touches to wreaths, and giving the final festal air to the rooms.

Presently Robert made his appearance as the bearer of Mr. Prendergast's flowers, and setting his back against a shutter, in his favourite attitude, stood looking as if he wanted to help, but knew not how. Phœbe, at least, was vividly conscious of his presence, but she was supporting a long festoon with which Owen was adorning a pier-glass, and could hardly even turn her head to watch him.

'Oh, horrid!' cried Lucilla, retreating backwards to look at Ratia's performance; 'for love or money, a bit of clematis!'

'Where shall I find one?' said Robert, unseeing the masses waving on the cloister, if, good youth, he even knew what clematis was.

'You there, Mr. Fulmort!' exclaimed Rashe; 'for goodness gracious sake, go out to tennis or something with the other men. I've ordered them all out, or there'll be no good to be got out of Cilly.'

Phœbe flashed out in his defence, 'You are letting Owen alone.'

'Ah! by the bye, that wreath of yours has taken an unconscionable time!' said Miss Charteris, beginning to laugh; but Phœbe's grave, straightforward eyes met her with such a look as absolutely silenced her merriment into a mere mutter of 'What a little chit it is!' Honora, who was about indignantly to assume the protection of her charge, recognised in her what was fully competent to take care of herself.

'Away with both of you,' said Lucilla; 'here is Edna come for a last rehearsal, and I wont have you making her nervous. Take away that Robin, will you, Owen?'

Horatia flew gustily to greet and reassure the school-mistress as she entered, trembling, although moving with the dignity that seemed to be her form of embarrassment. Lucilla meanwhile sped to the others near the window. 'You must go,' she said, 'or I shall never screw her up; it is a sudden access of stage fright. She is as pale as death.'

Owen stepped back to judge of the paleness, and Robert contrived to say, 'Cannot you grant me a few words, Lucy?'

'The most impossible thing you could have asked,' she replied. 'There's Rashe's encouragement quite done for her now!'

She bounded back to the much-overcome Edna, while Phœbe herself, perceiving how ill-advised an opportunity Robert had chosen, stepped out with him into the cloister, saying, 'She can't help it, dear Robin; she cannot think, just now.'

'When can she?' he asked, almost with asperity.

'Think how full her hands are, how much excited she is,' pleaded Phœbe, feeling that this was no fair moment for the crisis.

'Ireland?' almost groaned Robert, but at the same moment grasped her roughly to hinder her from replying, for Owen was close upon them, and he was the person to whom Robert would have been most reluctant to display his feelings.

Catching intuitively at his meaning, Phœbe directed her attention to some clematis on the opposite side of the cloister, and called both her companions to gather it for her, glad to be with Robert and to relieve Miss Murrell of the presence of another spectator. Charles Charteris coming up, carried the two young men to inspect some of his doings out of doors, and Phœbe returned with her wreaths of creepers to find that the poor schoolmistress had become quite hysterical, and had been taken away by Lucilla.

Rashe summoned her at the same time to the decoration of the music-room, and on entering, stopped in amusement, and made her a sign in silence to look into a large pier-glass, which stood so as to reflect through an open door what was passing in the little fanciful boudoir beyond, a place fitted like a tent, and full of quaint Dresden china and toys of *bijouterie*. There was a complete picture within the glass. Lucilla, her fair face seen in profile, more soft and gentle than she often allowed it to appear, was kneeling beside the couch where half reclined the tall, handsome Edna, whose raven hair, and pale, fine features made her like a heroine, as she nervously held the hands which Lucilla had placed within her grasp. There was a low murmur of voices, one soothing, the other half sobbing, but nothing reached the outer room distinctly, till, as Phœbe was holding a long wreath, which Ratia was tying up, she heard—'Oh! but it is so different with me from you young ladies who are used to company and all. I dare say that young lady would not be timid.'

'What young lady, Edna? Not the one with the auburn hair?'

Ratia made an ecstatic face which disgusted Phœbe.

'Oh, no!—the young lady whom Mr. Sandbrook was helping. I dare say she would not mind singing—or anything,' came amid sobs.

Ratia nodded, looked excessively arch, and formed a word with her lips, which Phœbe thought was 'jealous,' but could not imagine what she could mean by it.

'I don't know why you should think poor Phœbe Fulmort so brazen. She is a mere child, taking a holiday from her strict governess.'

Phœbe laughed back an answer to Rashe's pantomime, which in this case she understood.

'She has not had half your training in boldness, with your inspectors and examinations, and all those horrid things. Why, you never thought of taking fright before, even when you have sung to people here. Why should you, now?'

'It is so different, now—so many more people. Oh, so different! I shall never be able.'

'Not at all. You will quite forget all about yourself and your fears when the time comes. You don't know the exhilaration of a room full of people, all lights and music! That symphony will lift you into another world, and you will feel quite ready for "Men must work and women must weep."'

'If I can only begin—but oh! Miss Sandbrook, shall you be far away from me?'

'No, I promise you not. I will bring you down, if you will come to Ratia's room when you are dressed.

The black silk and the lilac ribbon Owen and I chose for you; I must see you in it.'

'Dear Miss Sandbrook, you are so kind! What shall I do when you have left?'

'You are going yourself for the holidays, silly puss!'

'Ah! but no one else sympathizes or enters into my feelings.'

'Feelings!' said Lucilla, lightly, yet sadly. 'Don't indulge in them, Edna; they are no end of a torment.'

'Ah! but if they prey on one, one cannot help it.'

Rashe made a face of great distaste. Phœbe felt as if it were becoming too confidential to permit of listening, all the more as she heard Lucilla's reply.

'That's what comes of being tall, and stately, and dignified! There's so much less of me that I can carry off my troubles twice as well."

'Oh, dear Miss Sandbrook, you can have no troubles!'

'Haven't I? Oh, Edna, if you knew! You that have a mother can never know what it is to be like me! I'm keeping it all at bay, lest I should break down; but I'm in the horridest bother and trouble.'

Not knowing what might come next, ashamed of having listened to so much, yet with one gleam of renewed hope, Phœbe resolutely disobeyed Ratia's frowns and gestures, and made her presence known by decided movements and words spoken aloud.

She saw the immediate effect in Edna Murrell's violent start; but Lucilla, without moving, at once began to sing, straining her thin though sweet voice, as though to surmount a certain tremulousness. Edna joined, and the melody was lovely to hear; but Phœbe was longing all the time for Robert to be at hand for this softer moment, and she hoped all the more when, the practising being over, and Edna dismissed, Lucy came springing towards her, notifying her presence by a caress—to outward appearance merely playful, but in reality a convulsive clasp of vehement affection—and Phœbe was sure that there had been tears in those eyes that seemed to do nothing but laugh.

The security that this wild elf was true at heart was, however, not enough for Phœbe. There was the knowledge that each moment's delay would drive Robert farther aloof, and that it was a mere chance whether he should encounter this creature of impulse at a propitious instant. Nay, who could tell what was best for him after all? Even Phœbe's faithful acceptance of her on his word had undergone sundry severe shocks, and she had rising doubts whether Lucy, such as she saw her, could be what would make him happy.

If the secrets of every guest at a *fête* were told, would any be found unmixedly happy? Would there be no one devoid of cares of their own or of other people's, or if exempt from these, undisturbed by the absence of the right individual or by the presence of the wrong one, by mishaps of deportment, difficulties of dress, or want of notice? Perhaps, after all, it may be best to have some one abiding anxiety, strong enough to destroy tedium, and exclude the pettier distresses, which are harder to contend with, though less dignified; and most wholesome of all is it that this should be an interest entirely external. So, after all, Phœbe's enjoyment might hardly have been increased had her thoughts been more free from Robin's troubles, when she came down dressed for her first party, so like a lily of the valley in her delicate dress, that Owen acknowledged that it justified her choice, and murmured something of 'in vernal green and virgin white, her festal robes, arrayed.' Phœbe was only distressed at what she thought the profanation of quoting from such a source in compliment to her. Honora was gratified to find the lines in his memory upon any terms. Poor dear Honor, in one case at least believing all things, hoping all things!

Phœbe ought to have made the most of her compliment. It was all she obtained in that line. Juliana herself could not have taken umbrage at her success. Nobody imagined her come out, no one attempted to disturb her from under Miss Charlecote's wing, and she kept close to her the whole afternoon, sometimes sitting upon a haycock, sometimes walking in the shrubbery, listening to the band, or looking at the archery, in company with dignified clergyman, or elderly lady, astonished to meet Honor Charlecote in so unwonted a scene. Owen Sandbrook was never far off. He took them to eat ices, conducted them to good points of view, found seats for them, and told them who every one was, with droll comments or anecdotes, which entertained them so much, that Phœbe almost wished that Robin had not made her sensible of the grain of irreverence that seasoned all Owen's most brilliant sallies.

They saw little of the others. Mr. and Mrs. Charteris walked about together, the one cordial, the other stately and gorgeous, and Miss Charlecote came in for her due and passing share of their politeness. Rashe once invited Phœbe to shoot, but had too many on her hands to be solicitous about one. Flirting no longer herself, Rashe's delight was in those who did flirt, and in any assembly her extreme and unscrupulous good-nature made her invaluable to all who wanted to have themselves taken off their own hands, or pushed into those of others. She ordered people about, started amusements, hunted gentlemen up, found partners, and shook up the bashful. Rashe Charteris was the life of everything. How little was wanting to make her kind-hearted activity admirable!

Lucilla never came in their way at all. She was only seen in full and eager occupation embellishing the archery, or forcing the 'decidedly pious' to be fascinated by her gracious self-adaptation. Robert was equally inaccessible, always watching her, but keeping aloof from his sister, and only consorting at times with Mr. Prendergast.

It was seven o'clock when this act of the drama was finally over, and the party staying in the house met round a hurried meal. Rashe lounging and yawning, laughing and quizzing, in a way amazing to Phœbe;

Lucilla in the very summit of spirits, rattling and laughing away in full swing. Thence the party dispersed to dress, but Honora had no sooner reached her room than she said, 'I must go and find Lucy. I must do my duty by her, little hope as I have. She has avoided me all day; I must seek her now.'

What a difference time and discipline had made in one formerly so timid and gentle as to be alarmed at the least encounter, and nervous at wandering about a strange house. Nervous and frightened, indeed, she still was, but self-control kept this in check, and her dislike was not allowed to hold her back from her duty. Humfrey's representative was seldom permitted to be weak. But there are times when the difference between man and woman is felt in their dealings with others. Strength can be mild, but what is strained can seldom be gentle, and when she knocked at Horatia Charteris's door, her face, from very unhappiness and effort, was sorrowfully reproachful, as she felt herself an unwelcome apparition to the two cousins, who lay on their bed still laughing over the day's events.

Rashe, who was still in her morning dress, at once gave way, saying she must go and speak to Lolly, and hastened out of the room. Lucy, in her dishabille, sat crouched upon the bed, her white bare shoulders and floating hair, together with the defiant glance of the blue eye, and the hand moodily compressing the lips, reminding Honor of the little creature who had been summarily carried into her house sixteen years since. She came towards her, but there was no invitation to give the caress that she yearned to bestow, and she leant against the bed, trembling, as she said, 'Lucy, my poor child, I am come that you may not throw away your last chance without knowing it. You do not realize what you are about. If you cast aside esteem and reliance, how can you expect to retain the affection you sometimes seem to prize?'

'If I am not trusted, what's the good of affection?'

'How can you expect trust when you go beyond the

bounds of discretion ?' said Honor, with voice scarcely steadied into her desired firmness.

'I can, I do!'

'Lucy, listen to me.' She gave way to her natural piteous, pleading tone : 'I verily believe that this is the very turn. Remember how often a moment has decided the fate of a life !' She saw the expression relax into some alarm, and continued : 'The Fulmorts do not say so, but I see by their manner that his final decision will be influenced by your present proceedings. You have trifled with him too long, and with his mind made up to the ministry, he cannot continue to think of one who persists in outraging decorum.'

Those words were effort enough, and had better have been unsaid. 'That is as people may think,' was all the answer.

'As he thinks ?'

'How do I know what he thinks ?'

Heartsick at such mere fencing, Honor was silent at first, then said, 'I, for one, shall rate your good opinion by your endeavour to deserve it. Who can suppose that you value what you are willing to risk for an unladylike bet, or an unfeminine sporting expedition ?'

'You may tell him so,' said Lucilla, her voice quivering with passion.

'You think a look will bring him back, but you may find that a true man is no slave. Prove his affection misplaced, and he will tear it away.'

Had Honora been discreet as she was good, she would have left those words to settle down ; but, woman that she was, she knew not when to stop, and coaxingly coming to the small bundle of perverseness, she touched the shoulder, and said, 'Now you wont make an object of yourself to-night ?'

The shoulder shook in the old fashion.

'At least you will not go to Ireland.'

'Yes, I shall.'

'Miss Charlecote, I beg your pardon——' cried Rashe, bursting in—(oh ! that she had been five seconds earlier)—' but dressing is imperative. People are beginning to come.'

Honora retreated in utter discomfiture.

'Rashe! Rashe! I'm in for it!' cried Lucilla, as the door shut, springing up with a look of terror.

'Proposed by deputy?' exclaimed Horatia, aghast.

'No, no!' gasped Lucilla; 'it's this Ireland of yours —that—that——' and she well-nigh sobbed.

'My bonny bell! I knew you would not be bullied into deserting.'

'Oh! Rashe, she was very hard on me. Every one is but you!' and Lucilla threw herself into her cousin's arms in a paroxysm of feeling; but their maid's knock brought her back to composure sooner than poor Honora, who shed many a tear over this last defeat, as, looking mournfully to Phœbe, she said, 'I have done, Phœbe. I can say no more to her. She will not hear anything from me. Oh! what have I done that my child should be hardened against me!'

Phœbe could offer nothing but caresses full of indignant sorrow, and there was evidently soothing in them, for Miss Charlecote's tears became softer, and she fondly smoothed Phœbe's fair hair, saying, as she drew the clinging arms closer round her: 'My little woodbine, you must twine round your brother and comfort him, but you can spare some sweetness for me too. There, I will dress. I will not keep you from the party.'

'I do not care for that; only to see Robin.'

'We must take our place in the crowd,' sighed Honora, beginning her toilet; 'and you will enjoy it when you are there. Your first quadrille is promised to Owen, is it not?'

'Yes,' said Phœbe, dreamily, and she would have gone back to Robin's sorrows, but Honora had learnt that there were subjects to be set aside when it was incumbent on her to be presentable, and directed the talk to speculations whether the poor schoolmistress would have nerve to sing; and somehow she talked up Phœbe's spirits to such a hopeful pitch, that the little maiden absolutely was crossed by a gleam of satisfaction from the ungrateful recollection that poor Miss Charlecote had done with the affair. Against her will, she had detected the antagonism between the two, and bad as it was of Lucy, was certain that she was more likely to be amenable where there was no interference from her best friend.

The music-room was already crowded when the two made their way into it, and Honora's inclination was to deposit herself on the nearest seat, but she owed something otherwise to her young charge, and Phœbe's eyes had already found a lonely black figure with arms crossed, and lowering brow. Simultaneously they moved towards him, and he towards them. 'Is she come down?' he asked.

Phœbe shook her head, but at the same moment another door near the orchestra admitted a small white butterfly-figure, leading in a tall queenly apparition in black, whom she placed in a chair adjacent to the bejewelled prima donna of the night—a great contrast with her dust-coloured German hair and complexion, and good-natured plain face.

Robert's face cleared with relief; he evidently detected nothing *outré* in Lucilla's aspect, and was rejoicing in the concession. Woman's eyes saw further; a sigh from Honora, an amused murmur around him, caused him to bend his looks on Phœbe. She knew his eyes were interrogating her, but could not bear to let her own reply, and kept them on the ground. He was moving towards Lucilla, who, having consigned her *protégée* to the good-humoured German, had come more among the guests, and was exchanging greetings and answering comments with all her most brilliant airs of saucy animation.

And who could quarrel with that fairy vision? Her rich double-skirted watered silk was bordered with exquisitely made and coloured flies, radiant with the hues of the peacock, the gold pheasant, the jay, parrots of all tints, everything rich and rare in plumage. A coronal of the same encircled her glossy hair, the tiny plumes contrasting with the blonde ringlets, and the *bonâ fide* hooks ostentatiously displayed; lesser and more innocuous flies edged the sleeves, corsage, shoes, and gloves; and her fan, which she used as skilfully as Jenny Wren, presented a Watteau-like picture of an angling scene. Anything more daintily, quaintly pretty could not be imagined, and the male part of the assembly would have unanimously concurred in Sir Harry Buller's 'three cheers for the queen of the anglers.'

But towards the party most concerned in her movements, Lucilla came not; and Phœbe, understanding a design to keep as near as might be to Miss Murrell, tried to suggest it as the cause, and looking round, saw Owen standing by Miss Charlecote, with somewhat of an uneasy countenance.

'Terribly hot here,' he said, restlessly; 'suffocating, aren't you, Honor? Come and take a turn in the cloister; the fountain is stunning by moonlight.'

No proposal could have been more agreeable to Honora; and Phœbe was afraid of losing her chaperon, though she would rather have adhered to her brother, and the barbs of that wicked little angler were tearing him far too deeply to permit him to move out of sight of his tormentor.

But for this, the change would have been delicious. The white lights and deep shadows from the calm, grave moon contrasted with the long gleams of lamplight from every window, reddened by the curtains within; the flowers shone out with a strange whiteness, the taller ones almost like spiritual shapes; the burnished orange leaves glistened, the water rose high in silvery spray, and fell back into the blackness of the basin, made more visible by one trembling, shimmering reflection; the dark blue sky above seemed shut into a vault by the enclosing buildings, and one solitary planet shone out in the lustrous neighbourhood of the moon. So still, so solemn, so cool! Honora felt it as repose, and pensively began to admire—Owen chimed in with her. Feverish thoughts and perturbations were always gladly soothed away in her company. Phœbe alone stood barely confessing the beauty, and suppressing impatience at their making so much of it; not yet knowing enough of care or passion to seek repose, and much more absorbed in human, than in any other form of nature.

The music was her first hope of deliverance from her namesake in the sky; but, behold, her companions chose to prefer hearing that grand instrumental piece softened by distance; and even Madame Hedwig's quivering notes did not bring them in. However, at the first sounds of the accompaniment to the 'Three Fishers' Wives,' Owen pulled back the curtain, and handed the two ladies back into the room, by a window much nearer to the orchestra than that by which they had gone out, not far from where Edna Murrell had just risen, her hands nervously clasped together, her colour rapidly varying, and her eyes roaming about as though in quest of something. Indeed, through all the music, the slight sounds of the entrance at the window did not escape her, and at the instant when she should have begun to sing, Phœbe felt those black eyes levelled on herself with a look that startled her; they were at once removed, the head turned away; there was an attempt at the first words, but they died away on her lips; there was a sudden whiteness, Lucilla and the German both tried to reseat her; but with readier judgment Owen made two long steps, gathered her up in his strong arms, and bore her through the curtains and out at the open window like a mere infant.

'Don't come, don't—it will only make more fuss—nobody has seen. Go to Madame Hedwig; tell her from me to go on to her next, and cover her retreat,' said Lucilla, as fast as the words would come, signing back Honora, and hastily disappearing between the curtains.

There was a command in Lucilla's gestures which always made obedience the first instinct even with Honora, and her impulse to assist thus counteracted, she had time to recollect that Lucy might be supposed to know best what to do with the schoolmistress, and that to dispose of her among her ladies' maid friends was doubtless the kindest measure.

'I must say I am glad,' she said; 'the poor thing cannot be quite so much spoilt as they wished.'

The concert proceeded, and in the next pause Honor fell into conversation with a pleasant lady who had brought one pair of young daughters in the morning, and now was doing the same duty by an elder pair.

Phœbe was standing near the window when a touch on her arm and a whispered 'Help! hush!' made her look round. Holding the curtain apart, so as to form the least possible aperture, and with one finger on her lip, was Lucy's face, the eyes brimming over with laughter, as she pointed to her head—three of the hooks had set their barbs deep into the crimson satin curtain, and held her a prisoner!

'Hush! I'll never forgive you if you betray me,' she whispered, drawing Phœbe by the arm behind the curtain; 'I should expire on the spot to be found in Absalom's case. All that little goose's fault—I never reckoned on having to rush about this way. Can't you do it? Don't spare scissors,' and Lucilla produced a pair from under her skirt. 'Rashe and I always go provided.'

'How is she?—where is she?' asked Phœbe.

'That's exactly what I can't tell. He took her out to the fountain; she was quite like a dead thing. Water wouldn't make her come to, and I ran for some salts; I wouldn't call anybody, for it was too romantic a condition to have Owen discovered in, with a fainting maiden in his arms. Such a rummage as I had. My own things are all jumbled up, I don't know how, and Rashe keeps nothing bigger than globules, only fit for fainting lady-birds, so I went to Lolly's, but her bottles have all gold heads, and are full of uncanny-looking compounds, and I made a raid at last on sweet Honey's rational old dressing-case, poked out her keys from her pocket, and got in ; wasting interminable time. Well, when I got back to my fainting damsel, *non est inventus.*'

'*Inventa,*' murmured the spirit of Miss Fennimore within Phœbe. 'But what? had she got well?'

'So I suppose. Gone off to the servants' rooms, no doubt; as there is no White Lady in the fountain to spirit them both away. What, haven't you done that, yet?'

'O! Lucy, stand still, please, or you'll get another hook in.'

'Give me the scissors; I know I could do it quicker. Never mind the curtain, I say; nobody will care.'

She put up her hand, and shook head and feet to the entanglement of a third hook; but Phœbe, decided damsel that she was, used her superior height to keep her mastery, held up the scissors, pressed the fidgety shoulder into quiescence, and kept her down while she extricated her, without fatal detriment to the satin, though with scanty thanks, for the liberation was no sooner accomplished than the sprite was off, throwing out a word about Rashe wanting her.

Phœbe emerged to find that she had not been missed, and presently the concert was over, and tea coming round, there was a change of places. Robert came towards her. 'I am going,' he said.

'Oh! Robert, when dancing would be one chance?'

'She does not mean to give me that chance; I would not ask it while she is in that dress. It is answer sufficient. Good night, Phœbe; enjoy yourself.'

Enjoy herself! A fine injunction, when her brother was going away in such a mood! Yet who would have suspected that rosy, honest apple face of any grievance, save that her partner was missing?

Honora was vexed and concerned at his neglect, but

Phœbe appeased her by reporting what Lucy had said. 'Thoughtless! reckless!' sighed Honora; 'if Lucy *would* leave the poor girl on his hands, of course he is obliged to make some arrangement for getting her home! I never knew such people as they are here! Well, Phœbe, you *shall* have a partner next time!'

Phœbe had one, thanks chiefly to Rashe, and somehow the rapid motion shook her out of her troubles, and made her care much less for Robin's sorrows than she had done two minutes before. She was much more absorbed in hopes for another partner.

Alas! he did not come; neither then nor for the ensuing. Owen's value began to rise.

Miss Charlecote did not again bestir herself in the cause, partly from abstract hatred of waltzes, partly from the constant expectation of Owen's re-appearance, and latterly from being occupied in a discussion with the excellent mother upon young girls reading novels.

At last, after a *galoppe*, at which Phœbe had looked on with wishful eyes, Lucilla dropped breathless into the chair which she relinquished to her.

'Well, Phœbe, how do you like it?'

'Oh! very much,' rather ruefully; 'at least it would be if——'

'If you had any partners, eh, poor child? Hasn't Owen turned up?'

'It's that billiard-room; I tried to make Charlie shut it up. But we'll disinter him; I'll rush in like a sky-rocket, and scatter the gentlemen to all quarters.'

'No, no, don't!' cried Phœbe, alarmed, and catching hold of her. 'It is not that, but Robin is gone.'

'Atrocious,' returned Cilly, disconcerted, but resolved that Phœbe should not perceive it; 'so we are both under a severe infliction,—both ashamed of our brothers.'

'I am not ashamed of mine,' said Phœbe, in a tone of gravity.

'Ah! there's the truant,' said Lucilla, turning aside. 'Owen, where have you hidden yourself? I hope you are ready to sink into the earth with shame at hearing you have rubbed off the bloom from a young lady's first ball.'

'No! it was not he who did so,' stoutly replied Phœbe.

'Ah! it was all the consequence of the green and white; I told you it was a sinister omen,' said Owen, chasing away a shade of perplexity from his brow, and assuming a certain air that Phœbe had never seen before, and did not like. 'At least you will be merciful, and allow me to retrieve my character.'

'You have nothing to retrieve,' said Phœbe, in the most straightforward manner; 'it was very good in you to take care of poor Miss Murrell. What became of her? Lucy said you would know.'

'I—I?' he exclaimed, so vehemently as to startle her by the fear of having ignorantly committed some egregious blunder; 'I'm the last person to know.'

'The last to be seen with the murdered always falls under suspicion,' said Lucilla.

'Drowned in the fountain?' cried Owen, affecting horror.

'Then you must have done it,' said his sister, 'for when I came back, after ransacking the house for salts, you had both disappeared. Have you been washing your hands all this time after the murder?'

'Nothing can clear me but an appeal to the fountain,' said Owen; 'will you come and look in, Phœbe? It is more delicious than ever.'

But Phœbe had had enough of the moonlight, did not relish the subject, and was not pleased with Owen's manner; so she refused by a most decided 'No, thank you,' causing Lucy to laugh at her for thinking Owen dangerous.

'At least you will vouchsafe to trust yourself with me for the Lancers,' said Owen, as Cilla's partner came to claim her, and Phœbe rejoiced in anything to change the tone of the conversation; still, however, asking, as he led her off, what had become of the poor schoolmistress.

'Gone home, very sensibly,' said Owen; 'if she is wise she will know how to trust to Cilly's invitations! People that do everything at once never do anything well. It is quite a rest to turn to any one like you, Phœbe, who are content with one thing at a time! I wish——'

'Well then, let us dance,' said Phœbe, abruptly; 'I can't do that well enough to talk, too.'

It was not that Owen had not said the like things to her many times before; it was his eagerness and fervour that gave her an uncomfortable feeling. She was not sure that he was not laughing at her by putting on these devoted airs, and she felt herself grown up enough to put an end to being treated as a child. He made her a profound bow in a mockery of acquiescence, and preserved absolute silence during the first figures, but she caught his eye several times gazing on her with looks such as another might have interpreted into mingled regret and admiration, but which were to her simply discomfiting and disagreeable. and when he spoke again, it was not in banter, but half in sadness. 'Phœbe, how do you like all this?'

'I think I could like it very much.'

'I am almost sorry to hear you say so; anything that should tend to make you resemble others is detestable.'

'I should be very sorry not to be like other people.'

'Phœbe, you do not know how much of the pleasure of my life would be lost if you were to become a mere conventional young lady.'

Phœbe had no notion of being the pleasure of any one's life except Robin's and Maria's, and was rather affronted that Owen should profess to enjoy her childish ignorance and *naïveté*.

'I believe,' she said, 'I was rude just now when I told you not to talk. I am sorry for it; I shall know better next time.'

'Your knowing better is exactly what I deprecate.

But there it is ; unconsciousness is the charm of simplicity. It is the very thing aimed at by Rashe and Cilly, and all their crew, with their eccentricities.'

'I am sorry for it,' seriously returned Phœbe, who had by this time, by quiet resistance, caused him to land her under the lee of Miss Charlecote, instead of promenading with her about the room. He wanted her to dance with him again, saying she owed it to him for having sacrificed the first to common humanity, but great as was the pleasure of a polka, she shrank from him in this complimentary mood, and declared she should dance no more that evening. He appealed to Honora, who, disliking to have her boy baulked of even a polka, asked Phœbe if she were *very* tired, and considering her 'rather not' as equivalent to such a confession, proposed a retreat to their own room.

Phœbe was sorry to leave the brilliant scene, and no longer to be able to watch Lucilla, but she wanted to shake Owen off, and readily consented. She shut her door after one good night. She was too much grieved and disappointed to converse, and could not bear to discuss whether the last hope were indeed gone, and whether Lucilla had decided her lot without choosing to know it. Alas! how many turning points may be missed by those who never watch !

How little did Phœbe herself perceive the shoal past which her self-respect had just safely guided her!

'I wonder if those were ball-room manners? What a pity if they were, for then I shall not like balls,' was all the thought that she had leisure to bestow on her own share in the night's diversions, as through the subsequent hours she dozed and dreamt, and mused and slept again, with the feverish limbs and cramp-tormented feet of one new to balls ; sometimes teased by entangling fishing flies, sometimes interminably detained in the moonlight, sometimes with Miss Fennimore waiting for an exercise, and the words not to be found in the dictionary ; and even this unpleasant counterfeit of sleep deserting her after her usual time for waking, and leaving her to construct various fabrics of possibilities for Robin and Lucy.

She was up in fair time, and had written a long and particular account to Bertha of everything in the festivities not recorded in this narrative, before Miss Charlecote awoke from the compensating morning slumber that had succeeded a sad and unrestful night. Late as they were, they were down-stairs before any one but the well-seasoned Rashe, who sat beguiling the time with a Bradshaw, and who did *not* tell them how intolerably cross Cilly had been all the morning.

Nor would any one have suspected it who had seen her, last of all, come down at a quarter to eleven, in the most exultant spirits, talking the height of rodomontade with the gentlemen guests, and dallying with her breakfast, while Phœbe's heart was throbbing at the sight of two grave figures, her brother and the curate, slowly marching up and down the cloister, in waiting till this was over.

And there sat Lucilla inventing adventures for an imaginary tour to be brought out on her return by the name of 'Girls in Galway'—' From the Soirée to the Salmon'—' Flirts and Foolsheads,' as Owen and Charles discontentedly muttered to each other, or, as Mr. Calthorp proposed, 'The Angels and the Anglers.' The ball was to be the opening chapter, Lord William entreated for her costume as the frontispiece, and Mr. Calthorp begged her to re-assume it, and let her cousin photograph her on the spot.

Lucilla objected to the impracticability of white silk, the inconvenience of unpacking the apparatus, the nuisance of dressing, the lack of time; but Rashe was delighted with the idea, and made light of all, and the gentlemen pressed her strongly, till with rather more of a consent than a refusal, she rose from her nearly untasted breakfast, and began to move away.

'Cilla,' said Mr. Prendergast, at the window, 'can I have a word with you?'

'At your service,' she answered, as she came out to

him, and saw that Robert had left him. 'Only be quick; they want to photograph me in my ball-dress.'

'You wont let them do it, though,' said the curate.

'White comes out hideous,' said Lucilla; 'I suppose you would not have a copy, if I took one off for you?'

'No; I don't like those visitors of yours well enough to see you turned into a merry-andrew to please them.'

'So that's what Robert Fulmort told you I did last night,' said Lucilla, blushing at last, and thoroughly.

'No, indeed; you didn't?' he said, regarding her with an astonished glance.

'I *did* wear a dress trimmed with salmon-flies, because of a bet with Lord William,' said Lucilla, the suffusion deepening on brow, cheek, and throat, as the confiding esteem of her fatherly friend effected what nothing else could accomplish. She would have given the world to have justified his opinion of his late rector's little daughter, and her spirit seemed gone, though the worst he did was to shake his head at her.

'If you did not know it, why did you call me *that?*' she asked.

'A merry-andrew?' he answered; 'I never meant that you had been one. No; only an old friend like me doesn't like the notion of your going and dressing up in the morning to amuse a lot of scamps.'

'I wont,' said Lucilla, very low.

'Well, then,' began Mr. Prendergast, as in haste to proceed to his own subject; but she cut him short.

'It is not about Ireland?'

'No; I know nothing about young ladies; and if Mr. Charteris and your excellent friend there have nothing to say against it, I can't.'

'My excellent friend had so much to say against it, that I was pestered into vowing I would go! Tell me not, Mr. Prendergast,—I should not mind giving up to you;' and she looked full of hope.

'That would be beginning at the wrong end, Cilla; you are not my charge.'

'You are my clergyman,' she said, pettishly.

'You are not my parishioner,' he answered.

'Pish!' she said; 'when you know I want you to tell me.'

'Why, you say you have made the engagement.'

'So what I said when she fretted me past endurance, must bind me!'

Be it observed that, like all who only knew Hiltonbury through Lucilla, Mr. Prendergast attributed any blemishes which he might detect in her to the injudicious training of an old maid; so he sympathized. 'Ah! ladies of a certain age never get on with young ones! But I thought it was all settled before with Miss Charteris.'

'I never quite said I would go, only we got ready for the sake of the fun of talking of it, and now Rashe has grown horridly eager about it. She did not care at first—only to please me.'

'Then wouldn't it be using her ill to disappoint her, now? You couldn't do it, Cilla. Why, you have given your word, and she is quite old enough for anything. Wouldn't Miss Charlecote see it so?'

To regard Ratia as a mature personage robbed the project of romance, and to find herself bound in honour by her inconsiderate rattle was one of the rude shocks which often occur to the indiscriminate of tongue; but the curate had too much on his mind to dwell on what concerned him more remotely, and proceeded, 'I came to see whether you could help me about poor Miss Murrell. You made no arrangement for her getting home last night?'

'No!'

'Ah, you young people! But it is my fault; I should have recollected young heads. Then I am afraid it must have been——'

'What?'

'She was seen on the river very late last night with a stranger. He went up to the school with her, remained about a quarter of an hour, and then rowed up the river again. I am afraid it is not the first time she has been seen with him.'

'But, Mr. Prendergast, she was here till at least ten! She fainted away just as she was to have sung, and we carried her out into the cloister. When she recovered she went away to the housekeeper's room—' (a bold assertion, built on Owen's partially heard reply to Phœbe). 'I'll ask the maids.'

'It is of no use, Cilla; she allows it herself.'

'And pray,' cried Lucilla, rallying her sauciness, 'how do you propose ever to have banns to publish, if young men and maidens are never to meet by water nor by land?'

'Then you do know something?'

'No; only that such matters are not commonly blazoned in the commencement.'

'I don't wish her to blazon it, but if she would only act openly by me,' said the distressed curate. 'I wish nothing more than that she were safe married; and then if you ladies appoint another beauty, I'll give up the place, and live at —— college.'

'We'll advertise for the female Chimpanzee, and depend upon it she will marry at the end of six weeks. So you have attacked her in person. What did she say?'

'Nothing that she could help. She stood with those great eyes cast down, looking like a statue, and sometimes vouchsafing "yes, sir," or "no, sir." It was "no, sir," when I asked if her mother knew. I am afraid it must be something very unsatisfactory, Cilla; but she might say more to you if you were not going away.'

'Oh! Mr. Prendergast, why did you not come sooner?'

'I did come an hour ago, but you were not come down.'

'I'll walk on at once; the carriage can pick me up. I'll fetch my hat. Poor Edna! I'll soon make her satisfy your mind. Has any one surmised who it can be?'

'The notion is that it is one of your musicians—very dangerous, I am afraid; and I say, Cilla, did you ever do such a thing—you couldn't, I suppose—as lend her Shelley's poems?'

'I? No; certainly not.'

'There was a copy lying on the table in her little parlour, as if she had been writing something out from it. It is very odd, but it was in that peculiar olive-green morocco that some of the books in your father's library were bound in.'

'Not mine, certainly,' said Lucilla. 'Good Honor Charlecote would have run crazy if she thought I had touched a Shelley; a very odd study for Edna. But as to the olive-green, of course it was bound under the same star as ours.'

'Cilly, Cilly, now or never! photograph or not?' screamed Rashe, from behind her three-legged camera.

'Not!' was Lucilla's cavalier answer. 'Pack up; have done with it, Rashe. Pick me up at the school.'

Away she flew headlong, the patient and disconcerted Horatia following her to her room to extract hurried explanations, and worse than no answers as to the sundries to be packed at the last moment, while she hastily put on hat and mantle, and was flying down again, when her brother, with outspread arms, nearly caught her in her spring. 'Hollo! what's up?'

'Don't stop me, Owen! I'm going to walk on with Mr. Prendergast and be picked up. I must speak to Edna Murrell.'

'Nonsense! The carriage will be out in five minutes.'

'I must go, Owen. There's some story of a demon in human shape on the water with her last night, and Mr. Prendergast can't get a word out of her.'

'Is that any reason you should go ramping about, prying into people's affairs?'

'But, Owen, they will send her away. They will take away her character.'

'The—the—the more reason you should have nothing to do with it,' he exclaimed. 'It is no business for you, and I wont have you meddle in it.'

Such a strong and sudden assumption of fraternal authority took away her breath; and then, in terror lest he should know cause for this detention, she said—

'Owen! you don't guess who it was?'

'How should I?' he roughly answered. 'Some villanous slander, of course, there is, but it is no business of yours to be straking off to make it worse.'

'I should not make it worse.'

'Women always make things worse. Are you satisfied now?' as the carriage was seen coming round.

'That is only to be packed.'

'Packed with folly, yes! Look here! 11.20, and the train at 12.5!'

'I will miss the train, go up later, and sleep in London.'

'Stuff and nonsense! Who is going to take you? Not I.'

In Lucilla's desperation in the cause of her favourite Edna, she went through a rapid self-debate. Honor would gladly wait for her for such a cause; she could sleep at Woolstone Lane, and thence go on to join Horatia in her visit in Derbyshire, escorted by a Hiltonbury servant. But what would that entail? She would be at their mercy. Robert would obtain his advantage—it would be all over with her! Pride arose; Edna's cause sank. How many destinies were fixed in the few seconds while she stood with one foot forward, spinning her black hat by the elastic band!

'Too late, Mr. Prendergast; I cannot go,' she said, as she saw him waiting for her at the door. 'Don't be angry with me, and don't let the womankind prejudice you against poor Edna. You forgive me! It is really too late.'

'Forgive *you?*' smiled Mr. Prendergast, pressing her caressing hand in his great, lank grasp; 'what for?'

'Oh, because it is too late; and I can't help it. But don't be hard with her. Good-bye.'

Too late! Why did Lucilla repeat those words so often? Was it a relief to that irreflective nature to believe the die irrevocably cast, and the responsibility of decision over? Or why did she ask forgiveness of the only one whom she was not offending, but because there was a sense of need of pardon where she would not stoop to ask it.

Miss Charlecote and the Fulmorts, Rashe and Cilly, were to be transported to London by the same train, leaving Owen behind to help Charles Charteris entertain some guests still remaining, Honora promising him to wait in town until Lucilla should absolutely have started for Ireland, when she would supply him with the means of pursuit.

Lucilla's delay and change of mind made the final departure so late that it was needful to drive excessively fast, and the train was barely caught in time. The party were obliged to separate, and Robert took Phœbe into a different carriage from that where the other three found places.

In the ten minutes' transit by railway, Lucy, always softened by parting, was like another being towards Honor, and talked eagerly of 'coming home' for Christmas, sent messages to Hiltonbury friends, and did everything short of retractation to efface the painful impression she had left.

'Sweetest Honey!' she whispered, as they moved on after the tickets had been taken, thrusting her pretty head over into Honor's place. 'Nobody's looking, give me a kiss, and say you don't bear malice, though your kitten has been in a scratching humour.'

'Malice! no, indeed!' said Honor, fondly; 'but, oh! remember, dear child, that frolics may be at too dear a price.'

She longed to say more, but the final stop was made, and their roads diverged. Honor thought that Lucy looked white and trembling, with an uneasy eye, as though she would have given much to have been going home with her.

Nor was the consoling fancy unfounded. Lucilla's nerves were not at their usual pitch, and an undefined sense of loss of a safeguard was coming over her. Moreover, the desire for a last word to Robert was growing every moment, and he *would* keep on hunting out those boxes, as if they mattered to anybody.

She turned round on his substitute, and said, 'I've not spoken to Robin all this time. No wonder his feathers are ruffled. Make my peace with him, Phœbe dear.'

On the very platform, in that moment of bustle, Phœbe conscientiously and reasonably began, 'Will you tell me how much you mean by that?'

'Cilly—King's-cross—1.15,' cried Ratia, snatching at her arm.

'Oh! the slave one is! Next time we meet, Phœbe, the redbreast will be in a white tie, I shall——'

Hurry and agitation were making her flippant, and Robert was nearer than she deemed. He was assisting her to her seat, and then held out his hand, but never raised his eyes. 'Good-bye, Robin,' she said; 'Reason herself shall meet you at the Holt at Christmas.'

'Good-bye,' he said, but without a word of augury, and loosed her hand. Her fingers clung one moment, but he drew his away, called 'King's-cross to the coachman, and she was whirled off. Angler as she was, she no longer felt her prey answer her pull. Had the line snapped?

When Owen next appeared in Woolstone Lane he looked fagged and harassed, but talked of all things in sky, earth, or air, politics, literature, or gossip, took the bottom of the table, and treated the Parsonses as his guests. Honora, however, felt that something was amiss; perhaps Lucilla engaged to Lord William; and when, after luncheon, he followed her to the cedar room, she began with a desponding 'Well?'

'Well, she is off!'

'Alone with Rashe?'

'Alone with Rashe. Why, sweet Honey, you look gratified!'

'I had begun to fear some fresh news,' said Honor, smiling with effort. 'I am sure that something is wrong. You do not look well, my dear. How flushed you are, and your forehead is so hot!' as she put her hand on his brow.

'Oh, nothing!' he said, caressingly, holding it there. 'I'm glad to have got away from the Castle; Charlie and his set drink an intolerable lot of wine. I'll not be there again in a hurry.'

'I am glad of that. I wish you had come away with us.'

'I wish to heaven I had!' cried Owen; 'but it could not be helped! So now for my wild goose chase. Cross to-morrow night; only you were good enough to say you would find ways and means.'

'There, that is what I intended, including your Midsummer quarter. Don't you think it enough?' as she detected a look of dissatisfaction.

'You are very good. It is a tremendous shame; but you see, Honor dear, when one is across the water, one may as well go the whole animal. If this wise sister of mine does not get into a mess, there is a good deal I could do—plenty of sport. Little Henniker and some Westminster fellows in the —th are at Kilkenny.'

'You would like to spend the vacation in Ireland,' said Honor, with some disappointment. 'Well, if you go for my pleasure, it is but fair you should have your own. Shall I advance your September allowance?'

'Thank you. You do spoil one abominably, you concoction of honey and all things sweet. But the fact is, I've got uncommonly hard-up of late; no one would believe how ruinous it is being with the Charterises. I believe money evaporates in the atmosphere.'

'Betting?' asked Honor, gasping and aghast.

'On my honour, I assure you not *there*,' cried Owen,

eagerly. 'I never did bet there but once, and that was Lolly's doing; and I could not get out of it. Jew that she is! I wonder what Uncle Kit would say to that house now.'

'You are out of it, and I shall not regret the purchase of your disgust at their ways, Owen. It may be better for you to be in Ireland than to be tempted to go to them for the shooting season. How much do you want? You know, my dear, if there be anything else, I had rather pay anything that is right than have you in debt.'

'You were always the sweetest, best Honey living!' cried Owen, with much agitation; 'and it is a shame——' but there he stopped, and ended in a more ordinary tone—'shame to prey on you, as we both do, and with no better return.'

'Never mind, dear Owen,' she said, with moisture in her eye; 'your real happiness is the only return I want. Come, tell me your difficulty; most likely I can help you.'

'I've nothing to tell,' said Owen, with alarmed impetuosity; 'only that I'm a fool, like every one else, and—and—if you would only double that——'

'Double that! Owen, things cannot be right.'

'I told you they were not right,' was the impatient answer, 'or I should not be vexing you and myself; and,' as though to smooth away his rough commencement, 'what a comfort to have a Honey that will have patience!'

She shook her head, perplexed. 'Owen, I wish you could tell me more. I do not like debts. You know, dear boy, I grudge nothing I can do for you in my lifetime; but for your own sake, you must learn not to spend more than you will be able to afford. Indulgence now will be a penance to you by and by.'

Honora dreaded overdoing lectures to Owen. She knew that an old maid's advice to a young man was dangerous work, and her boy's submissive patience always excited her gratitude and forbearance, so she

desisted, in hopes of a confession, looking at him with such tenderness that he was moved to exclaim—
'Honor dear, you are the best and worst-used woman on earth! Would to Heaven that we had requited you better!'

'I have no cause of complaint against you, Owen,' she said, fondly; 'you have always been the joy and comfort of my heart;' and as he turned aside, as though stricken by the words, 'whatever you may have to reproach yourself with, it is not with hurting me; I only wish to remind you of higher and more stringent duties than those to myself. If you have erred, as I cannot but fear, will you not let me try and smooth the way back?'

'Impossible,' murmured Owen; 'there are things that can never be undone.'

'Not undone, but repented,' said Honor, convinced that he had been led astray by his cousin Charles, and felt bound not to expose him; 'so repented as to become stepping-stones in our progress.'

He only shook his head with a groan.

'The more sorrow, the better hope,' she began; but the impatient movement of his foot warned her that she was only torturing him, and she proceeded,—'Well, I trust you implicitly; I can understand that there may be confidences that ought not to pass between us, and will give you what you require to help you out of your difficulty. I wish you had a father, or any one who could be of more use to you, my poor boy!' and she began to fill up the cheque to the utmost of his demand.

'It is too much—too much,' cried Owen. 'Honor, I must tell you at all costs. What will you think when——'

'I do not wish to purchase a confession, Owen,' she said; 'you know best whether it be a fit one to make to me, or whether for the sake of others you ought to withhold it.'

He was checked, and did not answer.

'I see how it is,' continued Honor; 'my boy, as far as I am concerned, I look on your confession as made. You will be much alone while thus hovering near your sister among the mountains and by the streams. Let it be a time of reflection, and of making your peace with Another. You may do so the more earnestly for not having cast off the burthen on me. You are no child now, to whom your poor Honey's pardon almost seems an absolution. I sometimes think we went on with that too long.'

'No fear of my ever being a boy again,' said Owen, heavily, as he put the draft into his purse, and then bent his tall person to kiss her with the caressing fondness of his childhood, almost compensating for what his sister caused her to undergo.

Then, at the door, he turned to say, ' Remember, you would not hear.' He was gone, having left a thorn with Honor, in the doubt whether she ought not to have accepted his confidence ; but her abstinence had been such a mortification both of curiosity and of hostility to the Charterises that she could not but commend herself for it. She had strong faith in the efficacy of trust upon an honourable mind, and though it was evident that Owen had, in his own eyes, greatly transgressed, she reserved the hope that his error was magnified by his own consciousness, and admired the generosity that refused to betray another. She believed his present suffering to be the beginning of that growth in true religion which is often founded on some shock leading to self-distrust.

Alas ! how many falls have been counted by mothers as the preludes to rising again, like the clearing showers of a stormy day.

CHAPTER VIII.

Fearless she had tracked his feet
To this rocky, wild retreat,
And when morning met his view,
Her mild glances met it too.
Ah! your saints have cruel hearts,
Sternly from his bed he starts,
And with rude, repulsive shock,
Hurls her from the beetling rock.—T. MOORE.

HE deed was done. Conventionalities were defied, vaunts fulfilled, and Lucilla sat on a camp-stool on the deck of the steamer, watching the Welsh mountains rise, grow dim, and vanish gradually.

Horatia, in common with all the rest of the womankind, was prostrate on the cabin floor, treating Cilly's smiles and roses as aggravations of her misery. Had there been a sharer in her exultation, the gay pitching and dancing of the steamer would have been charming to Lucy, but when she retreated from the scene of wretchedness below, she felt herself lonely, and was conscious of some surprise among the surviving gentlemen at her re-appearance.

She took out a book as a protection, and read more continuously than she had done since *Vanity Fair* had come to the Holt, and she had been pleased to mark Honora's annoyance at every page she turned.

But July light faded, and only left her the poor

amusement of looking over the side for the phosphorescence of the water, and watching the smoke of the funnel lose itself overhead. The silent stars and sparkling waves would have set Phœbe's dutiful science on the alert, or transported Honor's inward ear by the chant of creation, but to her they were of moderate interest, and her imagination fell a prey to the memory of the eyes averted, and hand withdrawn. 'I'll be exemplary when this is over,' said she to herself, and at length her head nodded till she dropped into a giddy doze, whence with a chilly start she awoke, as the monotonous jog and bounce of the steamer were exchanged for a snort of arrival, among mysterious lanes of sparkling lights apparently rising from the waters.

She had slept just long enough to lose the lovely entrance of Dublin Bay, stiffen her limbs, and confuse her brains, and she stood still as the stream of passengers began to rush trampling by her, feeling bewildered and forlorn. Her cousin's voice was welcome, though over-loud and somewhat piteous. 'Where are you, stewardess? where's the young lady? Oh! Cilly, there you are. To leave me alone all this time, and here's the stewardess saying we must go ashore at once, or lose the train. Oh! the luggage, and I've lost my plaid,' and ghastly in the lamplight, limp and tottering, Rashe Charteris clasped her arm for support, and made her feel doubly savage and bewildered. Her first movement was to enjoin silence, then to gaze about for the goods. A gentleman took pity on the two ladies, and told them not to be deluded into trying to catch the train; there would be another in an hour's time, and if they had any one to meet them, they would most easily be found where they were.

'We have no one—we are alone,' said Lucilla; and his chivalry was so far awakened that he handed them to the pier, and undertook to find their boxes. Rashe was absolutely subdued, and hung shivering and helpless on her cousin, who felt as though dreaming in the strange scene of darkness made visible by the bright circles round the lamps, across which rapidly flitted the cloaked forms of travellers presiding over queer, wild, caricature-like shapes, each bending low under the weight of trunk or bag, in a procession like a magic lantern, save for the Babel of shrieks, cries, and expostulations everywhere in light or gloom.

A bell rang, an engine roared and rattled off. 'The train!' sighed Horatia; 'we shall have to stay here all night.'

'Nonsense,' said Lucy, ready to shake her; 'there is another in an hour. Stay quiet, do, or he will never find us.'

'Porter, ma'am—porrterr——'

'No, no, thank you,' cried Lucilla, darting on her rod-case and carriage-bag to rescue them from a freckled countenance, with claws attached.

'We shall lose everything, Cilla; that's your trusting to a stranger!'

'All right; thank you!' as she recognised her possessions, borne on various backs towards the station, whither the traveller escorted them, and where things looked more civilized. Ratia began to resume her senses, though weak and hungry. She was sorely discomfited at having to wait, and could not, like the seasoned voyagers, settle herself to repose on the long leathern couches of the waiting-room, but wandered, wobegone and impatient, scolding her cousin for choosing such an hour for their passage, for her desertion and general bad management. The merry, good-natured Rashe had disappeared in the sea-sick, cross, and weary wight, whose sole solace was grumbling, but her dolefulness only made Lucilla more mirthful. Here they were, and happen what would, it should only be 'such fun.' Recovered from the moment's bewilderment, Lucy announced that she felt as if she were at a ball, and whispered a proposal of astonishing the natives by a polka in the great empty boarded space. 'The suggestion would immortalize us ; come !' And she threatened mischievously to seize the waist of the still giddy and aching-headed Horatia, who repulsed her with sufficient roughness and alarm to set her off laughing at having been supposed to be in earnest.

The hurry of the train came at last; they hastened down-stairs and found the train awaiting them, were told their luggage was safe, and after sitting till they were tired, shot onwards watching the beautiful glimpses of the lights in the ships off Kingstown. They would gladly have gone on all night without another disembarkation and scramble, but the Dublin station came only too soon ; they were disgorged, and hastened after goods. Forth came trunk and portmanteau. Alas! none of theirs! Nothing with them but two carriage-bags and two rod-cases!

'It seems to be a common predicament,' said Lucilla; 'here are at least half-a-dozen in the same case.'

'Horrible management. We shall never see it more.'

'Nay, take comfort in the general lot. It will turn up to-morrow ; and meantime sleep is not packed up in our boxes. Come, let's be off. What noises! How do these drivers keep from running over one another. Each seems ready to whip every one's beast but his own. Don't you feel yourself in Ireland, Rashe? Arrah! I shall begin to scream, too, if I stand here much longer.'

'We can't go in that thing—a fly!'

'Don't exist here, Rashe—vermin is unknown. Submit to your fate——' and ere another objection could be uttered, Cilly threw bags and rods into an inside car, and pushed her cousin after them, chattering all the time, to poor Horatia's distraction. 'Oh! delicious! A cross between a baker's cart and a Van Amburg. A little more, and it would overbalance and carry the horse head over heels! Take care,

Rashe; you'll pound me into dust if you slip down over me.'

'I can't help it! Oh! the vilest thing in creation.'

'Such fun! To be taken when well shaken. Here we go up, up, up; and here we go down, down, down! Ha! ware fishing-rod! This is what it is to travel. No one ever described the experiences of an inside car!'

'Because no one in their senses would undergo such misery!'

'But you don't regard the beauties, Rashe, beauties of nature and art combined—see the lights reflected in the river—what a width. Oh! why don't they treat the Thames as they do the Liffey?'

'I can't see, I shall soon be dead! and getting to an inn without luggage, it's not respectable.'

'If you depart this life on the way, the want of luggage will concern me the most, my dear. Depend on it, other people have driven up in inside cars, minus luggage, in the memory of man, in this City of Dublin. Are you such a worldling base as to depend for your respectability on a paltry leathern trunk?'

Lucilla's confidence did not appear misplaced, for neither waiters nor chambermaids seemed surprised, but assured them that people usually missed their luggage by that train, and asseverated that it would appear next morning.

Lucilla awoke determined to be full of frolic and enjoyment, and Horatia, refreshed by her night's rest, was more easily able to detect 'such fun' than on the previous night; so the two cousins sat down amicably to breakfast on the Sunday morning, and inquired about church-services.

'My mallard's tail hat is odd "go to meeting" head-gear,' said Cilla, 'but one cannot lapse into heathenism; so where, Rashe?'

'Wouldn't it be fun to look into a Roman Catholic affair?'

'No,' said Cilly, decidedly; 'where I go it shall be the genuine article. I don't like curiosities in religion.'

'It's a curiosity to go to church at twelve o'clock! If you are so orthodox, let us wait for St. Patrick's this afternoon.'

'And in the mean time? It is but eleven this minute, and St. Patrick's is not till three. There's nothing to be done but to watch Irish nature in the street. Oh! I never before knew the perfection of Carleton's illustration. See that woman and her cap, and the man's round eyebrows and projecting lips with shillelagh written on them. Would it be Sabbath-breaking to perpetrate a sketch?'

But as Ratia was advancing to the window, Lucy suddenly started back, seized her and whirled her away, crying, 'The wretch! I know him now! I could not make him out last night.'

'Who?' exclaimed Rashe, starting determinedly to the window, but detained by the two small but resolute hands clasped round her waist.

'That black-whiskered valet of Mr. Calthorp's. If that man has the insolence to dog me and spy me, I'll not stay in Ireland another day.'

'O what fun!' burst out Horatia. 'It becomes romantic!'

'Atrocious impertinence!' said Lucilla, passionately. 'Why do you stand there laughing?'

'At you, my dear,' gasped Ratia, sinking on the sofa in her spasm of mirth. 'At your reception of chivalrous devotion.'

'Pretty chivalry to come and spy and beset ladies alone.'

'He has not beset us yet. Don't flatter yourself!'

'What do you mean by that, Horatia?'

'Do you want to try your pistols on me? The waiter could show us the way to the Fifteen Acres, only you see it is Sunday.'

'I want,' said Lucy, all tragedy and no comedy,

'to know why you talk of my *flattering* myself that I am insulted, and my plans upset.'

'Why?' said Rashe, a little sneeringly. 'Why, a little professed beauty like you would be so disappointed not to be pursued, that she is obliged to be always seeing phantoms that give her no peace.'

'Thank you,' coolly returned Cilly. 'Very well, I'll say no more about it, but if I find that man to be in Ireland, the same day I go home!'

Horatia gave a long, loud, provoking laugh. Lucilla felt it was for her dignity to let the subject drop, and betook herself to the only volumes attainable, Bradshaw and her book of flies; while Miss Charteris repaired to the window to investigate for herself the question of the pursuer, and made enlivening remarks on the two congregations, the one returning from mass, the other going to church, but these were not appreciated. It seemed as though the young ladies had but one set of spirits between them, which were gained by the one as soon as lost by the other.

It was rather a dull day. Fast as they were, the two girls shrank from rambling alone in streets thronged with figures that they associated with ruffianly destitution. Sunday had brought all to light, and the large handsome streets were beset with barefooted children, elf-locked women, and lounging, beetle-browed men, such as Lucy had only seen in the purlieus of Whittingtonia, in alleys looked into, but never entered by the civilized. In reality 'rich and rare' was so true that they might have walked there more secure from insult, than in many better regulated regions, but it was difficult to believe so, especially in attire then so novel as to be very remarkable, and the absence of protection lost its charm when there was no one to admire the bravado.

She did her best to embalm it for future appreciation by journalizing, making the voyage out a far better joke than she had found it, and describing the inside car in the true style of the facetious traveller.

Nothing so drives away fun, as the desire to be funny, and she began to grow weary of her work, and disgusted at her own lumbering attempts at pen-and-ink mirth; but they sufficed to make Rashe laugh, they would be quite good enough for Lord William, would grievously annoy Honora Charlecote, would be mentioned in all the periodicals, and give them the name of the Angel Anglers all the next season. Was not that enough to go to Ireland and write a witty tour for?

The outside car took them to St. Patrick's, and they had their first real enjoyment in the lazy liveliness of the vehicle, and the droll ciceroneship of the driver, who contrived to convey such compliments to their pretty faces, as only an Irishman could have given without offence.

Lucilla sprang down with exhilarated spirits, and even wished for Honor to share her indignation at the slovenliness around the cathedral, and the absence of close or cloister; nay, though she had taken an aversion to Strafford as a hero of Honor's, she forgave him, and resolved to belabour the House of Cork handsomely in her journal, when she beheld the six-storied monument, and imagined it, as he had found it, in the Altar's very place. 'Would that he had created an absolute Boylean vacuum!' What a grand *bon mot* for her journal!

However, either the spirit of indignation at the sight of the unkneeling congregation, or else the familiar words of the beautiful musical service, made her more than usually devout, and stirred up something within her that could only be appeased by the resolution that the singing in Robert Fulmort's parish should be super-excellent. After the service, the carman persuaded them to drive in the Phœnix Park, where they enjoyed the beautiful broken ground, the picturesque thickets, the grass whose colour reminded them that they were in the Emerald Isle, the purple outlines of the Wicklow hills, whence they thought they detected a fresh mountain breeze. They only wondered to find this delightful place so little frequented. In England, a Sunday would have filled it with holiday strollers, whereas here, they only encountered a very few, and those chiefly gentlefolks. The populace preferred sitting on the doorsteps, or lounging against the houses, as if they were making studies of themselves for caricatures; and were evidently so much struck with the young ladies' attire, that the shelter of the hotel was gladly welcomed.

Lucilla was alone in the sitting-room when the waiter came to lay the cloth. He looked round, as if to secure secresy, and then remarked in a low confidential voice, 'There's been a gentleman inquiring for you, ma'am.'

'Who was it?' said Lucy, with feigned coolness.

'It was when you were at church, ma'am; he wished to know whether two ladies had arrived here, Miss Charteris and Miss Sandbrook.'

'Did he leave his card?'

'He did not, ma'am,'his call was to be a secret; he said it was only to be sure whether you had arrived.'

'Then, he did not give his name?'

'He did, ma'am, for he desired to be let know what route the young ladies took when they left,' quoth the man, with a comical look, as though he were imparting a most delightful secret.

'Was he Mr. Calthorp?'

'I said I'd not mention his name,' said the waiter, with, however, such decided assent, that, as at the same moment he quitted the room and Horatia entered it, Cilly exclaimed, 'There, Rashe, what do you say now to the phantom of my vanity? Here has he been asking for us, and what route we meant taking.'

'He! Who?'

'Who?—why, who should it be? The waiter has just told me.'

VOL. I.   X

'You absurd girl!'

'Well, ask him yourself.'

So when the waiter came up, Miss Charteris demanded, 'Has Mr. Calthorp been calling here?'

'What was the name, ma'am, if you please?'

'Calthorp. Has Mr. Calthorp been calling here?'

'Cawthorne? Was it Colonel Cawthorne, of the Royal Hussars, ma'am? He was here yesterday, but not to-day.'

'I said Calthorp. Has a Mr. Calthorp been inquiring for us to-day?'

'I have not heard, ma'am, I'll inquire,' said he, looking alert, and again disappearing, while Horatia looked as proud of herself as Cilly had done just before.

He came back again, while Lucilla was repeating his communication, and assured Miss Charteris that no such person had called.

'Then, what gentleman has been here, making inquiries about us?'

'Gentleman! Indeed, ma'am, I don't understand your meaning.'

'Have you not been telling this young lady that a gentleman has been asking after us, and desiring to be informed what route we intended to take?'

'Ah, sure!' said the waiter, as if recollecting himself, 'I did mention it. Some gentleman did just ask me in a careless sort of way who the two beautiful young ladies might be, and where they were going. Such young ladies always create a sensation, as you must be aware, ma'am, and I own I did speak of it to the young lady, because I thought she had seen the attraction of the gentleman's eyes.'

So perfectly assured did he look, that Lucilla felt a moment's doubt whether her memory served her as to his former words, but just as she raised her eyes and opened her lips in refutation, she met a glance from him full of ludicrous reassurance, evidently meaning that he was guarding his own secret and hers. He was gone the next moment, and Horatia turned upon her, with exultant merriment.

'I always heard that Ireland was a mendacious country,' said Cilly.

'And a country where people lose the sight of their eyes and ears,' laughed Rashe. 'O what a foundation for the second act of the drama !'

'Of which the third will be my going home by the next steamer.'

'Because a stranger asked who we were ?'

Each had her own interpretation of the double-faced waiter's assertion, and it served them to dispute upon all the evening.

Lucilla was persuaded that he imagined her an injured beauty, reft from her faithful adorer by her stern aunt or duenna, and that he considered himself to be doing her a kindness by keeping her informed of her hero's vicinity, while he denied it to her companion; but she scorned to enter into an explanation, or make any disavowal, and found the few displeased words she spoke were received with compassion, as at the dictation of the stern monitress.

Horatia, on the other hand, could not easily resign the comical version that Lucilla's inordinate opinion of her own attractions had made her imagine Mr. Calthorp's valet in the street, and discover his master in the chance inquirer whom the waiter had mentioned; and as Cilly could not aver that the man had actually told her in so many words that it was Mr. Calthorp, Horatia had a right to her opinion, and though she knew she had been a young lady a good many years, she could not easily adopt the suggestion that she could pass for Cilly's cruel duenna.

Lucilla grew sullen, and talked of going home by the next steamer; Rashe, far from ready for another sea voyage, called herself ill used, and represented the absurdity of returning on a false alarm. Cilla was staggered, and thought what it would be, if Mr. Calthorp, smoking his cigar at his club, heard that she had fled from his imaginary pursuit. Besides, the luggage must be recovered, so she let Horatia go on arranging for an excursion for the Monday, only observing that it must not be in Dublin.

'No, bonnets are needful there. What do you think of Howth and Ireland's Eye, the place where Kirwan murdered his wife?' said Rashe, with great gusto, for she had a strong turn for the horrid murders in the newspaper.

'Too near, and too smart,' sulked Lucy.

'Well, then, Glendalough, that is wild, and far off enough, and may be done in a day from Dublin. I'll ring and find out.'

'Not from that man.'

'Oh! we shall see Calthorps peopling the hill-sides! Well, let us have the landlord.'

It was found that both the Devil's Glen and the Seven Churches might be visited if they started by the seven o'clock train, and returned late at night, and Lucilla agreeing, the evening went off as best it might, the cousins being glad to get out of each other's company at nine, that they might be up early the next morning. Lucy had not liked Ratia so little since the days of her infantine tyranny.

The morning, however, raised their spirits, and sent them off in a more friendly humour, enjoying the bustle and excitement, that was meat and drink to them, and exclaiming at the exquisite views of sea and rugged coast along beautiful Kilmeny bay. When they left the train, they were delighted with their outside car, and reclined on their opposite sides in enchantment with the fern-bordered lanes, winding between noble trees, between which came inviting glimpses of exquisitely green meadows and hill sides. They stopped at a park-looking gate, leading to the Devil's Glen, which they were to traverse on foot, meeting the car at the other end.

Here there was just enough life and adventure to charm them, as they gaily trod the path, winding picturesquely beside the dashing, dancing, foaming stream, now between bare salient bluffs of dark rock, now between glades of verdant thicket, or bold shouldering slopes of purple heath, and soft bent grass. They were constantly crying out with delight, as they bounded from one point of view to another, sometimes climbing among loose stones, leading between ferns and hazel stems to a well planted hermitage, sometimes springing across the streamlet upon stepping-stones. At the end of the wood another lodge gate brought them beyond the private grounds, that showed care, even in their rusticity, and they came out on the open hill-side in true mountain air, soft turf beneath their feet, the stream rushing away at the bottom of the slope, and the view closed in with blue mountains, on which the clouds marked purple shadows. This was freedom! this was enjoyment! this was worth the journey! and Cilla's elastic feet sprang along as if she had been a young kid. How much was delight in the scenery, how much in the scramble, need not be analyzed.

There was plenty of scrambling before it was over. A woman who had been lying in wait for tourists at the gate, guided them to the bend of the glen, where they were to climb up to pay their respects to the waterfall. The ascent was not far from perpendicular, only rendered accessible by the slope of fallen debris at the base, and a few steps cut out from one projecting rock to another, up to a narrow shelf, whence the cascade was to be looked down on. The more adventurous spirits went on to a rock overhanging the fall, and with a curious chink or cranny, forming a window with a seat, and called King O'Toole's chair. Each girl perched herself there, and was complimented on her strong head and active limbs, and all their powers were needed in the long breathless pull up craggy stepping-stones, then over steep slippery turf ere they gained the summit of the bank. Spent, though still gasping out, 'such fun!' they threw themselves on their backs upon the thymy grass, and lay still for several seconds ere they sat up to look back at the thickly wooded ravine, winding crevice-like in and out between the overlapping skirts of the hills, whose rugged heads cut off the horizon. Then merrily sharing the first instalment of luncheon with their barefooted guide, they turned their faces onwards, where all their way seemed one bare gray moor, rising far off into the outline of Luggela, a peak overhanging the semblance of a crater.

Nothing afforded them much more mirth than a rude bridge, consisting of a single row of square-headed unconnected posts along the heads of which Cilla three times hopped backwards and forwards for the mere drollery of the thing, with vigour unabated by the long walk over the dreary moorland fields with their stone walls.

By the side of the guide's cabin the car awaited them, and mile after mile they drove on through treeless wastes, the few houses with their thatch anchored down by stones, showing what winds must sweep along those unsheltered tracts. The desolate solitude began to weary the volatile pair into silence; ere the mountains rose closer to them, they crossed a bridge over a stony stream begirt with meadows, and following its course came into sight of their goal.

Here was Glendalough, a *cul de sac* between the mountains, that shelved down, enclosing it on all sides save the entrance, through which the river issued. Their summits were bare, of the gray stone that lay in fragments everywhere, but their sides were clothed with the lovely Irish green pastureland, intermixed with brushwood and trees, and a beauteous meadow surrounded the white ring-like beach of pure white sand and pebbles bordering the outer lake, whose gray waters sparkled in the sun. Its twin lake, divided from it by so narrow a belt of ground, that the white beaches lay on their green setting, like the outline of a figure of 8, had a more wild and gloomy aspect, lying deeper within the hollow, and the hills coming sheer down on it at the further end in all their grayness unsoftened by any verdure. The gray was that of absolute black and white intermingled in the grain of the stone, and this was peculiarly gloomy, but in the summer sunshine it served but to set off the brilliance of the verdure, and the whole air of the valley was so bright, that Cilly declared that it had been traduced, and that no skylark of sense need object thereto.

Losing sight of the lakes as they entered the shabby little town, they sprang off the car before a small inn, and ere their feet were on the ground were appropriated by one of a shoal of guides, in dress and speech an ultra Irishman, exaggerating his part as a sort of buffoon for the travellers. Rashe was diverted by his humours, Cilla thought them in bad taste, and would fain have escaped from his brogue and his antics, with some perception that the scene ought to be left to make its impression in peace.

Small peace, however, was there among the scores of men, women, and children, within the rude walls containing the most noted relics; all beset the visitors with offers of stockings, lace, or stones from the hills; and the chatter of the guide was a lesser nuisance for which she was forced to compound for the sake of his protection. When he had cleared away his compatriots, she was able to see the remains of two of the Seven Churches, the Cathedral, and St. Kevin's Kitchen, both of enduring gray stone, covered with yellow lichen, which gave a remarkable golden tint to their extreme old age. Architecture there was next to none. St. Kevin's so-called kitchen had a cylindrical tower, crowned by an extinguisher, and within the roofless walls was a flat stone, once the altar, and still a station for pilgrims; and the cathedral contained two broken coffin-lids with floriated crosses, but it was merely four rude roofless walls, enclosing less space than a cottage kitchen, and less ornamental than many a barn. The whole space was encumbered with regular modern headstones, ugly as the worst that English graveyards could show, and alternating between the names of Byrne and O'Toole, families who, as the guide said, would come 'hundreds of miles to lie there.' It was a grand thought, that those two lines, in wealth or in poverty, had been constant to that one wild mountain burying-place, in splendour or in ruin, for more than twelve centuries.

Here, some steps from the cathedral on the top of the slope, was the chief grandeur of the view. A noble old carved granite cross, eight or ten feet high, stood upon the brow, bending slightly to one side, and beyond lay the valley cherishing its treasure of the twin lakelets, girt in by the band across them, nestled in the soft lining of copsewood and meadow, and protected by the lofty massive hills above. In front, but below, and somewhat to the right, lay another enclosure, containing the ivied gable of St. Mary's Church, and the tall column-like Round Tower, both with the same peculiar golden hoariness. The sight struck Lucilla with admiration and wonder, but the next moment she heard the guide exhorting Rashe to embrace the stem of the cross, telling her that if she could clasp her arms round it, she would be sure of a handsome and rich husband within the year.

Half superstitious, and always eager for fun, Horatia spread her arms in the endeavour, but her hands could not have met without the aid of the guide, who dragged them together, and celebrated the exploit with a hurrah of congratulation, while she laughed triumphantly, and called on her companion to try her luck. But Lucy was disgusted, and bluntly refused, knowing her grasp to be far too small, unable to endure the touch of the guide, and maybe shrinking from the failure of the augury.

'Ah! to be shure, an' it's not such a purty young lady as yourself that need be taking the trouble,' did not fall pleasantly on her ears, and still less Ratia's laugh and exclamation, 'You make too sure, do you? Have a care. There were black looks at parting! But you need not be afraid, if handsome be a part of the spell.'

There was no answer, and Horatia saw that the outspoken raillery that Cilly had once courted now gave offence. She guessed that something was amiss, but did not know that what had once been secure had been wilfully imperilled, and that suspense was awakening new feelings of delicacy and tenderness.

The light words and vulgar forecasting had, in spite of herself, transported Lucilla from the rocky thicket where she was walking, even to the cedar room at Woolstone Lane, and conjured up before her that grave, massive brow, and the eye that would not meet her. She had hurried to these wilds to escape that influence, and it was holding her tighter than ever. To hasten home on account of Mr. Calthorp's pursuit would be the most effectual vindication of the feminine dignity that she might have impaired in Robert's eyes, but to do this on what Ratia insisted on believing a false alarm would be the height of absurdity. She was determined on extracting proofs sufficient to justify her return, and every moment seemed an hour until she could feel herself free to set her face homewards. A strange impatience seized her at every spot where the guide stopped them to admire, and Ratia's encouragement of his witticisms provoked her excessively.

With a kind of despair she found herself required, before taking boat for St. Kevin's Cave, to mount into a wood to admire another waterfall.

'See two waterfalls,' she muttered, 'and you have seen them all. There are only two kinds, one a bucket of water thrown down from the roof of a house, the other over the staircase. Either the water is a fiction, or you can't get at them for the wet!'

'That was a splendid fellow at the Devil's Glen.'

'There's as good a one any day at the lock on the canal at home! only we do not delude people into coming to see it. Up such places, too!'

'Cilly, for shame. What, tired and giving in?'

'Not tired in the least; only this place is not worth getting late for the train.'

'Will the young lady take my hand, I'd be proud to have the honour of helping her up,' said the guide; but Lucilla disdainfully rejected his aid, and climbed among the stones and brushwood aloof from the others, Ratia talking in high glee to the Irishman, and adventurously scrambling.

'Cilly, here it is,' she cried, from beneath a projecting elbow of rock; 'you look down on it. It's a delicious fall. I declare one can get into it;' and, by the aid of a tree, she lowered herself down on a flat stone, whence she could see the cascade better than above. 'This is stunning. I vow one can get right into the bed of the stream right across. Don't be slow, Cilly, this is the prime fun of all!'

'You care for the romp and nothing else,' grumbled Lucilla. That boisterous merriment was hateful to her, when feeling that the demeanour of gentlewomen must be their protection, and with all her high spirit, she was terrified lest insult or remark should be occasioned. Her signs of remonstrance were only received with a derisive outburst, as Rashe climbed down into the midst of the bed of the stream. 'Come, Cilla, or I shall indite a page in the diary, headed Faint heart—Ah!' as her foot slipped on the stones, and she fell backwards, but with instant efforts at rising, such as assured her cousin that no harm was done, 'Nay, nonsensical clambering will be the word,' she said.

'Serves you right for getting into such places! What! Hurt?' as Horatia, after resting in a sitting posture, tried to get up, but paused, with a cry.

'Nothing,' she said, 'I'll——' but another attempt ended in the same way. Cilla sprang to her, followed by the guide, imprecating bad luck to the slippery stones. Herself standing in the water, Lucilla drew her cousin upright, and with a good deal of help from the guide, and much suffering, brought her up the high bank, and down the rough steep descent through the wood.

She had given her back and side a severe twist, but she moved less painfully on more level ground, and, supported between Lucilla and the guide, whom the mischance had converted from a comedy clown to a delicately considerate assistant, she set out for the inn where the car had been left. The progress lasted for two doleful hours, every step worse than the last, and, much exhausted, she at length sank upon the sofa in the little sitting-room of the inn.

The landlady was urgent that the wet clothes should be taken off, and the back rubbed with whisky, but Cilla stood agitating her small soaked foot, and insisting that the car should come round at once, since the wet had dried on them, and they had best lose no time in returning to Dublin, or at least to Bray.

But Rashe cried out that the car would be the death of her; she could not stir without a night's rest.

'And be all the stiffer to-morrow? Once on the car, you will be very comfortable——'

'Oh, no! I can't! This is a horrid place. Of all the unlucky things that could have happened——'

'Then,' said Cilla, fancying a little coercion would be wholesome, 'don't be faint-hearted. You will be glad to-morrow that I had the sense to make you move to-day. I shall order the car.'

'Indeed!' cried Horatia, her temper yielding to pain and annoyance; 'you seem to forget that this expedition is mine! I am paymaster, and have the only right to decide.'

Lucilla felt the taunt base, as recalling to her the dependent position into which she had carelessly rushed, relying on the family feeling that had hitherto made all things as one. 'Henceforth,' said she, 'I take my share of all that we spend. I will not sell my free will.'

'So you mean to leave me here alone?' said Horatia, with positive tears of pain, weariness, and vexation, at the cruel unfriendliness of the girl she had petted.

'Nonsense! I must abide by your fate. I only hate to see people chicken-hearted, and thought you wanted shaking up. I stay so long as you own me an independent agent.'

The discussion was given up, when it was announced that a room was ready; and Rashe underwent so much in climbing the stairs, that Cilly thought she could not have been worse on the car.

The apartment was not much behind that at the village inn at Hiltonbury. In fact, it had gay curtains and a grand figured blind, but the doors at the Charlecote Arms had no such independent habits of opening, the carpet would have been whole, and the chairs would not have quaked beneath Lucy's grasshopper weight; when down she sat in doleful resignation, having undressed her cousin, sent her *chaussure* to dry, and dismissed the car, with a sense of bidding farewell to the civilized world, and entering a desert island, devoid of the zest of Robinson Crusoe.

What an endless evening it was, and how the ladies detested each other! There lay Horatia, not hurt enough for alarm, but quite cross enough to silence pity, suffering at every move, and sore at Cilly's want of compassion; and here sat Lucilla, thoroughly disgusted with her cousin, her situation, and her expedition. Believing the strain a trifle, she not unjustly despised the want of resolution that had shrunk from so expedient an exertion as the journey, and felt injured by the selfish want of consideration that had condemned her to this awkward position in this forlorn little inn, without even the few toilette necessaries that they had with them at Dublin, and with no place to sit in, for the sitting-room below stairs served as a coffee-room, where sundry male tourists were imbibing whisky, the fumes of which ascended to the young ladies above, long before they could obtain their own meal.

The chops were curiosities; and as to the tea, the grounds, apparently the peat of the valley, filled up nearly an eighth of the cup, causing Lucilla in lugubrious mirth to talk of 'That lake whose gloomy tea, ne'er saw Hyson nor Bohea,' when Rashe fretfully retorted, 'It is very unkind in you to grumble at everything, when you know I can't help it!'

'I was not grumbling, I only wanted to enliven you.'

'Queer enlivenment!'

Nor did Lucilla's attempts at body curing succeed better. Her rubbing only evoked screeches, and her advice was scornfully rejected. Horatia was a determined homœopath, and sighed for the globules in her wandering box, and as whisky and tobacco both became increasingly fragrant, averred again and again that nothing should induce her to stay here another night.

Nothing? Lucilla found her in the morning in all the aches and flushes of a feverish cold, her sprain severely painful, her eyes swollen, her throat so sore, that in alarm Cilly besought her to send for advice; but Rashe regarded a murderous allopathist as near akin to an executioner, and only bewailed the want of her minikin doses.

Giving up the hope of an immediate departure, Lucilla despatched a messenger to Bray, thence to telegraph for the luggage; and the day was spent in fears lest their landlord at Dublin might detain their goods as those of suspicious characters.

Other excitement there was none, not even in quarrelling, for Rashe was in a sleepy state, only roused by interludes of gloomy tea and greasy broth; and outside, the clouds had closed down, such clouds as she had never seen, blotting out lake and mountain with an impervious gray curtain, seeming to bathe rather than to rain on the place. She longed to dash out into it, but Ratia's example warned her against drenching her only garments, though indoors the dryness was only comparative. Everything she touched, herself included, seemed pervaded by a damp, limp rawness, that she vainly tried to dispel by ordering a fire. The turf smouldered, the smoke came into the room, and made their eyes water, and Rashe insisted that the fire should be put out.

Cilla almost envied her sleep, as she sat disconsolate in the window, watching the comparative density of the rain, and listening to the extraordinary howls and shrieks in the town, which kept her constantly expecting that a murder or a rebellion would come to relieve the monotony of the day, till she found that nothing ensued, and no one took any notice.

She tried to sketch from memory, but nothing would hinder that least pleasant of occupations— thought. Either she imagined every unpleasant chance of detention, she worried herself about Robert Fulmort, or marvelled what Mr. Prendergast and the censorious ladies would do with Edna Murrell. Many a time did she hold her watch to her ear, suspecting it of having stopped, so slowly did it loiter through the weary hours. Eleven o'clock when she hoped it was one—half-past two when it felt like five.

By real five, the mist was thinner, showing first nearer, then remoter objects; the coarse slates of the roofs opposite emerged polished and dripping, and the cloud finally took its leave, some heavy flakes, like cotton wool, hanging on the hill-side, and every rock shining, every leaf glistening. Verdure and rosy cheeks both resulted from a perpetual vapour bath.

Lucilla rejoiced in her liberty, and hurried out of doors, but leaning out of the coffee-room window, loungers were seen who made her sensible of the awkwardness of her position, and she looked about for yesterday's guide as a friend, but he was not at hand, and her uneasy gaze brought round her numbers, begging or offering guidance. She wished to retreat, but would not, and walked briskly along the side of the valley opposite to that she had yesterday visited, in search of the other four churches. Two fragments were at the junction of the lakes, another was entirely destroyed, but the last, called the Abbey, stood in ruins within the same wall as the Round Tower, which rosé straight, round, mysterious, defying inquiry, as it caught the evening light on its summit, even as it had done for so many centuries past.

Not that Cilla thought of the riddles of that tower, far less of the early Christianity of the isle of saints, of which these ruins and their wild legend were the only vestiges, nor of the mysticism that planted clusters of churches in sevens as analogous to the seven stars of the Apocalypse. Even the rugged glories of the landscape chiefly addressed themselves to her as good to sketch, her highest flight in admiration of the picturesque. In the state of mind ascribed to the ancients, she only felt the weird unhomelikeness of the place, as though she were at the ends of the earth, unable to return, and always depressed by solitude ; she could have wept. Was it for this that she had risked the love that had been her own from childhood, and broken with the friend to whom her father had commended her? Was it worth while to defy their censures for this dreary spot, this weak-spirited, exacting, unrefined companion, and the insult of Mr. Calthorp's pursuit?

Naturally shrewd, well-knowing the world, and guarded by a real attachment, Lucilla had never regarded the millionaire's attentions as more than idle amusement in watching the frolics of a beauty, and had suffered them as adding to her own diversion; but his secretly following her, no doubt to derive mirth from her proceedings, revealed to her that woman could not permit such terms without loss of dignity, and her cheek burnt at the thought of the ludicrous light in which he might place her present predicament before a conclave of gentlemen.

The thought was intolerable. To escape it by rapid motion, she turned hastily to leave the enclosure. A figure was climbing over the steps in the wall with outstretched hand, as if he expected her to cling to him, and Mr. Calthorp, springing forward, eagerly exclaimed in familiar, patronizing tones, 'Miss Sandbrook! They told me you were gone this way.' Then, in a very different voice at the unexpected look and bow that he encountered: 'I hope Miss Charteris's accident is not serious.'

'Thank you, not serious,' was the freezing reply.

'I am glad. How did it occur?'

'It was a fall.' He should have no good story wherewith to regale his friends.

'Going on well, I trust? Chancing to be at Dublin, I heard by accident you were here, and fearing that there might be a difficulty, I ran down in the hope of being of service to you.'

'Thank you,' in the least thankful of tones.

'Is there nothing I can do for you?'

'Thank you, nothing.'

'Could I not obtain some advice for Miss Charteris?'

'Thank you, she wishes for none.'

'I am sure'—he spoke eagerly—'that in some way I could be of use to you. I shall remain at hand. I cannot bear that you should be alone in this remote place.'

'Thank you, we will not put you to inconvenience. We intended to be alone.'

'I see you esteem it a great liberty,' said poor Mr. Calthorp; 'but you must forgive my impulse to see whether I could be of any assistance to you. I will do as you desire, but at least you will let me leave Stefano with you; he is a fellow full of resources, who would make you comfortable here, and me easy about you.'

'Thank you, we require no one.'

Those 'thank you's' were intolerable, but her defensive reserve and dignity attracted the gentleman more than all her dashing brilliancy, and he became more urgent. 'You cannot ask me to leave you entirely to yourselves under such circumstances.'

'I more than ask it, I insist upon it. Good morning.'

'Miss Sandbrook, do not go till you have heard and forgiven me.'

'I will not hear you, Mr. Calthorp. This is neither the time nor place,' said Lucilla, iuly more and more perturbed, but moving along with slow, quiet steps, and betraying no emotion. 'The object of our journey was totally defeated by meeting any of our ordinary acquaintance, and but for this mischance I should have been on my way home to-day.'

'Oh! Miss Sandbrook, do you class me among your ordinary acquaintance?'

It was all she could do to hinder her walk from losing its calm slowness, and before she could divest her intended reply of undignified sharpness, he continued: 'Who could have betrayed my presence? But for this, I meant that you should never have been aware that I was hovering near to watch over you.'

'Yes, to collect good stories for your club.'

'This is injustice! Flagrant injustice, Miss Sandbrook! Will you not credit the anxiety that irresistibly impelled me to be ever at hand in case you should need a protector?'

'No,' was the point blank reply.

'How shall I convince you?' he cried, vehemently. 'What have I done that you should refuse to believe in the feelings that prompted me?'

'What have you done?' said Lucilla, whose blood was up. 'You have taken a liberty, which is the best proof of what your feelings are, and every moment that you force your presence on me adds to the offence!'

She saw that she had succeeded. He stood still, bowed, and answered not, possibly deeming this the most effective means of recalling her; but from first to last he had not known Lucilla Sandbrook.

The eager, protecting familiarity of his first address had given her such a shock that she felt certain that she had no guard but herself from positively insulting advances; and though abstaining from all quickening of pace, her heart throbbed violently in the fear of hearing him following her, and the inn was a haven of refuge.

She flew up to her bed-room to tear about like a panther, as if by violence to work down the tumult in her breast. She had proved the truth of Honora's warning, that beyond the pale of ordinary *convenances*, a woman is exposed to insult, and however sufficient she may be for her own protection, the very fact of having to defend herself is well nigh degradation. It was not owning the error. It was the agony of humiliation, not the meekness of humility, and she was as angry with Miss Charlecote for the prediction as with Mr. Calthorp for having fulfilled it, enraged with Horatia, and desperate at her present imprisoned condition, unable to escape, and liable to be still haunted by her enemy.

At last she saw the discomfited swain re-enter the inn, his car come round, and finally drive off with him; and then she felt what a blank was her victory. If she breathed freely, it was at the cost of an increased sense of solitude and severance from the habitable world.

Hitherto she had kept away from her cousin, trusting that the visit might remain a secret, too mortifying to both parties to be divulged, but she found Horatia in a state of eager anticipation, awakened from the torpor to watch for tidings of a happy conclusion to their difficulties, and preparing jests on the pettish ingratitude with which she expected Lucilla to requite the services that would be nevertheless accepted.

Gone! Sent away! Not even commissioned to find the boxes. Horatia's consternation and irritation knew no bounds. Lucilla was no less indignant that she could imagine it possible to become dependent on his good offices, or to permit him to remain in the neighbourhood. Rashe angrily scoffed at her new-born scruples, and complained of her want of consideration for herself. Cilla reproached her cousin with utter absence of any sense of propriety and decorum. Rashe talked of ingratitude, and her sore throat being by this time past conversation, she came to tears. Cilla, who could not bear to see any one unhappy, tried many a 'never mind,' many a 'didn't mean,' many a fair augury for the morrow, but all in vain, and night came down upon the Angel Anglers more forlorn and less friendly than ever! and, with all the invalid's discomforts so much aggravated by the tears and the altercation that escape from this gloomy shore appeared infinitely remote.

There was an essential difference of tone of mind between those brought up at Hiltonbury or at Castle Blanch, and though high spirits had long concealed the unlikeness, it had now been made bare, and Lucy could not conquer her disgust and disappointment.

Sunshine was on Luggela, and Horatia's ailments were abating, so, as her temper was not alleviated, Lucilla thought peace would be best preserved by sallying out to sketch. A drawing from behind the cross became so engrossing that she was sorry to find it time for the early dinner, and her artistic pride was only allayed by the conviction that she should always hate what recalled Glendalough.

Rashe was better, and was up and dressed. Hopes of departure produced amity, and they were almost lively over their veal broth, when sounds of arrival made Lucilla groan at the prospect of cockney tourists obstructing the completion of her drawing.

'There's a gentleman asking to see you, Miss.'

'I can see no one.'

'Cilla, now do.'

'Tell him I cannot see him,' repeated Lucy, imperiously.

'How can you be so silly? he may have heard of our boxes.'

'I would toss them into the lake rather than take them from him.'

'Eh! pray let me be present when you perform the ceremony! Cilla in the heroics! Whom is she expecting?' said a voice outside the door, ever ajar, a voice that made Lucilla clasp her hands in ecstasy.

'You, Owen! come in,' cried Horatia, writhing herself up.

'Owen, old Owen! that's right,' burst from Cilla, as she sprang to him.

'Right! Ah! that is not the greeting I expected; I was thinking how to guard my eyes. So, you have had enough of the unprotected dodge! What has Rashe been doing to herself? A desperate leap down the Falls of Niagara.'

Horatia was diffuse in the narration; but, after the first, Lucy did not speak. She began by arming herself against her brother's derision, but presently felt perplexed by detecting on his countenance something unwontedly grave and preoccupied. She was sure that his attention was far away from Rashe's long story, and she abruptly interrupted it with, 'How came you here, Owen?'

He did not seem to hear, and she demanded, 'Is anything the matter? Are you come to fetch us because any one is ill?'

Starting, he said, 'No, oh no!'

'Then what brought you here? a family council, or Honor Charlecote?'

'Honor Charlecote,' he repeated mistily: then, making an effort, 'Yes, good old soul, she gave me a vacation tour on condition that I should keep an eye on you. Go on, Rashe; what were you saying?'

'Didn't you hear me, Owen? Why, Calthorp, the great Calthorp, is in our wake. Cilly is frantic.'

'Calthorp about!' exclaimed Owen, with a start of dismay. 'Where?'

'I've disposed of him,' quoth Lucilla; 'he'll not trouble us again.'

'Which way is he gone?'

'I would not tell you if I knew.'

'Don't be such an idiot,' he petulantly answered; 'I want nothing of the fellow, only to know whether he is clean gone. Are you sure whether he went by Bray?'

'I told you I neither knew nor cared.'

'Could you have believed, Owen,' said Rashe, plaintively, 'that she was so absurd as never even to tell him to inquire for our boxes?'

'Owen knows better;' but Lucilla stopped, surprised to see that his thoughts were again astray. Giving a constrained smile, he asked, 'Well, what next?'

'To find our boxes,' they answered in a breath.

'Your boxes? Didn't I tell you I've got them here?'

'Owen, you're a trump,' cried Rashe.

'How on earth did you know about them?' inquired his sister.

'Very simply; crossed from Liverpool yesterday, reconnoitered at your hotel, was shown your telegram, went to the luggage office, routed out that the things were taking a gentle tour to Limerick, got them back this morning, and came on. And what are you after next?'

'Home,' jerked out Lucy, without looking up, thinking how welcome he would have been yesterday, without the goods.

'Yes, home,' said Horatia. 'This abominable sprain will hinder my throwing a line, or jolting on Irish roads, and if Cilla is to be in agonies when she sees a man on the horizon, we might as well never have come.'

'Will you help me to carry home this poor invalid warrior, Owen?' said Lucilla; 'she will permit you.'

'I'll put you into the steamer,' said Owen; 'but, you see, I have made my arrangements for doing Killarney and the rest of it.'

'I declare,' said Rashe, recovering benevolence with

comfort, 'if they would send Scott from the Castle to meet me at Holyhead, Cilly might as well go on with you. You would be sufficient to keep off the Calthorps.'

'I'm afraid that's no go,' hesitated Owen. 'You see I had made my plans, trusting to your bold assertions that you would suffer no one to approach.'

'Oh! never mind. It was no proposal of mine. I've had enough of Ireland,' returned Lucy, somewhat aggrieved.

'How soon shall you be sufficiently repaired for a start, Ratia?' asked Owen, turning quickly round to her. 'To-morrow? No! Well, I'll come over and see.'

'Going away?' cried the ladies, by no means willing to part with their guardian.

'Yes, I must. Expecting that we should be parallels never meeting, I had to provide for myself.'

'I see,' said Rashe; 'he has a merry party at Newragh Bridge, and will sit up over whist and punch till midnight!'

'You don't pretend to put yourselves in competition,' said he, snatching at the idea hastily.

'Oh! no,' said his sister, with an annoyed gesture. 'I never expect you to prefer me and my comfort to ny one.'

'Indeed, Cilla, I'm sorry,' he answered gently, but in perplexity, 'but I never reckoned on being wanted, and engagements are engagements.'

'I'm sure I don't want you when anything pleasanter is going forward,' she answered, with vexation in her tone.

'I'll be here by eleven or twelve,' he replied, avoiding the altercation; 'but I must get back now. I shall be waited for.'

'Who is it that can't wait?' asked Rashe.

'Oh! just an English acquaintance of mine. There, good-bye! I wish I had come in time to surprise the modern St. Kevin! Are you sure there was no drowning in the lake!'

'You know it was blessed to drown no one after Kathleen.'

'Reassuring! Only mind you put a chapter about it into the tour.' Under the cover of these words he was gone.

'I declare there's some mystery about his companion!' exclaimed Horatia. 'Suppose it were Calthorp himself?'

'Owen is not so lost to respect for his sister.'

'But did you not see how little he was surprised, and how much pre-occupied?'

'Very likely; but no one but you could imagine him capable of such an outrage.'

'You have been crazy ever since you entered Ireland, and expect every one else to be the same. Seriously, what damage did you anticipate from a little civility?'

'If you begin upon that, I shall go out and finish my sketch, and not unpack one of the boxes.'

Nevertheless, Lucilla spent much fretting guess-work on her cousin's surmise. She relied too much on Owen's sense of propriety to entertain the idea that he could be forwarding a pursuit so obviously insolent, but a still wilder conjecture had been set afloat in her mind. Could the nameless one be Robert Fulmort? Though aware of the anonymous nature of brother's friends, the secrecy struck her as unusually guarded; and to one so used to devotion, it seemed no extraordinary homage that another admirer should be drawn along at a respectful distance, a satellite to her erratic course; nay, probably all had been concerted in Woolstone Lane, and therewith the naughty girl crested her head, and prepared to take offence. After all, it could not be, or why should Owen have been bent on returning, and be so independent of her? Far more probably he had met a college friend or a Westminster schoolfellow, some of whom were in regiments quartered in Ireland, and on the morrow would bring him to do the lions of Glendalough, among which might be reckoned the Angel Anglers!

That possibility might have added some grains to the satisfaction of making a respectable toilette next day. Certain it is that Miss Sandbrook's mountain costume was an exquisite feat of elaborate simplicity, and that the completion of her sketch was interrupted by many a backward look down the pass, and many a contradictory mood, sometimes boding almost as harsh a reception for Robert as for Mr. Calthorp, sometimes relenting in the thrill of hope, sometimes accusing herself of arrant folly, and expecting as a *pis aller* the diversion of dazzling and tormenting an Oxonian, or a soldier or two! Be the meeting what it might, she preferred that it should be out of Horatia's sight, and so drew on and on to the detriment of her distances.

Positively it was past twelve, and the desire to be surprised unconcernedly occupied could no longer obviate her restlessness, so she packed up her hair-pencil, and, walking back to the inn, found Rashe in solitary possession of the coffee-room.

'You have missed him, Cilly.'

'Owen? No one else?'

'No, not the Calthorp; I am sorry for you.'

'But who was here? tell me, Rashe.'

'Owen, I tell you,' repeated Horatia, playing with her impatience.

'Tell me; I will know whether he has any one with him.'

'Alack for your disappointment, for the waste of that blue bow; not a soul came here but himself.'

'And where is he? how did I miss him?' said Lucilla, forcibly repressing the mortification for which her cousin was watching.

'Gone. As I was not in travelling trim, and you not forthcoming, he could not wait; but we are to be off to-morrow at ten o'clock.'

'Why did he not come out to find me? Did you tell him I was close by?'

'He had to join his friend, and go to the Vale of Avoca. I've found out the man, Cilla. No, don't look so much on the *qui vive;* it's only Jack Hastings.'

'Jack Hastings!' said Lucilla, her looks fallen. 'No wonder he would not bring him here.'

'Why not, poor fellow? I used to know him very well before he was up the spout.'

'I wish Owen had not fallen in with him,' said the sister, gravely. 'Are you certain it is so, Rashe?'

'I taxed him with it, and he did not deny it; only put it from him, laughing. What's the harm? Poor Jack was always a good-natured, honourable fellow, uncommonly clever and amusing—a well-read man, too; and Owen is safe enough—no one could try to borrow of him.'

'What would Honor's feelings be?' said Lucilla, with more fellow-feeling for her than for months past. Lax as was the sister's tolerance, she was startled at his becoming the associate of an avowedly loose character under the stigma of the world, and with perilous abilities and agreeableness; and it was another of Horatia's offences against proper feeling, not only to regard such evil communications with indifference, but absolutely to wish to be brought into contact with a person of this description in their present isolated state. Displeased and uneasy, Lucilla assumed the *rôle* of petulance and quarrelsomeness for the rest of the day, and revenged herself to the best of her abilities upon Rashe and Owen, by refusing to go to inspect the scene of Kathleen's fatal repulse.

True to his appointment, Owen arrived alone on a car chosen with all regard to Horatia's comfort, and was most actively attentive in settling on it the ladies and their luggage, stretching himself out on the opposite side, his face raised to the clouds, as he whistled an air; but his eye was still restless, and his sister resolved on questioning him.

Opportunities were, however, rare; whether or not with the design of warding off a *tête-à-tête*, he devoted himself to his cousin's service in a manner rare to her since she had laid herself out to be treated as though her name were Horace instead of Horatia. However, Lucilla was not the woman to be balked of a settled purpose; and at their hotel, at Dublin, she nailed him fast by turning back on him when Horatia bade them good night. 'Well, what do you want?' he asked, annoyed.

'I want to speak to you.'

'I hope it is to beg me to write to ask Honor to receive you at home, and promise to behave like a decent and respectable person.'

'I want neither a judge nor an intercessor in you.'

'Come, Lucy, it really would be for every one's good if you would go and take care of poor Honor. You have been using her vilely, and I should think you'd had enough of Rashe for one while.'

'If I have used her vilely, at least I have dealt openly by her,' said Lucilla. 'She has always seen the worst of me on the surface. Can you bear to talk of her when you know how you are treating her?'

He coloured violently, and his furious gesture would have intimidated most sisters; but she stood her ground, and answered his stammering demand what she dared to imply.

'You may go into a passion, but you cannot hinder me from esteeming it shameful to make her mission a cover for associating with one whom she would regard with so much horror as Jack Hastings.'

'Jack Hastings!' cried Owen, to her amazement, bursting into a fit of laughter, loud, long, and explosive. 'Well done, Rashe!'

'You told her so.'

'She told me so, and one does not contradict a lady.'

'Something must have put it into her head.'

'Only to be accounted for by an unrequited attachment,' laughed Owen; 'depend on it, a comparison of dates would show Hastings's incarceration to have been the epoch of Rashe's taking to the high masculine line—

'"If e'er she loved, 'twas him alone
Who lived within the jug of stone."'

'For shame, Owen; Rashe never was in love.'

But he went on laughing at Rashe's disappointment at his solitary arrival till she said, tartly, 'You cannot wonder at our thinking you must have some reason for neither mentioning your companion's name nor bringing him with you.'

'In fact, no man not under a cloud could abstain from paying homage to the queen of the anglers.'

It was so true as to raise an angry spot on her cheek, and provoke the hasty excuse, 'It would have been obvious to have brought your friend to see your cousin and sister.'

'One broken-backed, both unwashed! O, the sincerity of the resistance I overheard! No gentleman admitted, forsooth! O, for a lodge in some vast wilderness! Yes; St. Anthony would have found it a wilderness indeed without his temptations. What would St. Dunstan have been minus the black gentleman's nose, or St. Kevin but for Kathleen? It was a fortunate interposition that Calthorp turned up the day before I came, or I might have had to drag the lake for you.'

This personal attack only made her persist. 'It was very different when we were alone or with you; you know very well that there could have been no objection.'

'No objection on your side, certainly, so I perceive; but suppose there were no desire on the other?'

'Oh!' in a piqued voice, 'I know many men don't care for ladies' society, but I don't see why they should be nameless.'

'I thought you would deem such a name unworthy to be mentioned.'

'Well, but who is the shy man? Is it the little Henniker, who used to look as if he would dive under the table when you brought him from Westminster?'

'If I told you, you would remember it against the poor creature for life, as a deliberate insult and want of taste. Good night.'

He took his hat, and went out, leaving Lucy balancing her guesses between Ensign Henniker and him whom she could not mention. Her rejection of Mr. Calthorp might have occasioned the present secrecy, and she was content to leave herself the pleasant mystery, in the hope of having it dispelled by her last glance of Kingstown quay.

In that hope, she rocked herself to sleep, and next morning was so extra vivacious as to be a sore trial to poor Rashe, in the anticipation of the *peine forte et dure* of St. George's Channel. Owen was also in high spirits, but a pattern of consideration and kind attention, as he saw the ladies on board, and provided for their comfort, not leaving them till the last moment.

Lucilla's heart had beaten fast from the moment she had reached Kingstown; she was keeping her hand free to wave a most encouraging kiss, and as her eye roamed over the heads upon the quay without a recognition, she felt absolutely baffled and cheated; and gloriously as the Bay of Dublin spread itself before her, she was conscious only of wrath and mortification, and of a bitter sense of dreariness and desertion. Nobody cared for her, not even her brother!

CHAPTER IX.

> My pride, that took
> Fully easily all impressions from below,
> Would not look up, or half despised the height
> To which I could not, or I would not climb.
> I thought I could not breathe in that fine air.
> IDYLLS OF THE KING.

'AN you come and take a turn in the Temple - gardens, Phœbe ? ' asked Robert, on the way from church, the day after Owen's visit to Woolstone Lane.

Phœbe rejoiced, for she had scarcely seen him since his return from Castle Blanch, and his state of mind was a mystery to her. It was long, however, before he afforded her any clue. He paced on, grave and abstracted, and they had many times gone up and down the least frequented path, before he abruptly said, 'I have asked Mr. Parsons to give me a title for Holy Orders.'

'I don't quite know what that means.'

'How simple you are, Phœbe,' he said, impatiently; 'it means that St. Wulstan's should be my first curacy. May my labours be accepted as an endeavour to atone for some of the evil we cause here.'

'Dear Robin ! what did Mr. Parsons say ? Was he not very glad ?'

'No ; there lies the doubt.'

'Doubt?'

'Yes. He told me that he had engaged as many

curates as he has means for. I answered that my stipend need be no consideration, for I only wished to spend on the parish, but he was not satisfied. Many incumbents don't like to have curates of independent means; I believe it has an amateur appearance.'

'Mr. Parsons cannot think you would not be devoted.'

'I hope to convince him that I may be trusted. It is all that is left me now.'

'It will be very cruel to you, and to the poor people, if he will not,' said Phœbe, warmly; 'what will papa and Mervyn say?'

'I shall not mention it till all is settled; I have my father's consent to my choice of a profession, and I do not think myself bound to let him dictate my course as a minister. I owe a higher duty, and if his business scatters the seeds of vice, surely "obedience in the Lord" should not prevent me from trying to counteract them.'

It was a case of conscience to be only judged by himself, and where even a sister like Phœbe could do little but hope for the best, so she expressed a cheerful hope that her father must know that it was right, and that he would care less, now that he was away, and pleased with Augusta's prospects.

'Yes,' said Robert, 'he already thinks me such a fool, that it may be indifferent to him in what particular manner I act it out.'

'And how does it stand with Mr. Parsons?'

'He will give me an answer to-morrow evening, provided I continue in the same mind. There is no chance of my not doing so. My time of suspense is over!' and the words absolutely sounded like relief, though the set stern face, and the long breaths at each pause told another tale.

'I did not think she would really have gone!' said Phœbe.

'This once, and we will mention her no more. It is not merely this expedition, but all I saw at Wrapworth convinced me that I should risk my faithfulness to my calling by connecting myself with one who, with all her loveliness and generosity, lives upon excitement. She is the very light of poor Prendergast's eyes, and he cannot endure to say a word in her dispraise; she is constantly doing acts of kindness in his parish, and is much beloved there, yet he could not conceal how much trouble she gives him by her want of judgment and wilfulness; patronizing and forgetting capriciously, and attending to no remonstrance. You saw yourself the treatment of that schoolmistress. I thought the more of this, because Prendergast is so fond of her, and does her full justice. No; her very aspect proves that a parish priest has no business to think of her.'

Large tears swelled in Phœbe's eyes. The first vision of her youth was melting away, and she detected no relenting in his grave resolute voice.

'Shall you tell her?' was all she could say.

'That is the question. At one time she gave me reason to think that she accepted a claim to be considered in my plans, and understood what I never concealed. Latterly she has appeared to withdraw all encouragement, to reject every advance, and yet—— Phœbe, tell me whether she has given you any reason to suppose that she ever was in earnest with me?'

'I know she respects and likes you better than any one, and speaks of you like no one else,' said Phœbe; then pausing, and speaking more diffidently, though with a smile, 'I think she looks up to you so much, that she is afraid to put herself in your power, for fear she should be made to give up her odd ways in spite of herself, and yet that she has no notion of losing you. Did you see her face at the station?'

'I would not! I could not meet her eyes! I snatched my hand from the little clinging fingers;' and Robert's voice almost became a gasp. 'It was not fit that the spell should be renewed. She would be miserable, I under constant temptation, if I endeavoured to make her share my work! Best as it is! She has so cast me off that my honour is no longer bound to her; but I cannot tell whether it be due to her to let her know how it is with me, or whether it would be mere coxcombry.'

'The Sunday that she spent here,' said Phœbe, slowly, 'she had a talk with me. I wrote it down. Miss Fennimore says it is the safest way——'

'Where is it?' cried Robert.

'I kept it in my pocket-book, for fear any one should see it, and it should do harm. Here it is, if it will help you. I am afraid I made things worse, but I did not know what to say.'

It was one of the boldest experiments ever made by a sister; for what man could brook the sight of an unvarnished statement of his proxy's pleading, or help imputing the failure to the go-between?

'I would not have had this happen for a thousand pounds!' was his acknowledgment. 'Child as you are, Phœbe, had you not sense to know, that no woman could endure to have that said, which should scarcely be implied? I wonder no longer at her studied avoidance.'

'If it be all my bad management, cannot it be set right?' humbly and hopefully said Phœbe.

'There is no right!' he said. 'There, take it back. It settles the question. The security you childishly showed, was treated as offensive presumption on my part. It would be presuming yet farther to make a formal withdrawal of what was never accepted.'

'Then is it my doing? Have I made mischief between you, and put you apart?' said poor Phœbe, in great distress. 'Can't I make up for it?'

'You? No, you were only an over plain-spoken child, and brought about the crisis that must have come somehow. It is not what you have done, or not done; it is what Lucy Sandbrook has said and done, that shows that I must have done with her for ever.'

'And yet,' said Phœbe, taking this as forgiveness,

'you see she never believed that you would give her up. If she did, I am sure she would not have gone.'

'She thinks her power over me stronger than my principles. She challenges me—desires you to tell me so. We shall see.'

He spoke as a man whose steadfastness had been defied, and who was piqued on proving it to the utmost. Such feelings may savour of the wrath of man, they may need the purifying of chastening, and they often impel far beyond the bounds of sober judgment; but no doubt they likewise frequently render that easy which would otherwise have appeared impossible, and which, if done in haste, may be regretted, but not repented, at leisure.

Under some circumstances, the harshness of youth is a healthy symptom, proving force of character and conviction, though that is only when the foremost victim is self. Robert was far from perfect, and it might be doubted whether he were entering the right track in the right way, but at least his heart was sound, and there was a fair hope that his failings, in working their punishment, might work their cure.

It was in a thorough brotherly and Christian spirit that before entering the house he compelled himself to say, 'Don't vex yourself, Phœbe, I know you did the best you could, as kindly as you could. It made no real difference, and it was best that she should know the truth.'

'Thank you, dear Robin,' cried Phœbe, grateful for the consolation; 'I am glad you do not think I misrepresented.'

'You are always accurate,' he answered. 'If you did anything undesirable, it was representing at all. But that is nothing to the purpose. It is all over now, and thank you for your constant good will and patience, my dear. There! now then it is an understood thing that her name is never spoken between us.'

Meanwhile, Robert's proposal was under discussion by the elders. Mr. Parsons had no abstract dread of a wealthy curate, but he hesitated to accept gratuitous services, and distrusted plans formed under the impulse of disappointment or of enthusiasm, since in the event of a change, both parties might be embarrassed. There was danger too of collisions with his family, and Mr. Parsons took counsel with Miss Charlecote, knowing indeed that where her affections were concerned, her opinions must be taken with a qualification, but relying on the good sense formed by rectitude of purpose.

Honor's affection for Robert Fulmort had always been moderated by Owen's antagonism; her moderation in superlatives commanded explicit credence, and Mr. Parsons inferred more, instead of less, than she expressed; better able as he was to estimate that manly character, gaining force with growth, and though slow to discern between good and evil, always firm to the duty when it was once perceived, and thus rising with the elevation of the standard. The undemonstrative temper, and tardiness in adopting extra habits of religious observance and profession, which had disappointed Honor, struck the clergyman as evidences both of sincerity and evenness of development, proving the sterling reality of what had been attained.

'Not taking, but trusty,' judged the vicar.

But the lad was an angry lover. How tantalizing to be offered a fourth curate, with a long purse, only to find St. Wulstan's serving as an outlet for a lover's quarrel, and the youth restless and restive ere the end of his diaconate!

'How savage you are,' said his wife; 'as if the parish would be hurt by his help or his presence. If he goes, let him go—some other help will come.'

'And don't deprive him of the advantage of a good master,' said Honor.

'This wretched cure is not worth flattery,' he said, smiling.

'Nay,' said Mrs. Parsons, 'how often have I heard you rejoice that you started here.'

'Under Mr. Charlecote—yes.'

'You are the depository of his traditions,' said Honor, 'hand them on to Robert. I wish nothing better for Owen.'

Mr. Parsons wished something better for himself, and averted a reply, by speaking of Robert as accepted.

Robert's next request was to be made useful in the parish, while preparing for his ordination in the autumn Ember week ; and though there were demurs as to unnecessarily anticipating the strain on health and strength, he obtained his wish in mercy to a state only to be alleviated by the realities of labour.

So few difficulties were started by his family, that Honora suspected that Mr. Fulmort, always chiefly occupied by what was immediately before him, hardly realized that by taking an assistant curacy at St. Wulstan's, his son became one of the pastors of Whittington-streets, great and little, Richard-courts, Cicely-row, Alice-lane, Cat-alley, and Turnagain-corner. Scarcely, however, was this settled, when a despatch arrived from Dublin, headed, 'The Fast Fly Fishers ; or, the modern St. Kevin,' containing in Ingoldsby legend-like rhymes, the entire narration of the Glendalough predicament of the 'Fast and Fair,' and concluding with a piece of prose, by the same author, assuring his sweet Honey that the poem, though strange, was true, that he had just seen the angelic anglers on board the steamer, and it would not be for lack of good advice on his part, if Lucy did not present herself at Woolstone Lane, to partake of the dish called humble pie, on the derivation whereof antiquaries were divided.

Half amused, half vexed by his levity, and wholly relieved and hopeful, Honora could not help showing Owen's performance to Phœbe for the sake of its cleverness ; but she found the child too young and simple to enter into it, for the whole effect was an entreaty that Robert might not see it, only hear the facts.

Rather annoyed by this want of appreciation of

Owen's wit, Honora saw, nevertheless, that Phœbe had come to a right conclusion. The breach was not likely to be diminished by finding that the wilful girl had exposed herself to ridicule, and the Fulmort nature had so little sense of the ludicrous, that this good-natured brotherly satire would be taken for mere derision.

So Honor left it to Phœbe to give her own version, only wishing that the catastrophe had come to his knowledge before his arrangements had been made with Mr. Parsons.

Phœbe had some difficulty in telling her story. Robert at first silenced her peremptorily, but after ten minutes relented, and said, moodily, 'Well, let me hear!' He listened without relaxing a muscle of his rigid countenance; and when Phœbe ended by saying that Miss Charlecote had ordered Lucy's room to be prepared, thinking that she might present herself at any moment, he said, 'Take care that you warn me when she comes. I shall leave town that minute.'

'Robert, Robert, if she come home grieved and knowing better——'

'I will not see her!' he repeated. 'I made her taking this journey the test! The result is nothing to me! Phœbe, I trust to you that no intended good-nature of Miss Charlecote's should bring us together. Promise me.'

Phœbe could do nothing but promise, and not another sentence could she obtain from her brother, indeed his face looked so formidable in its sternness, that she would have been a bold maiden to have tried.

Honora augured truly, that not only was his stern nature deeply offended, but that he was quite as much in dread of coming under the power of Lucy's fascinations, as Cilla had ever been of his strength. Such mutual aversion was really a token of the force of influence upon each, and Honor assured Phœbe that all would come right. 'Let her only come home and be good, and you will see, Phœbe! She will not be the worse for an alarm, nor even for waiting till after his two years at St. Wulstan's.'

The reception of the travellers at Castle Blanch was certainly not mortifying by creating any excitement. Charles Charteris said his worst in the words, 'One week!' and his wife was glad to have some one to write her notes.

This indifference fretted Lucy. She found herself loathing the perfumy rooms, the sleepy voice, and hardly able to sit still in her restless impatience of Lolly's platitudes and Charles's *insouciance*, while Rashe could never be liked again. Even a lecture from Honor Charlecote would have been infinitely preferable, and one grim look of Robert's would be bliss!

No one knew whether Miss Charlecote were still in town, nor whether Augusta Fulmort were to be married in England or abroad; and as to Miss Murrell, Lolly languidly wondered what it was that she had heard.

Hungering for some one whom she could trust, Lucilla took an early breakfast in her own room, and walked to Wrapworth, hoping to catch the curate lingering over his coffee and letters. From a distance, however, she espied his form disappearing in the school-porch, and approaching, heard his voice reading prayers, and the children's chanted response. Coming to the oriel, she looked in. There were the rows of shiny heads, fair, brown, and black; there were the long sable back and chopped-hay locks of the curate; but where a queen-like figure had of old been wont to preside, she beheld a tallow face, with sandy hair under the most precise of net caps, and a straight thread-paper shape in scanty gray stuff, and white apron.

Dizzy with wrathful consternation, Cilla threw herself on one of the seats of the porch, shaking her foot, and biting her lip, frantic to know the truth, yet too much incensed to enter, even when the hum of united voices ceased, the rushing sound of rising was over, and measured footsteps pattered to the classes, where the manly interrogations sounded alternately with the shrill little answers.

Clump, clump, came the heavy feet of a laggard, her head bent over her book, her thick lips vainly conning the unlearned task, unaware of the presence of the young lady, till Lucilla touched her, saying, 'What, Martha, a ten o'clock scholar?'

She gave a little cry, opened her staring eyes, and dropped a curtsey.

'Whom have you here for mistress?' asked Lucilla.

'Please, ma'am, governess is runned away.'

'What do you mean?'

'Yes, ma'am,' replied the girl, developing powers of volubility such as scholastic relations with her had left unsuspected. 'She ran away last Saturday was a week, and there was nobody to open the school when we came to it a Sunday morning; and we had holidays all last week, ma'am; and mother was terrified* out of her life; and father, he said he wouldn't have me never go for to do no such thing, and that he didn't want no fine ladies, as was always spiting of me.'

'Every one will seem to spite you, if you keep no better hours,' said Lucy, little edified by Martha's virtuous indignation.

The girl had scarcely entered the school before the clergyman stood on the threshold, and was seized by both hands, with the words, 'O Mr. Prendergast, what is this?'

'You here, Cilla? What's the matter? What has brought you back?'

'Had you not heard? A sprain of Ratia's, and other things. Never mind. What's all this?'

'Ah! I knew you would be sadly grieved!'

'So you did frighten her away!'

---

* Terrify, to tease or worry.

'I never meant it. I tried to act for the best. She was spoken to, by myself and others, but nobody could make any impression, and we could only give her notice to go at the harvest holidays. She took it with her usual grand air——'

'Which is really misery and despair. Oh, why did I go? Go on!'

'I wrote to the mother, advising her, if possible, to come and be with the girl till the holidays. That was on Thursday week, and the old woman promised to come on the Monday—wrote a very proper letter, allowing for the Methodistical phrases—but on the Saturday it was observed that the house was not opened, and on Sunday morning I got a note—if you'll come in I'll show it to you.'

He presently discovered it among multitudinous other papers on his chimney-piece. Within a lady-like envelope was a thick, satin-paper, queen's-sized note, containing these words:

'REVEREND SIR,—It is with the deepest feelings of regret for the unsatisfactory appearance of my late conduct that I venture to address you, but time will enable me to account for all, and I can at the present moment only entreat you to pardon any inconvenience I may have occasioned by the precipitancy of my departure. Credit me, reverend and dear sir, it was only the law of necessity that could have compelled me to act in a manner that may appear questionable. Your feeling heart will excuse my reserve when you are informed of the whole. In the mean time, I am only permitted to mention that this morning I became a happy wife. With heartfelt thanks for all the kindness I have received, I remain,

'Reverend sir,
'Your obedient servant,
'EDNA.'

'Not one message to me?' exclaimed Lucilla.

'Her not having had the impudence is the only redeeming thing!'

'I did not think she would have left no word for me,' said Lucy, who knew she had been kinder than her wont, and was really wounded. 'Happy wife! Who can it be?'

'Happy wife!' repeated the curate. 'It is miserable fool, most likely, by this time.'

'No surname signed! What's the post mark? Only Charing-cross. Could you find out nothing, or did you not think it worth while to look?'

'What do you take me for, Cilla? I inquired at the station, but she had not been there, and on the Monday I went to London and saw the mother, who was in great distress, for she had had a letter much like mine, only more unsatisfactory, throwing out absurd hints about grandeur and prosperity—poor deluded simpleton!'

'She distinctly says she is married.'

'Yes, but she gives no name nor place. What's that worth? After such duplicity as she has been practising so long, I don't know how to take her statement. Those people are pleased to talk of a marriage in the sight of heaven, when they mean the devil's own work!'

'No, no! I will not think it!'

'Then don't, my dear. You were very young and innocent, and thought no harm.'

'I'm not young—I'm not innocent!' furiously said Cilly. 'Tell me downright all you suspect.'

'I'm not given to suspecting,' said the poor clergyman, half in deprecation, half in reproof; 'but I am afraid it is a bad business. If she had married a servant, or any one in her own rank, there would have been no need of concealing the name, at least from her mother. I feared at first that it was one of your cousin Charles's friends, but there seems more reason to suppose that one of the musical people at your concert at the Castle may have thought her voice a good speculation for the stage.'

'He would marry her to secure her gains.'

'If so, why the secrecy?'

'Mrs. Jenkins has taught you to make it as bad as possible,' burst out Lucy. 'O, why was not I at home? Is it too late to trace her and proclaim her innocence?'

'I was wishing for your help. I went to Mr. Charteris to ask who the performers were, but he knew nothing about them, and said you and his sister had managed it all.'

'The director was Derval. He is fairly respectable, at least I know nothing to the contrary. I'll make Charlie write. There was an Italian, with a black beard and a bass voice, whom we have had several times. I saw him looking at her. Just tell me what sort of woman is the mother. She lets lodgings, does not she?'

'Yes, in Little Whittington-street.'

'Dear me! I trust she is no friend of Honor Charlecote's.'

'Out of her beat, I should think. She dissents.'

'What a blessing! I beg your pardon, but if anything could be an aggravation, it would be Honor Charlecote's moralities.'

'So you were not aware of the dissent?'

'And you are going to set that down as more deceit, as if it were the poor thing's business to denounce her mother. Now, to show you that I can be sure that Edna was brought up to the Church, I will tell you her antecedents. He father was Sir Thomas Deane's butler; they lived in the village, and she was very much in the nursery with the Miss Deanes—had some lessons from the governess. There was some notion of making her a nursery governess, but Sir Thomas died, the ladies went abroad, taking her father with them; Edna was sent to a training school, and the mother went to live in the City with a relation who let lodgings, and who has since died, leaving the concern to Mrs. Murrell, whose husband was killed by an upset of the carriage on the Alps.'

'I heard all that, and plenty besides! Poor woman, she was in such distress that one could not but let her pour it all out, but I declare the din rang in my ears the whole night after! A very nice, respectable-looking body she was, with jet-black eyes like diamonds, and a rosy, countrified complexion, quite a treat to see in that grimy place, her widow's cap as white as snow, but oh, such a tongue! She would give me all her spiritual experiences—how she was converted by an awakening minister in Cat-alley, and yet had a great respect for such ministers of the Church as fed their flocks with sincere milk, mixed up with the biography of all the shopmen and clerks who ever lodged there, and to whom she acted as a mother!'

'It was not their fault that she did not act as a mother-in-law. Edna has told me of the unpleasantness of being at home on account of the young men.'

'Exactly! I was spared none of the chances she might have had, but the only thing worthy of note was about a cashier who surreptitiously brought a friend from the "hopera," to overhear her singing hymns on the Sunday evening, and thus led to an offer on his part to have her brought out on the stage.'

'Ha! could that have come to anything?'

'No. Mrs. Murrell's suspicions took that direction, and we hunted down the cashier and the friend, but they were quite exonerated. It only proves that her voice has an unfortunate value.'

'If she be gone off with the Italian bass, I can't say I think it a fatal sign that she was slow to present him to her domestic Mause Headrigg, who no doubt would deliberately prefer the boards of her coffin to the boards of the theatre. Well, come along—we will get a letter from Charles, and rescue her—I mean, clear her.'

'Wont you look into school, and see how we go on?

The women complained so much of having their children on their hands, though I am sure they had sent them to school seldom enough of late, that I got this young woman from Mrs. Stuart's asylum till the holidays. I think we shall let her stay on, she has a good deal of method, and all seem pleased with the change.'

'You have your wish of a fright. No, I thank you! I'm not so glad as the rest of you to get rid of refinement and superiority.'

There was no answer, and more touched by silence than reply, she hastily said, 'Never mind! I dare say she may do better for the children, but you know, I, who am hard of caring for any one, did care for poor Edna, and I can't stand pæans over your new broom.'

Mr. Prendergast gave a smile such as was only evoked by his late rector's little daughter, and answered, 'No one can be more concerned than I. She was not in her place here, that was certain, and I ought to have minded that she was not thrust into temptation. I shall remember it with shame to my dying day.'

'Which means to say that so should I.'

'No, you did not know so much of the evils of the world.'

'I told you before, Mr. Pendy, that I am twenty times more sophisticated than you are. You talk of knowing the world! I wish I didn't. I'm tired of everybody!'

And on the way home she described her expedition, and had the pleasure of the curate's sympathy, if not his entire approval. Perhaps there was no other being whom she so thoroughly treated as a friend, actually like a woman friend, chiefly because he thoroughly believed in her, and was very blind to her faults. Robert would have given worlds to have found her *once*, what Mr. Prendergast found her *always*.

She left him to wait in the drawing-room, while she went on her mission, but presently rushed back in a fury. Nobody cared a straw for the catastrophe. Lolly begged her not to be so excited about a trifle, it made her quite nervous; and the others laughed at her; Rashe pretended to think it a fine chance to have changed 'the life of an early Christian,' for the triumphs of the stage; and Charles scouted the idea of writing to the man's employer. 'He call Derval to account for all the tricks of his fiddlers and singers? Much obliged!'

Mr. Prendergast decided on going to town by the next train, to make inquiries of Derval himself, without further loss of time, and Cilly declared that she would go with him and force the conceited professor to attend; but the curate, who had never found any difficulty in enforcing his own dignity, and thought it no business for a young lady, declined her company, unless, he said, she were going to spend the day with Miss Charlecote.

'I've a great mind to go to her for good and all. Let her fall upon me for all and sundry. It will do me good to hear a decent woman speak again! besides, poor old soul, she will be so highly gratified, that she will be quite meek' (and so will some one else, quoth the perverse little heart); 'I'll put up a few things, and not delay you.'

'This is very sudden!' said the curate, wishing to keep the peace between her and her friends, and not willing that his sunbeam should fleet 'so like the Borealis race!' 'Will it not annoy your cousins?'

'They ought to be annoyed!'

'And are you certain that you would find Miss Charlecote in town? I thought her stay was to be short.'

'I'm certain of nothing, but that every place is detestable.'

'What would you do if you did not find her?'

'Go on to Euston-square. Do you think I don't know my way to Hiltonbury, or that I should not get welcome enough—ay, and too much—there?'

'Then if you are so uncertain of her movements, do you not think you had better let me learn them before you start. She might not even be gone home, and you would not like to come back here again ; if——'

'Like a dog that has been out hunting,' said Lucilla, who could bear opposition from this quarter as from no other. 'You wont take the responsibility, that's the fact. Well, you may go and reconnoitre, if you will; but mind, if you say one word of what brings you to town, I shall never go near the Holt at all. To hear—whenever the Raymonds, or any other of the godly school-keeping sort come to dinner—of the direful effects of certificated schoolmistresses, would drive me to such distraction that I cannot answer for the consequences.'

'I am sure it is not a fact to proclaim.'

'Ah! but if you run against Mr. Parsons, you'll never abstain from telling him of his stray lamb, nor from condoling with him upon the wolf in Cat-alley. Now there's a fair hope of his having more on his hands than to get his fingers scratched by meddling with the cats, and so that this may remain unknown. So consider yourself sworn to secrecy.'

Mr. Prendergast promised. The good man was a bit of a gossip, so perhaps her precaution was not thrown away, for he could hardly have helped seeking the sympathy of a brother pastor, especially of him to whose fold the wanderer primarily belonged. Nor did Lucy feel certain of not telling the whole herself in some unguarded moment of confidence. All she cared for was, that the story should not transpire through some other source, and be brandished over her head as an illustration of all the maxims that she had so often spurned. She ran after Mr. Prendergast after he had taken leave, to warn him against calling in Woolstone Lane, and desired him instead to go to Masters's shop, where it was sure to be known whether Miss Charlecote were in town or not.

Mr. Prendergast secretly did grateful honour to the consideration that would not let him plod all the weary way into the City. Little did he guess that it was one part mistrust of his silence, and three parts reviving pride, which forbade that Honora should know that he had received any such commission.

The day was spent in pleasant anticipations of the gratitude and satisfaction that would be excited by her magnanimous return, and her pardon to Honor and to Robert for having been in the right. She knew she could own it so graciously that Robert would be overpowered with compunction, and for ever beholden to her; and now that the Charterises were so unmitigatedly hateful, it was time to lay herself out for goodness, and fling him the rein, with only now and then a jerk to remind him that she was a free agent.

A long-talked-of journey on the Continent was to come to pass as soon as Horatia's strain was well. In spite of wealth and splendour, Eloïsa had found herself disappointed in the step that she had hoped her marriage would give her into the most *élite* circles. Languid and indolent as her mind was, she could not but perceive that where Ratia was intimate and at ease, she continued on terms of form and ceremony, and her husband felt more keenly that the society in his house was not what it had been in his mother's time. They both became restless, and Lolly, who had already lived much abroad, dreaded the dulness of an English winter in the country ; while Charles knew that he had already spent more than he liked to recollect, and that the only means of keeping her contented at Castle Blanch, would be to continue most ruinous expenses.

With all these secret motives, the tour was projected as a scheme of amusement, and the details were discussed between Charles and Rashe with great animation, making the soberness of Hiltonbury appear both tedious and sombre, though all the time Lucy felt that there she should again meet that which her heart both feared and yearned for, and without which these pleasures would be but shadows of enjoyment. Yet that they were not including her in their party, gave her a sense of angry neglect and impatience. She wanted to reject their invitation indignantly, and make a merit of the sacrifice.

The after-dinner discussion was in full progress when she was called out to speak to Mr. Prendergast. Heated, wearied, and choking with dust, he would not come beyond the hall, but before going home he had walked all this distance to tell her the result of his expedition. Derval had not been uncivil, but evidently thought the suspicion an affront to his *corps*, which at present was dispersed by the end of the season. The Italian bass was a married man, and had returned to his own country. The clue had failed. The poor leaf must be left to drift upon unknown winds.

'But,' said the curate, by way of compensation, 'at Masters's I found Miss Charlecote herself, and gave your message.'

'I gave no message.'

'No, no, because you would not send me up into the City; but I told her all you would have had me say, and how nearly you had come up with me, only I would not let you, for fear she should have left town.'

Cilla's face did not conceal her annoyance, but not understanding her in the least, he continued, 'I'm sure no one could speak more kindly or considerately than she did. Her eyes filled with tears, and she must be heartily fond of you at the bottom, though maybe rather injudicious and strict; but after what I told her, you need have no fears.'

'Did you ever know me have any?'

'Ah, well! you don't like the word; but at any rate she thinks you behaved with great spirit and discretion under the circumstances, and quite overlooks any little imprudence. She hopes to see you the day after to-morrow, and will write and tell you so.'

Perhaps no intentional slander ever gave the object greater annoyance than Cilly experienced on learning that the good curate had, in the innocence of his heart, represented her as in a state of proper feeling, and interceded for her; and it was all the worse because it was impossible to her to damp his kind satisfaction, otherwise than by a brief 'Thank you,' the tone of which he did not comprehend.

'Was she alone?' she asked.

'Didn't I tell you the young lady was with her, and the brother?'

'Robert Fulmort!' and Cilla's heart sank at finding that it could not have been he who had been with Owen.

'Ay, the young fellow that slept at my house. He has taken a curacy at St. Wulstan's.'

'Did he tell you so?' with an ill-concealed start of consternation.

'Not he; lads have strange manners. I should have thought, after the terms we were upon here, he need not have been quite so much absorbed in his book as never to speak!'

'He has plenty in him instead of manners,' said Lucilla; 'but I'll take him in hand for it.'

Though Lucilla's instinct of defence had spoken up for Robert, she felt hurt at his treatment of her old friend, and could only excuse it by a strong fit of conscious moodiness. His taking the curacy was only explicable, she thought, as a mode of showing his displeasure with herself, since he could not ask her to marry into Whittingtonia; but 'That must be all nonsense,' thought she; 'I will soon have him down off his high horse, and Mr. Parsons will never keep him to his engagement—silly fellow to have made it—or if he does, I shall only have the longer to plague him. It will do him good. Let me see! he will come down to-morrow with Honor's note. I'll put on my lilac muslin with the innocent little frill, and do my hair under his favourite net, and look like such a horrid little meek ringdove that he will be perfectly disgusted with himself for having ever taken me for a fishing eagle. He will be abject, and I'll be generous, and not give another peck till it has grown intolerably stupid to go on being good, or till he presumes!'

For the first time for many days, Lucilla awoke with the impression that something pleasant was about to befall her, and her wild heart was in a state of glad flutter as she donned the quiet dress, and found that the subdued colouring and graver style rendered her more softly lovely than she had ever seen herself.

The letters were on the breakfast table when she came down, the earliest as usual, and one was from Honor Charlecote, the first sight striking her with vexation, as discomfiting her hopes that it would come by a welcome bearer. Yet that might be no reason why he should not yet run down.

She tore it open.

'My dearest Lucy,—Until I met Mr. Prendergast yesterday, I was not sure that you had actually returned, or I would not have delayed an hour in assuring you, if you could doubt it, that my pardon is ever ready for you.'

('Many thanks,' was the muttered comment. 'O that poor, dear, stupid man! would that I had stopped his mouth!')

'I never doubted that your refinement and sense of propriety would be revolted at the consequences of what I always saw to be mere thoughtlessness——'

('Dearly beloved of an old maid is, I told you so!')

'—— but I am delighted to hear that my dear child showed so much true delicacy and dignity in her trying predicament——'

('Delighted to find her dear child not absolutely lost to decorum! Thanks again.')

'—— and I console myself for the pain it has given by the trust that experience has proved a better teacher than precept.'

('Where did she find that grand sentence?')

'So that good may result from past evil and present suffering, and that you may have learnt to distrust those who would lead you to disregard the dictates of your own better sense.'

('Meaning her own self!')
'I have said all this by letter that we may cast aside all that is painful when we meet, and only to feel that I am welcoming my child, doubly dear, because she comes owning her error.'

('I dare say! We like to be magnanimous, don't we? O, Mr. Prendergast, I could beat you!')

'Our first kiss shall seal your pardon, dearest, and not a word shall pass to remind you of this distressing page in your history.'

('Distressing! Excellent fun it was. I shall make her hear my diary, if I persuade myself to encounter this intolerable kiss of peace. It will be a mercy if I don't serve her as the thief in the fable did his mother when he was going to be hanged.')

'I will meet you at the station by any train on Saturday that you like to appoint, and early next week we will go down to what I am sure you have felt is your only true home.'

('Have I? Oh! she has heard of their journey, and thinks this my only alternative. As if I could not go with them if I chose—I wish they would ask me, though. They shall! I'll not be driven up to the Holt as my last resource, and live there under a system of mild browbeating, because I can't help it. No, no! Robin shall find it takes a vast deal of persuasion to bend me to swallow so much pardon in milk and water. I wonder if there's time to change this spooney simplicity, and come out in something spicy, with a dash of the Bloomer. But, maybe, there's some news of him in the other sheet, now she has delivered her conscience of her rigmarole. Oh! here it is—')

'Phœbe will go home with us, as she is, according to the family system, not summoned to her sister's wedding. Robert leaves London on Saturday morning, to fetch his books, &c., from Oxford, Mr. Parsons having consented to give him a title for Holy Orders, and to let him assist in the parish until the next

Ember week. I think, dear girl, that it should not be concealed from you that this step was taken as soon as he heard that you had actually sailed for Ireland, and that he does not intend to return until we are in the country.'

('Does he not? Another act of coercion! I suppose you put him up to this, madam, as a pleasing course of discipline. You think you have the whip hand of me, do you? Pooh! See if he'll stay at Oxford!')

'I feel for the grief I'm inflicting——'

('Oh, so you complacently think "now I *have* made her sorry!"')

'—— but I believe uncertainty, waiting, and heart sickness would cost you far more. Trust me, as one who has felt it, that it is far better to feel oneself unworthy than to learn to doubt or distrust the worthiness or constancy of another.'

('My father, to wit! A pretty thing to say to his daughter! What right has she to be pining and complaining after him? He, the unworthy one? I'll never forgive that conceited inference! Just because he could not stand sentiment! Master Robert gone! Wont I soon have him repenting of his outbreak?')

'I have no doubt that his feelings are unchanged, and that he is solely influenced by principle. He is evidently exceedingly unhappy under all his reserve——'

('He shall be more so, till he behaves himself, and comes back humble! I've no notion of his flying out in this way.')

'—— and though I have not exchanged a word with him on the subject, I am certain that his good opinion will be retrieved, with infinite joy to himself, as soon as you make it possible for his judgment to be satisfied with your conduct and sentiments. Grieved as I am, it is with a hopeful sorrow, for I am sure that nothing is wanting on your part but that consistency and sobriety of behaviour of which you have newly learnt the necessity on other grounds. The Parsonses have gone to their own house, so you will not find any one here but two who will feel for you in silence, and we shall soon be in the quiet of the Holt, where you shall have all that can give you peace or comfort from your ever-loving old H. C.'

'Feel for me! Never. Don't you wish you may get it? Teach the catechism and feed caterpillars till such time as it pleases Mrs. Honor to write up and say "the specimen is tame!" How nice! No, no. I'll not be frightened into their lording it over me! I know a better way! Let Mr. Robert find out how little I care, and get himself heartily sick of St. Wulstan's, till it is "turn again Whittington indeed!" Poor fellow, I hate it, but he must be cured of his airs, and have a good fright. Why don't they ask me to go to Paris with them? Where can I go, if they don't. To Mary Cranford's? Stupid place, but I *will* show that I'm not so hard up as to have no place but the Holt to go to! If it were only possible to stay with Mr. Prendergast, it would be best of all! Can't I tell him to catch a chaperon for me? Then he would think Honor a regular dragon, which would be a shame, for it was nobody's fault but his! I shall tell him I'm like the Christian religion, for which people are always making apologies that it doesn't want! Two years! Patience! It will be very good for Robin, and four-and-twenty is quite soon enough to bite off one's wings, and found an ant-hill. As to being bullied into being kissed, pitied, pardoned, and trained by Honor, I'll never sink so low! No, at *no* price.'

Poor Mr. Prendergast! Did ever a more innocent mischief-maker exist?

Poor Honora! Little did she guess that the letter written in such love, such sympathy, such longing hope, would only excite fierce rebellion.

Yet it was at the words of Moses that the king's heart was hardened; and what was the end? He was taken at his word. 'Thou shalt see my face no more.'

To be asked to join the party on their tour had become Lucilla's prime desire, if only that she might not feel neglected, or driven back to Hiltonbury by absolute necessity; and when the husband and wife came down, the wish was uppermost in her mind.

Eloïsa remarked on her quiet style of dress, and observed that it would be quite the thing in Paris, where people were so much less *outré* than here.

'I have nothing to do with Paris.'

'Oh! surely you go with us!' said Eloïsa; 'I like to take you out, because you are in so different a style of beauty, and you talk and save one trouble! Will not she go, Charles?'

'You see, Lolly wants you for effect!' he said, sneeringly. 'But you are always welcome, Cilly; we are wofully slow when you aint there to keep us going, and I should like to show you a thing or two. I only did not ask you, because I thought you had not hit it off with Rashe, or have you made it up?'

'Oh! Rashe and I understand each other,' said Cilly, secure that though she would never treat Rashe with her former confidence, yet as long as they travelled *en grand seigneur*, there was no fear of collisions of temper.

'Rashe is a good creature,' said Lolly, 'but she is so fast and so eccentric that I like to have you, Cilly; you look so much younger, and more ladylike.'

'One thing more,' said Charles, in his character of head of the family; 'shouldn't you look up Miss Charlecote, Cilly? There's Owen straining the leash pretty hard, and you must look about you, that she does not take up with these new pets of hers and cheat you.'

'The Fulmorts? Stuff! They have more already than they know what to do with.'

'The very reason she will leave them the more. I declare, Cilly,' he added, half in jest, half in earnest, 'the only security for you and Owen is in a double marriage. Perhaps she projects it. You fire up as if she had!'

'If she had, do you think I should go back?' said Cilly, trying to answer lightly, though her cheeks were in a flame. 'No, no, I am not going to let slip a chance of Paris.'

She stopped short, dismayed at having committed herself, and Horatia coming down, was told by acclamation that Cilly was going.

'Of course she is,' said forgiving and forgetting Rashe. 'Little Cilly left behind, to serve for food to the Rouge Dragon? No, no! I should have no fun in life without her.'

Rashe forgot the past far more easily than Cilla could ever do. There was a certain guilty delight in writing—

'MY DEAR HONOR,—Many thanks for your letter, and intended *kindnesses*. The scene must, however, be deferred, as my cousins mean to winter at Paris, and I can't resist the chance of hooking a Marshal, or a Prince or two. Rashe's strain was a great sell, but we had capital fun, and shall hope for more success another season. I would send you my diary if it were written out fair. We go so soon that I can't run up to London, so I hope no one will be disturbed on my account.

'Your affectionate CILLY.'

No need to say how often Lucilla would have liked to have recalled that note for addition or diminution, how many misgivings she suffered on her peculiar mode of catching Robins, how frequent were her disgusts with her cousin, and how often she felt like a captive—the captive of her own self-will.

'That's right!' said Horatia to Lolly. 'I was mortally afraid she would stay at home to fall a prey to the incipient parson, but now he is choked off, and Calthorp is really in earnest, we shall have the dear little morsel doing well yet.'

CHAPTER X.

O ye, who never knew the joys
Of friendship, satisfied with noise,
　Fandango, ball, and rout,
Blush, when I tell you how a bird
A prison, with a friend preferred,
　To liberty without.
　　　　　　　　　Cowper.

HAD Lucilla Sandbrook realized the effect of her note, she would never have dashed it off; but, like all heedless people, pain out of her immediate ken was nothing to her.

After the loving hopes raised by the Curate's report, and after her own tender and forgiving letter, Honor was pierced to the quick by the scornful levity of those few lines. Of the ingratitude to herself, she thought but little in comparison with the heartless contempt towards Robert, and the miserable light-mindedness that it manifested.

'My poor, poor child!' was all she said, as she saw Phœbe looking with terror at her countenance; 'yes, there is an end of it. Let Robert never vex himself about her again.'

Phœbe took up the note, read it over and over again, and then said low and gravely, 'It is very cruel.'

'Poor child, she was born to the Charteris nature, and cannot help it! Like seeks like, and with Paris before her, she can see and feel nothing else.'

Phœbe vaguely suspected that there might be a

shadow of injustice in this conclusion. She knew that Miss Charlecote imagined Lucilla to be more frivolous than was the case, and surmised that there was more offended pride than mere levity in the letter. Insight into character is a natural, not an acquired endowment; and many of poor Honor's troubles had been caused by her deficiency in that which was intuitive to Phœbe, though far from consciously. That perception made her stand thoughtful, wondering whether what the letter betrayed were folly or temper, and whether, like Miss Charlecote, she ought altogether to quench her indignation in contemptuous pity.

'There, my dear,' said Honor, recovering herself, after having sat with ashy face and clasped hands for many moments. 'It will not bear to be spoken or thought of. Let us go to something else. Only, Phœbe, my child, do not leave her out of your prayers.'

Phœbe clung about her neck, kissed and fondled her, and felt her cheeks wet with tears, in the passionate tenderness of the returning caress.

The resolve was kept of not going back to the subject, but Honora went about all day with a soft, tardy step, and subdued voice, like one who has stood beside a death-bed.

When Phœbe heard those stricken tones striving to be cheerful, she could not find pardon for the wrong that had not been done to herself. She dreaded telling Robert that no one was coming whom he need avoid, though without dwelling on the tone of the refusal. To her surprise, he heard her short, matter-of-fact communication without any token of anger or of grief, made no remark, and if he changed countenance at all, it was to put on an air of gloomy satisfaction, as though another weight even in the most undesirable scale were preferable to any remnant of balancing, and compunction for possible injustice were removed.

Could Lucilla but have seen that face, she would

have doubted of her means of reducing him to
obedience.

The course he had adopted might indeed be the
more excellent way in the end, but at present even
his self-devotion was not in such a spirit as to afford
much consolation to Honor. If good were to arise
out of sorrow, the painful seed-time was not yet over.
His looks were stern even to harshness, and his
unhappiness seemed disposed to vent itself in doing
his work after his own fashion, brooking no interference.

He had taken a lodging over a baker's shop at
Turnagain Corner. Honor thought it fair for the
locality, and knew something of the people, but to
Phœbe it was horror and dismay. The two small
rooms, the painted cupboard, the cut paper in the
grate, the pictures in yellow gauze, with the flies
walking about on them, the round mirror, the pattern
of the carpet, and the close, narrow street, struck her
as absolutely shocking, and she came to Miss Charlecote with tears in her eyes, to entreat her to remon-
strate, and tell Robin it was his duty to live like a
gentleman.

'My dear,' said Honor, rather shocked at a speech
so like the ordinary Fulmort mind, 'I have no fears
of Robert not living like a gentleman.'

'I know—not in the real sense,' said Phœbe, blushing, 'but surely he ought not to live in this dismal
poky place, with such mean furniture, when he can
afford better.'

'I am afraid the parish affords few better lodgings,
Phœbe, and it is his duty to live where his work lies.
You appreciated his self-denial, I thought? Do you
not like him to make a sacrifice?'

'I ought,' said Phœbe, her mind taking little pleasure in those acts of self-devotion that were the delight
of her friend. 'If it be his duty, it cannot be helped,
but I cannot be happy at leaving him to be uncomfortable—perhaps ill.'

Coming down from the romance of martyrdom which had made her expect Phœbe to be as willing to see her brother bear hardships in the London streets, as she had herself been to dismiss Owen the first to his wigwam, Honor took the more homely view of arguing on the health and quietness of Turnagain Corner, the excellence of the landlady, and the fact that her own cockney eyes had far less unreasonable expectations than those trained to the luxuries of Beauchamp. But by far the most efficient solace was an expedition for the purchase of various amenities of life, on which Phœbe expended the last of her father's gift. The next morning was spent in great secrecy at the lodgings, where Phœbe was so notable and joyous in her labours, that Honor drew the conclusion that housewifery was her true element; and science, art, and literature only acquired, because they had been made her duties, reckoning all the more on the charming order that would rule in Owen Sandbrook's parsonage.

All troubles and disappointments had faded from the young girl's mind, as she gazed round exulting on the sacred prints on the walls, the delicate statuettes, and well-filled spill-holder and match-box on the mantelshelf, the solid inkstand and appurtenances upon the handsome table-cover, the comfortable easy chair, and the book-cases, whose contents had been reduced to order due, and knew that the bedroom bore equal testimony to her skill; while the good landlady gazed in admiration, acknowledging that she hardly knew her own rooms, and promising with all her heart to take care of her lodger.

Alas! when, on the way to the station, Honor and Phœbe made an unexpected raid to bring some last improvements, Robert was detected in the act of undoing their work, and denuding his room of even its original luxuries. Phœbe spoke not, but her face showed her discomfiture, and Honora attacked him openly.

'I never meant you to know it,' he said, looking rather foolish.

'Then to ingratitude you added treachery.'

'It is not that I do not feel your kindness——'

'But you are determined not to feel it!'

'No, no! only, this is no position for mere luxuries. My fellow curates——'

'Will use such conveniences of life as come to them naturally,' said Honor, who had lived long enough to be afraid of the freaks of asceticism. 'Hear me, Robert. You are not wise in thrusting aside all that brings home to you your little sister's love. You think it cannot be forgotten, but it is not well to cast away these daily memorials. I know you have much to make you severe—nay, morose—but if you become so, you will never do your work efficiently. You may repel, but never invite; frighten, but not soothe.'

'You want me to think my efficiency dependent on arm-chairs and table-covers.'

'I know you will be harder to all for living in needless discomfort, and that you will be gentler to all for constantly meeting tokens of your sister's affection. Had you sought these comforts for yourself, the case would be different; but, Robert, candidly, which of you is the self-pleasing, which the mortified one, at this moment?'

Robert could not but look convicted as his eyes fell on the innocent face, with the tears just kept back by strong effort, and the struggling smile of pardon.

'Never mind, Robin,' said Phœbe, as she saw his air of vexation; 'I know you never meant unkindness. Do as you think right, only pray think of what Miss Charlecote says.'

'She has one thing more to say,' added Honor. 'Do you think that throwing aside Phœbe's little services will make you fitter to go among the little children?'

There was no answer, but a reluctant approach to a

smile gave Phœbe courage to effect her restorations, and her whispered 'You will not disturb them?' met with an affirmative satisfactory to herself.

Perhaps he felt as of old, when the lady of the Holt had struck him for his cruelty to the mouse, or expelled him for his bad language. The same temper remained, although self-revenge had become the only outlet. He knew what it was that he had taken for devoted self-denial.

'Yes, Robin,' were Miss Charlecote's parting words, as she went back to days of her own long past. 'Wilful doing right seldom tends to good, above all when it begins by exaggeration of duty.'

And Robert was left with thoughts such as perchance might render him a more tractable subordinate for Mr. Parsons, instead of getting into training for the Order of St. Dominic.

Phœbe had to return less joyfully than she had gone forth. Her first bright star of anticipation had faded, and she had partaken deeply of the griefs of the two whom she loved so well. Not only had she to leave the one to his gloomy lodgings in the City, and the toil that was to deaden suffering, but the other must be parted with at the station, to return to the lonely house, where not even old Ponto would meet her— his last hour having, to every one's grief, come in her absence.

Phœbe could not bear the thought of that solitary return, and even at the peril of great disappointment to her sisters, begged to sleep that first night at the Holt, but Honor thanked her, and laughed it off. 'No, no! my dear, I am used to be alone, and depend upon it, there will be such an arrear of farm business for me, that I should hardly have time to speak to you. You need not be uneasy for me, dear one, there is always relief in having a great deal to do, and I shall know you are near, to come if I want you. There's a great deal in that knowledge, Phœbe.'

'If I were of any use——'

'Yes, Phœbe, this visit has made you my friend instead of my playfellow.'

Phœbe's deepening colour showed her intense gratification.

'And there are the Sundays,' added Honor. 'I trust Miss Fennimore will let you come to luncheon, and to the second service with me.'

'I will try very hard!'

For Phœbe could not help feeling like the canary, who sees his owner's hand held out to catch him after his flight, or the pony who marks his groom at the gate of the paddock. Cage and rein were not grievous, but liberty was over, and free will began to sink into submission, as the chimneys of home came nearer, even though the anticipation of her sister's happiness grew more and more on her, and compensated for all.

Shrieks of ecstasy greeted her; she was held as fast as though her sisters feared to lose her again, and Miss Fennimore showed absolute warmth of welcome. Foreign tongues were dispensed with, and it was a festival evening of chatter, and display of purchases, presents and commissions. The evidences of Phœbe's industry were approved. Her abstracts of her reading, her notes of museums and exhibitions, her drawing, needlework, and new pieces of music, exceeded Miss Fennimore's hopes, and appalled her sisters.

'You did all that,' cried Bertha, profiting by Miss Fennimore's absence; 'I hope to goodness she wont make it a precedent.'

'Wasn't it very tiresome?' asked Maria.

'Sometimes; but it made me comfortable, as if I had a backbone for my day.'

'But didn't you want to feel like a lady?'

'I don't think I felt otherwise, Maria.'

'Like a grown-up lady, like mamma and my sisters?'

'O examples!' cried Bertha. 'No wonder Maria thinks doing nothing the great thing to grow up for. But, Phœbe, how could you be so stupid as to go and do all this heap? You might as well have stayed at home.'

'Miss Fennimore desired me!'

'The very reason why I'd have read stories, and made pictures out of them, just to feel myself beyond her talons.'

'Talents, not talons,' said Maria. 'Cats have talons, people have talents.'

'Sometimes both, sometimes neither,' observed Bertha. 'No explanation, Phœbe, what's the use? I want to know if Owen Sandbrook didn't call you little Miss Precision?'

'Something like it.'

'And you went on when he was there?'

'Generally.'

'Oh! what opportunities are wasted on some people. Wouldn't I have had fun? But of course he saw you were a poor little not-come-out thing, and never spoke to you. Oh! if Miss Charlecote would ask me to London!'

'And me!' chimed in Maria.

'Well, what would you do?'

'Not act like a goose, and bring home dry abstracts. I'd make Miss Charlecote take me everywhere, and quite forget all my science, unless I wanted to amaze some wonderful genius. Oh dear! wont I make Augusta look foolish some of these days? She really thinks that steel attracts lightning! Do you think Miss Charlecote's society will appreciate me, Phœbe?'

'And me?' again asked Maria.

Phœbe laughed heartily, but did not like Bertha's scoffing mirth at Maria's question. Glad as she was to be at home, her glimpse of the outer world had so enlarged her perceptions, that she could not help remarking the unchildlike acuteness of the younger girl, and the obtuse comprehension of the elder; and she feared that she had become discontented and fault-finding after her visit. Moreover, when Bertha spoke much English, a certain hesitation occurred in her speech which was apt to pass unnoticed in her foreign tongues, but which jarred unpleasantly on her sister's ear, and only increased when noticed.

At nine, when Phœbe rose as usual to wish good night, Miss Fennimore told her that she need not for the future retire before ten, the hour to which she had of late become accustomed. It was a great boon, especially as she was assured that the additional hour should be at her own disposal.

'You have shown that you can be trusted with your time, my dear. But not to-night,' as Phœbe was turning to her desk; 'remember how long I have suffered a famine of conversation. What! were you not sensible of your own value in that respect?'

'I thought you instructed me; I did not know you conversed with me.'

'There's a difference between one susceptible of instruction, and anything so flippant and volatile as Bertha,' said Miss Fennimore, smiling. 'And poor Maria!'

'She is so good and kind! If she could only see a few things, and people, and learn to talk!'

'Silence and unobtrusiveness are the only useful lessons for her, poor girl!' then observing Phœbe's bewildered looks, 'My dear, I was forced to speak to Bertha because she was growing jealous of Maria's exemptions; but you, who have been constantly shielding and supplying her deficiencies, you do not tell me that you were not aware of them?'

'I always knew she was not clever,' said Phœbe, her looks of alarmed surprise puzzling Miss Fennimore, who in all her philosophy had never dreamt of the unconscious instinct of affection.

'I could not have thought it,' she said.

'Thought what? Pray tell me! O what is the matter with poor Maria?'

'Then, my dear, you really had never perceived that poor Maria is not—has not the usual amount of capacity—that she cannot be treated as otherwise than peficient.'

'Does mamma know it?' faintly asked Phœbe, tears slowly filling her eyes.

Miss Fennimore paused, inwardly rating Mrs. Fulmort's powers little above those of her daughter. 'I am not sure,' she said; 'your sister Juliana certainly does, and in spite of the present pain, I believe it best that your eyes should be opened.'

'That I may take care of her.'

'Yes, you can do much in developing her faculties, as well as in sheltering her from being thrust into positions to which she would be unequal. You do so already. Though her weakness was apparent to me the first week I was in the house, yet, owing to your kind guardianship, I never perceived its extent till you were absent. I could not have imagined so much tact and vigilance could have been unconscious. Nay, dear child, it is no cause for tears. Her life may perhaps be happier than that of many of more complete intellect.'

'I ought not to cry,' owned Phœbe, the tears quietly flowing all the time. 'Such people cannot do wrong in the same way as we can.'

'Ah! Phœbe, till we come to the infinite, how shall the finite pronounce what is wrong.'

Phœbe did not understand, but felt that she was not in Miss Charlecote's atmosphere, and from the heavenly, 'from him to whom little is given, little will be required,' came to the earthly, and said, imploring, 'And you will never be hard on her again!'

'I trust I have not been hard on her. I shall task her less, and only endeavour to give her habits of quiet occupation, and make her manners retiring. It was this relaxation of discipline, together with Bertha's sad habit of teasing, which was intolerable in your absence, that induced me to explain to her the state of the case.'

'How shocked she must have been.'

'Not quite as you were. Her first remark was that it was as if she were next in age to you.'

'She is not old enough to understand.'

The governess shook her head. 'Nay, when I found her teasing again, she told me it was a psychological experiment. Little monkey, she laid hold of some books of mine, and will never rest till she has come to some conclusion as to what is wanting in Maria.'

'Too young to feel what it means,' repeated Phœbe.

She was no great acquisition as a companion, for she neither spoke nor stirred, so that the governess would have thought her drowsy, but for the uprightness of the straight back, and the steady fold of the fingers on the knee. Much as Miss Fennimore detested the sight of inaction, she respected the reverie consequent on the blow she had given. It was a refreshing contrast with Bertha's levity; and she meditated why her system had made the one sister only accurate and methodical, while the other seemed to be losing heart in mind, and becoming hard and shrewd.

There was a fresh element in Phœbe's life. The native respect for 'the innocent' had sprung up within her, and her spirit seemed to expand into protecting wings with which to hover over her sister as a charge peculiarly her own. Here was the new impulse needed to help her when subsiding into the monotony and task-work of the schoolroom, and to occupy her in the stead of the more exciting hopes and fears that she had partaken in London.

Miss Fennimore wisely relaxed her rule over Phœbe, since she had shown that liberty was regarded as no motive for idleness; so though the maiden still scrupulously accomplished a considerable amount of study, she was allowed to portion it out as suited her inclination, and was no longer forbidden to interrupt herself for the sake of her sisters. It was infinite. comfort to be no longer obliged to deafen her ears to the piteous whine of fretful incapacity, and to witness the sullen heaviness of faculties overtasked, and temper goaded into torpor. The fact once faced, the result was relief; Maria was spared and considered, and Phœbe found the governess much kinder, not only to her sister but to herself. Absence had taught the value of the elder pupil, and friendly terms of equality were beginning to be established.

Phœbe's freedom did not include solitary walks, and on week days she seldom saw Miss Charlecote, and then only to hear natural history, the only moderately safe ground between the two elder ladies. What was natural science with the one, was natural history with the other. One went deep in systems and classifications, and thrust Linnæus into the dark ages; the other had observed, collected, and drawn specimens with the enthusiasm of a Londoner for the country, till she had a valuable little museum of her own gathering, and was a handbook for the county curiosities. Star, bird, flower, and insect, were more than resources, they were the friends of her lonely life, and awoke many a keen feeling of interest, many an aspiration of admiring adoration that carried her through her dreary hours. And though Miss Fennimore thought her science puerile, her credulity extensive, and her observations inaccurate, yet she deemed even this lady-like dabbling worthy of respect as an element of rational pleasure and self-training, and tried to make Bertha respect it, and abstain from inundating Miss Charlecote with sesquipedalian names for systems and families, and, above all, from her principal delight, setting the two ladies together by the ears, by appealing to her governess to support her abuse of Linnæus as an old 'dictionary maker,' or for some bold geological theory that poor Honor was utterly unprepared to swallow.

Bertha was somewhat like the wren, who, rising on the eagle's head, thought itself the monarch of the birds, but Honor was by no means convinced that she was not merely blindfolded on the back of Clavileno Aligero. There was neither love nor admiration wasted between Honor and Miss Fennimore, and

Phœbe preferred their being apart. She enjoyed her Sunday afternoons, short enough, for school must not be neglected, but Honor shyly acceded to Phœbe's entreaty to be allowed to sit by her class and learn by her teaching.

It was an effort. Honor shrank from exposing her own misty metaphors, hesitating repetitions, and trivial queries to so clear a head, trained in distinct reasoning, but it was the very teaching that the scientific young lady most desired, and she treasured up every hint, afterwards pursuing the subject with a resolution to complete the chain of evidence, and asking questions sometimes rather perplexing to Honor, accustomed as she was to take everything for granted. Out came authorities, and Honor found herself examining into the grounds of her own half-knowledge, gaining fresh ideas, correcting old ones, and obtaining subjects of interest for many an hour after her young friend had left her.

While, at home, Phœbe, after running the gauntlet of Bertha's diversion at her putting herself to school, when Scripture lessons were long ago done with, would delight Maria with long murmuring discourses, often stories about the scholars, but always conveying some point of religious instruction. It was a subject to which Maria was less impervious than to any other; she readily learnt to croon over the simple hymns that Phœbe brought home, and when once a Scripture story had found entrance to her mind, would beg to have it marked in her Bible, and recur to it frequently.

Miss Fennimore left her entirely to Phœbe at these times, keeping Bertha from molesting her by sarcastic queries, or by remarks on the sing-song hymns, such as made Phœbe sometimes suspect that Maria's love for these topics rendered them the more distasteful to the younger girl. She tried to keep them as much sheltered as possible, but was still sometimes disconcerted by Bertha's mischievous laugh, or by finding Miss Fennimore's eyes fixed in attention.

Phœbe's last hour on these evenings was spent in laying up her new lore in her diligently kept notebook, weighing it and endeavouring to range it in logical sequence, which she had been duly trained to consider the test of reasoning. If she sometimes became bewildered, and detected insufficient premises for true conclusions, if she could not think allegory or analogy the evidence it was made at the Sunday-school, and which Miss Charlecote esteemed as absolute proof, her sound heart and loving faith always decided her that she should discover the link in time; and the doctrine had too strong a hold on her convictions and affections for her to doubt that the chain of argument existed, though she had not yet found it. It was not the work for which so young a head was intended, and perhaps it was well that she was interrupted by the arrival at home of the heads of the family.

Augusta and her husband were to spend the winter abroad; Juliana had met some friends, whom she had accompanied to their home, and though she had exacted that Phœbe should not come out, yet the eldest daughter at home was necessarily brought somewhat forward. Phœbe was summoned to the family meals, and went out driving with her mother, or riding with her father, but was at other times in the schoolroom, where indeed she was the most happy.

The life downstairs was new to her, and she had not been trained to the talk there expected of her. The one event of her life, her visit to London, gave evident dissatisfaction. There were growls whenever Robert was mentioned, and Phœbe found that though permission had been given for his taking the curacy, it had been without understanding his true intentions with regard to Whittingtonia. Something had evidently passed between him and his father and brother, while on their way through London, which had caused them to regard him as likely to be a thorn in their side; and Phœbe could not but fear that he would meet them in no spirit of conciliation, would rather prefer a little persecution, and would lean to the side of pastoral rather than filial duty, whenever they might clash. Even if he should refrain from speaking his full mind to his father, he was likely to use no precautions with his brother, and Phœbe was uneasy whenever either went up for their weekly visit of inspection at the office.

Her mother gently complained. 'Honora Charlecote's doing, I suppose. He should have considered more! Such a wretched place, no genteel family near! Your papa would never let me go near it. But he must buy an excellent living soon, where no one will know his connexion with the trade.'

The only sympathy Phœbe met with at home on Robert's ordination, was in an unexpected quarter. 'Then your brother has kept his resolution,' said Miss Fennimore. 'Under his reserve there is the temper that formed the active ascetics of the middle ages. His doctrine has a strong mediæval tinge, and with sufficient strength of purpose, may lead to like results.'

When Phœbe proudly told Miss Charlecote of this remark, they agreed that it was a valuable testimony, both to the doctrines and the results. Honor had had a letter from Robert, that made her feel by force of contrast that Owen was more than three years from a like conception of clerical duty.

The storm came at last. By order of the Court of Chancery, there was put up for sale a dreary section of Whittingtonia, in dire decay, and remote from civilization. The firm of Fulmort and Son had long had their eyes on it, as an eligible spot for a palace for the supply of their commodity; and what was their rage when their agent was out-bidden, and the tenements knocked down to an unknown customer for a fancy price? After much alarm lest a rival distiller should be invading their territory, their wrath came to a height when it finally appeared that the new owner of the six ruinous houses in Cicely Row was no other than the Reverend Robert Mervyn Fulmort, with the purpose of building a church and schools for Whittingtonia at his own expense.

Mervyn came home furious. High words had passed between the brothers, and his report of them so inflamed Mr. Fulmort, that he inveighed violently against the malice and treachery that scrupled not to undermine a father. Never speaking to Robert again, casting him off, and exposing the vicar for upholding filial insolence and undutifulness, were the mildest of his threats. They seemed to imagine that Robert was making this outlay, supposing that he would yet be made equal in fortune by his father to the others, and there was constant repetition that he was to expect not a farthing—he had had his share, and should have no more. There was only a scoff at Phœbe's innocence, when she expressed her certainty that he looked for no compensation, knowing that he had been provided for, and was to have nothing from his father; and Phœbe trembled under such abuse of her favourite brother, till she could bear it no longer, and seizing the moment of Mervyn's absence, she came up to her father, and said, in as coaxing a tone as she could, 'Papa, should not every one work to the utmost in his trade?'

'What of that, little one?'

'Then pray don't be angry with Robert for acting up to his,' said Phœbe, clasping her hands, and resting them fondly on his shoulder.

'Act up to a fool's head! Parsons should mind their business, and not fly in their fathers' faces.'

'Isn't it their work to make people more good?' continued Phœbe, with an unconscious wiliness, looking more simple than her wont.

'Let him begin with himself, then! Learn his duty to his father! A jackanapes; trying to damage my business under my very nose.'

'If those poor people are in such need of having good done to them——'

'Scum of the earth! Much use trying to do good to them!'

'Ah! but if it be his work to try? and if he wanted a place to build a school——'

'You're in league with him, I suppose.'

'No, papa! It surprised me very much. Even Mr. Parsons knew nothing of his plans. Robert only wrote to me when it was done, that now he hoped to save a few of the children that are turned out in the streets to steal.'

'Steal! They'll steal all his property! A proper fool your uncle was to leave it all to a lad like that. The sure way to spoil him! I could have trebled all your fortunes if that capital had been in my hands, and now to see him throw it to the dogs! Phœbe, I can't stand it. Conscience? I hate such coxcombry! As if men would not make beasts of themselves whether his worship were in the business or not.'

'Yes!' ventured Phœbe, 'but at least he has no part in their doing so.'

'Much you know about it,' said her father, again shielding himself with his newspaper, but so much less angrily than she had dared to expect, that even while flushed and trembling, she felt grateful to him as more placable than Mervyn. She knew not the power of her own sweet face and gently honest manner, nor of the novelty of an attentive daughter.

When the neighbours remarked on Mrs. Fulmort's improved looks and spirits, and wondered whether they were the effect of the Rhine or of 'getting off' her eldest daughter, they knew not how many fewer dull hours she had to spend. Phœbe visited her in her bedroom, talked at luncheon, amused her drives, coaxed her into the garden, read to her when she rested before dinner, and sang to her afterwards. Phœbe likewise brought her sister's attainments more into notice, though at the expense of Bertha's contempt for mamma's preference for Maria's staring fuchsias and feeble singing, above her own bold chalks from models and scientific music, and indignation at Phœbe's constantly bringing Maria forward rather than her own clever self.

Droning narrative, long drawn out, had as much charm for Mrs. Fulmort as for Maria. If she did not always listen, she liked the voice, and she sometimes awoke into descriptions of the dresses, parties, and acquaintance of her youth, before trifling had sunk into dreary insipidity under the weight of too much wealth, too little health, and 'nothing to do.'

'My dear,' she said, 'I am glad you are not out. Quiet evenings are so good for my nerves; but you are a fine girl, and will soon want society.'

'Not at all, mamma; I like being at home with you.'

'No, my dear! I shall like to take you out and see you dressed. You must have advantages, or how are you to marry?'

'There's no hurry,' said Phœbe, smiling.

'Yes, my dear, girls always get soured if they do not marry!'

'Not Miss Charlecote, mamma.'

'Ah! but Honor Charlecote was an heiress, and could have had plenty of offers. Don't talk of not marrying, Phœbe, I beg.'

'No,' said Phœbe, gravely. 'I should like to marry some one very good and wise, who could help me out of all my difficulties.'

'Bless me, Phœbe! I hope you did not meet any poor curate at that place of Honor Charlecote's. Your papa would never consent.'

'I never met anybody, mamma,' said Phœbe, smiling. 'I was only thinking what he should be like.'

'Well, what?' said Mrs. Fulmort, with girlish curiosity. 'Not that it's any use settling. I always thought I would marry a marquis's younger son, because it is such a pretty title, and that he should play on the guitar. But he must not be an officer, Phœbe; we have had trouble enough about that.'

'I don't know what he is to be, mamma,' said

Phœbe, earnestly, 'except that he should be as sensible as Miss Fennimore, and as good as Miss Charlecote. Perhaps a man could put both into one, and then he could lead me, and always show me the reason of what is right.'

'Phœbe, Phœbe! you will never get married if you wait for a philosopher. Your papa would never like a very clever genius, or an author.'

'I don't want him to be a genius, but he must be wise.'

'Oh, my dear! That comes of the way young ladies are brought up. What would the Miss Berrilees have said, where I was at school at Bath, if one of their young ladies had talked of wanting to marry a wise man?'

Phœbe gave a faint smile, and said, 'What was Mr. Charlecote like, mamma, whose brass was put up the day Robert was locked into the Church?'

'Humfrey Charlecote, my dear? The dearest, most good-hearted man that ever lived. Everybody liked him. There was no one that did not feel as if they had lost a brother when he was taken off in that sudden way.'

'And was not he very wise, mamma?'

'Bless me, Phœbe, what could have put that into your head? Humfrey Charlecote a wise man? He was just a common, old-fashioned, hearty country squire. It was only that he was so friendly and kind-hearted that made every one trust him, and ask his advice.'

'I should like to have known him,' said Phœbe, with a sigh.

'Ah, if you married any one like that! But there's no use waiting! There's nobody left like him, and I wont have you an old maid! You are prettier than either of your sisters—more like me when I came away from Miss Berrilees, and had a gold-sprigged muslin for the Assize Ball, and Humfrey Charlecote danced with me.'

Phœbe fell into speculations on the wisdom whose counsel all asked, and which had left such an impression of affectionate honour. She would gladly lean on such an one, but if no one of the like mould remained, she thought she could never bear the responsibilities of marriage.

Meantime she erected Humfrey Charlecote's image into a species of judge, laying before this vision of a wise man all her perplexities between Miss Charlecote's religion and Miss Fennimore's reason, and all her practical doubts between Robert's conflicting duties. Strangely enough, the question, 'What would Mr. Charlecote have thought?' often aided her to cast the balance. Though it was still Phœbe who decided, it was Phœbe drawn out of herself, and strengthened by her mask.

With vivid interest, such as for a living man would have amounted to love, she seized and hoarded each particle of intelligence that she could gain respecting the object of her admiration. Honora herself, though far more naturally enthusiastic, had, with her dreamy nature and diffused raptures, never been capable of thus reverencing him, nor of the intensity of feeling of one whose restrained imagination and unromantic education gave force to all her sensations. Yet this deep individual regard was a more wholesome tribute than Honor had ever paid to him, or to her other idol, for to Phœbe it was a step, lifting her to things above and beyond, a guide on the road, never a vision obscuring the true object.

Six weeks had quietly passed, when, like a domestic thunderbolt, came Juliana's notification of her intention to return home at the end of a week. Mrs. Fulmort, clinging to her single thread of comfort, hoped that Phœbe might still be allowed to come to her boudoir, but the gentlemen more boldly declared that they wanted Phœbe, and would not have her driven back into the school-room; to which the mother only replied with fears that Juliana would be in a dreadful temper, whereon Mervyn responded, 'Let her! Never mind her, Phœbe. Stick up for yourself, and we'll put her down.'

Except for knowing that she was useful to her mother, Phœbe would have thankfully retired into the west wing rather than have given umbrage. Mervyn's partisanship was particularly alarming, and, endeavour as she might to hope that Juliana would be amiable enough to be disarmed by her own humility and unobtrusiveness, she lived under the impression of disagreeables impending.

One morning at breakfast, Mr. Fulmort, after grumbling out his wonder at Juliana's writing to him, suddenly changed his tone into, 'Hollo! what's this? "My engagement"——'

'By Jove!' shouted Mervyn; 'too good to be true. So she's done it. I didn't think he'd been such an ass, having had one escape.'

'Who?' continued Mr. Fulmort, puzzling, as he held the letter far off—'engagement to dear—dear Devil, does she say?'

'The only fit match,' muttered Mervyn, laughing.

'No, no, sir! Bevil—Sir Bevil Acton.'

'What! not the fellow that gave us so much trouble! He had not a sixpence; but she must please herself now.'

'You don't mean that you didn't know what she went with the Merivales for?—five thousand a year and a baronetcy, eh?'

'The deuce! If I had known that, he might have had her long ago.'

'It's quite recent,' said Mervyn. 'A mere chance; and he has been knocking about in the colonies these ten years—might have cut his wisdom teeth.'

'Ten years—not half-a-dozen!' said Mr. Fulmort.

'Ten!' reiterated Mervyn. 'It was just before I went to old Raymond's. Acton took me to dine at the mess. He was a nice fellow then, and deserved better luck.'

'Ten years' constancy!' said Phœbe, who had been looking from one to the other in wonder, trying to collect intelligence. 'Do tell me.'

'Whew!' whistled Mervyn. 'Juliana hadn't her sharp nose nor her sharp tongue when first she came out. Acton was quartered at Elverslope, and got smitten. She flirted with him all the winter; but I fancy she didn't give you much trouble when he came to the point, eh, sir?'

'I thought him an impudent young dog for thinking of a girl of her prospects; but if he had this to look to!—I was sorry for him, too! Ten years ago,' mused Mr. Fulmort.

'And she has liked no one since?'

'Or, no one has liked her, which comes to the same,' said Mervyn. 'The regiment went to the Cape, and there was an end of it, till we fell in with the Merivales on board the steamer; and they mentioned their neighbour, Sir Bevil Acton, come into his property, and been settled near them a year or two. Fine sport it was, to see Juliana angling for an invitation, brushing up her friendship with Minnie Merivale—amiable to the last degree! My stars! what work she must have had to play good temper all these six weeks, and how we shall have to pay for it!'

'Or Acton will,' said Mr. Fulmort, with a hearty chuckle of triumphant good humour.

Was it a misfortune to Phœbe to have been so much refined by education as to be grated on by the vulgar tone of those nearest to her? It was well for her that she could still put it aside as their way, even while following her own instinct. Mervyn and Juliana had been on cat and dog terms all their lives; he was certain to sneer at all that concerned her, and Phœbe reserved her belief that an attachment, nipped in the bud, was ready to blossom in sunshine. She ran up with the news to her mother.

'Juliana going to be married! Well, my dear, you may be introduced at once! How comfortable you and I shall be in the little brougham.'

Phœbe begged to be told what the intended was like.

'Let me see—was he the one that won the steeple-chase? No; that was the one that Augusta liked. We knew so many young men, that I could never tell which was which; and your sisters were always talking about them till it quite ran through my poor head, such merry girls as they were!'

'And poor Juliana never was so merry after he was gone.'

'I don't remember,' replied this careful mother; 'but you know she never could have meant anything, for he had nothing, and you with your fortunes are a match for anybody! Phœbe, my dear, we must go to London next spring, and you shall marry a nobleman. I must see you a titled lady as well as your sisters.'

'I've no objection, provided he is my wise man,' said Phœbe.

Juliana had found the means of making herself welcome, and her marriage a cause of unmixed jubilation in her family. Prosperity made her affable, and instead of suppressing Phœbe, she made her useful, and treated her as a confidante, telling her of all the previous intimacy, and all the secret sufferings in dear Bevil's absence, but passing lightly over the last happy meeting, which Phœbe respected as too sacred to be talked of.

The little maiden's hopes of a perfect brother in the constant knight rose high, and his appearance and demeanour did not disappoint them. He had a fine soldierly figure, and that air of a thorough gentleman which Phœbe's Holt experience had taught her to appreciate; his manners were peculiarly gentle and kind, especially to Mrs. Fulmort; and Phœbe did not like him the less for showing traces of the effects of wounds and climate, and a grave, subdued air, almost amounting to melancholy. But before he had been three days at Beauchamp, Juliana made a virulent attack on the privileges of her younger sisters. Perhaps it was the consequence of poor Maria's volunteer to Sir Bevil—

'I am glad Juliana is going with you, for now no one will be cross to me;' but it seemed to verify the poor girl's words, that she should be hunted like a strange cat if she were found beyond her own precincts, and that the other two should be treated much in the same manner. Bertha stood up for her rights, declaring that what mamma and Miss Fennimore allowed, she would not give up for Juliana; but the only result was an admonition to the governess, and a fierce remonstrance to the poor meek mother. Phœbe, who only wished to retire from the stage in peace, had a more difficult part to play.

'What's the matter now?' demanded Mervyn, making his way up to her as she sat in a remote corner of the drawing-room, in the evening. 'Why were you not at dinner?'

'There was no room, I believe.'

'Nonsense! our table dines eight-and-twenty, and there were not twenty.'

'That was a large party, and you know I am not out.'

'You don't look like it in that long-sleeved white affair, and nothing on your head either. Where are those ivy-leaves you had yesterday—real, weren't they?'

'They were not liked.'

'Not liked! they were the prettiest things I have seen for a long time. Acton said they made you look like a nymph—the green suits that shiny light hair of yours, and makes you like a picture.'

'Yes, they made me look forward and affected.'

'Now who told you that? Has the Fennimore got to her old tricks?'

'Oh no, no!'

'I see! a jealous toad! I heard him telling her that you reminded him of her in old times. The spiteful vixen! Well, Phœbe, if you cut her out, I bargain for board and lodging at Acton Manor. This will be no place for a quiet, meek soul like me!'

Phœbe tried to laugh, but looked distressed, uncomprehending, and far from wishing to comprehend. She could not escape, for Mervyn had penned her up, and went on. 'You don't pretend that you don't see how it is! That unlucky fellow is heartily sick of his bargain, but you see he was too soft to withstand her throwing herself right at his head, and doing the "worm in the bud," and the cruel father, green and yellow melancholy, &c., ever since they were inhumanly parted.'

'For shame, Mervyn. You don't really believe it is all out of honour.'

'I should never have believed a man of his years could be so green; but some men get crotchets about honour in the army, especially if they get elderly there.'

'It is very noble, if it be right, and he can take those vows from his heart,' moralized Phœbe. 'But no, Mervyn, she cannot think so. No woman could take any one on such terms.'

'Wouldn't she, though?' sneered her brother. 'She'd have him, if grim death were hanging on to his other hand. People aren't particular, when they are nigh upon their third ten.'

'Don't tell me such things! I don't believe them; but they ought never to be suggested.'

'You ought to thank me for teaching you knowledge of the world.'

He was called off, but heavy at her heart lay the text, 'The knowledge of wickedness is not wisdom.'

Mervyn's confidences were serious troubles to Phœbe. Gratifying as it was to be singled out by his favour, it was distressing to be the repository of what she knew ought never to have been spoken, prompted by a coarse tone of mind, and couched in language that, though he meant it to be restrained, sometimes seemed to her like the hobgoblins' whispers to Christian. Oh! how unlike her other brother! Robert had troubles, Mervyn grievances, and she saw which were the worst to bear. It was a pleasing novelty to find a patient listener, and he used it to the utmost, while she often doubted whether to hear without remonstrance were not undutiful, yet found opposition rather increased the evil by the storm of ill-temper that it provoked.

This last communication was dreadful to her, yet she could not but feel that it might be a wholesome warning to avoid giving offence to the jealousy, which when once pointed out to her, she could not prevent herself from tracing in Juliana's petulance towards herself, and resolve to force her into the background. Even Bertha was more often brought forward, for in spite of a tongue and temper cast somewhat in a similar mould, she was rather a favourite with Juliana, whom she was not unlikely to resemble, except that her much more elaborate and accurate training might give her both more power and more self-control.

As Mervyn insinuated, Juliana was prudent in not lengthening out the engagement, and the marriage was fixed for Christmas week, but it was not to take place at Hiltonbury. Sir Bevil was bashful, and dreaded county festivities, and Juliana wished to escape from Maria as a bridesmaid, so they preferred the privacy of an hotel and a London church. Phœbe could not decently be excluded, and her heart leapt with the hope of seeing Robert, though so unwelcome was his name in the family that she could not make out on what terms he stood, whether proscribed, or only disapproved, and while sure that he would strive to be with her, she foresaw that the pleasure would be at the cost of much pain. Owen Sandbrook was spending his vacation at the Holt, and Miss Charlecote looked so bright as she walked to church leaning on his arm, that Phœbe had no regrets in leaving her. Indeed, the damsel greatly preferred the Holt in his absence. She did not understand his discursive comments on all things in art or nature, and he was in a mood of flighty fitful spirits, which perplexed her alike by their wild, satirical mirth, and their mournful sentiment. She thought Miss Charlecote was worried and perplexed at times by his tone; but there was no doubt of his affection and attention for his 'Sweet Honey,' and Phœbe rejoiced that her own absence should be at so opportune a moment.

Sir Bevil went to make his preparations at home, whence he was to come and join the Fulmorts the day after their arrival in town. Mrs. Fulmort was dragged out in the morning, and deposited at Farrance's in time for luncheon, a few minutes before a compact little brougham set down Lady Bannerman, jollier than ever in velvet and sable, and more scientific in cutlets and pale ale. Her good nature was full blown. She was ready to chaperon her sisters anywhere, invited the party to the Christmas dinner, and undertook the grand *soirée* after the wedding. She proposed to take Juliana at once out shopping, only lamenting that there was no room for Phœbe, and was so universally benevolent, that in the absence of the bride elect, Phœbe ventured to ask whether she saw anything of Robert.

'Robert? Yes, he called when we first came to town, and we asked him to dinner; but he said it was a fast day; and you know Sir Nicholas would never encourage that sort of thing.'

'How was he?'

'He looked odder than ever, and so ill and cadaverous. No wonder! poking himself up in such a horrid place, where one can't notice him.'

'Did he seem in tolerable spirits?'

'I don't know. He always was silent and glum; and now he seems wrapt up in nothing but ragged schools and those disgusting City missions. I'm sure we can't subscribe, so expensive as it is living in town. Imagine, mamma, what we are giving our cook!'

Juliana returned, and the two sisters went out, leaving Phœbe to extract entertainment for her mother from the scenes passing in the street.

Presently a gentleman's handsome cabriolet and distinguished-looking horse were affording food for their descriptions, when, to her surprise, Sir Bevil emerged from it, and presently entered the room. He had come intending to take out his betrothed, and in her absence transferred the offer to her sister. Phœbe demurred, on more accounts than she could mention, but her mother remembering what a drive in a stylish equipage with a military baronet would once have been to herself, overruled her objections, and hurried her away to prepare. She quickly returned, a cheery spectacle in her russet dress and brown straw bonnet, and her scarlet neck-tie, the robin red-breast's livery which she loved.

'Your cheeks should be a refreshing sight to the Londoners, Phœbe,' said Sir Bevil, with his rare, but most pleasant smile. 'Where shall we go? You don't seem much to care for the Park. I'm at your service wherever you like to go.' And as Phœbe hesitated, with cheeks trebly beneficial to the Londoners, he kindly added, 'Well, what is it? Never mind what! I'm open to anything—even Madame Tussaud's.'

'If I might go to see Robert. Augusta said he was looking ill.'

'My dear!' interposed her mother, 'you can't think of it. Such a dreadful place, and such a distance.'

'It is only a little way beyond St. Paul's, and there are no bad streets, dear mamma. I have been there with Miss Charlecote. But if it be too far, or you don't like driving into the City, never mind,' she continued, turning to Sir Bevil; 'I ought to have said nothing about it.'

But Sir Bevil, reading the ardour of the wish in the honest face, pronounced the expedition an excellent idea, and carried her off with her eyes as round and sparkling as those of the children going to Christmas parties. He stole glances at her as if her fresh innocent looks were an absolute treat to him, and when he talked, it was of Robert in his boyhood. 'I remember him at twelve years old, a sturdy young ruffian, with an excellent notion of standing up for himself.'

Phœbe listened with delight to some characteristic anecdotes of Robert's youth, and wondered whether he would be appreciated now. She did not think Sir Bevil held the same opinions as Robert or Miss Charlecote; he was an upright, high-minded soldier, with honour and subordination his chief religion, and not likely to enter into Robert's peculiarities. She was in some difficulty when she was asked whether her brother were not under some cloud, or had not been taking a line of his own—a gentler form of inquiry, which she could answer with the simple truth.

'Yes, he would not take a share in the business, because he thought it promoted evil, and he felt it right to do parish work at St. Wulstan's, because our profits chiefly come from thence. It does not please at home, because they think he could have done better for himself, and he sometimes is obliged to interfere with Mervyn's plans.'

Sir Bevil made the less answer because they were in the full current of London traffic, and his proud chesnut was snuffing the hat of an omnibus conductor. Careful driving was needed, and Phœbe was praised for never even looking frightened, then again for her organ of locality and the skilful pilotage with which she unerringly and unhesitatingly found the way through the Whittingtonian labyrinths; and as the disgusted tiger pealed at the knocker of Turnagain Corner, she was told she would be a useful guide in the South African bush. 'At home,' was the welcome reply, and in another second, her arms were round Robert's neck. There was a thorough brotherly greeting between him and Sir Bevil; each saw in the other a man to be respected, and Robert could not but be grateful to the man who brought him Phœbe.

Her eyes were on the alert to judge how he had been using himself in the last half-year. He looked thin, yet that might be owing to his highly clerical coat, and some of his rural ruddiness was gone, but there was no want of health of form or face, only the spareness and vigour of thorough working condition. His expression was still grave even to sadness, and sternness seemed gathering round his thin lips. Heavy of heart he doubtless was still, but she was struck by the absence of the undefined restlessness that had for years been habitual to both brothers, and which had lately so increased on Mervyn, that there was a relief in watching a face free from it, and telling not indeed of happiness, but of a mind made up to do without it.

She supposed that his room ought to satisfy her, for though untidy in female eyes, it did not betray ultra self-neglect. The fire was brisk, there was a respectable luncheon on the table, and he had even treated himself to the *Guardian*, some new books, and a beautiful photograph of a foreign cathedral. The room was littered with half-unrolled plans, which had to be cleared before the guests could find seats, and he had evidently been beguiling his luncheon with the perusal of some large MS. sheets, red-taped together at the upper corner.

'That's handsome,' said Sir Bevil. 'What is it for? A school or almshouses?'

'Something of both,' said Robert, his colour rising. 'We want a place for disposing of the destitute children that swarm in this district.'

'Oh, show me!' cried Phœbe. 'Is it to be at that place in Cicely Row?'

'I hope so.'

The stiff sheets were unrolled, the designs explained. There was to be a range of buildings round a court, consisting of day-schools, a home for orphans, a *crèche* for infants, a reading-room for adults, and apartments for the clergy of the Church which was to form one side of the quadrangle. Sir Bevil was much interested, and made useful criticisms. 'But,' he objected, 'what is the use of building new churches in the City, when there is no filling those you have?'

'St. Wulstan's is better filled than formerly,' said Robert. 'The pew system is the chief enemy there;

but even without that, it would not hold a tenth part of the Whittingtonian population, would they come to it, which they will not. The Church must come to them, and with special services at their own times. They need an absolute mission, on entirely different terms from the Woolstone quarter.'

'And are you about to head the mission?'

'To endeavour to take a share in it.'

'And who is to be at the cost of this?' pursued Sir Bevil. 'Have you a subscription list?'

Robert coloured again as he answered, 'Why, no; we can do without that so far.'

Phœbe understood, and her face must have revealed the truth to Sir Bevil, for laying his hand on Robert's arm, he said, 'My good fellow, you don't mean that you are answerable for all this?'

'You know I have something of my own.'

'You will not leave much of it at this rate. How about the endowment?'

'I shall live upon the endowment.'

'Have you considered? You will be tied to this place for ever.'

'That is one of my objects,' replied Robert, and in reply to a look of astonished interrogation, 'myself and all that is mine would be far too little to atone for a fraction of the evil that our house is every day perpetrating here.'

'I should hate the business myself,' said the baronet; 'but don't you see it in a strong light?'

'Every hour I spend here shows me that I do not see it strongly enough.'

And there followed some appalling instances of the effects of the multiplicity of gin-palaces, things that it well nigh broke Robert's heart to witness, absorbed as he was in the novelty of his work, fresh in feeling, and never able to divest himself of a sense of being a sharer in the guilt and ruin.

Sir Bevil listened at first with interest, then tried to lead away from the subject; but it was Robert's single idea, and he kept them to it till their departure, when Phœbe's first words were, as they drove from the door, ' Oh, thank you, you do not know how much happier you have made me.'

Her companion smiled, saying, ' I need not ask which is the favourite brother.'

' Mervyn is very kind to me,' quickly answered Phœbe.

' But Robert is the oracle ! eh ?' he said, kindly and merrily.

' Robert has been everything to us younger ones,' she answered. ' I am still more glad that you like him.'

His grave face not responding as she expected, she feared that he had been bored, that he thought Robert righteous over much, or disapproved his opinions; but his answer was worth having when it came. ' I know nothing about his views; I never looked into the subject; but when I see a young man giving up a lucrative prospect for conscience sake, and devoting himself to work in that sink of iniquity, I see there must be something in him. I can't judge if he goes about it in a wrong-headed way, but I should be proud of such a fellow instead of discarding him.'

' Oh, thank you !' cried Phœbe, with ecstasy that made him laugh, and quite differently from the made-up laughter she had been used to hear from him.

' What are you thanking me for ?' he said. ' I do not imagine that I shall be able to serve him. I'll talk to your father about him, but he must be the best judge of the discipline of his own family.'

' I was not thinking of your doing anything,' said Phœbe ; ' but a kind word about Robert does make me very grateful.'

There was a long silence, only diversified by an astonished nod from Mervyn driving back from the office. Just before setting her down, Sir Bevil said, ' I wonder whether your brother would let us give something to his church. Will you find out what it shall be, and let me know ? As a gift from Juliana and myself—you understand.'

It was lucky for Phœbe that she had brought home a good stock of satisfaction to support her, for she found herself in the direst disgrace, and her mother too much cowed to venture on more than a feeble self-defensive murmur that she had told Phœbe it would never do. Convinced in her own conscience that she had done nothing blameworthy, Phœbe knew that it was the shortest way not to defend herself, and the storm was blowing over when Mervyn came in, charmed to mortify Juliana by compliments to Phœbe on 'doing it stylishly, careering in Acton's turn-out,' but when the elder sister explained where she had been, Mervyn, too, deserted her, and turned away with a fierce imprecation on his brother, such as was misery to Phœbe's ears. He was sourly ill-humoured all the evening ; Juliana wreaked her displeasure on Sir Bevil in ungraciousness, till such silence and gloom descended on him, that he was like another man from him who had smiled on Phœbe in the afternoon.

Yet, though dismayed at the offence she had given, and grieved at these evidences of Robert's ill-odour with his family, Phœbe could not regret having seized her single chance of seeing Robert's dwelling for herself, nor the having made him known to Sir Bevil. The one had made her satisfied, the other hopeful, even while she recollected, with foreboding, that truth sometimes comes not with peace, but with a sword, to set at variance parent and child, and make foes of them of the same household.

Juliana never forgave that drive. She continued bitter towards Phœbe, and kept such a watch over her and Sir Bevil, that the jealous surveillance became palpable to both. Sir Bevil really wanted to tell Phœbe the unsatisfactory result of his pleading for Robert ; she wanted to tell him of Robert's gratitude for his offered gift ; but the exchange of any words in private was out of their power, and each silently felt that it was best to make no move towards one another till the unworthy jealousy should have died away.

Though Sir Bevil had elicited nothing but abuse of 'pig-headed folly,' his espousal of the young clergyman's cause was not without effect. Robert was not treated with more open disfavour than he had often previously endured, and was free to visit the party at Farrance's, if he chose to run the risk of encountering his father's blunt coldness, Mervyn's sulky dislike, and Juliana's sharp satire, but as he generally came so as to find his mother and Phœbe alone, some precious moments compensated for the various disagreeables. Nor did these affect him nearly as much as they did his sister. It was, in fact, one of his remaining unwholesome symptoms that he rather enjoyed persecution, and took no pains to avoid giving offence. If he meant to be uncompromising, he sometimes was simply provoking, and Phœbe feared that Sir Bevil thought him an unpromising *protégé*.

He was asked to the Christmas dinner at the Bannermans', and did not fulfil Augusta's prediction that he would say it was a fast day, and refuse. That evening gave Phœbe her best *tête-à-tête* with him, but she observed that all was about Whittingtonia, not one word of the past summer, not so much as an inquiry for Miss Charlecote. Evidently that page in his history was closed for ever, and if he should carry out his designs in their present form, a wife at the intended institution would be an impossibility. How near the dearest may be to one another, and yet how little can they guess at what they would most desire to know!

Sir Bevil had insisted on his being asked to perform the ceremony, and she longed to understand whether his refusal were really on the score of his being a deacon, or if he had any further motive. His own family were affronted, though glad to be left free to request the services of the greatest dignitary of their acquaintance, and Sir Bevil's blunt 'No, no, poor fellow! say no more about it,' made her suppose that he suspected that Robert's vehemence in his parish was meant to work off a disappointment.

It was a dreary wedding, in spite of London grandeur. In all her success, Juliana could not help looking pinched and ill at ease, her wreath and veil hardening instead of softening her features, and her bridegroom's studious cheerfulness and forced laughs became him less than his usual silent dejection. The Admiral was useful in getting up stock wedding-wit, but Phœbe wondered how any one could laugh at it; and her fellow-bridesmaids, all her seniors, seemed to her, as perhaps she might to them, like thoughtless children, playing with the surface of things. She pitied Sir Bevil, and saw little chance of happinessfor either, yet heard only congratulations, and had to be bright, busy, and helpful, under a broad, stiff, white watered silk scarf, beneath which Juliana had endeavoured to extinguish her, but in which her tall, rounded shape looked to great advadtage. Indeed, that young rosy face, and the innocently pensive wondering eyes were so sweet, that the bride had to endure hearing admiration of her sister from all quarters, and the Acton bridemaidens whispered rather like those at Netherby Hall.

It was over, and Phœbe was the reigning Miss Fulmort. Her friends were delighted for her and for themselves, and her mother entered on the full enjoyment of the little brougham.

CHAPTER XI.

> When some dear scheme
> Of our life doth seem
> Shivered at once like a broken dream;
> And our hearts to reel
> Like ships that feel
> A sharp rock grating against their keel.—C. F. A.

IT was high summer; and in spite of cholera-averting thunder-storms, the close streets, and the odour of the Thames were becoming insufferable. Mr. Parsons arranged a series of breathing times for his clerical staff, but could make Robert Fulmort accept none. He was strong and healthy, ravenous of work, impervious to disgusts, and rejected holidays as burdensome and hateful. Where should he go? What could he do? What would become of his wild scholars without him, and who would superintend his buildings?

Mr. Parsons was fain to let him have his own way, as had happened in some previous instances, specially the edifice in Cicely Row, where the incumbent would have paused, but the curate rushed on with resolute zeal and impetuosity, taking measures so decidedly ere his intentions were revealed, that neither remonstrance nor prevention were easy, and a species of annoyed, doubtful admiration alone was possible. It was sometimes a gratifying reflection to the vicar, that when the buildings were finished, Whittingtonia would become a district, and its busy curate be no longer under his jurisdiction.

Meantime Robert was left with a companion in priest's orders, but newer to the parish than himself, to conduct the services at St. Wulstan's, while the other curates were taking holiday, and the vicar at his son's country-house. To see how contentedly, nay, pleasureably, 'Fulmort' endured perpetual broiling, passing from frying school to grilling pavement, and seething human hive, was constant edification to his colleague, who, fresh from the calm university, felt such a life to be a slow martyrdom, and wished his liking for the deacon were in better proportion to his esteem.

'A child to be baptized at 8, Little Whittington-street,' he said, with resigned despair, as at the vestry door he received a message from a small maid, one afternoon, when the air looked lurid yellow with sultry fire.

'I'll go,' replied Robert, with the alacrity that sometimes almost irritated his fellows; and off he sped, with alert steps, at which his friend gazed with the sensation of watching a salamander.

Little Whittington-street, where it was not warehouses, was chiefly occupied by small tradesfolk, or by lodging houses for the numerous 'young men' employed in the City. It was one of the most respectable parts of that quarter, but being much given to dissent, was little frequented by the clergy, who had too much immorality to contend with, to have leisure to speak against schism.

When he rang at No. 8, the little maid ushered him down a narrow, dark staircase, and announcing, 'Please, ma'am, here's the minister,' admitted him into a small room, feeling like a cellar, the window opening into an area. It was crowded with gay and substantial furniture, and contained two women, one lying on a couch, partially hidden by a screen, the other an elderly person, in a widow's cap, with an infant in her arms.

'Good morning, sir, we were sorry to trouble you, but I felt certain, as I told my daughter, that a minister of the Gospel would not tarry in time of need. Not that I put my trust in ordinances, sir; I have been blest with the enlightening of the new birth, but my daughter, sir, she follows the Church. Yes, sir, the poor little lamb is a sad sufferer in this vale of tears. So wasted away, you see; you would not think he was nine weeks old. We would have brought him to church before, sir, only my daughter's hillness, and her 'usband's habsence. It was always her wish, sir, and I was not against it, for many true Christians have found grace in the Church, sir.'

Robert considered whether to address himself to the young mother, whose averted face and uneasy movements seemed to show that this stream of words was distressing to her. He thought silence would be best procured by his assumption of his office, and quietly made his preparations, opened his book, and took his place.

The young woman, raising herself with difficulty, said in a low, sweet voice, 'The gentleman is ready, mother.'

As there was no pressing danger, he read the previous collects, the elder female responding with devout groans, the younger sinking on her knees, her face hidden in her wasted hands. He took the little feeble being in his arms, and demanded the name.

'Hoeing Charterhouse,' replied the grandmother.

He looked interrogative, and Hoeing Charterhouse was repeated.

'Owen Charteris,' said the low, sweet voice.

A thrill shot over his whole frame, as his look met a large, full, liquid pair of dark eyes, such as once seen could never be forgotten, though dropped again instantly, while a burning blush arose, instantly veiled by the hands, which hid all up to the dark hair.

Recalling himself by an effort, he repeated the too familiar name, and baptized the child, bending his head over it afterwards in deep compassion and mental entreaty both for its welfare, and his own guidance in the tissue of wrongdoing thus disclosed. A hasty, stealthy glance at the hands covering the mother's face, showed him the ring on her fourth finger, and as they rose from their knees, he said, 'I am to register this child as Owen Charteris Sandbrook.'

With a look of deadly terror, she faintly exclaimed, 'I have done it! You know him, sir; you will not betray him!'

'I know you, too,' said Robert, sternly. 'You were the schoolmistress at Wrapworth!'

'I was, sir. It was all my fault. Oh! promise me, sir, never to betray him; it would be the ruin of his prospects for ever!' And she came towards him, her hands clasped in entreaty, her large eyes shining with feverish lustre, her face wasted but still lovely, a piteous contrast to the queenly being of a year ago in her pretty schoolroom.

'Compose yourself,' said Robert, gravely; 'I hope never to betray any one. I confess that I am shocked, but I will endeavour to act rightly.'

'I am sure, sir,' broke in Mrs. Murrell, with double volume, after her interval of quiescence, 'it is not to be expected but what a gentleman's friends would be offended. It was none of my wish, sir, being that I never knew a word of it till she was married and it was too late, or I would have warned her against broken cisterns. But as for her, sir, she is as innocent as a miserable sinner can be in a fallen world. It was the young gentleman as sought her out. I always misdoubted the ladies noticing her, and making her take part with men-singers and women-singers, and such vanities as is pleasing to the unregenerate heart. Ah! sir, without grace, where are we? Not that he was ever other than most honourable with her, or she would never have listened to him not for a moment, but she was over-persuaded, sir, and folks said what they hadn't no right to say, and the minister, he was 'ard on her, and so, you see, sir, she took fright and married him out of 'and, trusting to a harm of flesh, and went to Hireland with him. She just writ me a note, which filled my 'art with fear and trembling, a 'nonymous note, with only Hedna signed to it; and I waited, with failing eyes and sorrow of heart, till one day in autumn he brings her back to me, and here she has been ever since, dwining away in a nervous fever, as the doctors call it, as it's a misery to see her, and he never coming nigh her.'

'Once,' murmured Edna, who had several times tried to interrupt.

'Once, ay, for one hour at Christmas.'

'He is known here; he can't venture often,' interposed the wife; and there was a further whisper, 'he couldn't stay, he couldn't bear it.'

But the dejected accents were lost in the old woman's voice,—'Now, sir, if you know him or his family, I wouldn't be wishing to do him no hinjury, nor to ruinate his prospects, being, as he says, that the rich lady will make him her hare; but, sir, if you have any power with him as a godly minister or the friend of his youth, may be——'

'He is only waiting till he has a curacy—a house of his own—mother!'

'No, Edna, hold your peace. It is not fit that I should see my only child cut down as the grass of the field, and left a burthen upon me, a lone woman, while he is eating of the fat of the land. I say it is scandalous that he should leave her here, and take no notice; not coming near her since one hour at Christmas, and only just sending her a few pounds now and then; not once coming to see his own child!'

'He could not; he is abroad!' pleaded Edna.

'He tells you he is abroad!' exclaimed Robert.

'He went to Paris at Easter. He promised to come when he comes home.'

'You poor thing!' burst out Robert. 'He is deceiving you! He came back at the end of three weeks. I heard from my sister that she saw him on Sunday.'

Robert heartily rued his abruptness, as the poor young wife sank back in a deadly swoon. The grandmother hurried to apply remedies, insisting that the gentleman should not go, and continuing all the time her version of her daughter's wrongs. Her last remnant of patience had vanished on learning this deception, and she only wanted to publish her daughter's claims, proceeding to establish them by hastening in search of the marriage certificate as soon as Edna had begun to revive, but sooner than Robert was satisfied to be left alone with the inanimate, helpless form on the couch.

He was startled when Edna raised her hand, and strove to speak,—'Sir, do not tell—do not tell my mother where he is. She must not fret him—she must not tell his friends—he would be angry.'

She ceased as her mother returned with the certificate of the marriage, contracted last July before the registrar of the huge suburban Union to which Wrapworth belonged, the centre of which was so remote, that the pseudo-banns of Owen Charteris Sandbrook and Edna Murrell had attracted no attention.

'It was very wrong,' feebly said Edna; 'I drew him into it! I loved him so much; and they all talked so after I went in the boat with him, that I thought my character was gone, and I begged him to save me from them. It was my fault, sir; and I've the punishment. You'll not betray him, sir; only don't let that young lady, your sister, trust to him. Not yet. My baby and I shall soon be out of her way.'

The calm languor of her tone was almost fearful, and even as she spoke a shuddering seized her, making her tremble convulsively, her teeth knocking together, and the couch shaking under her.

'You must have instant advice,' cried Robert. 'I will fetch some one.'

'You wont betray him,' almost shrieked Edna. 'A little while—stay a little while—he will be free of me.'

There was delirium in look and voice, and he was compelled to pause and assure her that he was only going for the doctor, and would come again before taking any other step.

It was not till the medical man had been summoned that his mind recurred to the words about his sister. He might have dismissed them as merely the jealous suspicion of the deserted wife, but that he remembered Lucilla's hint as to an attachment between Owen and Phœbe, and he knew that such would have been most welcome to Miss Charlecote.

'My Phœbe, my one bright spot!' was his inward cry, 'must your guileless happiness be quenched! O, I would rather have it all over again myself than that one pang should come near you, in your sweetness and innocence, the blessing of us all! And I not near to guard nor warn! What may not be passing even now? Unprincipled, hard-hearted deceiver, walking at large among those gentle, unsuspicious women—trading on their innocent trust! Would that I had disclosed the villany I knew of!'

His hand clenched, his brow lowered, and his mouth was set so savagely, that the passing policeman looked in wonder from the dangerous face to the clerical dress.

Early next morning he was at No. 8, and learnt that Mrs. Brook, as the maid called her, had been very ill all night, and that the doctor was still with her. Begging to see the doctor, Robert found that high fever had set in, an aggravation of the low nervous fever that had been consuming her strength all the spring, and her condition was already such that there was little hope of her surviving the present attack. She had been raving all night about the young lady with whom Mr. Sandbrook had been walking by moonlight, and when the door of the little adjoining bed-room was open, her moans and broken words were plainly audible.

Robert asked whether he should fetch her husband, and Mrs. Murrell caught at the offer. Owen's presence was the single hope of restoring her, and at least he ought to behold the wreck that he had wrought. Mrs. Murrell gave a terrible thrust by saying, 'that the young lady at least ought to be let know, that she might not be trusting to him.'

'Do not fear, Mrs. Murrell,' he said, almost under his breath. 'My only doubt is, whether I can meet Owen Sandbrook as a Christian should.'

Cutting off her counsels on the unconverted nature, he strode off to find his colleague, whom he perplexed by a few rapid words on the necessity of going into the country for the day. His impatient condition required vehement action; and with a sense of hurrying to rescue Phœbe, he could scarcely brook the slightest delay till he was on his way to Hiltonbury, nor till the train spared him all action, could he pause to collect his strength, guard his resentment, or adjust his measures for warning, but not betraying. He could think of no honourable mode of dealing, save carrying off Owen to London with him at once, sacrificing the sight of his sister for the present, and either writing or going to her afterwards, when the mode of dealing the blow should be more evident. It cost him keen suffering to believe that this was the sole right course, but he had bound himself to it by his promise to the poor suffering wife, blaming himself for continually putting his sister before her in his plans.

At Elverslope, on his demand for a fly for Hiltonbury, he was answered that all were engaged for the Horticultural Show in the Forest; but the people at the station, knowing him well, made willing exertions to procure a vehicle for him, and a taxed cart soon making its appearance, he desired to be taken, not to the Holt, but to the Forest, where he had no doubt that he should find the object of his search.

This Horticultural Show was the great gaiety of the year. The society had originated with Humfrey Charlecote, for the benefit of the poor as well as the rich; and the summer exhibition always took place under the trees of a fragment of the old Forest, which still survived at about five miles from Hiltonbury. The day was a county holiday. The delicate orchid and the crowned pine were there, with the hairy gooseberry, the cabbage and potato, and the homely cottage-garden nosegay from many a woodland hamlet. The young ladies competed in collections of dried flowers for a prize botany book; and the subscriptions were so arranged that on this festival each poorer member might, with two companions, be provided with a hearty meal; while grandees and farmers had a luncheon-tent of their own, and regarded the day as a county pic-nic.

It was a favourite affair with all, intensely enjoyed, and full of good neighbourhood. Humfrey Charlecote's spirit never seemed to have deserted it; it was a gathering of distant friends, a delight of children as of the full-grown; and while the young were frantic for its gipsying fun, their elders seldom failed to attend, if only in remembrance of poor Mr. Charlecote, 'who had begged one and all not to let it drop.'

Above all, Honora felt it due to Humfrey to have prize-roots and fruits from the Holt, and would have thought herself fallen, indeed, had the hardest rain kept her from the rendezvous, with one wagon carrying the cottagers' articles, and another a troop of school children. No doubt the Forest would be the place to find Owen Sandbrook, but for the rest——

From the very extremity of his perplexity, Robert's mind sought relief in external objects. So joyous were the associations with the Forest road on a horticultural day, that the familiar spots could not but revive them. Those green glades, where the graceful beeches retreated, making cool green galleries with their slender

gleaming stems, reminded him of his putting his new
pony to speed to come up with the Holt carriage; that
scathed oak had a tradition of lightning connected with
it; yonder was the spot where he had shown Lucilla a
herd of deer; here the rising ground whence the whole
scene could be viewed, and from force of habit he felt
exhilarated as he gazed down the slope of heather,
where the fine old oaks and beeches, receding, had left
an open space, now covered with the well-known tents;
there the large one, broadly striped with green, containing the show; there the white marquees for the
eaters; the union jack's gay colours floating lazily
from a pole in the Outlaw's Knoll; the dark, full
foliage of the forest, and purple tints of the heather
setting off the bright female groups in their delicate
summer gaieties. Vehicles of all degrees—smart ba-
rouche, lengthy britzschka, light gig, dashing pony carriage, rattling shanderadan, and gorgeous wagon—
were drawn up in treble file, minus their steeds; the
sounds of well-known tunes from the band were wafted
on the wind, and such an air of jocund peace and festivity pervaded the whole, that for a moment he had a
sense of holiday-making ere he sighed at the shade that
he was bringing on that scene of merriment.

Reaching the barrier, he paid his entrance-money,
and desiring the carriage to wait, walked rapidly down
the hill. On one side of the road was the gradual
sweep of open heath, on the other was a rapid slope,
shaded by trees, and covered with fern, growing tall
and grand as it approached the moist ground in the
hollow below. Voices made him turn his head in that
direction. Aloof from the rest of the throng, he beheld
two figures half-way down the bank, so nearly hidden
among the luxuriant wing-like fronds of the Osmond
royal which they were gathering, that at first only
their hats were discernible—a broad grey one, with
drooping feather, and a light Oxford boating straw hat.
The merry ring of the clear girlish voice, the deep-
toned replies, told him more than his first glance did;

and with one inward ejaculation for self-command, he turned aside to the descent.

The rustling among the copsewood caught the ear of Phœbe, who was the highest up, and, springing up like a fawn in the covert, she cried,—'Robin! dear Robin! how delicious!' but ere she had made three bounds towards him, his face brought her to a pause, and, in an awe-struck voice, she asked, 'Robert, what is it?'

'It does not concern you, dearest; at least, I hope not. I want Owen Sandbrook.'

'Then it is *she*. O Robin, can you bear it?' she whispered, clinging to him, terrified by the agitated fondness of his embrace.

'I know nothing of *her*,' was his answer, interrupted by Owen, who, raising his handsome, ruddy face from beneath, shouted mirthfully—

'Ha! Phœbe, what interloper have you caught? What, Fulmort, not quite grilled in the Wulstonian oven?'

'I was in search of you. Wait there, Phœbe,' said Robert, advancing to meet Owen, with a gravity of countenance that provoked an impatient gesture, and the question—

'Come, have it out! Do you mean that you have been ferreting out some old scrape of mine?'

'I mean,' said Robert, looking steadily at him, 'that I have been called in to baptize your sick child. Your wife is dying, and you must hasten if you would see her alive.'

'That wont do. You know better than that,' returned Owen, with ill-concealed agitation, partaking of anger. 'She was quite recovered when last I heard, but she is a famous hand at getting up a scene; and that mother of hers would drive Job out of his senses. They have worked on your weak mind. I was an ass to trust to the old woman's dissent for hindering them from finding you out, and getting up a scene.'

'They did not. It was by accident that I was the

person who answered the summons. They knew neither me nor my name, so you may acquit them of any preparation. I recognised your name, which I was desired to give to the child; and then, in spite of wasting, terror, and deadly sickness, I knew the mother. She has been pining under low nervous fever, still believing you on the Continent; and the discovery that she had been deceived, was such a shock as to bring on a violent attack, which she is not likely to have strength to survive.'

'I never told her I was still abroad,' said Owen, in a fretful tone of self-defence. 'I only had my letters forwarded through my scout; for I knew I should have no peace nor safety if the old woman knew where to find me, and preach me crazy; and I could not be going to see after her, for, thanks to Honor Charlecote and her schools, every child in Whittingtonia knows me by sight. I told her to be patient till I had a curacy, and was independent; but it seems she could not be. I'll run up as soon as I can get some plea for getting away from the Holt.'

'Death will leave no time for your excuses,' said Robert. 'By setting off at once, you may catch the five o'clock express at W——.'

'Well, it is your object to have a grand explosion! When I am cut out, you and Cilly may make a good thing of it. I wish you joy! Ha! by Jove!' he muttered, as he saw Phœbe waiting out of earshot. And then, turning from Robert, who was dumb in the effort to control a passionate reply, he called out, 'Good by, Phœbe; I beg your pardon, but you see I am summoned. Family claims are imperative!'

'What is the matter?' said the maiden, terrified not only at his tone, but at the gestures of her brother of fierce, suppressed menace towards him, despairing protection towards her.

'Why, he has told you! Matter enough, isn't it? I'm a married man. I ask your compassion!' with a bitter laugh.

'It is you who have told her,' said Robert, who, after a desperate effort, had forced all violence from his voice and language. 'Traitor as you consider me, your secret had not crossed my lips. But no—there is no time to waste on disputes. Your wife is sinking under neglect; and her seeing you once more may depend on your not loitering away these moments.'

'I don't believe it. Canting and tragedy queening. Taking him in! I know better!' muttered Owen, suddenly, as he moved up the bank.

'O Robin, how can he be so hard?' whispered Phœbe, as she met her brother's eyes wistfully fixed on her face.

'He is altogether selfish and heartless,' returned Robert, in the same inaudible voice. 'My Phœbe, give me this one comfort. You never listened to him.'

'There was nothing to listen to,' said Phœbe, turning her clear, surprised eyes on him. 'You couldn't think him so bad as that. O Robin, how silly!'

'What were you doing here?' he asked, holding her arm tight.

'Only Miss Fennimore wanted some Osmunda, and Miss Charlecote sent him to show me where it grew; because she was talking to Lady Raymond.'

The free simplicity of her look made Robert breathe freely. Charity was coming back to him.

At the same moment Owen turned, his face flushed, and full of emotion, but the obduracy gone.

'I may take a long leave! When you see Honor Charlecote, Fulmort ——'

'I shall not see her. I am going back with you,' said Robert, instantly deciding, now that he felt that he could both leave Phœbe, and trust himself with the offender.

'You think I want to escape!'

'No; but I have duties to return to. Besides, you will find a scene for which you are little prepared; and which will cost you the more for your present mood. I may be of use there. Your secret is safe with Phœbe and me. I promised your wife to keep it, and we will not rob you of the benefit of free confession.'

'And what is to explain my absence? No, no, the secret is one no longer, and it has been intolerable enough already,' said Owen, recklessly. 'Poor Honor, it will be a grievous business, and little Phœbe will be a kind messenger. Wont you, Phœbe? I leave my cause in your hands.'

'But,' faltered Phœbe, 'she should hear who——'

'Simple child, you can't draw inferences. Cilla wouldn't have asked. Don't you remember her darling at Wrapworth? People shouldn't throw such splendid women in one's way, especially when they are made of such inflammable materials, and take fire at a civil word. So ill, poor thing! Now, Robert, on your honour, has not the mother been working on you?'

'I tell you not what the mother told me, but what the medical man said. Low nervous fever set in long ago, and she has never recovered her confinement. Heat and closeness were already destroying her, when my disclosure that you were not abroad, as she had been led to believe, brought on fainting, and almost immediate delirium. This was last evening, she was worse this morning.'

'Poor girl, poor girl!' muttered Owen, his face almost convulsed with emotion. 'There was no helping it. She would have drowned herself if I had not taken her with me—quite capable of it! after those intolerable women at Wrapworth had opened fire. I wish women's tongues were cut out by act of parliament. So, Phœbe, tell poor Honor that I know I am unpardonable, but I am sincerely sorry for her. I fell into it, there's no knowing how, and she would pity me, and so would you, if you knew what I have gone through. Good-bye, Phœbe. Most likely I shall never see you again. Wont you shake hands, and tell me you are sorry for me?'

'I should be, if you seemed more sorry for your wife

than yourself,' she said, holding out her hand, but by no means prepared for his not only pressing it with fervour, but carrying it to his lips.

Then, as Robert started forward with an impulse of snatching her from him, he almost threw it from his grasp, and with a long sigh very like bitter regret, and a murmur that resembled 'That's a *little* angel,' he mounted the bank. Robert only tarried to say, 'May I be able to bear with him! Phœbe, do your best for poor Miss Charlecote. I will write.'

Phœbe sat down at the foot of a tree, veiled by the waving ferns, to take breath and understand what had passed. Her first act was to strike one hand across the other, as though to obliterate the kiss, then to draw off her glove, and drop it in the deepest of the fern, never to be worn again. Hateful! With that poor neglected wife pining to death in those stifling city streets, to be making sport in those forest glades. Shame! shame! But oh! worst of all was his patronizing pity for Miss Charlecote! Phœbe's own mission to Miss Charlecote was dreadful enough, and she could have sat for hours deliberating on the mode of carrying grief and dismay to her friend, who had looked so joyous and exulting with her boy by her side as she drove upon the ground; but there was no time to be lost, and rousing herself into action with strong effort, Phœbe left the fern brake, walking like one in a dream, and exchanging civilities with various persons who wondered to see her alone, made her way to the principal marquee, where luncheon had taken place, and which always served as the *rendezvous*. Here sat mammas, keeping up talk enough for civility, and peeping out restlessly to cluck their broods together; here gentlemen stood in knots, talking county business; servants congregated in the rear, to call the carriages; stragglers gradually streamed together, and 'Oh! here you are,' was the staple exclamation.

It was uttered by Mrs. Fulmort as Phœbe appeared, and was followed by plaintive inquiries for her sisters, and assurances that it would have been better to have stayed in the cool tent, and gone home at once. Phœbe consoled her by ordering the carriage, and explaining that her sisters were at hand with some other girls, then begged leave to go home with Miss Charlecote for the night.

'My dear, what shall I do with the others without you? Maria has such odd tricks, and Bertha is so teasing without you! You promised they should not tire me!'

'I will beg them to be good, dear mamma; I am very sorry, but it is only this once. She will be alone. Owen Sandbrook is obliged to go away.'

'I can't think what she should want of you,' moaned her mother, 'so used as she is to be alone. Did she ask you?'

'No, she does not know yet. I am to tell her, and that is why I want you to be so kind as to spare me, dear mamma.'

'My dear, it will not do for you to be carrying young men's secrets, at least not Owen Sandbrook's. Your papa would not like it, my dear, until she had acknowledged him for her heir. You have lost your glove, too, Phœbe, and you look so heated, you had better come back with me,' said Mrs. Fulmort, who would not have withstood for a moment a decree from either of her other daughters.

'Indeed,' said Phœbe, 'you need not fear, mamma. It is nothing of that sort, quite the contrary.'

'Quite the contrary! You don't tell me that he has formed another attachment, just when I made sure of your settling at last at the Holt, and you such a favourite with Honor Charlecote. Not one of those plain Miss Raymonds, I hope.'

'I must not tell, till she has heard,' said Phœbe, 'so please say nothing about it. It will vex poor Miss Charlecote sadly, so pray let no one suspect, and I will come back and tell you to-morrow, by the time you are dressed.'

Mrs. Fulmort was so much uplifted by the promise of the grand secret that she made no more opposition, and Maria and Bertha hurried in with Phœbe's glove, which, with the peculiar fidelity of property wilfully lost, had fallen into their hands while searching for Robert. Both declared they had seen him on the hill, and clamorously demanded him of Phœbe. Her answer 'he is not in the forest, you will not find him,' was too conscious fully to have satisfied the shrewd Bertha, but for the pleasure of discoursing to the other girls upon double gangers, of whom she had stealthily read in some prohibited German literature of her governess's.

Leaving her to astonish them, Phœbe took up a position near Miss Charlecote, who was talking to the good matronly-looking Lady Raymond, and on the first opportunity offered herself as a companion. On the way home, Honor, much pleased, was proposing to find Owen, and walk through a beautiful and less frequented forest path, when she saw her own carriage coming up with that from Beauchamp, and lamented the mistake which must take her away as soon as Owen could be found.

'I ventured to order it,' said Phœbe; 'I thought you might prefer it. Owen is gone. He left a message with me for you.'

Experience of former blows taught Honora to ask no questions, and to go through the offices of politeness as usual. But Lady Raymond, long a friend of hers, though barely acquainted with Mrs. Fulmort, and never having seen Phœbe before, living as she did on the opposite side of the county, took a moment for turning round to the young girl, and saying with a friendly motherly warmth, far from mere curiosity, 'I am sure you have bad news for Miss Charlecote. I see you cannot speak of it now, but you must promise me to send to Moorcroft, if Sir John or I can be of any use.'

Phœbe could only give a thankful grasp of the kind

hand. The Raymonds were rather despised at home for plain habits, strong religious opinions, and scanty fortunes, but she knew they were Miss Charlecote's great friends and advisers.

Not till the gay crowd had been left behind did Honor turn to Phœbe, and say gently, 'My dear, if he is gone off in any foolish way, you had better tell me at once, that something may be done.'

'He is gone with Robert,' said Phœbe. 'Bertha did really see Robert. He had made a sad discovery, and came for Owen. Do you remember that pretty schoolmistress at Wrapworth?'

Never had Phœbe seen such a blanched face and dilated eyes as were turned on her, with the gaspin words, 'Impossible! they would not have told you.'

'They were obliged,' said Phœbe; 'they had to hurry for the train, for she is very ill indeed.'

Honor leant back with folded hands and closed eyes, so that Phœbe almost felt as if she had killed her. 'I suppose Robert was right to fetch him,' she said; 'but their telling you!'

'Owen told me he fancied Robert had done so,' said Phœbe, 'and called out to me something about family claims, and a married man.'

'Married!' cried Honora, starting forward. 'You are sure!'

'Quite sure,' repeated Phœbe; 'he desired me to tell you I was to say he knew he was unpardonable, but he had suffered a great deal, and he was grieved at the sorrow you would feel.'

Having faithfully discharged her message, Phœbe could not help being vexed at the relenting, 'Poor fellow!'

Honor was no longer confounded, as at the first sentences, and though still cast down, was more relieved than her young friend could understand, asking all that had passed between the young men, and when all had been told, leaning back in silence until, when almost at home, she laid her hand on Phœbe's arm, and said, 'My child, never think yourself safe from idols.'

She then sought her own room, and Phœbe feared that her presence was intrusive, for she saw her hostess no more till tea-time, when the wan face and placid smile almost made her weep at first, then wonder at the calm unconstrained manner in which her amusement was provided for, and feel ready to beg not to be treated like a child or a stranger. When parting for the night, however, Honor tenderly said, 'Thanks, my dear, for giving up the evening to me.'

'I have only been an oppression to you.'

'You did me the greatest good. I did not want discussion; I only wanted kindness. I wish I had you always, but it is better not. Their uncle was right. I spoil every one.'

'Pray do not say so. You have been our great blessing. If you knew how we wish to comfort you.'

'You do comfort me. I can watch Robert realizing my visions for others, and you, my twilight moon, my autumn flower. But I must not love you too much, Phœbe. They all suffer for my inordinate affection. But it is too late to talk. Good night, sweet one.'

'Shall you sleep?' said Phœbe, wistfully lingering.

'Yes; I don't enter into it enough to be haunted. Ah! you have never learnt what it is to feel heavy with trouble. I believe I shall not dwell on it till I know more. There may be much excuse; she may have been artful, and at least Owen dealt fairly by her in one respect. I can better suppose her unworthy, than him cruelly neglectful.'

In that hope Honor slept, and was not more depressed than Phœbe had seen her under Lucilla's desertion. She put off her judgment till she should hear more, went about her usual occupations, and sent Phœbe home till letters should come, when they would meet again.

Both heard from Robert by the next post, and his letter to Miss Charlecote related all that he had been able to collect from Mrs. Murrell, or from Owen himself. The narrative is here given more fully than he was able to make it. Edna Murrell, born with the susceptible organization of a musical temperament, had in her earliest childhood been so treated as to foster refined tastes and aspirations, such as disgusted her with the respectable vulgarity of her home. The pet of the nursery and school-room looked down on the lodge kitchen and parlour, and her discontent was a matter of vanity with her parents, as a sign of her superiority, while plausibility and caution were continually enjoined on her rather by example than precept, and she was often aware of her mother's indulgence of erratic propensities in religion, unknown either to her father or his employers.

Unexceptionable as had been her training-school education, the high cultivation and soundness of doctrine had so acted on her as to keep her farther aloof from her mother, whose far more heartfelt religion appeared to her both distasteful and contemptible, and whose advice was thus cast aside as prejudiced and sectarian.

Such was the preparation for the unprotected life of a schoolmistress in a house by herself. Servants and small tradesfolk were no companions to her, and were offended by her ladylike demeanour; and her refuge was in books that served but to increase the perils of sham romance, and in enthusiastic adoration of the young lady, whose manners apparently placed her on an equality, although her beauty and musical talents were in truth only serving as a toy.

Her face and voice had already been thrust on Owen's notice before the adventure with the bargeman had constituted the young gentleman the hero of her grateful imagination, and commenced an intercourse, for which his sister's inconsiderate patronage gave ample opportunities. His head was full of the theory of fusion of classes, and of the innate refinement, freshness of intellect, and vigour of perception of the unsophisticated, at least so he thought, and when he lent her books, commenting on favourite passages, and talked poetry or popular science to her, he imagined himself walking in the steps of those who were asserting the claims of intelligence to cultivation, and sowing broadcast the seeds of art, literature, and emancipation. Perhaps he knew not how often he was betrayed into tokens of admiration, sufficient to inflame such a disposition as he had to deal with, and if he were aware of his influence, and her adoration, it idly flattered and amused him, without thought of the consequences.

On the night when she had fainted at the sight of his attention to Phœbe, she was left on his hands in a state when all caution and reserve gave way, and her violent agitation fully awakened him to the perception of the expectations he had caused, the force of the feelings he had aroused. A mixture of pity, vanity, and affection towards the beautiful creature before him had led to a response such as did not disappoint her, and there matters might have rested for the present, but that their interview had been observed. Edna, terror-stricken, believing herself irretrievably disgraced, had thrown herself on his mercy in a frantic condition, such as made him dread exposure for himself, as well as suspense for her tempestuous nature.

With all his faults, the pure atmosphere in which he had grown up, together with the tone of his associates, comparatively free from the grosser and more hard-hearted forms of vice, had concurred with poor Edna's real modesty and principle in obtaining the sanction of marriage, for her flight with him from the censure of Wrapworth, and the rebukes of her mother. Throughout, his feeling had been chiefly stirred up by the actual sight of her beauty, and excited by her fervid passion. When absent from her, there had been always regrets and hesitations, such as would have prevailed, save for his compassion, and dread of the effects of her desperation, both for her and for himself. The unpardonable manner in which he knew himself to have acted, made it needful to plunge deeper for the very sake of concealment.

Yet, once married, he would have been far safer if he had confessed the fact to his only true friend, since it must surely come to light some time or other, but he had bred himself up in the habit of schoolboy shuffling, hiding everything to the last moment, and he could not bear to be cast off by the Charterises, be pitied and laughed at by his Oxford friends, nor to risk Honor Charlecote's favour, perhaps her inheritance. Return to Oxford the victim of an attachment to a village schoolmistress! Better never return thither at all, as would be but too probably the case! No! the secret must be kept till his first start in life should be secure; and he talked to Edna of his future curacy, while she fed her fancy with visions of lovely parsonages and 'clergymen's ladies' in a world of pensive bliss, and after the honeymoon in Ireland, promised to wait patiently, provided her mother might know all.

Owen had not realized the home to which he was obliged to resign his wife, nor his mother-in-law's powers of tongue. There were real difficulties in the way of his visiting her. It was the one neighbourhood in London where his person might be known, and if he avoided daylight, he became the object of espial to the disappointed lodgers, who would have been delighted to identify the 'Mr. Brook,' who had monopolized the object of their admiration. These perils, the various disagreeables, and especially Mrs. Murrell's complaints and demands for money, had so much annoyed Owen, who felt himself the injured party in the connexion, that he had not only avoided the place, but endeavoured to dismiss the whole humiliating affair from his mind, trying to hinder himself from being harassed by letters, and when forced to attend to the representations of the women, sending a few kind words and promises, with such money as he could spare, always backed, however, by threats of the consequences of a disclosure, which he vaguely intimated would ruin his prospects for life.

Little did the thoughtless boy comprehend the cruelty of his neglect. In the underground rooms of the City lodging-house, the voluntary prison of the shamefaced, half-owned wife, the overwrought headache, incidental to her former profession, made her its prey; nervous fever came on as the suspense became more trying, and morbid excitement alternated with torpor and depression. Medical advice was long deferred, and that which was at last sought was not equal to her needs. It remained for the physician summoned by Owen, in his horror at her delirium, to discover that her brain had long been in a state of irritation, which had become aggravated to such a degree that death was even to be desired. Could she yet survive, it could hardly be to the use of her intellect.

Robert described poor Owen's impetuous misery, and the cares which he lavished on the unconscious sufferer, mentioning him with warmth and tenderness that amazed Honor, from one so stern of judgment. Nay, Robert was more alive to the palliations of Owen's conduct than she was herself. She grieved over the complicated deceit, and resented the cruelty to the wife with the keen severity of secluded womanhood, unable to realize the temptations of young-manhood.

'Why could he not have told me?' she said. 'I could so easily have forgiven him for generous love, if I alone had been offended, and there had been no falsehood; but, after the way he has used us all, and chiefly that poor young thing, I can never feel that he is the same.'

And, though 'the heart that knew no guile had been saved from suffering, the thought of the intimacy that she had encouraged, and the wishes she had entertained for Phœbe, filled her with such dismay, that it required the sight of the innocent, serene face, and the sound of the happy, unembarrassed voice, to reassure her that her darling's peace had not been wrecked. For, though Owen had never overpassed the bounds of the familiar intercourse of childhood, there had been an implication of preference in his look and tone ; nor had there been error in the intuition of poor Edna's jealous passion. Something there was of involuntary reverence that had never been commanded by the far more beautiful and gifted girl who had taken him captive.

So great was the shock that Honora moved about mechanically, hardly able to think. She knew that in time she should pardon her boy; but she could not yearn to do so till she had seen him repent. He had sinned too deeply against others to be taken home at once to her heart, even though she grieved over him with deep, loving pity, and sought to find the original germs of error rather in herself than in him.

Had she encouraged deceit by credulous trust? Alas! alas! that should but have taught him generosity. It was the old story. Fond affection had led her to put herself into a position to which Providence did not call her, and to which she was, therefore, unequal. Fond affection had blinded her eyes, and fostered in its object the very faults most hateful to her. She could only humble herself before her Maker for the recurring sin, and entreat for her own pardon, and for that of the offender with whose sins she charged herself.

And to man she humbled herself by her confession to Captain Charteris, and by throwing herself unreservedly on the advice of Mr. Saville and Sir John Raymond, for her future conduct towards the culprit. If he were suffering now for her rejection of the counsel of manhood and experience, it was right that they should deal with him now, and she would try to bear it. And she also tried as much as possible to soften the blow to Lucilla, who was still abroad with her cousins.

VOL. I.   E E

CHAPTER XII.

A little grain of conscience made him sour.
TENNYSON.

'A PENNY for your thoughts, Cilly,' said Horatia, sliding in on the slippery boards of a great bare room of a lodging-house at the celebrated Spa of Spitzwasserfitzung.

'My thoughts? I was trying to recollect the third line of

'Sated at home, of wife and children tired,
Sated abroad, all seen and naught admired.'

'Bless me, how grand! Worth twopence. So good how Shakspeare, as the Princess Ottilie would say!'

'Twopence for its sincerity! It is not for your sake that I am not in Old England.'

'Not for that of the three flaxen-haired princesses, with religious opinions to be accommodated to those of the crowned heads they may marry?'

'I'm sick of the three, and their raptures. I wish I was as ignorant as you, and that Shakspeare had never been read at the Holt.'

'This is a sudden change. I thought Spitzwasserfitzung and its princesses had brought halcyon days.'

'Halcyon days will never come till we get home.'

'Which Lolly will never do. She passes for somebody here, and will never endure Castle Blanch again.'

'I'll make Owen come and take me home.'

'No,' said Rashe, seriously, 'don't bring Owen here. If Lolly likes to keep Charles where gaming is man's sole resource, don't run Owen into that scrape.'

'What a despicable set you are!' sighed Lucilla. 'I wonder why I stay with you.'

'You might almost as well be gone,' said Ratia. 'You aren't half so useful in keeping things going as you were once; and you wont be ornamental long, if you let your spirits be so uncertain.'

'And pray how is that to be helped? No, don't come out with that stupid thing.'

'Commonplace because it is reasonable. You would have plenty of excitement in the engagement, and then no end of change, and settle down into a blooming little matron, with all the business of the world on your hands. You have got him into excellent training by keeping him dangling so long; and it is the only chance of keeping your looks or your temper. By the time I come and stay with you, you'll be so agreeable you wont know yourself——'

'Blessings on that hideous post-horn for stopping your mouth!' cried Lucilla, springing up. 'Not that letters ever come to me.'

Letters and Mr. and Mrs. Charteris all entered together, and Rashe was busy with her own share, when Lucilla came forward with a determined face, unlike her recent listless look, and said, 'I am wanted at home. I shall start by the diligence to-night.'

'How now?' said Charles. 'The old lady wanting you to make her will?'

'No,' said Lucilla, with dignity. 'My brother's wife is very ill. I must go to her.'

'Is she demented?' asked Charles, looking at his sister.

'Raving,' was the answer. 'She has been so the whole morning. I shall cut off her hair, and get ice for her head.'

'I tell simple truth,' returned Cilla. 'Here is a letter from Honor Charlecote, solving the two mysteries of last summer. Owen's companion, who Rashe would have it was Jack Hastings——'

'Ha! married, then! The cool hand! And, verily, but that Cilly takes it so easily, I should imagine it was her singing prodigy—eh? It was, then?'

'Absurd idiot!' exclaimed Charles. 'There, he is done for now!'

'Yes,' drawled Eloïsa; 'one never could notice a low person like that.'

'She is my sister, remember!' cried Lucilla, with stamping foot and flashing eye.

'Cunning rogue!' continued Horatia. 'How did he manage to give no suspicion? Oh! what fun! No wonder she looked green and yellow when he was flirting with the little Fulmort! Let's hear all, Cilly—how, when, and where?'

'At the Registrar's, at R——, July 14th, 1854,' returned Lucilla, with defiant gravity.

'Last July!' said Charles. 'Ha! the young donkey was under age—hadn't consent of guardian. I don't believe the marriage will hold water. I'll write to Stevens this minute.'

'Well, that would be luck!' exclaimed Rashe.

'Much better than he deserves,' added Charles, 'to be such a fool as to run into the noose and marry the girl.'

Lucilla was trembling from head to foot, and a light gleamed in her eyes; but she spoke so quietly, that her cousins did not apprehend her intention in the question—

'You mean what you say?'

'Of course I do,' said Charles. 'I'm not sure of the law, and some of the big-wigs are very cantankerous about declaring an affair of this sort null; but I imagine there is a fair chance of his getting quit for some annual allowance to her; and I'll do my best, even if I had to go to London about it. A man is never ruined till he is married.'

'Thank you,' returned Lucilla, her lips trembling

with bitter irony. 'Now I know what you all are made of. We are obliged for your offered exertion, but we are not inclined to become traitors.'

'Cilly! I thought you had more sense! You are no child!'

'I am a woman—I feel for womanhood. I am a sister—I feel for my brother's honour.'

Charles burst into a laugh. Eloïsa remonstrated—'My dear, consider the disgrace to the whole family—a village schoolmistress!'

'Our ideas differ as to disgrace,' said Lucilla. 'Let me go, Ratia; I must pack for the diligence.'

The brother and sister threw themselves between her and the door. 'Are you insane, Cilly? What do you mean should become of you? Are you going to join the *ménage*, and teach the A B C?'

'I am going to own my sister while yet there is time,' said Lucilla. 'While you are meditating how to make her a deserted outcast, death is more merciful. Pining under the miseries of an unowned marriage, she is fast dying of pressure on the brain. I am going in the hope of hearing her call me sister. I am going to take charge of her child, and stand by my brother.'

'Dying, poor thing! Why did you not tell us before?' said Horatia, sobered.

'I did not know it was to save Charles so much *kind trouble*,' said Lucilla. 'Let me go, Rashe; you cannot detain me.'

'I do believe she is delighted,' said Horatia, releasing her.

In truth, she was inspirited by perceiving any door of escape. Any vivid sensation was welcome in the irksome vacancy that pursued her in the absence of immediate excitement. Devoid of the interest of opposition, and of the bracing changes to the Holt, her intercourse with the Charterises had become a weariness and vexation of spirit. Idle foreign life deteriorated them, and her principle and delicacy suffered frequent offences; but like all living wilfully in temptation, she seemed under a spell, only to be broken by an act of self-humiliation to which she would not bend. Longing for the wholesome atmosphere of Hiltonbury, she could not brook to purchase her entrance there by permitting herself to be pardoned. There was one who she fully intended should come and entreat her return, and the terms of her capitulation had many a time been arranged with herself; but when he came not, though her heart ached after him, pride still forbade one homeward step, lest it should seem to be in quest of him, or in compliance with his wishes.

Here, then, was a summons to England—nay, into his very parish—without compromising her pride or forcing her to show deference to rejected counsel. Nay, in contrast with her cousins, she felt her sentiments so lofty and generous that she was filled with the gladness of conscious goodness, so like the days of her early childhood, that a happy dew suffused her eyes, and she seemed to hear the voice of old Thames. Her loathing for the views of her cousins had borne down all resentment at her brother's folly and Edna's presumption; and relieved that it was not worse, and full of pity for the girl she had really loved, Honor's grieved displeasure and Charles's kind project together made her the ardent partisan of the young wife. Because Honor intimated that the girl had been artful, and had forced herself on Owen, Lucilla was resolved that her favourite had been the most perfect of heroines; and that circumstance alone should bear such blame as could not be thrown on Honor herself and the Wrapworth gossipry. Poor circumstance!

The journey gave her no concern. The way was direct to Ostend, and Spitzwasserfitzung contained a '*pension*' which was a great resort of incipient English governesses, so that there were no difficulties such as to give her enterprising spirit the least concern. She refused the escort that Rashe would have pressed upon her, and made her farewells with quiet resolution. No further remonstrance was offered; and though each party knew that what had passed would be a barrier for ever, good breeding preferred an indifferent parting. There were light, cheery words, but under the full consciousness that the friendship begun in perverseness had ended in contempt.

Horatia turned aside with a good-natured 'Poor child! she will soon wish herself back.' Lucilla, taking her last glance, sighed as she thought, 'My father did not like them. But for Honor, I would never have taken up with them.'

Without misadventure, Lucilla arrived at London Bridge, and took a cab for Woolstone Lane, where she must seek more exact intelligence of the locality of those she sought. So long had her eye been weary of novelty, while her mind was ill at ease, that even Holborn in the August sun was refreshingly homelike; and begrimed Queen Anne, 'sitting in the sun' before St. Paul's, wore a benignant aspect to glances full of hope and self-approval. An effort was necessary to recal how melancholy was the occasion of her journey, and all mournful anticipation was lost in the spirit of partisanship and patronage—yes, and in that pervading consciousness that each moment brought her nearer to Whittingtonia.

Great was the amaze of good Mrs. Jones, the housekeeper, at the arrival of Miss Lucy, and equal disappointment that she would neither eat nor rest, nor accept a convoy to No. 8, Little Whittington Street. She tripped off thither the instant she had ascertained the number of the house, and heard that her brother was there, and his wife still living.

She had formed to herself no image of the scenes before her, and was entirely unprepared by reflection when she rang at the door. As soon as she mentioned her name, the little maid conducted her downstairs, and she found herself in the sitting-room, face to face with Robert Fulmort.

Without showing surprise or emotion, or relaxing

his grave, listening air, he merely bowed his head, and held out his hand. There was an atmosphere of awe about the room, as though she had interrupted a religious office; and she stood still in the solemn hush, her lips parted, her bosom heaving. The opposite door was ajar, and from within came a kind of sobbing moan, and a low, feeble, faltering voice faintly singing—

> 'For men must work, and women must weep,
> And the sooner 'tis over, the sooner to sleep.'

The choking thrill of unwonted tears rushed over Lucilla, and she shuddered. Robert looked disappointed as he caught the notes; then placing a seat for Lucilla said, very low, 'We hoped she would waken sensible. Her mother begged me to be at hand.'

'Has she never been sensible?'

'They hoped so, at one time, last night. She seemed to know him.'

'Is he there?'

Robert only sighed assent, for again the voice was heard—'I must get up. Miss Sandbrook wants me. She says I sha'n't be afraid when the time comes; but oh!—so many, many faces—all their eyes looking; and where is he?—why doesn't he look? Oh! Miss Sandbrook, don't bring that young lady here—I know—I know it is why he never comes—keep her away——'

The voice turned to shrieking sobs. There were sounds of feet and hurried movements, and Owen came out, gasping for breath, and his face flushed. 'I can't bear it,' he said, with his hands over his face.

'Can I be of use?' asked Robert.

'No; the nurse can hold her;' and he leant his arms on the mantelpiece, his frame shaken with long-drawn sobs. He had never even seen his sister, and she was too much appalled to speak or move.

When the sounds ceased, Owen looked up to listen, and Robert said, 'Still no consciousness?'

'No, better not. What would she gain by it?'

'It must be better not, if so ordained,' said Robert.

'Pshaw! what are last feelings and words? As if a blighted life and such suffering were not sure of compensation. There's more justice in Heaven than in your system!'

He was gone; and Robert with a deep sigh said, 'I am not judging. I trust there were tokens of repentance and forgiveness; but it is painful, as her mother feels it, to hear how her mind runs on light songs and poetry.'

'Mechanically!'

'True; and delirium is no criterion of the state of mind. But it is very mournful. In her occupation, one would have thought habit alone would have made her ear catch other chimes.'

Lucilla remembered with a pang that she had sympathized with Edna's weariness of the monotony of hymn and catechism. Thinking poetry rather dull and tiresome, she had little guessed at the effect of sentimental songs and volumes of L. E. L., and the like, on an inflammable mind, when once taught to slake her thirsty imagination beyond the S. P. C. K. She did not marvel at the set look of pain with which Robert heard passionate verses of Shelley and Byron fall from those dying lips. They must have been conned by heart, and have been the favourite study, or they could hardly thus recur.

'I must go,' said Robert, after a time; 'I am doing no good here. You will take care of your brother, if it is over before I return. Where are you?'

'My things are in Woolstone Lane.'

'I meant to get him there. I will come back by seven o'clock; but I must go to the school.'

'May I go in there?'

'You had better not. It is a fearful sight, and you cannot be of use. I wish you could be out of hearing; but the house is full.'

'One moment, Robert—the child?'

'Sent to a nurse, when every sound was agony.'

He stepped into the sick room, and brought out Mrs. Murrell, who began with a curtsey, but eagerly pressed

Lucilla's offered hand. Subdued by sorrow and watching, she was touchingly meek and resigned, enduring with the patience of real faith, and only speaking to entreat that Mr. Fulmort would pray with her for her poor child. Never had Lucilla so prayed; and ere she had suppressed her tears, ere rising from her knees, Robert was gone.

She spent the ensuing hours of that summer evening, seated in the arm-chair, barely moving, listening to the ticking of the clock, and the thunder of the streets, and at times hearkening to the sounds in the inner chamber, the wanderings feebler and more rare, but the fearful convulsions more frequent, seeming, as it were, to be tearing away the last remnant of life. These moments of horror-struck suspense were the only breaks, save when Owen rushed out unable to bear the sight, and stood, with hidden face, in such absorption of distress as to be unconscious of her awe-struck attempts to obtain his attention, or when Mrs. Murrell came to fetch something, order her maid, or relieve herself by a few sad words to her guest. Gratified by the eager sisterly acknowledgment of poor Edna, she touched Lucilla deeply by speaking of her daughter's fondness for Miss Sandbrook, grief at having given cause for being thought ungrateful, and assurances that the secret never could have been kept had they met the day after the *soirée*. Many had been the poor thing's speculations how Miss Sandbrook would receive her marriage, but always with confidence in her final mercy and justice; and when Lucilla heard of the prolonged wretchedness, the hope deferred, the evil reports and suspicions of neighbours and lodgers, the failing health, and cruel disappointment, and looked round at the dismal little stifling dungeon where this fair and gifted being had pined and sunk beneath slander and desertion, hot tears of indignation filled her eyes, and with fingers clenching together, she said, 'Oh that I had known it sooner! Edna was right. I will be the person to see justice done to her!'

And when left alone she cast about for the most open mode of proclaiming Edna Murrell her brother's honoured wife and her own beloved sister. The more it mortified the Charterises the better!

By the time Robert came back, the sole change was in the failing strength, and he insisted on conducting Lucilla to Woolstone Lane, Mrs. Murrell enforcing his advice so decidedly that there was no choice. She would not be denied one look at the sufferer, but what she saw was so miserably unlike the beautiful creature whom she remembered, that she recoiled, feeling the kindness that had forbidden her the spectacle, and passively left the house, still under the chill influence of the shock. She had tasted nothing since breakfasting on board the steamer, and on coming into the street the comparative coolness seemed to strike her through; she shivered, felt her knees give way, and grasped Robert's arm for support. He treated her with watchful, considerate solicitude, though with few words, and did not leave her till he had seen her safe under the charge of the housekeeper; when, in return for his assurance that he would watch over her brother, she promised to take food and go at once to rest.

Too weary at first to undress, and still thinking that Owen might be brought to her, she lay back on the couch in her own familiar little cedar room, feeling as if she recalled the day through the hazy medium of a dream, and as if she had not been in contact with Edna, nor Owen, nor Robert, but only with pale phantoms called by those names.

Robert especially! Engrossed and awe-stricken as she had been, still it came on her that something was gone that to her had constituted Robert Fulmort. Neither the change of dress, nor even the older and more settled expression of countenance, made the difference; but the want of that nameless, hesitating deference which in each word or action formerly seemed to implore her favour, or even when he dared to censure, did so under appeal to her mercy. Had he avoided her, she could have understood it; but his calm, authoritative self-possession was beyond her, though as yet she was not alarmed, for her mind was too much confused to perceive that her influence was lost; but it was uncomfortable, and part of this strange, unnatural world, as though the wax which she had been used to mould had suddenly lost its yielding nature and become marble.

Tired out, she at last went to bed, and slept soundly, but awoke early, and on coming down, found from the housekeeper that her brother had been brought home at two o'clock by Mr. Fulmort, and had gone to his room at once. All was over. Lucilla, longing to hear more, set out to see Mrs. Murrell, before he should come downstairs.

While the good woman was forced to bestir herself for her lodgers' breakfasts, Lucilla could steal a solitary moment to gaze on the pallid face to which death had restored much of its beauty. She pressed her lips on the regal brow, and spoke half aloud, 'Edna, Edna Sandbrook, sister Edna, you should have trusted me. You knew I would see justice done to you, and I will. You shall lie by my mother's side in our own churchyard, and Wrapworth shall know that she, whom they envied and maligned, was Owen Sandbrook's wife and my cherished sister.'

Poor Mrs. Murrell, with her swimming eyes and stock phrases, brought far more Christian sentiments to the bed of death. 'Poor, dear love, her father and I little thought it would end in this, when we used to be so proud of her. We should have minded that pride is not made for sinners. 'Favour is deceitful and beauty is vain;' and the Lord saw it well that we should be cast down and slanderous lips opened against us, that so we might feel our trust is in Him alone! Oh, it is good that even thus she was brought to turn to Him! But I thank—oh, I thank Him, that her father never lived to see this day!'

She wept such tears of true thankfulness and resignation, that Lucilla, almost abashed by the sight of piety beyond her comprehension, stood silent, till, with a change to the practical, Mrs. Murrell recovered herself, saying, 'If you please, ma'am, when had I best come and speak to the young gentleman? I ought to know what would be pleasing to him about the funeral.'

'We will arrange,' said Lucilla; 'she shall be buried with my mother and sister in Wrapworth churchyard.'

Though gratified, Mrs. Murrell demurred, lest it might be taken ill by the 'family' and by that godly minister whose kindness and sympathy at the time of Edna's evasion had made a deep impression: but Lucilla boldly undertook that the family *must* like it, and she would take care of the minister. Nor was the good woman insensible to the posthumous triumph over calumny, although still with a certain hankering after Kensal Green as a sweet place, with pious monuments, where she should herself be laid, and the Company that did things so reasonable and so handsome.

Lucilla hurried back to fulfil the mission of Nemesis to the Charterises, which she called justice to Edna, and by the nine o'clock post despatched three notes. One containing the notice for the *Times*—'On the 17th instant, at 8, Little Whittington-street, St. Wulstan's, Edna, the beloved wife of Owen Charteris Sandbrook, Esq.;' another was to order a complete array of mourning from her dressmaker; and the third was to the Reverend Peter Prendergast, in the most simple manner requesting him to arrange for the burial of her sister-in-law, at 5 P.M. on the ensuing Saturday, indicating the labourers who should act as bearers, and ending with, 'You will be relieved by hearing that she was no other than our dear Edna, married on the 14th of July, last year.'

She then beguiled the time with designs for gravestones, until she became uneasy at Owen's non-appearance, and longed to go and see after him; but she fancied he might have spent nights of watching, and thought sleep would be the best means of getting through the interval which appalled her mind, unused to contact with grief. Still his delay began to wear her spirits and expectation, so long wrought up to the meeting; and she was at least equally restless for the appearance of Robert, wanting to hear more from him, and above all certain that all her dreary cravings and vacancy would be appeased by one dialogue with him, on whatever topic it might be. She wished that she had obeyed that morning bell at St. Wulstan's. It would have disposed of half an hour, and she would have met him. 'For shame,' quoth the haughty spirit, 'now that has come into my head, I can't go at all.'

Her solitude continued till half-past ten, when she heard the welcome sound of Robert's voice, and flew to meet him, but was again checked by his irresponsive manner as he asked for Owen.

'I have not seen him. I do not know whether to knock, lest he should be asleep.'

'I hope he is. He has not been in bed for three nights. I will go and see.'

He was moving to the door, without lingering for a word more. She stopped him by saying, 'Pray hear first what I have settled with Mrs. Murrell.'

'She told me,' said Robert. 'Is it Owen's wish?'

'It ought to be. It must. Every public justice must be paid now.'

'Is it quite well judged, unless it were his strong desire? Have you considered the feelings of Mr. Prendergast or your relations?'

'There is nothing I consider more. If Charles thinks it more disgraceful to marry a Christian for love than a Jewess for money, he shall see that we are not of the same opinion.'

'I never pretend to judge of your motives.'

'Mercy, what have I gone and said?' ejaculated Lucilla, as the door closed after him. 'Why did I let it out, and make him think me a vixen? Better than a hypocrite, though! I always professed to show my worst. What's come to me, that I can't go on so contentedly? He must hear the Charteris' sentiments, though, that he may not think mine a gratuitous affront.'

Her explanation was at her tongue's end, but Robert only reappeared with her brother, whom he had found dressing. Owen just greeted his sister, but asked no questions, only dropping heavily into a chair, and let her bring him his breakfast. So young was he, still wanting six weeks to years of discretion; so youthful his appearance in spite of his size and strength, that it was almost absurd to regard him as a widower, and expect him to act as a man of mature age and feeling. There was much of the boy in his excessive and freely-indulged lassitude, and his half-sullen, half-shy reserve towards his sister. Knowing he had been in conversation with Robert, she felt it hard that before her he only leant his elbows on the table, yawned, and talked of his stiffness, until his friend, rising to leave them, he exerted himself to say, 'Don't go, Fulmort.'

'I am afraid I must. I leave you to your sister. (She noted that it was not 'Lucy.')

'But, I say, Fulmort, there are things to settle—funeral, and all that,' he said in a helpless voice, like a sulky schoolboy.

'Your sister has been arranging with Mrs. Murrell.'

'Yes, Owen,' said Lucilla, tears glistening in her eyes, and her voice thrilling with emotion; 'it is right and just that she should be with our mother and little Mary at home; so I have written to Mr. Prendergast.'

'Very well,' he languidly answered. 'Settle it as you will; only deliver me from the old woman!'

He was in no state for reproaches; but Lucilla was obliged to bite her lip to restrain a torrent of angry weeping.

At his urgent instance, Robert engaged to return to dinner, and went, leaving Lucilla with nothing to do but to watch those heavy slumberings on the sofa and proffer attentions that were received with the surliness of one too miserable to know what to do with himself. She yearned over him with a new awakening of tenderness, longing, yet unable, to console or soothe. The light surface-intercourse of the brother and sister, each selfishly refraining from stirring the depths of the other's mind, rendered them mere strangers in the time of trouble; and vainly did Lucy gaze wistfully at the swollen eyelids and flushed cheeks, watch every peevish gesture, and tend each sullen wish, with pitying sweetness ; she could not reach the inner man, nor touch the aching wound.

Towards evening, Mrs. Murrell's name was brought in, provoking a fretful injunction from Owen not to let him be molested with her cant. Lucilla sighed compliance, though vexed at his egotism, and went to the study, where she found that Mrs. Murrell had brought her grandson, her own most precious comforter, whom she feared she must resign 'to be bred up as a gentleman as he was, and despise his poor old granny; and she would say not a word, only if his papa would let her keep him till he had cut his first teeth, for he had always been tender, and she could not be easy to think that any one else had the charge of him.' She devoured him with kisses as she spoke, taking every precaution to keep her profuse tears from falling on him; and Lucilla, much moved, answered, 'Oh ! for the present, no one could wish to part him from you. Poor little fellow ! May I take him for a little while to my brother ? It may do him good.'

Cilly had rather have ridden a kicking horse than handled an infant. She did not think this a prepossessing specimen, but it was passive. She had always understood from books that this was the sure means of 'opening the sealed fountains of grief.' She remembered what little Mary had been to her father, and in hopes that parental instinct would make Owen know better what to do with her burden than she did, she entered the drawing-room, where a little murmuring sound caused Owen to start up on his elbow, exclaiming, 'What are you at ? Don't bring *that* here !'

'I thought you might wish to see him ?'

'What should I do with him?' asked Owen, in the same glum, childish tone, turning his face inwards as he lay down. 'Take it away. Aint I wretched enough already to please you?'

She gave up the point, much grieved and strongly drawn to the little helpless one, rejected by his father, misused and cast off like his mother. Would no one stand up for him? Yes, it must be her part. She was his champion! She would set him forth in the world, by her own toil if need were!

Sealing the promise with a kiss, she returned him to his grandmother, and talked of him as so entirely her personal concern, that the good woman went home to report to her inquiring friends that the young lady was ready to 'hact very feeling, and very 'andsome.' Probably desirous to avoid further reference to his unwelcome son and heir, Owen had betaken himself to the solace of his pipe, and was pacing the garden with steps now sauntering with depression, now impetuous with impatience, always moving too much like a caged wild beast to invite approach. She was disconsolately watching him from the window, when Mr. Fulmort was admitted. A year ago, what would he not have given for that unfeigned, simple welcome, as she looked up with eyes full of tears, saying, 'Oh, Robert, it is so grievous to see him!'

'Very sad,' was the mournful answer.

'You may be able to help him. He asks for you, but turns from me.'

'He has been obliged to rely on me, since we came to town,' said Robert.

'You must have been very kind!' she warmly exclaimed.

But he drew back from the effusion, saying, 'I did no more than was absolutely necessary. He does not lay himself open to true comfort.'

'Deaths never seemed half so miserable before,' cried Lucilla. 'Yet this poor thing had little to live for! Was it all poor Honor's tender softening that took off the edge to our imaginations?'

'It is not always so mournful!' shortly said Robert.

'No; even the mother bears it better, and not for want of heart.'

'She *is* a Christian,' said Robert.

'Poor Owen! It makes me remorseful. I wonder if I made too light of the line he took; yet what difference could I have made? Sisters go for so little; and as to influence, Honor overdid it.' Then, as he made no reply, 'Tell me, do you think my acquiescence did harm?'

'I cannot say. Your conscience must decide. It is not a case for me. I must go to him.'

It was deep mortification. Used to have the least hint of dawning seriousness thankfully cherished and fostered, it was a rude shock, when most in need of *épanchement du cœur* after her dreary day, to be thrown back on that incomprehensible process of self-examination; and by Robert, too!

She absolutely did not feel as if she were the same Lucilla. It was the sensation of doubt on her personal identity awakened in the good woman of the ballad when her little dog began to bark and wail at her.

She strove to enliven the dinner by talking of Hiltonbury, and of Juliana's marriage, thus awakening Owen into life and talkativeness so much in his light ordinary humour, as to startle them both. Lucilla would have encouraged it as preferable to his gloom, but it was decidedly repressed by Robert.

She had to repair to solitary restlessness in the drawing-room, and was left alone there till so late that Robert departed after a single cup of tea, cutting short a captious argument of Owen's about impossibility of proof, and truth being only true in a sense.

Owen's temper was, however, less morose; and when his sister was lighting his candle for him at night, kindly said, 'What a bore I've been all day, Lucy.'

'I am glad to be with you, dear Owen; I have no one else.'

'Eh? What's become of Rashe?'
'Never mention her again!'
'What? They've cut you?'
'I have cut them.'
She related what had passed.
Owen set his face into a frown. 'Even so, Charlie; doltishness less pardonable than villainy! You were right to cut the connexion, Lucy; it has been our curse. So now you will go back to poor Honor, and try to make it up to her.'
'I'm not going near Honor till she forgives you, and receives your child.'
'Then you will be very ridiculous,' said Owen, impatiently. 'She has no such rancour against me as you have against her, poor dear; but it is not in the nature of things that she should pass over this unlucky performance.'
'If it had been such a performance as Charles desired, I should have said so.'
'Pshaw! I hadn't the chance; and gloss it as you will, Lucy, there's no disguising it, she *would* have it, and I could not help it, but she was neglected, and it killed her!' He brought his hand down on the table with a heavy thump, which together with the words made his sister recoil. 'Could Honor treat me the same after that? And she not my mother, either! Why had not my father the sense to have married her? Then I could go to her and get rid of this intolerable weight!' and he groaned aloud.
'A mother could hardly love you more,' said Lucy, to her own surprise. 'If you will but go to her, when she sees you so unhappy.'
'Out of the question,' broke in Owen; 'I can't stay here! I would have gone this very night, but I can't be off till that poor thing—'
'Off!'
'Ay, to the diggings, somewhere, anywhere, to get away from it all!'
'Oh, Owen, do nothing mad!'

'I'm not going to do anything just now, I tell you. Don't be in a fright. I shan't take French leave of you. You'll find me to-morrow morning, worse luck. Good night.'

Lucilla was doubly glad to have come. Her pride approved his proposal, though her sisterly love would suffer, and she was anxious about the child; but the dawning confidence was at least a relief.

Next morning, he was better, and talked much too like his ordinary self, but relapsed afterwards for want of employment; and when a letter was brought to him, left by his wife to be read after her death, he broke down, and fell into a paroxysm of grief and despair, which still prevailed when a message came in to ask admission for Mr. Prendergast. Relieved to be out of sight of depression that her consolations only aggravated, and hoping for sympathy and counsel, Lucy hastened to the study with out-stretched hands, and was met with the warmth for which she had longed.

Still there was disappointment. In participation with Owen's grief, she had lost sight of his offences, and was not prepared for the commencement. 'Well, Cilla, I came up to talk to you. A terrible business this of Master Owen's.'

'It breaks one's heart to see him so wretched.'
'I hope he is. He ought to be.'
'Now, Mr. Prendergast.'

The curate held up both hands, deprecating her coaxing piteous look, and used his voice rather loudly to overpower hers, and say what he had prepared as a duty.

'Yes, yes, he is your brother, and all that. You may feel for him what you like. But I must say this: it was a shameful thing, and a betrayal of confidence, such as it grieves me to think of in his father's son. I am sorry for her, poor thing! whom I should have looked after better; and I am very sorry indeed for you, Cilla; but I must tell you that to bury the poor girl next to Mrs. Sandbrook, as your brother's wife, would be a scandal.'

'Don't speak so loud; he will hear.'

His mild face was unwontedly impatient as he said, 'I can see how you gave in to the wish; I don't blame you, but if you consider the example to the parish.'

'After what I told you in my letter, I don't see the evil of the example; unless it be your *esprit de corps* about the registrar, and they could not well have requested you to officiate.'

'Cilla, you were always saucy, but this is no time for nonsense. You can't defend them.'

'Perhaps you are of your Squire's opinion—that the bad example was in the marrying her at all.'

Mr. Prendergast looked so much shocked that Lucilla felt a blush rising, conscious that the tone of the society she had of late lived with had rendered her tongue less guarded, her cheek less shamefaced than erst, but she galloped on to hide her confusion. 'You were their great cause. If you had not gone and frightened her, they might have philandered on all this time, till the whole affair died of its own silliness.'

'Yes, no one was so much to blame as I. I will trust no living creature again. My carelessness opened the way to temptation, and Heaven knows, Lucilla, I have been infinitely more displeased with myself than with them.'

'Well, so am I with myself, for putting her in his way. Don't let us torment ourselves with playing the game backwards again—I hate it. Let's see to the next.'

'That is what I came for. Now, Cilla, though I would gladly do what I could for poor Owen, just think what work it will make with the girls at Wrapworth, who are nonsensical enough already, to have this poor runaway brought back to be buried as the wife of a fine young gentleman.'

'Poor Edna's history is no encouragement to look out for fine young gentlemen.'

'They will know the fact, and sink the circumstances.'

'So you are so innocent as to think they don't know! Depend upon it, every house in Wrapworth rings with it; and wont it be more improving to have the poor thing's grave to point the moral?'

'Cilla, you are a little witch. You always have your way, but I don't like it. It is not the right one.'

'Not right for Owen to make full compensation? Mind, it is not Edna Murrell, the eloped schoolmistress, but Mrs. Sandbrook, whom her husband wishes to bury among his family.'

'Poor lad, is he much cut up?'

'So much that I should hardly dare tell him if you had refused. He could not bear another indignity heaped on her, and a wound from you would cut deeper than from any one else. You should remember in judging him that he had no parent to disobey, and there was generosity in taking on him the risk rather than leave her to a broken heart and your tender mercy.'

'I fear his tender mercy has turned out worse than mine; but I am sorry for all he has brought on himself, poor lad!'

'Shall I try whether he can see you?'

'No, no; I had rather not. You say young Fulmort attends to him, and I could not speak to him with patience. Five o'clock, Saturday?'

'Yes; but that is not all. That poor child—Robert Fulmort, you, and I must be sponsors.'

'Cilla, Cilla, how can I answer how it will be brought up?'

'Some one must. Its father talks of leaving England, and it will be my charge. Will you not help me? you who always have helped me. My father's grandson;—you cannot refuse him, Mr. Pendy,' said she, using their old childish name for him.

He yielded to the united influence of his rector's daughter and the memory of his rector. Though no weak man, those two appeals always swayed him; and Lucilla's air, spirited when she defended, soft when she grieved, was quite irresistible; so she gained her point, and felt restored to herself by the exercise of power, and by making her wonted impression. Since one little dog had wagged his little tail, she no longer doubted 'If I be I;' yet this only rendered her more nervously desirous of obtaining the like recognition from the other, and she positively wearied after one of Robert's old wistful looks.

A *tête-à-tête* with him was necessary on many accounts, and she lay in wait to obtain a few moments alone with him in the study. He complied neither eagerly nor reluctantly, bowed his head without remark when she told him about the funeral, and took the sponsorship as a matter of course. 'Very well; I suppose there is no one else to be found. Is it your brother's thought?'

'I told him.'

'So I feared.'

'Oh! Robert, we must take double care for the poor little thing.'

'I will do my best,' he answered.

'Do you know what Owen intends?' said Lucilla, in low, alarmed accents.

'He has told you? It is a wild purpose; but I doubt whether to dissuade him, except for your sake,' he added, with his first softening towards her, like balm to the sore spot in her heart.

'Never mind me, I can take care of myself,' she said, while the muscles of her throat ached and quivered with emotion. 'I would not detain him to be pitied, and forgiven.'

'Do not send him away in pride;' said Robert, sadly.

'Am not I humbled enough?' she said; and her drooping head and eye seemed to thrill him with their wonted power.

One step he made towards her, but checked himself, and said in a matter-of-fact tone, 'Currie, the architect, has a brother, a civil engineer, just going out to Canada to lay out a railway. It might be an opening for Owen to go as his assistant—unless you thought it beneath him.'

These last words were caused by her uncontrollable look of disappointment. But it was not the proposal: no; but the change of manner that struck her. The quiet indifferent voice was like water quenching a struggling spark, but in a moment she recovered her powers. 'Beneath him! Oh, no. I told you we were humbled. I always longed for his independence, and I am glad that he should not go alone.'

'The work would suit his mathematical and scientific turn. Then, since you do not object, I will see whether he would like it, or if it be practicable, in case Miss Charlecote should approve.'

Robert seized this opportunity of concluding the interview. Lucy ran upstairs for the fierce quarter-deck walking that served her instead of tears, as an ebullition that tired down her feelings by exhaustion.

Some of her misery was for Owen, but would the sting have been so acute had Robert Fulmort been more than the true friend?

Phœbe's warning, given in that very room, seemed engraven on each panel. 'If you go on as you are doing now, he does not think it would be right for a clergyman.'

Could Lucilla have looked through the floor, she would have seen Robert with elbows on the window-sill, and hands locked over his knitted brows; and could she have interpreted his short-drawn sighs, she would have heard, 'Poor child! poor child! It is not coquetry. That was injustice. She loves me. She loves me still! Why do I believe it only too late? Why is this trial sent me, since I am bound to the scheme that precludes my marriage? What use is it to see her as undisciplined—as unfit as ever? I know it! I always knew it. But I feel still a traitor to her! She had warning! She trusted the power of my attachment in spite of my judgment! Fickle to her, or a falterer to my higher pledge? Never! I must let her see the position—crush any hope—otherwise I cannot trust myself, nor deal fairly by her. Heaven help us both!'

When they next met, Robert had propounded his Canadian project, and Owen had caught at it. Idleness had never been his fault, and he wanted severe engrossing labour to stun pain and expel thought. He was urgent to know what standard of attainments would be needful, and finding Robert ignorant on this head, seized his hat, and dashed out in the gaslight to the nearest bookseller's for a treatise on surveying.

Robert was taken by surprise, or he might have gone too. He looked as if he meditated a move, but paused as Lucy said, 'Poor fellow, how glad he is of an object!'

'May it not be to his better feelings like sunshine to morning dew?' said Robert, sighing. 'I hear a very high character of Mr. Currie, and a right-minded, practical, scientific man may tell more on a disposition like his——'

'Than parsons and women,' said Lucilla, with a gleam of her old archness.

'Exactly so. He must see religion in the world, not out of it.'

'After all, I have not heard who is this Mr. Currie, and how you know him.'

'I know him through his brother, who is building the church in Cecily Row.'

'A church in Cecily Row! St. Cecilia's? Who is doing it? Honor Charlecote?'

'No; I am.'

'You! Tell me all about it,' said Lucilla, leaning forward to listen with the eager air of interest which, when not half so earnest, had been always bewitching.

Poor Robert looked away, and tried to think himself explaining his scheme to the Archdeacon. 'The place is in frightful disorder, filled with indescribable vice and misery, but there is a shadow of hope that a few may be worked on if something like a mission can be organized. Circumstances seemed to mark me out as the person to be at the cost of setting it on foot, my father's connexion with the parish giving it a claim on me. So I purchased the first site that was in the market, and the buildings are in progress, chapel, schools, orphanage, and rooms for myself and two other clergy. When all the rest is provided for, there will remain about two hundred and fifty pounds a year—just enough for three of us, living together.'

He durst not glance towards her, or he would have seen her cheek white as wax, and her eye seeking his in dismayed inquiry. There was a pause; then she forced herself to falter—'Yes. I suppose it is very right—very grand. It is settled?'

'The Archdeacon has seen the plans, the Bishop has consented.'

Long and deep was the silence that fell on both.

Lucilla knew her fate as well as if his long coat had been a cowl.

She would not, could not feel it yet. She must keep up appearances, so she fixed her eyes steadily on the drawing her idle hands were perpetrating on the back of a letter, and appeared absorbed in shading a Turk's head.

If Robert's motives had not been unmixed, if his zeal had been alloyed by temper, or his self-devotion by undutifulness; if his haste had been self-willed, or his judgment one-sided, this was an hour of retribution. Let her have all her faults, she was still the Lucy who had flown home to him for comfort. He felt as if he had dashed away the little bird that had sought refuge in his bosom.

Fain would he have implored her pardon, but for the stern resolution to abstain from any needless word or look, such as might serve to rivet the affection that ought to be withdrawn; and he was too manly and unselfish to indulge in discussion or regret, too late as it was to change the course to which he had offered himself and his means. To retract would have been a breach of promise—a hasty one, perhaps, but still an absolute vow publicly made; and in all his wretchedness he had at least the comfort of knowing the present duty.

Afraid of last words, he would not even take leave until Owen came in upon their silence, full of animation and eagerness to see how far his knowledge would serve him with the book that he had brought home. Robert then rose, and on Owen's pressing to know when he might see the engineer, promised to go in search of him the next day, but added that they must not expect to see himself till evening, since it would be a busy day.

Lucilla stood up, but speech was impossible. She was in no mood to affect indifference, yet she could neither be angry nor magnanimous. She seemed to have passed into a fresh stage of existence where she was not yet at home; and in the same dreamy way she went on drawing Red Indians, till by a sudden impulse she looked up and said, 'Owen, why should not I come out with you?'

He was intent on a problem, and did not hear.

'Owen, take me with you; I will make a home for you.'

'Eh?'

'Owen, let me come to Canada, and take care of you and your child.'

He burst out laughing. 'Well done, Cilly; that beats all!'

'Am I likely to be in play?'

'If not, you are crazy. As if a man could go surveying in the backwoods with a woman and a brat at his heels!'

Lucy's heart seemed to die within her. Nothing

was left to her: hopes and fears were alike extinct, and life a waste before her. Still and indifferent, she laid her down at night, and awoke in the morning, wishing still to prolong the oblivion of sleep. Anger with Robert would have been a solace, but his dejection forbade this; nor could she resent his high-flown notions of duty, and deem herself their victim, since she had slighted fair warning, and repelled his attempts to address her. She saw no resource save the Holt, now more hopelessly dreary and distasteful than ever, and she shrank both from writing to Honor, or ending her tantalizing intercourse with Robert. To watch over her brother was her only comfort, and one that must soon end.

He remained immersed in trigonometry, and she was glad he should be too much engrossed for the outbreaks of remorseful sorrow that were so terrible to witness, and carefully guarded him from all that could excite them.

Mrs. Murrell brought several letters that had been addressed to him at her house, and as Lucilla conveyed them to him, she thought their Oxford post-marks looked suspicious, especially as he thrust them aside with the back of his hand, returning without remark to A B and C D.

Presently a person asked to speak with Mr. Sandbrook; and supposing it was on business connected with the funeral, Lucilla went to him, and was surprised at recognising the valet of one of the gentlemen who had stayed at Castle Blanch. He was urgent to see Mr. Sandbrook himself; but she, resolved to avert all annoyances, refused to admit him, offering to take a message.

'Was it from his master?'

'Why, no, ma'am. In fact, I have left his lordship's service,' he said, hesitating. 'In point of fact, I am the principal. There was a little business to be settled with the young gentleman when he came into his fortune; and understanding that such was the case, since

I heard of him as settled in life, I have brought my account.'

'You mistake the person. My brother has come into no fortune, and has no expectation of any.'

'Indeed, ma'am!' exclaimed the man. 'I always understood that Mr. Owen Charteris Sandbrook was heir to a considerable property.'

'What of that?'

'Only this, ma'am,—that I hold a bond from that gentleman for the payment of 600*l.* upon the death of Miss Honora Charlecote, of the Holt, Hiltonbury, whose property I understood was entailed on him.' His tone was still respectful, but his hand shook with suppressed rage, and his eye was full of passion.

'Miss Charlecote is not dead,' steadily answered Lucilla. 'She is in perfect health, not fifty years old, and her property is entirely at her own disposal.'

Either the man's wrath was beyond control, or he thought it his interest to terrify the lady, for he broke into angry complaints of being swindled, with menaces of exposure; but Lucilla, never deficient in courage, preserved ready thought and firm demeanour.

'You had better take care,' she said. 'My brother is under age, and not liable. If you should recover what you have lent him, it can only be from our sense of honesty. Leave me your address and a copy of the bond, and I give you my word that you shall receive your due.'

The valet, grown rich in the service of a careless master, and richer by money-lending transactions with his master's friends, knew Miss Sandbrook, and was aware that a lady's word might be safer than a spendthrift's bond. He tried swaggering, in the hope of alarming her into a promise to fulfil his demand uninvestigated; but she was on her guard; and he, reflecting that she must probably apply to others for the means of paying, gave her the papers, and freed her from his presence.

Freed her from his presence! Yes, but only to leave her to the consciousness of the burthen of shame he had brought her. She saw why Owen thought himself past pardon. Speculation on the death of his benefactress! Borrowing on an inheritance that he had been forbidden to expect. Double-dyed deceit and baseness! Yesterday, she had said they were humbled enough. This was not humiliation, it was degradation! It was far too intolerable for standing still and feeling it. Lucilla's impetuous impulses always became her obstinate resolutions, and her pride rebounded to its height in the determination that Owen should leave England in debt to no man, were it at the cost of all she possessed.

Re-entering the drawing-room, she found that Owen had thrust the obnoxious letters into the waste-basket, each unopened envelope, with the contents, rent down the middle. She sat down on the floor, and took them out, saying, as she met his eye, 'I shall take these. I know what they are. They are my concern.'

'Folly!' he muttered. 'Don't you know I have the good luck to be a minor?'

'That is no excuse for dishonesty.'

'Look at home before you call names,' said Owen, growing enraged. 'Before you act spy on me, I should like to know who paid for your fine salmon-fly gown, and all the rest of it?'

'I never contracted debts in the trust that my age would enable me to defraud my creditors.'

'Who told you that I did? I tell you, Lucilla, I'll endure no such conduct from you. No sister has a right to say such things!' and starting up, his furious stamp shook the floor she sat upon, so close to her that it was as if the next would demolish her.

She did not move, except to look up all the length of the tall figure over her into the passion-flushed face. 'I should neither have said nor thought so, Owen,' she replied. 'I should have imputed these debts to mere heedless extravagance, like other people's—like my own, if you please—save for your own words, and for finding you capable of such treachery as borrowing on a *post-obit.*'

He walked about furiously, stammering interrogations on the mode of her discovery, and, as she explained, storming at her for having brought this down on him by the folly of putting 'that thing into the *Times.*' Why could she not have stayed away, instead of meddling where she was not wanted?

'I thought myself wanted when my brother was in trouble,' said Lucilla, mournfully, raising her face, which she had bent between her hands at the first swoop of the tempest. 'Heaven knows, I had no thought of spying. I came to stand by your wife, and comfort you. I only learnt all this in trying to shield you from intrusion. Oh, would that I knew it not! Would that I could think of you as I did an hour ago! Oh, Owen, though I have never shared your fondness for Honor Charlecote, I thought it genuine; I did not scorn it as fortune-hunting.'

'It was not! It never was!' cried the poor boy. 'Honor! Poor Honor! Lucy, I doubt if I could have felt for my mother as I do for her. O, if you could guess how I long for her dear voice in my ears, her soft hand on my head—' and he sank into his chair, hiding his face and sobbing aloud.

'Am I to believe that, when—' began Lucilla, slowly.

'The last resource of desperation,' cried Owen. 'What could I do with such a drain upon me; the old woman for ever clamouring for money, and threatening exposure? My allowance? Poor Honor meant well, but she gave me just enough to promote expensive habits without supplying them. There was nothing to fall back on—except the ways of the Castle Blanch folk.'

'Betting?'

He nodded. 'So when it went against me, and people would have it that I had expectations, it was not for me to contradict them. It was their business, not mine, to look out for themselves, and pretty handsomely they have done so. It would have been a very different percentage if I had been an eldest son. As it is, my bond is—what is it for, Lucy?'

'Six hundred.'

'How much do you think I have touched of that? Not two! Of that, three-fourths went to the harpies I fell in with at Paris, under Charles's auspices—and five-and-twenty there'—pointing in the direction of Whittington Street.

'Will the man be satisfied with the two hundred?'

'Don't he wish he may get it? But, Lucy, you are not to make a mess of it. I give you warning I shall go, and never be heard of more, if Honor is applied to.'

'I had rather die than do so.'

'You are not frantic enough to want to do it out of your own money? I say, give me those papers.'

He stooped and stretched out the powerful hand and arm, which when only half-grown had been giant-like in struggles with his tiny sister; but she only laid her two hands on the paper, with just sufficient resistance to make it a matter of strength on his side. They were man and woman, and what availed his muscles against her will? It came to parley. 'Now, Lucy, I have a right to think for you. As your brother, I cannot permit you to throw your substance to the dogs.'

'As your sister, I cannot allow you to rest dishonoured.'

'Not a whit more than any of your chosen friends. Every man leaves debts at Oxford. The extortion is framed on a scale to be unpaid.'

'Let it be! There shall be no stain on the name that once was my father's, if there be on the whole world beside.'

'Then,' with some sulkiness, 'you wont be content without beggaring me of my trumpery twenty-five hundred as soon as I am of age?'

'Not at all. Your child must live on that. Only one person can pay your debts without dishonouring you, and that is your elder sister.'

'Elder donkey,' was the ungrateful answer. 'Why, what would become of you? You'd have to be beholden to Honor for the clothes on your back!'

'I shall not go back to Honor; I shall earn my own livelihood.'

'Lucilla, are you distracted, or is it your object to make me so?'

'Only on one condition could I return to the Holt,' said Lucilla resolutely. 'If Honor would freely offer to receive your son, I would go to take care of him. Except for his sake, I had rather she would not. I will not go to be crushed with pardon and obligation, while you are proscribed. I will be independent, and help to support the boy.'

'Sure,' muttered Owen to himself, 'Lucifer is her patron saint. If I looked forward to anything, it was to her going home tame enough to make some amends to poor, dear Sweet Honey, but I might as well have hoped it of the panther of the wilderness! I declare I'll write to Honor this minute.'

He drew the paper before him. Lucilla started to her feet, looking more disgusted and discomfited than by any former shock. However, she managed to restrain any dissuasion, knowing that it was the only right and proper step in his power, and that she could never have looked Robert in the face again had she prevented the confession; but it was a bitter pill; above all, that it should be made for her sake. She rushed away, as usual, to fly up and down her room.

She might have spared herself that agony. Owen's resolution failed him. He could not bring himself to make the beginning, nor to couple the avowal of his offence with such presumption as an entreaty for his child's adoption, though he knew his sister's impulsive obstinacy well enough to be convinced that she would adhere pertinaciously to this condition. Faltering after the first line, he recurred to his former plan of postponing his letter till his plans should be so far matured that he could show that he would no longer be a pensioner on the bounty of his benefactress, and that he sought pardon for the sake of no material advantage. He knew that Robert had intimated his intention of writing after the funeral, and by this he would abide.

Late in the evening Robert brought the engineer's answer, that he had no objection to take out a pupil, and would provide board, lodging, and travelling expenses; but he required a considerable premium, and for three years would offer no salary. His standard of acquirements was high, but such as rather stimulated than discouraged Owen, who was delighted to find that an appointment had been made for a personal interview on the ensuing Monday.

It was evident that if these terms were accepted, the debts, if paid at all, must come out of Lucilla's fortune. Owen's own portion would barely clothe him and afford the merest pittance for his child until he should be able to earn something after his three years' apprenticeship. She trusted that he was convinced, and went upstairs some degrees less forlorn for having a decided plan; but a farther discovery awaited her, and one that concerned herself.

On her bed lay the mourning for which she had sent, tasteful and expensive, in her usual complete style, and near it an envelope. It flashed on her that her order had been dangerously unlimited, and she opened the cover in trepidation, but what was her dismay at the double, treble, quadruple foolscap? The present articles were but a fraction to the dreadful aggregate—the sum total numbered hundreds! In a dim hope of error she looked back at the items, 'Black lace dress: Dec. 2nd, 1852.'—She understood all. It dated from the death of her aunt. Previously, her wardrobe had been replenished as though she had been a daughter of the house, and nothing had marked the difference; indeed, the amply provided Horatia had probably intended that things were to go on as usual. Lucilla had been allowed to forget the existence of accounts, in a family which habitually ignored them. Things had gone smoothly; the beautiful little Miss Sandbrook was an advertisement to her milliners, and living among wealthy people, and reported to be on the verge of marriage with a millionaire, there had been no hesitation in allowing her unlimited credit.

Probably the dressmaker had been alarmed by the long absence of the family, and might have learnt from the servants how Lucilla had quitted them, therefore thinking it expedient to remind her of her liabilities. And not only did the present spectacle make her giddy, but she knew there was worse beyond. The Frenchwoman who supplied all extra adornments, among them the ball-dress whose far bitterer price she was paying, could make more appalling demands; and there must be other debts elsewhere, such that she doubted whether her entire fortune would clear both her brother and herself. What was the use of thinking? It must be done, and the sooner she knew the worst the better. She felt very ill-used, certain that her difficulties were caused by Horatia's inattention, and yet glad to be quit of an obligation that would have galled her as soon as she had become sensible of it. It was more than ever clear that she must work for herself, instead of returning to the Holt, as a dependant instead of a guest. Was she humbled enough?

The funeral day began by her writing notes to claim her bills, and to take steps to get her capital into her own hands. Owen drowned reflection in geometry, till it was time to go by the train to Wrapworth.

There Mr. Prendergast fancied he had secured secresy by eluding questions and giving orders at the latest possible moment. The concourse in the church and churchyard was no welcome sight to him, since he could not hope that the tall figure of the chief mourner could remain unrecognised. Worthy man, did he think that Wrapworth needed that sight to assure them of what each tongue had wagged about for many a day?

Owen behaved very properly and with much feeling. When not driving it out by other things, the fact was palpable to him that he had brought this fair young creature to her grave; and in the very scenes where her beauty and enthusiastic affection had captivated him, association revived his earlier admiration, and swept away his futile apology that she had brought the whole upon herself. A gust of pity, love, and remorse convulsed his frame, and though too proud to give way, his restrained anguish touched every heart, and almost earned him Mr. Prendergast's forgiveness.

Before going away, Lucilla privately begged Mr. Prendergast to come to town on Monday, to help her in some business. It happened to suit him particularly well, as he was to be in London for the greater part of the week, to meet some country cousins, and the appointment was made without her committing herself by saying for what she wanted him, lest reflection should convert him into an obstacle instead of an assistant.

The intervening Sunday, with Owen on her hands, was formidable to her imagination, but it turned out better than she expected. He asked her to walk to Westminster Abbey with him, the time and distance being an object to both, and he treated her with such gentle kindness, that she began to feel that something more sweet and precious than she had yet known from him might spring up, if they were not forced to separate. Once, on rising from kneeling, she saw him stealthily brushing off his tears, and his eyes were heavy and swollen, but, softened as she felt, his tone of feelings were a riddle beyond her power, between their keenness and their petulance, their manly depth and boyish levity, their remorse and their recklessness; and when he tried to throw them off, she could not but follow his lead.

'I suppose,' he said, late in the day, 'we shall mortify Fulmort if we don't go once to his shop. Otherwise, I like the article in style.'

'I am glad you should like it at all,' said Lucy, anxiously.

'I envy those who, like poor dear Honor, or that little Phœbe, can find life in the driest form,' said Owen.

'They would say it is our fault that we cannot find it.'

'Honor would think it her duty to say so. Phœbe has a wider range, and would be more logical. Is it our fault or misfortune that our ailments can't be cured by a paring of St. Bridget's thumb-nail, or by any nostrum, sacred or profane, that really cure their votaries? I regard it as a misfortune. Those are happiest who believe the most, and are eternally in a state in which their faith is working out its effects upon them mentally and physically. Happy people!'

'Really I think, unless you were one of those happy people, it is no more consistent in you to go to church than it would be in me to set up Rashe's globules.'

'No, don't tell me so, Lucy. There lie all my best associations. I venerate what the great, the good, the beloved receive as their blessing and inspiration. Sometimes I can assimilate myself, and catch an echo of what was happiness when I was a child at Honor's knee.'

The tears had welled into his eyes again, and he hurried away.

Lucilla had faith (or rather acquiescence) without feeling. Feeling without faith was a mystery to her. How much Owen believed or disbelieved she knew not, probably he could not himself have told. It was more uncertainty than denial, rather dislike to technical dogma than positive unbelief; and yet, with his predilections all on the side of faith, she could not, womanlike, understand why they did not bring his reason with them. After all, she decided, in her off-hand fashion, that there was quite enough that was distressing and perplexing without concerning herself about them!

Style, as Owen called it, was more attended to than formerly at St. Wulstan's, but was not in perfection. Robert, whose ear was not his strong point, did not shine in intoning, and the other curate preached. The impression seemed only to have weakened that of the morning, for Owen's remarks on coming out were on the English habit of having over much of everything, and on the superior sense of foreigners in holiday-making, instead of making a conscience of stultifying themselves with double and triple church-going.

Cilla agreed in part, but owned that she was glad to have done with Continental Sundays that had left her feeling good for nothing all the week, just as she had felt when once, as a child, to spite Honor, she had come down without saying her prayers.

'The burthen bound on her conscience by English prejudice,' said her brother, adding 'that this was the one oppressive edict of popular theology. It was mere self-defence to say that the dulness was Puritanical, since the best Anglican had a cut-and-dried pattern for all others.'

'But surely as a fact, Sunday observance is the great safeguard. All goes to the winds when that is given up.'

'The greater error to have rendered it grievous.'

Lucilla had no reply. She had not learnt the joy of the week's Easter-day. It had an habitual awe for her, not sacred delight; and she could not see that because it was one point where religion taught the world that it had laws of its own, besides those of mere expedience and morality, therefore the world complained, and would fain shake off the thraldom.

Owen relieved her by a voluntary proposal to turn down Whittington-street, and see the child. Perhaps he had an inkling that the chapel in Cat-alley would be in full play, and that the small maid would be in charge; besides it was gas-light, and the lodgers would be out. At any rate, softening was growing on him. He looked long and sorrowfully at the babe in its cradle, and at last said,—

'He will never be like her.'

'No; and I do not think him like you.'

'In fact, it is an ugly little mortal,' said Owen, after another investigation. 'Yet, it's very odd, Lucy, I should like him to live.'

'Very odd, indeed!' she said, nearly laughing.

'Well, I own, before ever I saw him, when they said he would die, I did think it was best for himself, and every one else. So, may be, it would; but you see I shouldn't like it. He will be a horrible expense, and it will be a great bore to know what to do with him; so absurd to have a son only twenty years younger than oneself; but I think I like him, after all. It is something to work for, to make up to him for what *she* suffered. And I say, Lucy,' his eye brightened, 'perhaps Honor will take to him! What a thing it would be if he turned out all she hoped of me, poor thing! I would be banished for life, if he could be in my place, and make it up to her. He might yet have the Holt!'

'You have not proposed sending him to her?'

'No, I am not so cool,' he sadly answered; 'but she is capable of anything in an impulse of forgiveness.'

He spent the evening over his letter; and, in spite of his sitting with his back towards his sister, she saw more than one sheet spoilt by large tears unperceived till they dropped, and felt a jealous pang in recognising the force of his affection for Honor. That love and compassion seemed contemptible to her, they were so inconsistent with his deception and disobedience; and she was impatient of seeing that, so far as he felt his errors at all, it was in their aspect towards his benefactress. His ingratitude towards her touched him in a more tender part than his far greater errors towards his wife. The last was so shocking and appalling, that he only half realized it, and, boy like, threw it from him; the other came home to the fondness that had been with him all his life, and which he missed every hour in his grief. Lucy positively dreaded his making such submission, or betraying such sorrow as might bring Honora down on them, full of pardon and beneficence. At least, she had the satisfaction of hearing 'I've said nothing about you, Cilla.'

'That's right!'

'Nor the child,' he continued, brushing up his hair from his brow. 'When I came to go over it, I did hate myself to such a degree that I could not say a word like asking a favour.'

Lucy was greatly relieved.

He looked like himself when he came down to breakfast, exhilarated by the restoration to activity, and the opening of a new path, though there was a subdued, grave look on his young brow not unsuited to his deep mourning.

He took up his last evening's production, looked at it with some satisfaction, and observed, 'Sweet old Honey! I do hope that letter may be a little comfort to her good old heart!'

Then he told that he had been dreaming of her looking into the cradle, and he could not tell whether it were himself or the boy that he had seen sitting on a haycock at Hiltonbury.

'Who knows but it may be a good omen,' said he, in his sanguine state. 'You said you would go to her, if she took the child.'

'I did not say I would not.'

'Well, don't make difficulties; pray don't, Lucilla. I want nothing for myself; but if I could see you and the child at the Holt, and hear her dear voice say one word of kindness, I could go out happy. Imagine if she should come to town!'

Lucilla had no mind to imagine any such thing.

END OF VOL. I.

NEW BOOKS AND NEW EDITIONS,

PUBLISHED BY

JOHN W. PARKER AND SON, WEST STRAND.

Faithful for Ever.
By COVENTRY PATMORE. 6s.

Wearing the Willow; or, Bride Fielding.
A Tale of Ireland and of Scotland Sixty Years Ago. By the Author of *The Nut-Brown Maids.* 9s.

Mademoiselle Mori.
A Tale of Modern Rome.
Second and Cheaper Edition. One Volume.

The Angel in the House.
By COVENTRY PATMORE. Third Edition, revised. 7s. 6d.

Chilcote Park; or, the Sisters.
By the Author of *Likes and Dislikes.* Foolscap octavo. 5s.

Likes and Dislikes; or, Passages in the Life of Emily Marsden. 6s.

Holmby House.
By G. J. WHYTE MELVILLE, Author of *Digby Grand.*
Second Edition. Two Volumes. 16s.

General Bounce.
By G. J. WHYTE MELVILLE. Second and Cheaper Edition. 5s.

The Two Mottoes.
By the Author of *Mademoiselle Mori.* 5s.

Aggesden Vicarage.
A Tale for the Young. Two Volumes. 9s.

The Nut-Brown Maids.
A Family Chronicle of the Days of Queen Elizabeth. 10s. 6d.

The Old Coalpit.
A Story for Boys. By E. J. MAY, Author of *Louis' School Days*. 4s. 6d.

Misrepresentation.
By ANNA HARRIETT DRURY. Two Volumes. 18s.

Friends and Fortune.
By Miss DRURY. Second Edition. 6s.

Dorothy.
Second Edition. 4s. 6d.

The Maiden Sisters.
By the Author of *Dorothy*. 5s.

Uncle Ralph.
By the same. 4s. 6d.

Still Waters.
By the same. Two Volumes. 9s.

De Cressy.
By the same. 4s. 6d.

The Recreations of A Country Parson;
Being a Selection from the Contributions of A. K. H. B. to *Fraser's Magazine*. Second Edition. 8vo. 9s.

The Saint's Tragedy.
By the Rev. CHARLES KINGSLEY. Third Edition. 5s.

Friends in Council.
Second Series. The Second Edition. 2 vols. 14s.
The First Series. New Edition. 2 vols. 9s.

Miscellanies.
By the Rev. CHARLES KINGSLEY. The Second Edition. 2 vols. 18s.

George Canning and his Times.
By A. GRANVILLE STAPLETON. 16s.

Shipwrecks of the Royal Navy.
By W. O. S. GILLY. The Third Edition. 5s.

Revolutions in English History.
By ROBERT VAUGHAN, D.D.
The First Volume, 'Revolutions of Race.' 8vo. 15s.

History of the Literature of Ancient Greece.
By Professor K. O. MÜLLER.
Translated by the Right Hon. Sir G. CORNEWALL LEWIS and J. W. DONALDSON, D.D., Classical Examiner in Lond. Univ.
3 vols. 8vo. 36s. The new portion separately, 2 vols. 20s.

Dissertations and Discussions, Political, Philosophical, and Historical.
By JOHN STUART MILL. 2 vols. 8vo. 24s.

Man and his Dwelling-Place.
An Essay towards the Interpretation of Nature. 9s.

Of the Plurality of Worlds.
An Essay. Fifth Edition. 6s.

Extracts from Jean Paul Richter.
Translated by Lady CHATTERTON. 3s. 6d.

The Crusaders.
Scenes, Events, and Characters from the Time of the Crusaders.
By THOMAS KEIGHTLEY. Fifth Edition, revised. 7s.

Major Hodson's Twelve Years of A Soldier's Life in India.
Edited by the Rev. GEORGE H. HODSON, M.A.
Third Edition, with Additions. 10s. 6d.

Spiritual Songs for the Sundays and Holydays throughout the Year.
By JOHN S. B. MONSELL, LL.D. Second Edition. 4s. 6d.

Night Lessons from Scripture.
Compiled by the Author of *Amy Herbert*. Roan, Red Edges. 3s.

Cecil and Mary; or, Phases of Life and Love:
A Missionary Poem. By JOSEPH EDWARD JACKSON. 4s.

Songs for the Suffering.
By T. DAVIS, M.A., Incumbent of Roundhay. s.

The Good News of God.
Sermons by the Rev. CHARLES KINGSLEY. Third Edition. 6s.

Sermons Preached in Westminster Abbey.
By RICHARD CHENEVIX TRENCH, D.D., Dean of Westminster.
Octavo. 10s. 6d.

Bacon's Essays.
With Annotations by Archbishop WHATELY.
Fifth Edition. Octavo. 10s. 6d.

Paley's Evidences of Christianity.
With Annotations by Archbishop WHATELY. 9s.

Paley's Moral Philosophy.
With Annotations by the Archbishop of DUBLIN. 8vo. 7s.

A Select Glossary of English Words used formerly in Senses different from their Present.
By the Dean of WESTMINSTER.
The Second Edition, Revised and Improved. 4s.

Intellectual Education, and its Influence on the Character and Happiness of Women.
By EMILY SHIRREFF. Post Octavo. 10s. 6d.

History of Normandy and of England.
By Sir FRANCIS PALGRAVE, Deputy Keeper of the Records.
Octavo. Volumes I. and II. 21s. each.

History of England.
By JAMES ANTHONY FROUDE.
The Fifth and Sixth Volumes, containing the Reigns of Edward the Sixth and Mary. 28s.
Volumes I. to IV. Second Edition, completing the Reign of Henry the Eighth. 54s.

History of England during the Reign of George the Third.
By WILLIAM MASSEY, M.P. Volumes I., II., and III., 12s. each.

The Spanish Conquest in America,
AND ITS RELATION TO THE HISTORY OF SLAVERY AND TO THE GOVERNMENT OF COLONIES.
By ARTHUR HELPS. Vols. I. and II., 28s.; Vol. III., 16s., Octavo.

The Kingdom and People of Siam.
With a Narrative of the Mission to that Country in 1855.
By Sir JOHN BOWRING, F.R.S. Two Vols., with Illustrations. 32s.

The Holy City;
Historical, Topographical, and Antiquarian Notices of Jerusalem.
By G. WILLIAMS, B.D.
Second Edition, with Illustrations and Additions and a Plan of Jerusalem. Two Volumes. 2l. 5s.

History of the Holy Sepulchre.
By Professor WILLIS. Reprinted from Williams's *Holy City.* 9s.

Plan of Jerusalem from the Ordnance Survey.
With a Memoir. 9s.; mounted on rollers, 18s.

The Earth and Man;
Or, Physical Geography in its Relation to the History of Mankind.
From the Work of GUYOT, with Notes and Copious Index.
Cheap Edition, 2s.

Hellas: The Home, the History, the Literature, and the Arts of the Ancient Greeks.
From the German of JACOBS. Foolscap Octavo. 4s. 6d.

The New Cratylus:
By J. W. DONALDSON, D.D., Classical Examiner in the University of London. Third Edition, revised and enlarged, 20s.

Varronianus.
By J. W. DONALDSON, D.D. Third Edition, Revised and Enlarged. 16s.

On the Classification and Geographical Distribution of the Mammalia.
'On the Gorilla' and 'On the Extinction and Transmutation of Species.'
By RICHARD OWEN, F.R.S. 8vo. 5s.

Dialogues on Divine Providence.
By a Fellow of a College. Foolscap Octavo. 3s. 6d.

God's Acre; or, Historical Notices relating to Churchyards.
By Mrs. STONE. Post Octavo. 10s. 6d.

The Cloister Life of Charles the Fifth.
By WILLIAM STIRLING, M.P. The Third Edition. 8s.

Arundines Cami.
Edited by the Rev. HENRY DRURY, M.A.
Fifth and Cheaper Edition. 7s. 6d.

Homeric Ballads.
The Greek Text, with an English Translation in Verse, and Introduction and Notes. By the late Dr. MAGINN. 6s.

A Long Vacation in Continental Picture Galleries.
By T. W. JEX BLAKE, M.A. 3s. 6d.

Remains of Bishop Copleston:
With Reminiscences of his Life, by the Archbishop of DUBLIN. 10s. 6d.

Evelyn's Life of Mrs. Godolphin.
Edited by the Bishop of OXFORD. Third Edition, with Portrait. 6s.

Companions of My Solitude.
Fifth Edition. 3s. 6d

Essays Written in Intervals of Business.
Seventh Edition. 2s. 6d.

Ancient and Modern Fish Tattle.
By the Rev. C. DAVID BADHAM. 12s.

Leaves from the Note Book of a Naturalist.
By the late W. J. BRODERIP, F.R.S. Post Octavo. 10s. 6d.

BY WILLIAM WHEWELL, D.D., F.R.S.
Master of Trinity College, Cambridge.

History of the Inductive Sciences.
The Third Edition, with Additions. 3 vols. 24s.

Novum Organon Renovatum.
Being the Second Part of a Third Edition of *The Philosophy of the Inductive Sciences*. With large Additions. 7s.

History of Scientific Ideas.
Being the First Part of a Third Edition of *The Philosophy of the Inductive Sciences*. 2 vols., with large Additions. 14s.

On the Philosophy of Discovery.
Being the Third and Concluding Part of a Third Edition of *The Philosophy of the Inductive Sciences*. 1 vol. 9s.

LONDON: JOHN W. PARKER AND SON, WEST STRAND.

www.ingramcontent.com/pod-product-compliance
Lightning Source LLC
Chambersburg PA
CBHW022111300426
44117CB00007B/667